Religions
of the
World

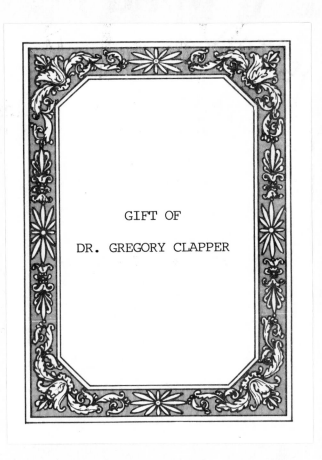

Religions

of the
World

Fourth Edition

Lewis M. Hopfe

96-729

MACMILLAN PUBLISHING COMPANY
New York
COLLIER MACMILLAN PUBLISHERS
London

Macmillan Publishing Company
866 Third Avenue, New York, New York 10022

Collier Macmillan Canada, Inc.

Library of Congress Cataloging-in-Publication Data

Hopfe, Lewis M.
  Religions of the world.

  Includes bibliographies and index.
  1. Religions. I. Title.
BL80.2.H66 1987   291   86–12693
ISBN 0-02-356930-1

Printing: 3 4 5 6 7   Year: 7 8 9 0 1 2 3

ACKNOWLEDGMENTS

Permission has been granted to quote from the following publications (listed in approximate order of quotation):

The Scripture quotations in this publication are from the Revised Standard Version of the Bible, copyrighted © 1971 and 1952 by the Division of Christian Education of the National Council of the Churches of Christ in the USA.

Monica Wilson, *Communal Rituals of the Nyakyusa.* Copyright © 1959 by the International African Institute, London. Reprinted by permission of the publisher.

Maria Leach, *The Beginning.* New York: Krishna Press, 1956. Reprinted by permission of the publisher.

Franklin Edgerton (Trans.) *Bhagavad Gita.* Cambridge, Mass.: Harvard University Press. Reprinted by permission of the publishers, copyright © 1944 by the President and Fellows of Harvard College; © 1972 by Eleanor Hill Edgerton.

A. L. Basham, in W. Theodore de Bary (Ed.), *Sources of Indian Tradition.* New York: Columbia University Press, 1958. Reprinted by permission of the publisher.

Lord Chalmers (Trans.), *Further Dialogues of the Buddha.* New York: Krishna Press, 1926. Reprinted by permission of the publisher.

E. J. Thomas (Trans.), *Early Buddhist Scriptures.* New York: Krishna Press, 1935. Reprinted by permission of the publisher.

Edward Conze (Trans.), *Buddhist Texts Through the Ages.* Oxford: Bruno Cassierer Publishers Ltd., 1954. Reprinted by permission of the publisher.

W. Theodore de Bary (Ed.), *Sources of Japanese Tradition.* New York: Columbia University Press, 1958. Reprinted by permission of the publisher.

S. E. Frost (Ed.), *The Sacred Writings of the World's Great Religions.* New York: Copeland and Lamm, Inc., 1943. Reprinted by permission of the publisher.

ISBN 0-02-356930-1

Arthur Waley (Trans.), *The Way and Its Power*. New York: Grove Press, and London: Allen & Unwin, 1958. Reprinted by permission of the publishers.

Arthur Waley (Trans.), *The Analects of Confucius*. London: Allen & Unwin, 1938. Reprinted by permission of the publisher.

Y. P. Mei (Trans.), in W. Theodore de Bary (Ed.), *Sources of Chinese Tradition*. New York: Columbia University Press, 1960. Reprinted by permission of the publisher.

M. Kitagawa, in Wing-Tait Chan et al. (Eds.), *The Great Asian Religions: An Anthology*. Copyright © 1969 by Macmillan Publishing Company. Reprinted by permission of the publisher.

R. C. Zaehner, *The Teachings of the Magi*. London: Allen & Unwin, 1956. Reprinted by permission of Darby & Son, Oxford.

R. C. Zaehner (Trans.), *Zuran: A Zoroastian Dilemma*. Oxford: Oxford Univesity Press, 1955. Reprinted by permission of the publisher.

Herbert Danby (Trans.), *The Mishnah*. Oxford: Oxford University Press, 1933. Reprinted by permission of the publisher.

Kirsopp Lake (Trans.), *The Apostolic Fathers, Vol. II*. Cambridge, Mass.: Harvard University Press, 1913. Reprinted by permission of the publishers and The Loeb Classical Library.

A. J. Arberry, *The Koran Interpreted*. Reprinted by permission of Macmillan Publishing Company. Copyright © 1955 by Allen & Unwin Ltd.

Shoghi Effendi (Trans.), *Gleanings from the Writings of Bahá'u'lláh*. Copyright © 1952, 1976 National Spiritual Assembly of the Bahá'ís of the United States.

S. Radhakrishnan, *The Principal Upanishads*. London: Allen & Unwin, 1953. Reprinted by permission of the publisher.

J. M. Rodwell (Trans.), *The Quran*. London: J. M. Dent & Sons Ltd., 1909. Reprinted by permission of the publisher.

For Gerry, Maria, and all the other pilgrims. . . .

Preface

Religions of the World is written for students who are beginning their work in world religions. It provides a concise and basic introduction to the major religions of today's world. The text begins by first introducing the reader to the study with a presentation on the definitions of religion and some of the theories of the origin of religion. This is followed by a chapter that discusses basic or primitive religions. In this section, one not only finds concepts important to contemporary basic religions but also concepts at the heart of many other religions. This is followed by chapters on Native American and African religions. The remainder of the text is divided into three sections. The first presents the religions native to India: Hinduism, Jainism, Buddhism, and Sikhism. The second major section discusses the religions of China and Japan: Taoism, Confucianism, and Shinto. The final section presents the religions that arose in the Middle East but which are almost worldwide in their scope: Zoroastrianism, Judaism, Christianity, and Islam. This edition of *Religions of the World* has added a chapter on Baha'i to this section.

The fourth edition of *Religions of the World* differs from previous editions in a number of important respects. The chapter on American Indian religions has been completely rewritten. Throughout the text, content has been updated and revised to reflect changes during recent years. Religions such as Christianity and Islam have undergone periods of rapid growth. Other religions such as Sikhism and Shia Islam have been in the headlines because of related national problems. Therefore, each chapter ends with a brief section on the state of the religion today. The fourth edition of *Religions of the World* also includes a revised collection of primary readings; it is believed that the student may learn religions better if he or she is able to understand a brief selection of scripture or other basic material. At the end of each chapter, a new section of study questions is included in order to focus the attention of the reader on the central themes of the chapter.

This edition of *Religions of the World* is the work of many people. I am indebted to the reviewers who have used this text and made helpful suggestions for its improvement: John H. Zimmerman, Kendall College; Harry Partin, Duke University; Lynda Sexson, Montana State University; Henry Carrigan, Emory University; Christopher Vecsey, Colgate University; and Franklin Proano, Ohio State University. Special thanks is given to Nora Treese and to Lee Ditkowsky for their help in the preparation of this manuscript, and to Helen McInnis, Robin Roy, and Wendy Polhemus at Macmillan for much patient work on behalf of the text.

L. M. H.

Contents

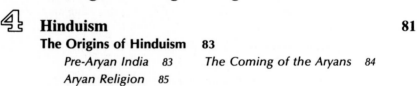

Religions Originating in India · 79

Religions Originating in the Middle East · 257

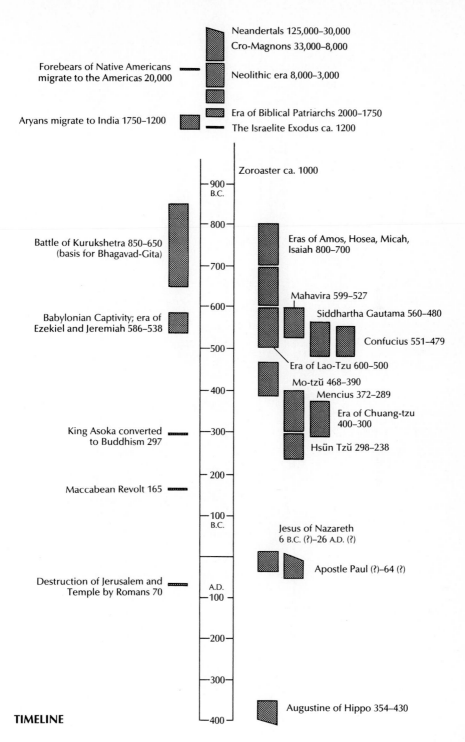

Neandertals 125,000–30,000

Cro-Magnons 33,000–8,000

Forebears of Native Americans migrate to the Americas 20,000

Neolithic era 8,000–3,000

Aryans migrate to India 1750–1200

Era of Biblical Patriarchs 2000–1750

The Israelite Exodus ca. 1200

Zoroaster ca. 1000

900 B.C.

800

Battle of Kurukshetra 850–650 (basis for Bhagavad-Gita)

Eras of Amos, Hosea, Micah, Isaiah 800–700

700

Mahavira 599–527

600

Siddhartha Gautama 560–480

Babylonian Captivity; era of Ezekiel and Jeremiah 586–538

Confucius 551–479

500

Era of Lao-Tzu 600–500

Mo-tzŭ 468–390

400

Mencius 372–289

Era of Chuang-tzu 400–300

King Asoka converted to Buddhism 297

300

Hsün Tzŭ 298–238

200

Maccabean Revolt 165

100 B.C.

Jesus of Nazareth 6 B.C. (?)–26 A.D. (?)

Apostle Paul (?)–64 (?)

Destruction of Jerusalem and Temple by Romans 70

A.D. 100

200

300

Augustine of Hippo 354–430

TIMELINE

400

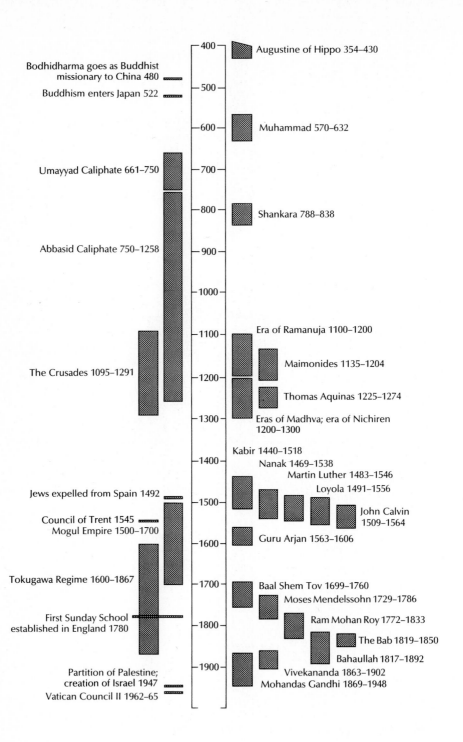

Bodhidharma goes as Buddhist missionary to China 480

Buddhism enters Japan 522

Umayyad Caliphate 661–750

Abbasid Caliphate 750–1258

The Crusades 1095–1291

Jews expelled from Spain 1492

Council of Trent 1545
Mogul Empire 1500–1700

Tokugawa Regime 1600–1867

First Sunday School established in England 1780

Partition of Palestine; creation of Israel 1947

Vatican Council II 1962–65

400 — Augustine of Hippo 354–430

500

600 — Muhammad 570–632

700

800 — Shankara 788–838

900

1000

1100 — Era of Ramanuja 1100–1200

Maimonides 1135–1204

1200

Thomas Aquinas 1225–1274

1300 — Eras of Madhva; era of Nichiren 1200–1300

Kabir 1440–1518

1400 — Nanak 1469–1538

Martin Luther 1483–1546

Loyola 1491–1556

1500 — John Calvin 1509–1564

Guru Arjan 1563–1606

1600

1700 — Baal Shem Tov 1699–1760

Moses Mendelssohn 1729–1786

Ram Mohan Roy 1772–1833

1800 — The Bab 1819–1850

Bahaullah 1817–1892

1900 — Vivekananda 1863–1902

Mohandas Gandhi 1869–1948

Overview

Religion: *The service and adoration of God or a god as expressed in forms of worship, in obedience to divine commands . . . and in the pursuit of a way of life regarded as incumbent on true believers.*
—Webster's New International Dictionary of the English Language, Second Edition

Why study religion?

Any student embarking upon a study of the religions of the world, whether it be for a semester, a year, or a lifetime, must question his or her reasons. After all, we have been told that religion is a personal matter and that while we should be informed about the nature of our own religion, the religion of others need scarcely concern us. We have heard that religions are of little real consequence; that we might more profitably spend our time studying subjects of immediate practical value in the pursuit of a career; that religions are becoming passé in a scientifically progressive world. Why, then, should any student take time from his or her academic career to study the religions of the world?

We might justify the study of religions in the same manner that we justify the study of Shakespeare or art history: the subject can be worth studying simply because the student is interested in it. Certainly anyone who is interested in the history of the world and in the antecedents of his or her own culture will find the study of world religions imperative. An art historian lecturing to a class on the art of sixteenth- and seventeenth-century Europe presented picture after picture of the art of that period, which was filled with religious themes. To his class he said, "Because you may have no religious interest yourself, please do not assume that the people of the past had none." Indeed, we could not understand the art of 90 percent of the world's cultures without knowing the religious themes of those cultures. Likewise the student of world literature must know religions. We cannot understand the Bhagavad-Gita without understanding Hinduism; we cannot truly understand Hermann Hesse's *Siddhartha* without a knowledge of Buddhism; we cannot understand the literature of Herman Melville without a knowledge of Christian themes; even the contemporary literature of a writer such as Philip Roth is misunderstood without a knowledge of Judaism.

Perhaps the greatest contribution that a knowledge of world religions can make to a citizen of the fourth quarter of the twentieth century is in the area of world politics. At the time of this writing, as at almost any time in history, major political conflicts have at their roots religious differences. Catholic Christians war against Protestant Christians; Muslims war against Eastern Orthodox Christians; Hindus war against Muslims; Buddhists war with Christians; and Jews struggle with Muslims. Certainly these conflicts have other dimensions, but the religious differences are imposing. If we are to understand these conflicts fully, we must know that Christians, Jews, Muslims, Hindus, and Buddhists have basic philosophical differences. This is not to say that people of different religions and cultures cannot live in peace together; it is to say that if there is to be peace, these differences must be known and respected. In the early 1960s, a young professor and his wife gave a dinner party on a Friday evening. The guest list included Jews, Catholics, and Muslims. The dinner entrée was ham! Needless to say, it was not a happy party. Whether the choice of food was made in ignorance or arrogance does not matter. The guests, because of their religions, were offended. The dinner party is all too frequently a microcosm of what happens in the larger world because of ignorance of the religions of the world.

A DEFINITION OF RELIGION

Assuming an interest in religions and a willingness to study them, what constitutes the subject matter of a course in world religions? Humankind has been on earth for a long, long time. Our cultures, historic and prehistoric, are too numerous to even begin to detail. Which cultures and religions shall we study? Whole texts have been written solely on prehistoric religions, not to mention the great families of religion, such as those found within Hinduism. Therefore, any one text or course on religions must of necessity be selective about its subject, and a definition of the subject is necessary.

The English word *religion* is derived from the Latin *religio*, which refers to the fear or awe one feels in the presence of a spirit or a god. The average person seeks to define religion in terms of a set of beliefs, having to do with the gods, through which one is taught a moral system. While elements of this definition may be found within many of the religions of the world, it cannot do justice to them all. For example, some religions may recognize the existence of gods but actually have very little to do with them. Jainism and to some extent early Buddhism may be called atheistic religions because their emphasis was on people's delivering themselves from their plights without the help of gods. There are also religions that are not naturally tied to moral systems. A majority of the religions that have existed upon earth have probably been far more concerned with humanity's proper relationship to gods, demons, and spirits than with ethical relationships between people. One distinctive characteristic of the religion of the early Hebrews was the ethical dimension that Yahweh required of them. This was also found in Zoroastrianism and was in turn passed on to Christianity and Islam. Modern adherents to those religions associate the word *religious* with the word *moral.* But among the majority of religions it is not necessarily so.

A definition of religion that is widely accepted today was offered by the late Paul Tillich, who identified religion as that which is of "ultimate concern."[1] Taking Tillich's definition one step further, some might say that in its basic form a person's religion is that which is so vital to that person that he or she would die for it. In this sense, then, the intense patriotism one finds in many nations could be called *religion.* Men and women have been known to die for their families. In terms of this definition their intense love for their family thus may be seen as their religion. However satisfying Tillich's definition may be, it is probably too broad for most of us. People have been known to have ultimate concern for their automobiles, their professions, their homes, food, and golf. Only in the broadest sense of the word can these things be considered *religions* or even *religious.* For the purposes of this book, a more restrictive definition must be used.

The contents of this text have been chosen from the hundreds of religions that have existed in the world on the following five bases: (1) They are religions that usually deal in some way with people's relationship to the unseen world of spirits, gods, demons. (2) They are religions that usually have developed a system of myths about the unseen world and rituals designed for communing with or propitiating the spirits. (3) They are religions that usually have developed a cult of organized rituals, temples, priests, and scriptures at some point in their history. (4) They are religions that usually have some statement about life beyond death, either as survival in some shadowy hades, in some version of heaven and hell, or through reincarnation. (5) Finally, the religions discussed in this text generally have attracted large followings, either currently or at some time in the past.

As there are many religions from which we must choose, so there are many methods by which we might deal with these religions. We might present the religions of the world in terms of their effects upon the societies that support them; in terms of their forms or style of

---

[1] See Paul Tillich, *The Protestant Era,* trans., James Luther Adams (Chicago: The University of Chicago Press, 1948), pp. xv, 59, and 273.

worship; in a comparative manner, in which each religion is compared with the others in terms of its outlook toward God, the nature of humankind, sin, and so on; or we might present the religions of the world in terms of their histories and their effects upon the histories of the nations where they were found. It is the intent of this text to combine some of these methods and to present the major religions of the world as simply and yet as thoroughly as possible. For each religion, four major points will be considered: (1) The world that produced this religion: What was the culture that hosted this religion? (2) The life of the founder(s): Where there is a founder, and where anything can be known of this person's life, what factors caused this person to found this religion? (3) The sacred texts: Where there are scriptures or sacred books, what does the literature tell us about this religion? (4) The major historical developments of this religion.

THE UNIVERSALITY OF RELIGION

Wherever people are found, there too religion resides. Occasionally religion is hard to find or pin down, but in the great metropolitan capitals and in the most primitive areas of the world, there are physical and cultural temples, pyramids, megaliths, and monuments that societies have raised at tremendous expense as an expression of their religion. Even when we explore the backwaters of time in prehistoric civilizations, we find altars, cave paintings, and special burials that point toward our religious nature. Indeed, there is no other phenomenon so pervasive, so consistent from society to society, as the search for gods.

THEORIES OF THE ORIGIN OF RELIGIONS

Where does religion come from? This is a very basic question, as our answer tends to reflect our view of the very nature of religion. Some would say that human beings developed religion because they were weak and ignorant of the forces of nature that surrounded them. They were at the mercy of these forces and therefore devised a scheme of gods and spirits that tended to explain the mysteries of the universe, and to whom they could pray for support. According to this view, religion was needed as a crutch to lean upon. The implication is that when human beings come to fully know and understand their universe, they will no longer need the crutch of religion to support them. Others would say that religion was developed by a few as a means of suppressing the masses. The traditional view held by those who are themselves religious is that God revealed religion and religious truths to human beings at some point in their development.

In the nineteenth century, when the social sciences were being developed and anthropologists were first beginning to investigate the remaining primitive cultures, certain theories of the origin of religion were proposed by pioneers in this field. No longer satisfied with mere guessing about the origin of religion or with the orthodox religious views on the subject, early anthropologists based their theories on their observations. These nineteenth- and early twentieth-century scholars, enamored of the belief that the biological theories of evolution taught by Darwin could be applied to the social sciences, investigated contemporary "primitive" religions, reread ancient reporters such as Herodotus, and hypothesized ad infinitum about the origin and development of the phenomenon of religion. A few of the more outstanding and enduring of their theories follow.

The Animistic Theories

The most outstanding exponent of one animistic theory of the origin of religion was the English scholar Sir Edward Burnett Tylor. In his book *Primitive Culture,* which was published in 1871, Tylor maintained that primitive people had difficulty in distinguishing dreams from reality. Therefore, when they dreamed of the recent dead, particularly outstanding members of their society, they believed that the dead were not really dead, or at least they continued to exist in some other form. On the basis of their visions of the ghosts of the dead in their dreams, primitive people came to believe in the existence of souls or spirits that continued to exist after physical death. According to Tylor, primitive peoples also believed that these souls (Latin, *anima*) were to be found not only in people but in all of nature. There were souls in stones, trees, animals, rivers, springs, volcanoes, and mountains. The entire world, the very air itself, was seen to be alive with spirits of all kinds. These spirits could be helpful or harmful to human beings, and they had personalities that could be offended or flattered. Therefore, it became a part of the life of primitive societies to pray to these spirits, to offer sacrifices to them, to seek to appease them, and to avoid offending them. From this animistic understanding of the world there arose the multiple deities that became the basis for the more developed religions of the world.

Another theory of the origin of religion that can be loosely defined as animistic was developed and propounded in 1891 by a Christian missionary to the Melanesian people, Bishop Codrington. In the course of his work Codrington discovered that the Melanesians believed in a mysterious and awesome force that inhabited all of nature and caused nature to act as it did toward humankind. The Melanesians called this force *mana,* and Bishop Codrington theorized that all primitive people had begun their religions with an awareness of such a force. Investigators studying other primitive cultures found a similar phenomenon, although it was called by other names. The theory that a force like *mana* existed in nature and was acknowledged by primitive societies differed from Tylor's animistic theory. The animists tended to recognize the unseen forces in nature as personal. One could communicate with these forces as well as flatter or offend them. Those who recognized a force like *mana* thought of it as an impersonal force. One did not offer sacrifices to it; one only sought to avoid its evil consequences. The Melanesians avoided the destructiveness of *mana* by establishing what they called *taboos.* For example, if a man married his sister and the marriage produced an evil effect or resulted in no children, then it might be construed that somehow marriage between brother and sister was responsible for the evil effect. Therefore, in later generations such a marriage would become a tribal taboo and be forbidden.

The Nature-Worship Theory

Another theory regarding the origin of religion was developed by the German scholar Max Müller. Müller taught at Oxford University in the last quarter of the nineteenth century and was primarily concerned with mythology and Indian religions. From his studies he became convinced that human beings first developed their religions from their observations of the forces of nature. According to this theory, primitive people became aware of the regularity of the seasons, the tides, and the phases of the moon. Their response to these forces in nature was to personalize them. Thus they gave a name to the sun, the moon, and so on, and began to describe the activities of these forces with tales that eventually became mythology. An example of this process is found in the Greek myth of Apollo and Daphne. Apollo was in love with Daphne, but she fled from him and was changed into a laurel tree. By searching out the etymology of these names, Müller found that Apollo was the name given to the sun and that Daphne was the name for the dawn. Thus the original myth is simply a primitive story describing the manner in which the sun chases away the dawn. In applying similar etymological studies to the mythologies of the world Müller became convinced he had found the key to the origin of all religions: Primitive people identified the forces in nature, personified them, created myths to describe their activities, and eventually developed pantheons and religions around them.

The Theory of Original Monotheism

A completely different approach to the origin of religion was presented early in the twentieth century by a Jesuit, Father Wilhelm Schmidt, in his book *Der Ursprung der Gottesidee.* Schmidt had examined the religions of many contemporary basic cultures in Australia and Africa and found that they all held a common belief in a distant high god. While the predominant form of religion for these primitives was animism or polytheism, there was always the belief that originally there had been one great god above all others. He may have been the creator of the world or the father of the many lesser deities. After initially establishing the world, this high god went away and now has little contact with the world. Some of the mythologies go on to say that one day he will return and reestablish himself. In these societies the local deities receive the majority of attention and worship, although the distant high god has a small part in mythology. Father Schmidt inferred from this phenomenon that primitive societies were originally monotheistic, but because the worship of one god was difficult, religion was corrupted into polytheism. Later, more advanced religions recovered the true monotheistic religion. Naturally, Schmidt was accused of allowing his Christian prejudices to be active in the formulation of this theory.

The Magic Theory

Between 1890 and 1915, Sir James George Frazer produced his encyclopedic work on religion, *The Golden Bough.* Unlike Codrington and Schmidt, Frazer did not personally study contemporary basic religions but rather constructed his theories from reading the reports of anthropologists, missionaries, and ancient writers such as Herodotus. On the basis of his studies, Frazer came to believe that humankind had gone through three phases of development regarding the spirit world. First, people had attempted to control the world of nature through magic. The magician is one who believes that through certain processes such as dances, rituals, formulae, incantations, and so on, nature can be forced to act in one's favor. For example, if people need rain they employ the services of a magician who leads the tribe in the proper rain magic (dances and incantations, for example). The premise behind magic is that if the ritual is done properly nature will have no choice but to cooperate. Finally, people came to realize that nature could not be coerced by magic. Therefore, in a second phase, people turned to religion, whose premise seems to be that nature can be implored to cooperate. Whereas the witch doctor might perform a rain dance, a priest would pray and offer sacrifice to the powers of nature, hoping to please them and thus bring rain. In a third phase, people turned from religion to science, in which a more rational understanding of nature is operative. Therefore the modern farmer who needs rain will turn neither to the magician nor to the priest but to the scientist, who will seed the clouds and cause it to rain. A skeptic might note that there is little proof that seeding the clouds produces rain any more frequently than did rain dances or prayers.

The Wish-Fulfillment Theory

One of the most influential thinkers of the nineteenth century was the German philosopher Ludwig Feuerbach. Feuerbach, who had originally been a theological student, taught that there were no gods and that belief in gods was merely wish fulfillment. People who were troubled and could not cope with the problems and challenges of life simply projected their wishes and developed gods and religions.

Two of the leading disciples of Feuerbach's thinking in the nineteenth and twentieth centuries were Karl Marx and Sigmund Freud. Each of these men took Feuerbach's position on the origin of religion and added his own distinctive touches. Marx saw the origin and development of religion in terms of his personal view of history and the economic and social struggle between classes. He said:

> Man makes religion, religion does not make man. Religion is the self-consciousness and self-esteem of man who has either not yet found himself or has already lost himself again. . . . Religion is the sigh of the oppressed creature, the heart of a heartless world, just as it is the spirit of spiritless conditions. It is the opium of the people.[2]

Marx also believed that religion was used by the ruling classes to suppress the under classes.

> The social principles of Christianity preach the necessity of a ruling and an oppressed class, and for the latter all they have to offer is the pious wish that the former may be charitable . . . The social principles of Christianity declare all the vile acts of oppressors against the oppressed to be either just punishment for original sin and for other sins, or trials which the Lord, in his infinite wisdom, ordains for the redeemed.[3]

Sigmund Freud, the founder of psychoanalysis, gave Feuerbach's ideas a psychological dimension. He saw religion as having originated from

---

[2] Karl Marx, "Contribution to the Critique of Hegel's Philosophy of Law," *Marx Engels on Religion* (Moscow: Progress Publishers, 1957), pp. 38, 39.
[3] Karl Marx, "The Communism of the Rheinishcher Beobachter," Ibid., p. 74.

the guilt that individuals supposedly feel in hating their fathers. Freud saw in the ancient Greek myth of Oedipus a pattern of human experience. Oedipus was a man who, through a long and tragic series of events, killed his father and married his mother. Freud said that in all males there was a similar tendency to desire our mothers and therefore to hate our fathers. Because of this subconscious hatred and ensuing guilt, Freud believed that we project a great father image in the sky and call him God. The truly healthy mature person, according to Freud, is content to stand alone and face the problems of life without gods or religions.

TYPES OF RELIGIONS

In the long period of human life on earth there have been hundreds of religions and religious systems. Since recorded history covers only the last five thousand years of our million-year existence, there are undoubtedly more unknown than known religions. In addition, many religious systems have lived and died within the relatively short span of recorded history. This text does not pretend to deal with all religions, historical or prehistorical. It deals only with religious systems that are active and viable today. These religions are grouped into four categories.

Basic or Primitive Religions

The term "basic religion" is generally applied to the religions of people in undeveloped areas of the world and to the religions of prehistoric peoples, about which we know very little. This category embraces a great variety of beliefs and practices, including animism, totemism, and demonism. In the following chapters we will examine American Indian religions and African religions as examples of the basic religions. Probably the most common characteristic of this group is an animistic view of nature. No one knows the numbers of persons whose religions may be categorized as basic.

Religions Originating in India

Four of the great religions of the world originated in India: Hinduism, Jainism, Buddhism, and Sikhism. India remains the home of Hinduism, Jainism, and Sikhism while Buddhism is now found in other Asian nations such as China, Japan, Korea, Vietnam, Cambodia, and Thailand. The basic beliefs of these religions are that there are many gods (Sikhism is the exception, taking its belief in one god from Islam) and that one person may lead many lives through a system of reincarnation. The goal of these religions is release from the cycle of life, death, and rebirth and the achievement of nonlife, which is called *moksha* or *Nirvana*. Sometimes this goal is achieved through the aid of the gods, but often believers are expected by their actions or lack thereof to work out their own release.

Religions Originating in China and Japan

Religions that originated in China and Japan include Taoism, Confucianism, and Shintoism. There is some question as to whether Taoism and Confucianism are truly religions, but since they have at times developed religious cults they are usually considered world religions. They have in common the belief in many gods and include the worship of nature, the worship or veneration of ancestors, and, in the case of Shinto, a reverence of the nation itself. Like most of the religions of India, they are relatively tolerant, allowing their adherents the freedom to accept and even adopt the religious positions of others.

Religions Originating in the Middle East

Religions originating in the Middle East include Zoroastrianism, Judaism, Christianity, and Islam. All four hold to the common belief in one supreme creator god. In contrast to the Indian religions, they believe that each person lives only one life. Christianity and Islam have been two of the great missionary religions of the world. Today their adherents are found all over the globe and number in the billions.

STUDY QUESTIONS

1. List several values that can come from a knowledge of the differing religious viewpoints in the world.

2. Define "religion."

3. What do we know about the origin of religions? What does this knowledge contribute to the way we view religion today?

4. Contrast the Marxist view of religion with that of Freud.

5. List the four types of religious systems and tell where each may be found.

Basic Religions

At one time in history human religions may have shared certain characteristics no longer visible in the contemporary religions that dominate the world. Through an examination of archaeological evidence and of certain cultures that are judged to be "primitive" by modern standards, the student of religions may be able to gain an insight into what the earliest religions may have been. At the same time, by studying the characteristics of these so-called basic religions of the past and present, the student will also learn more about the bases upon which such major contemporary religions as Hinduism, Christianity, and Islam rest. The key to an appropriate and valuable study of these religions is an openness and a willingness to appreciate their strengths and beauty.

CHAPTER 1

Characteristics of Basic Religions

The Venus of Laussel. The exaggerated breasts, hips, and abdomen indicate that this was an image connected with fertility worship. (*Courtesy of Collections Musée D'Aquitaine, Bordeaux, France.*)

It has its wild and demonic forms and can sink into an almost grisly horror and shuddering. It has its crude, barbaric antecedents and early manifestations, and again it may be developed into something beautiful and pure and glorious. It may become the hushed, trembling, and speechless humility of the creature in the presence of—whom or what! In the presence of that which is a mystery *inexpressible and above all creatures.*
—Rudolf Otto, The Idea of the Holy

Typically, the religions and total culture of prehistoric peoples and the current practices in geographical areas that are not technically classified as *civilized* are referred to as *primitive*. Unfortunately, the word *primitive* carries with it the connotations of backward, simple, even childlike. Thus the Christian or Muslim or Jew may tend to look down upon these religions as superstitious or uncivilized. However, the religion of the bushman of Australia or the Indian of the Americas may be fully as intricate in its rituals and mythology and as satisfying to its adherents as is the worship of the high-church Episcopalian. In studying the religions of the world we can assume no evolutionary scale that moves from basic religions to Zen Buddhism or any other highly developed religion of the so-called civilized world. There is satisfaction and beauty in all religions, and there is ugliness and baseness in all, too. Nevertheless, because basic religious elements are found in the religions of prehistoric people and people of the less-developed areas of the world, the term *basic religions* is not inappropriate.

It follows, of course, that of all the world's religions, we know least about these basic religions simply because they spring from prehistory or in out-of-the-way places that have not been penetrated by civilization. However, the study of these religions is extremely important. Elements of the basic religions are found to a greater or lesser degree in all religions. It is therefore important that we have an understanding of these elements and the manner in which they operate. Second, it is important that we study basic religions because they represent the majority of the total religious experience of humankind since the dawn of human history.

SOURCES OF INFORMATION
CONCERNING BASIC RELIGIONS

Humans have been active on planet Earth for a million or more years, depending upon which anthropologist one chooses to believe. However, we know but a tiny fraction of human history. Only within the last five or six thousand years has *Homo sapiens* utilized writing. While nonwritten sources such as cave paintings, burial sites, religious statuary, and archaeological remains indicate human culture and religious experiences, our strongest source of knowledge is the written record. Of the total period of time in which people have been upon Earth, we have written records of perhaps less than one-half of 1 percent. From these records we know a great deal about peoples' culture and religious experience, but there is an enormous amount we do not know.

There are two primary sources of information about basic religions. The first is contemporary basic religions. The anthropologist visits a contemporary basic culture and studies its religious beliefs and practices. From this study the anthropolgist may infer that many or all basic and prehistoric religions may have had similar attitudes and religious practices. Thus Bishop Codrington studied the Melanesian people in the nineteenth century and reported their awareness of the unseen force in nature called *mana*. He and others were led to believe that a similar awareness of a force like *mana* might have been humankind's original religious impetus.

However interesting the study of contemporary basic religions may

Stonehenge, located on the Salisbury Plain of southern England. It is believed that these massive stones were erected in the second millennium B.C. Their exact purpose is open to speculation, but the arrangement of the stones indicates to some a monument to magic. (*Courtesy of the British Tourist Authority.*)

be, it obviously leaves much to be desired as a source for knowledge of prehistoric basic religion. It is possible that the Melanesians of the nineteenth century were very different from civilized people, or even from pre-nineteenth century Melanesians. Their religious awareness and practices might have changed within the nineteenth century itself. They might only recently have adopted the belief in *mana,* or they could have been affected by the visits of former missionaries or traders, or even by the visit of the anthropologist. There is also the possibility that even if the anthropologist arrived and found a virgin primitive society in the exact state of prehistoric time, the anthropologist's observations and reporting might not be accurate. The anthropologist must learn the language of the group that is being studied and live with that group long enough to be thoroughly conversant with its customs and religions. The reliability of the chieftains and the priests with whom there is contact must also be taken into account. If any of these factors is missing, then the data that the anthropologist gathers can be questioned. Therefore, while the study of contemporary basic religions may be helpful, it cannot be relied upon to give a total picture of basic religions as they have always been.

A second source of information comes from the science of archaeology. Although human beings have always been interested in their past and have doubtless always attempted to investigate the physical remains of that past, the scientific examination of those remains is less than two hundred years old. In fact, most of the serious archaeological work that has been done has been achieved in the twentieth century.

Archaeologists, working very carefully, attempt to uncover the physical remains of past civilizations and reconstruct the life and history of their cultures. In their examinations of relatively recent cultures, such as the Roman or the Mayan, the task is simplified because of the wealth of buildings, burials, coinage, and other elaborate artifacts that these civilizations left. The task is further simplified when the cultures that are examined have been literate, and scrolls, clay tablets, and inscriptional material are found.

In dealing with distant prehistoric cultures, the task is more difficult. Here the main sources of information are likely to be burials, weapons, and tools, and the archaeologist must reconstruct very carefully. However, even in dealing with either distant or recent cultures, archaeological results depend upon the interpretations of the investigator. What one archaeologist calls a temple another may call a stable; controversy and mistakes within this field are too numerous to list. Therefore we must be very careful to give archaeological investigation its due value and no more. Some archaeologists may assure us that Neandertal people worshiped bears because bear skulls have been found in their burial sites. This may or may not be the case. Bear skulls may have been buried with these primitive people because they worshiped the bear, or bears may have been buried there as trophies of the hunt. Until the day when the Neandertals speak for themselves in one form or another, we cannot be certain about their religion.

PREHISTORIC BEGINNINGS OF BASIC RELIGIONS

Neandertal Religion

The earliest hominid for whom much evidence of religion remains is the so-called Neandertal. It is believed that Neandertals lived from approximately 125,000 to 30,000 B.C. and inhabited Europe, the Middle East, Western and Central Asia. While they were anatomically similar to modern *Homo sapiens,* Neandertal skeletons reveal that they were somewhat shorter and more muscular. More than one hundred sites of Neandertal life have been excavated. These sites reveal that these people were clever workers with tools of stone, bone, and wood. They also show that the Neandertals were the first humans to bury their dead. It is in the circumstances of these burials that one finds clues to Neandertal religion. Found in these burials are the remains of animal bones and stone tools. Some suggest that these remains indicate that the dead were buried with food and with their tools and weapons, perhaps as offerings to the gods or as a necessary accompaniment into the world of the dead. In addition, archaeologists have found bear skulls, apparently carefully arranged, in Neandertal burials; and this suggests a worshipful attitude toward the bear. None of this proves that Neandertals were religious or had any concept of life beyond the grave, however.

Cro-Magnon Religion

The forerunner of modern *Homo sapiens* who replaced the Neandertal approximately 30,000 years ago was the Cro-Magnon. Like the Neandertals, the Cro-Magnons did not leave any written records of culture or religion. Again, our only information comes from the work of archaeologists. Like the Neandertals, the Cro-Magnons apparently buried their dead with tools and weapons. Graves have also yielded ornaments with which the dead were buried. In addition, some

Cro-Magnon graves have yielded bones that were painted red. Archaeologists have interpreted these factors as indicating a concern for life beyond the grave.

The most outstanding artifacts associated with the Cro-Magnon are the famous paintings and engravings located on the walls and ceilings of caves. These pictures, located in dark recesses far from the entrances, were identified as Cro-Magnon and apparently had been placed in such difficult places to keep out the uninitiated. Their location had inadvertently protected them from damage for thousands of years. Most of these paintings depict animals being killed during a hunt. The an-

Cave art from Dordogne Valley, Lascaux. Typical of primitive religious art, this painting may be an example of imitative magic through which a hunter sought to insure success in a hunt. (*Courtesy of the French Government Tourist Office.*)

imals—bison, horses, wild boar, and bears—are shown with arrows and spears entering their bodies at critical points. While the animals are painted in a very lifelike fashion, the humans hunting them are depicted by mere stick figures. The most commonly held interpretation of these paintings is that they were placed on the hidden walls of the caves by priests or magicians of the Cro-Magnon people before the hunt. It is believed that by painting the animals being killed or by retracing the paintings, the priests were hoping to predict the events of a successful hunt. Similar practices are followed by the witch doctors of contemporary basic religions, either in the form of graphic art or a drama in which members of the tribe play the part of animals being killed during a hunt.

In addition to the cave paintings, which may have had religious significance, the Cro-Magnons also left figurines carved from stone. One of the best known of these is the so-called Venus of Willendorf, a small figurine depicting a female form. Although the figure has no face, her breasts, hips, and abdomen are greatly exaggerated. It is suggested that this figure was part of a fertility cult that may have been associated with Cro-Magnon religion.

Neolithic Religion

Since Neandertal and Cro-Magnon societies primarily utilized stone tools and weapons, their cultures are identified archaeologically as Stone Age cultures. The eras that followed the Cro-Magnon period also utilized stone weapons and implements, but they were much advanced in other ways. The Neolithic or late Stone Age ran from approximately 7000 to 3000 B.C. and was characterized by many new developments in civilization.

One of the most significant advances that greatly influenced the development of religion was the development of agriculture as a way of life. When primitive people found that they could live by planting seeds, harvesting their crops, and storing the crops against their future hunger, their lives changed enormously. For the first time people did not have to move constantly from place to place in search of wild game; they could settle and live in one place as long as the soil was fertile. This meant that they now needed more permanent dwellings and that they could live in larger groups. This in turn led to the development of cities that were located close to farming areas.

In Egypt, the advancement to agriculture led to the development of the ownership of land. The sciences of surveying and mathematics were developed to establish ownership of the fields after the annual flood of the delta by the river Nile. Above all else the development of agriculture gave people more leisure time than they had ever known.

They could, in effect, afford to sit back and allow the soil to provide them with their nourishment. For the first time, certain people in the community could afford to be free to devote their total time to the mysteries of religion. A true priesthood prior to an agricultural society is really unthinkable. In addition, agricultural society for the first time became dependent upon the fertility of nature. People became aware that one year would be a year of great harvest, while the next might be a year of drought. They became aware of the regularity of the seasons, the tides, the phases of the moon, and the movements of the stars. Each of these factors caused Neolithic people to develop religions based upon the fertility of the soil as well as the fertility of humans and animals. These factors also caused them to develop mythologies in which deities became personifications of the sun, the moon, the stars, and the seasons.

Archaeological remains from the Neolithic period give some indication of the religious attitudes of the time. Large burials from this era contain the bones of men, women, and animals along with tools, weapons, and ornaments. This suggests to some that Neolithic people may have buried the chieftain with his wives, servants, and favorite animals so that they might serve him in the next life.

It also appears that Neolithic societies erected megaliths in several parts of the world. The two best examples of this practice are the great stone monuments erected at Stonehenge in England and the hundreds of megaliths set up in the fields of Brittany in France. Apparently these massive stones were quarried at a distance and transported with great effort to the place where they were erected. Since Neolithic societies left no written records about these stones it is assumed by many that their purpose was at least in part religious, but this cannot be proved.

COMMON FEATURES OF BASIC RELIGIONS

The following features appear to be common to many of those basic religions that still exist, or at least existed in some form, in the nineteenth and twentieth centuries, when anthropologists began to study them. These features have also appeared in the historical religions of which we are aware. Many of these features are evident in one form or another in the so-called advanced or developed religions. Sacrifice, for example, appears in the earliest form of nearly every extant religion. Finally, some of the features not currently a part of religions are to be found subliminally in modern cultures. For instance, while few of the developed religions would admit that magic is part of their theology, belief in the lucky coin, the unlucky day, the avoidance of the number *thirteen*, and so on, is widely found, even in the most advanced societies of the twentieth century.

Animism

Tylor suggested that primitive people originally envisioned the world as alive with souls or spirits, and on the basis of this understanding of nature developed religions. Indeed, the belief that nature is alive with spirits that have feelings and can be communicated with is one of the most common to human religious experience. In many of the basic religions people seem to believe that they are not the only spirit, that animals, trees, stones, rivers, mountains, the heavenly bodies, the seas, and the earth itself have *anima* (spirit), and that these spirits can communicate with people, can be flattered or offended by them, and can either help or hurt them. Basic religions tend to see these forces as either personal, as in the case of the typical animist, or as impersonal vague forces, which are identified as mana by Bishop Codrington and others.

On the basis of an awareness of life in nature the basic religions tend to revere nature in a way in which modern religions do not. Before building a house upon a hill, primitive peoples might ask the permission of the hill; before cutting a tree, they might ask the tree's permission, offer a sacrifice to it, and promise to use every bit of the tree to good purpose; upon hunting an animal they might apologize to the animal for killing it and treat the corpse with great respect.

On the basis of an animistic understanding of life, basic religions and many advanced religions have revered or openly worshiped nearly everything in nature. Almost any animal one can think of has at some time or another been worshiped; stones have been worshiped or have been the sites where the gods have spoken to people or received the blood of their sacrifices; mountains have frequently been the objects of worship or the places of revelation; the seas and the creatures in them have been objects of veneration; trees have frequently been the objects of religious cults; the heavenly bodies, the sun, moon, and stars, play a part in nearly every religion; and fire, water, and the earth itself have become objects of worship or important elements in worship. The list of animistic expression is almost endless.

Modern people place historic stones at the corners of their new buildings; they build expensive, elaborate, and useless fireplaces. Christians bring evergreen trees into their homes to celebrate Christmas, knowing full well that there is no basic connection between an evergreen tree and the birth of Jesus; Muslims march around the sacred black stone and kiss it during their pilgrimage to Mecca; Hindus seek to bathe in the sacred river Ganges; the Parsee bring gifts of sandalwood to be burned in the sacred fire temple; and on and on. The animistic understanding of life is one of the most pervasive and influential of all the religious and nonreligious impulses of mankind.

Magic

When modern people speak of magic, they often think in terms of sleight-of-hand tricks or illusions performed by a professional whose job is to deceive and amuse them. In basic religions the term *magic* takes on far more serious meaning.

Magicians in basic societies attempt to control nature for either the benefit of their people or the detriment of their enemies. These magicians believe that if they perform their rituals, their formulae, their dances, or their incantations properly, they will in fact be able to control nature: they can make rain, cause the crops to be bountiful, create conditions for a successful hunt, or kill their enemies.

According to one theory, the line between religion and magic is drawn by the intent of the practitioner. Magicians believe that by performing rituals they can force nature to act as they desire, whereas the practitioners of religion only seek to implore the gods on their behalf. The magician knows his will shall be done, but the priest hopes that the gods will act favorably toward him. Actually the distinction between religion and magic is never that clear, and elements of magic appear in religion, elements of religion appear in magic. Sir James Frazer, a Scottish anthropologist, believed that magic was a phase through which humankind passed on its way to religion and ultimately to science.

The most common form of magic at work among basic societies is sympathetic or imitative magic. In this form of magic one attempts to coerce nature into some act by performing that act oneself, but on a smaller scale. An example of this is the so-called voodoo doll with which the magician seeks to do evil to enemies. The doll is created in the rough image of the enemy and may contain such personal elements of the enemy as bits of hair or nail parings. Since the doll looks like the victim, whatever is done to the doll will happen to the victim. If the doll is pierced with a needle through the leg, then the victim will be injured in the leg; if the doll is pierced through the heart, then the victim will be killed or at least have severe chest pains. In primitive societies many of the rain ceremonies are based upon imitative magic. Many believe that the Cro-Magnon cave paintings that showed animals being pierced by weapons during a hunt were made by priests seeking to work imitative magic.

Another aspect of magic frequently found in basic religions is the fetish. A fetish is any object that is used to control nature in a magical fashion. In modern society such objects are called good-luck charms. The fetish is used to bring good fortune to the one who possesses it and to ward off evil. In basic societies the fetish may be almost anything: a wooden stick, a stone or collection of stones, a bone, a feather, even a special weapon. Fetishes may be held singly or in a collection, or they may be used as ornamentation of some kind. Fetishism is never very far from even the most advanced human society. In any group of people one is likely to encounter a large collection of lucky coins, rabbits' feet, religious medallions, and so on. The value that most twentieth-century people place on their fetishes probably varies considerably from that which primitive people placed on theirs. Nevertheless, the existence of fetishes and other elements of basic religion in advanced and scientific societies speaks of their enduring appeal to the human race.

Divination

The prediction of the future through divination is a very important function in basic societies. Usually this is the work of priests or someone who is especially prepared for the task, and it is accomplished by various means. Frequently divination is done through the examination of the entrails of a sacrificed animal. Sometimes it is accomplished by observation of the flights of birds or the casting of sacred dice. In ancient China, a tortoiseshell was heated until it cracked, and the pattern of the cracks was interpreted as a prediction of the future. This was later refined into the practice of casting yarrow stalks, and these patterns were interpreted in a book called the *I Ching*. Among the ancient Greeks, the future was predicted when a priestess sat on a tripod and breathed fumes that escaped from the ground at Delphi. What she said after breathing the fumes was interpreted by a priest as the message from the gods regarding the future.

Frequently, primitive societies sought knowledge of the future from a member of the group who was believed to have been possessed by the spirits. Among the peoples of Siberia this person was called a *shaman*. While the word *shaman* often bears the connotation *"priest"* or *"magician,"* the original meaning related to one who was possessed by the spirits and spoke their messages to the group.

Taboo

In the primitive scheme of life there are certain actions that must be avoided lest the spirit world release harmful effects upon the person or group. These acts to be avoided are known by the Polynesian word *tabu.* Generally in basic societies, holy persons, places, and objects are considered taboo to the ordinary person. Chieftains, priests, sacred places, fetishes, and so on, are to be avoided by the unordained person except on very special occasions or when there is special preparation. In basic societies one does not touch the person of the chief, nor does one enter the sacred areas without great fear. Great harm can come to someone who violates these tribal taboos. In the Hebrew bible we find occasions when people either knowingly or accidentally violate taboos. II Kings 2:23–25 speaks of an occasion when boys mocked and taunted the prophet Elisha. As a result, the children were mauled by two bears. II Samuel 6:1–7 tells of a man who merely touched the ark of the covenant in order to prevent its falling off a cart and as a result was struck dead by God. Isaiah, chapter 6, relates the calling of the young man, Isaiah, and his great fear and awe as he entered the holy Temple of Yahweh, which was taboo. In many other cultures the person of the king is so sacred that it is considered taboo to come into his presence without special invitation. Until fairly recent times the Japanese people considered it taboo to look upon the face of the emperor, even when he toured the streets of a city.

Other examples are numerous. In some basic societies the birth of twins is so rare as to be considered taboo. Thus when twins are born they are either killed or exiled, or they are treated as special sacred persons. The dead are often the object of taboos. Among many cultures those who handle the dead for burial are considered ritually unclean, at least for a certain period of time. Women during their menstrual period are frequently considered taboo and are often required to live in houses separate from the rest of the group. Many cultures have developed taboos regarding certain foods. Usually the food set aside for the chieftain is forbidden to the rest of the community. Certain kinds of food, such as pork, beef, and shellfish, are considered by particular groups to be ritually unclean and thus taboo.

Totems

Another practice found in some basic religions, but by no means all, is that of totemism. Totemism was first identified by white settlers in the eighteenth century when they found the practice among American Indians. Totemism was later identified within other basic societies in other parts of the world. The word *totem* is a corruption of the Ojibwa word *ototeman.*

Totemism is apparently based upon the feeling of kinship that exists between humans and other creatures or objects in nature. As such it is an extension and expression of animism. Generally it involves

A collection of totem poles in the village of northwest coast American Indians. These massive wooden poles are carved with the images of various animals and figures that are totem to the people of the village. (*Courtesy of the Department of Library Services, American Museum of Natural History.*)

some form of identification between a tribe or a clan and an animal, although totems in some parts of the world have been identified as plants or even as the sun, moon, or stars. For example, a clan may believe that it is basically related to the bear. The bear may be the ancestor of the clan, the clan may possess the characteristics of the bear (strength, ferocity, or size), or clan members may believe that when they die they will take the form of the bear. If the bear is the totem of the clan, members may not eat or kill this animal except in cases of self-defense, or on very sacred occasions, when they may eat its flesh in a ceremonial meal, which has the effect of binding the clan closer together. Members of another, neighboring clan, whose totem is the deer, may hunt and eat the bear while members of the first clan may hunt and eat the deer.

Highly developed societies, although they do not clearly and religiously adhere to totemism, still retain the vestiges of this practice. Nations are symbolized by animals, such as the eagle, the bear, or the lion, and schools choose mascots to symbolize the spirit of their athletic teams.

Sacrifice

One of the most common practices in all the religions of the world is sacrifice. Throughout history one finds people offering sacrifices of nearly every imaginable material to the gods, the spirits, the demons, and the ancestors. Most often the sacrifices are animals, which are slaughtered and then burned or cooked and eaten before the gods. However, the sacrifice of nearly every other item of value can be found. People have sacrificed grain, wine, milk, water, wood, tools, weapons, and jewelry to the gods. Occasionally religions will call for the sacrifice of a human, but this is a relatively rare practice. Usually the human who is sacrificed is an enemy who has been taken prisoner in a battle, but on infrequent occasions it is a beloved child or a young person who has been chosen especially for the altar.[1] Human sacrifice is rarely mentioned in religious literature and is usually considered an extreme but effective method of persuading the gods.[2]

The act of sacrifice has a variety of meanings. Originally it was probably considered a means of feeding the residents of the spirit world. How does one feed the spirits? One may pour water, wine, and milk on the ground and believe that as the fluid is soaked up the spirits are drinking it. One may leave food in a sacred place and assume that when the food has disappeared the gods have been fed. Or one may burn meat or grain, and the gods may inhale the smoke of the offerings. Thus the spirit world is sustained by the human world and acts favorably toward it.

At other times the sacrifice is understood simply as a gift of some sort to the spirit world. Gifts of tools, weapons, ornaments, money, incense, or even tobacco may be left in sacred places for the spirits by a person who wishes the favor of the spirits or who simply wishes to avoid offending them.

Sacrifice in some basic religions also implies the establishment of a communal bond between spirits and human beings. The worshiper

[1] Recent archaeological investigation at the ancient city of Carthage reveals that this rather advanced culture burned hundreds of its children as sacrifices over the history of the city.

[2] Human sacrifice is mentioned only occasionally in the Hebrew Bible, for example. When it is mentioned it is regarded as the supreme and outstanding sacrifice, which is usually prompted by extremely rare circumstances. See Genesis 22, Judges 11, II Kings 3:27, and Micah 6:7.

brings food to the sacred place, burns a portion of it for the gods, and then eats a portion of it or shares it with the clan. Thus the spirits and the living share a meal together, and their bond is renewed and strengthened.

Rites of Passage

Another almost universal practice among basic societies is the establishment of certain rituals at key points in the life of the individual. These are called rites of passage. The usually recognized key points in life are birth, puberty, marriage, and death. In developed societies the ceremonies at birth are most important. Frequently this is the occasion for circumcision, baptism, and so on. The infant is officially recognized as a member of the community, given a name, and at least symbolically initiated into the religion of the group.

The rites of passage at puberty are preceded by a period of instruction in the basic knowledge of the society, as well as in the arts of survival, hunting, agriculture, fire making, and so on. At puberty the child may have to undergo an ordeal of some kind. Among some American Indians, children are expected to live apart from their families for a while, fast, and seek a vision from the spirits. Among other basic societies children may be painted white or given some other highly visible mark and be sent away to live alone until the paint or the mark disappears. During this time they are expected to fend entirely for themselves. Some children are not lucky or skillful enough to survive this period. Those who do survive and return are then initiated into full adulthood in the society. The individual may also be circumcised, or given some other mark of identity, such as facial scars. During these ceremonies the young person will be more fully instructed in the religious traditions, secrets, and lore of the society and thereafter may take his or her place as a fully matured member of the group.[3] The counterpart to the puberty rites of passage in more modern societies is confirmation for Christian youths and Bar Mitzvah or Bat Mitzvah for Jewish young people.[4]

Other key points at which religious rituals and symbols are important are marriage and death. Marriage is frequently celebrated with fertility rituals of one kind or another and with the full attention of religious functionaries. The passage at death is likewise given the attention of religious rituals, both at the time of death and at the burial.

---

[3] For examples of these rites see the chapters on American Indian and African religions.
[4] Some have suggested that the twentieth-century secular version of the puberty rite of passage is the acquisition of a driver's license, with its intensive preparation, its ordeal, and the admission to adulthood of those who "pass."

Ancestor Veneration

One final characteristic of basic religions is the veneration or worship of deceased members of the family. Tylor theorized that primitive people dreamed of their departed family and friends and therefore assumed that they were not truly dead or gone but simply living in another realm. Whether this was the occasion of the beginning of religion or not is a matter of speculation. However, from what is known of basic religions, it is apparent that these people recognized that the dead lived on in some form, at least for a time, and that the dead could either help or hurt the living.

These people greatly feared the evil that the dead might do and frequently took great pains to prevent the dead from returning from their graves to harm the living. Bodies were buried with large stones on them or with stakes implanted in their chests, apparently to prevent them from roaming. Among some basic societies the names of the dead were dropped from common usage for a time, and the houses in which they died were burned to discourage their return.

At the same time, people also seemed to feel that the dead could benefit the living. Therefore steps were taken to please the dead. Their possessions, tools, weapons, favorite foods, ornaments and sometimes even their wives and servants were sent into the grave with them. Graves and tombs were decorated and elaborately cared for in order that the dead might be comfortable. Among the ancient Chinese, grave mounds were rebuilt each year, and offerings of food, drink, flowers, and even blankets were left for the comfort of the deceased. Perhaps no people made such a great effort to placate the deceased as the ancient Chinese. Their special concern was to keep alive the memory of their ancestors by memorizing their names and biographies and passing this information on to future generations.

STUDY QUESTIONS

1. Why do we speak of "basic" religions rather than "primitive" religions?

2. What are the two primary sources of information about basic religions? How trustworthy are these sources?

3. What do we believe was the purpose of the Cro-Magnon cave paintings?

4. Define "animism," and give several examples of surviving animism in modern life.

5. Distinguish "magic" from "religion."

6. List several examples of imitative or sympathetic magic.

7. Are there any taboos in modern life? How are they like those in basic societies? How are they different?

8. In your culture, what are the rites of passage?

SUGGESTED READING

Eliade, Mircea. *The Sacred and the Profane.* Translated by Willard Trask. New York: Harper Torchbooks, 1961.

Evans-Pritchard, E. E. *Theories of Primitive Religion.* Oxford: At the Clarendon Press, 1965.

Frazer, Sir James. *The New Golden Bough.* Abridgment by Theodore H. Gaster. New York: Criterion Books, 1959.

Malinowski, Bronislaw. *Magic, Science and Religion, and Other Essays.* Boston: Beacon Press, 1948.

Otto, Rudolf. *The Idea of the Holy.* Translated by John W. Harvey. London: Oxford University Press, 1948.

CHAPTER 2

American Indian Religions

Tu-Bang-Vin-Tiwa, chief priest of antelope fraternity, makes an offering at the shrine of the spider woman, and prays. (*Courtesy of Southwest Museum, Los Angeles, Calif.*)

Holy Mother Earth, the trees and all nature, are witnesses of your thoughts and deeds.
    —*A Winnebago Wise Saying*

One of the earliest and most enduring forms of religion is that practiced by the various American Indian peoples. Because of the role played by Indians in American history over the past four hundred years, their religious practices have been of interest not only to scholars but to the general public. In recent years, the rise of the American Indian movement and its publications have focused more attention on this subject.

When speaking of the religion of Native Americans, we must be aware that we are not speaking of a monolithic structure. The people identified as American Indians arrived on the North American continent between 15,000 and 20,000 years ago. Since then they have lived in nearly every section of the Americas. They have survived in many different climates, with differing lifestyles. Some American Indian tribes have been hunting and gathering societies, while others have had settled agricultural communities. Most people tend to identify the American Indian with those groups that roamed the western plains of North America in the nineteenth century. The lives of these people were centered on the pursuit of the bison. However, many of these tribes had at one time been primarily agricultural. Because of such a long time span, and the many differing lifestyles, it is difficult to talk about one set "American Indian Religion."

In studying these religions one must also be aware of the relative poverty of sources. With American Indian life covering perhaps 20,000 years, there are literary sources from only the last four hundred years. Frequently these sources have been the reports of Christian missionaries, who may or may not have been sympathetic or objective witnesses. Furthermore, the great bulk of information on American Indian religions has been written during the last one hundred years, after the Indians had come in contact with Western civilization, its religions, and its technology. Scholars often debate whether some aspect of these religions truly reflects "pure" Indian religion, or whether it developed in response to some aspect of Christianity.[1]

Our primary source of knowledge about Indian religions prior to

---

[1] A case in point is the debate over Indian eschatology. Did Indians believe in life after death, heaven, and hell? Where evidence emerges supporting these features, the charge is made that it is the result of contact with Christianity.

the coming of Europeans is archaeology. While archaeology can show much about the total culture of any people, it is of little value in revealing precise religious data. Since pre-Columbian Indians were basically pre-literate people, our knowledge of their religious beliefs is very limited.

In order to describe American Indian religion we have two major options: we can either describe the specific religion of one tribe at one period in history, or we can make general statements about the entire field of these religions. In this text we will take the second path. Following are some characteristics found in many of the better-known American Indian religions.

THE SPIRIT WORLD

To investigate the religions of Native Americans, one might begin by asking if these religions were basically polytheistic or monotheistic. Did they recognize one supreme God or multiple deities? Did Indians follow the theological patterns of Islam and Judaism, or were they more like the polytheistic Graeco-Roman religions, with their many gods? Unfortunately, there are no easy answers to these questions. In one sense, American Indian religions were polytheistic. All of nature seemed to be alive with spirits. Near at hand were the spirits that took the forms of animals and appeared in visions. There were also the guardian spirits of the various animals. There were the spirits of the dead who lived in the land of the dead. Nature was personified in many spirits. At the heart of nature was Mother Earth, who was able to provide the bounty of the earth. Thunder and lightning were also believed to be individual deities. Therefore, in the broadest sense of the word, American Indian religions were *polytheistic.* They believed that many levels of gods and spirits existed in the universe.

However, many forms of Native American religion believed that, in addition to the multiple spirits of nature, there was a single Supreme Being. American Indians believed in the Supreme Being in a manner found in many basic religions. The position that these religions took was that, above and beyond all the lesser deities, there was a high God. However, this high God was distant and apart from the concerns of earth. The day-to-day matters of life were the business of the nature spirits. It was to these spirits that one prayed and gave attention. The high God was appealed to only rarely, perhaps in the case of extreme emergency. The high God was rarely mentioned in religious conversation. He simply existed. Many of the varieties of American Indian religions took this attitude toward the Supreme Being. He was not conceived of as the creator of the universe, since Indians usually had no creation myth. The Supreme Being was not spoken of or prayed to on a regular basis. The only time prayers were directed to the Supreme Being was at the time of the Sun Dance. Thus, American Indian religions had some of the qualities of both monotheism and polytheism.

ANIMISM

Much is made of the contrast between the Indian attitude toward nature and that of the Europeans who came to America. Generally it is said that the Indians had a reverent attitude toward the land, trees, rivers, and mountains. On the other hand, the Europeans tended to look upon nature as something to be used and exploited. Thus they were willing to sacrifice the beauty and even the life of the land in order to build a technology that would make life more comfortable and pleasant. Whether or not this is an accurate characterization of either Indians or Europeans is a matter of debate. One may find examples of Indians who seemed to abuse their environment and of Europeans who loved and respected nature. However, it would appear that in general American Indians had a more reverent attitude toward nature than European Americans.

The term *animism* has been applied to American Indian religions by some scholars. In the strictest sense of the word, an animist is one who believes that the inanimate world of trees, rocks, rivers, and so on, is actually alive. The animist believes that the spirits that exist in nature have the power to either help or harm. Therefore the animist offers some form of worship to these spirits. Although American Indian religions may not be animistic in the most narrow sense, they do believe that the Supreme Being lives in all creation. If the Supreme Being lives and manifests itself in nature, nature should be respected and cared for. Therefore nature is not seen as an object to be subjugated and tamed by humankind. Rather, one must seek to live in harmony with nature. Hunting was permitted, but only under special circumstances. It was a religious pursuit in which the hunter saw the animal as a fellow creature, with a similar spirit. Therefore, a hunter prayed to the spirit of the animal before the hunt. Only those animals that were absolutely needed were killed. After the hunt, one asked the animal for forgiveness. Care was taken to use every piece of the slaughtered animal. Its meat was eaten, its hide used for clothing materials, and its bones were used for implements. Nothing was wasted. Sometimes the bones of the animal were buried in such a way so that it might be resuscitated in a future resurrection. These practices were in marked contrast to the actions of the white hunters, who slaughtered great herds of buffalo for their hides or tongues and left the bulk of the animal to rot.

Among agricultural Indians there was a reverent and prayerful attitude toward the soil, plants, and trees. The soil was often personified as "Mother Earth." Planting and harvesting were surrounded with rituals and taboos. Even the gathering of clay for the production of pottery was done with an understanding of the life in the soil. The Papago women of southern Arizona spoke to the clay that they dug for pots: "I take only what I need. It is to cook for my children."[2] Even the cutting of wood had religious overtones. One made an offering to the tree before cutting it. No wood was to be wasted. Indians believed the trees had feelings that had to be respected.

The reverent attitude of the American Indian toward nature, and its contrast to that of many whites, is best summarized in the words of a Wintu:

> The White people never cared for land or deer or bear. When we Indians kill meat, we eat it all up. When we dig roots we make little holes. When we build houses, we make little holes. When we burn grass for grasshoppers, we don't ruin things. We shake down acorns and pinenuts. We don't chop down the trees. We only use dead wood. But the White people plow up the ground, pull down the trees, kill everything. The tree says, "Don't. I am sore, Don't hurt me." But they chop it down and cut it up. The spirit of the land hates them. They blast out trees and stir it up to its depths. They saw up the trees. That hurts them. The Indians never hurt anything, but the White people destroy all. They blast rocks and scatter them on the ground. The rock says, "Don't. You are hurting me." But the White people pay no attention. When the Indians use rocks, they take little round ones for their cooking. . . . How can the spirit of the earth like the White man? . . . Everywhere the White man has touched it, it is sore.[3]

CONTROLS OVER THE SPIRIT WORLD

American Indian religions did not tend to see the universe under the control of one supreme god, in the pattern of such religions as Judaism or Islam. Neither did they see it as being under the direction of many gods in a pantheon, as in many Eastern religions or in the Graeco-Roman world view. Instead, they were primarily interested in the day-to-day life among the multiple spirits that are found in the world. The bulk of their religious attention was directed toward achieving good

[2] Ruth M. Underhill, *Red Man's Religion* (Chicago: The University of Chicago Press, 1965), p. 116.

[3] T. C. McLuhan, *Touch the Earth* (New York: Outerbridge & Dienstfrey, 1971), p. 15.

relations with the spirits of the earth, the forests, streams, and the animals on which they depended.

Sacrifice

Most of the religions of the world have practiced some form of sacrifice as a means of pleasing the deities. Throughout history religions have sacrificed animals, grain, wine, beer, and sometimes humans. This element is almost entirely missing from American Indian religions. Occasionally they sacrificed dogs, but rarely were there human sacrifices. Sometimes various rituals, such as the Sun Dance, allowed self-torment or sacrifice. But the great blood sacrifices found in many religions were not a part of Indian worship. Perhaps the animistic spirit of the American Indian felt that human or animal blood poured out to the spirits would be wasteful.

Taboos

One of the ways Native Americans protected themselves from evil that might come from the spirit world was through taboos. The concept of taboo, as it applies to American Indian religions, may be defined in the following manner.

> Taboo are all actions, circumstances, persons, objects, etc., which owing to their dangerousness fall outside the normal everyday categories of existence.[4]

A collection of widely held taboos among American Indians was in regard to menstruating women. In many cultures women are believed to have special powers for either good or evil, but the menstruating woman is thought to be particularly powerful. It is during this time that she is obviously set apart by the spirit world as one who can participate in the miracle of child production. Many American Indians believed in the unusual power of a women at these times in her life. Therefore, during menstruation a woman was to be kept away from ordinary society. In some communities she was required to leave her family and live in a special location. At this time her power could make her especially damaging to the magic necessary for a hunt. It was believed by some that even a glance from a menstruating woman could destroy the hunting ability of a man for the rest of his life. Her gaze could also destroy the magic of hunting weapons, and her presence in the forests might drive away the game forever.

[4] Ake Hultkrantz, *Belief and Worship in Native North America* (Syracuse, New York: Syracuse University Press, 1981), p. 171.

Sacred bags of the Horn Society of the Blood Indian tribe. These bags would likely contain various religious items believed by these Plains Indians to have great medicinal or religious power. (*Courtesy of E. S. Curtis, Southwest Museum, Los Angeles, Calif.*)

Another taboo widely observed by American Indians was the avoidance of the dead. No matter how beloved the dead may have been in life, after death it was feared that the spirit would continue to stay around its former home and perhaps attempt to take its former friends and family. At best, the spirits of the dead might haunt their families, causing them bad dreams. This fear of the dead was particularly apparent among some of the tribes of western America.

> A particular reaction against anything associated with death, the dead person, his belongings, the lodge in which he died, characterizes Athapascan and, to a certain degree, Shoshoni-Paiute, Yuman, and Piman peoples in western North America. . . . The Southern Athapascans in Arizona, New Mexico, and Texas, have a fright of death which ascends to morbid proportions.[5]

Because of the taboo state of the dead, steps were taken to keep them in the grave and away from contact with the human world. Sometimes the names of the dead were not spoken for years after their death. They were buried by special members of the tribe apart from

[5] Ibid., p. 94.

the immediate family, and these corpse handlers were considered to be ritually unclean for a period of time after they had touched the body. They were separated from the tribe for a period of perhaps ten days and forbidden to eat the regular food of the tribe.

Ceremonies and Rituals

Along with the observance of taboos, American Indians sought to control the forces of the spirit world with ceremonies. As is the case with many other religions, ceremonies were extremely important to Native American religions. The purpose of their ceremonies, rituals, and dances was not necessarily for worship; they were a means of renewing the partnership between humans and the spirit world. Frequently they involved dancing, fasting, ordeals, bathing, and the observance of certain taboos.

One of the most common elements in American Indian religions was the use of the dance as a means of contacting the spirit world in preparation for some special event in life. The dance was an event in which the entire community participated. It was used to prepare the tribe for the hunt, for the agricultural season, or for war. It was also used in the rites of passage. Whatever the occasion, the dance was usually accompanied by song, the beating of drums, and the shaking of rattles. The song might be made up of only a few lines that would be repeated over and over again. The drum beat might be nothing more than several people beating on a log with sticks, but the effect of hours of song and steady rhythm was hypnotic. Long hours of dancing in this atmosphere prepared the participants for contact with the spirit world.

Among the American Indian tribes whose livelihood depended on hunting, rituals prepared the hunters for their work. Hunting, like agriculture, tends to develop highly religious societies, because of its capricious nature. During one season the hunters may go forth and find an abundance of game. They may find their weapons extremely accurate and effective. In the next season, the same hunters may find game scarce or their weapons virtually useless. Therefore the spirits of the animals and the hunters themselves, along with their weapons, must be properly prepared to insure success. It is believed that the cave paintings of France, from the Cro-Magnon era, were attempts to depict the game being killed, an effort to ensure a successful hunt. The following is a description of a Pueblo ritual before a hunt.

> One of my most dramatic memories is that of standing in the plaza of a Pueblo, in the dark of a January morning, to watch the Mother of Game bring in the deer. It was almost dawn when we heard the hunter's call

from the hillside. Then shadowy forms came bounding down through the pinon trees. At first we could barely see the shaking horns and dappled hides. Then the sun's rays picked out men on all fours, with deerskins over their backs and painted staves in their hands to simulate forelegs. They leaped and gamboled before the people while around them pranced little boys who seemed actually to have the spirit of fawns.

In their midst was a beautiful Pueblo woman with long black hair, in all the regalia of white boots and embroidered *manta*. She was their Owner, the Mother of Game. But she was also Earth Mother, the source of all live things including men. She led the animals where they would be good targets for the hunters, and one by one, they were symbolically killed.[6]

A ritual such as this could be called sympathetic or imitative magic. Those persons imitating the game animals in the ceremony are symbolically called forth and killed, in the belief that during the actual hunt the real animals will similarly be killed.

Because of the identification of a kindred spirit between the American Indians and their game, the ritual of the hunt also included a merciful killing of the animal and festive treatment of its body. For example, we have reports in which Indians apologized to the animal before they killed it. Afterwards, the body of the animal was brought back to the tribe and treated as an honored guest.

Visions

In order to gain special power at some point in life, Native Americans often sought visions that would put them in contact with the spirit world. Visions were especially sought for children at puberty. Early in life children were taught that one day they must go alone into the wilderness and seek a vision of the spirit world. Usually at age nine or ten, the child was sent away from his or her family and was required to live alone until he or she received a vision. The quest for the vision was nearly always accompanied by several days of fasting. Usually the child lived without food, perhaps without water, and with only the barest of possessions and clothing. This was done so that the child might appear poor and humble before the spirits. Sometimes the child's face and body might be painted in order to resemble some special member of his or her tribe. Under such conditions the child awaited the vision. The spirits might appear in a vision or in a dream, in the guise of animals. If this were the case, the animal that appeared became the special guardian of the child, and the child's name might be changed to include this animal. At other times the vision might be of a man or woman. If the vision did not appear after two or three

---

[6]Underhill, *Red Man's Religion*, pp. 117, 118.

days of fasting and prayer, the child might feel compelled to take more extreme measures. One might cut his or her flesh or even chop off a finger as a sign of sincerity. When the vision finally came the child returned to the tribe as a fuller member of the group, having passed through this rite of passage.

Visions were sought by American Indians at other times in life. They were particularly important on the eve of great battles when extraordinary strength was needed to achieve honors. Visions were also connected with hunting. This was particularly true during the days of the great buffalo hunts in the nineteenth century.

An example of a communal effort toward achieving visions was the Sun Dance, which was practiced by the Plains Indians. Usually this dance took place in the summer months, when the heat of the sun was at its peak. Participants in the dance were seeking a vision that would give them unusual spiritual power or healing. They would gather in a lodge especially built for the purpose. The dance usually lasted three days and nights. During this time the dancers would fast and dance continually. On some occasions and among some tribes, the Sun Dance involved self-torture. Among the Oglala Sioux the dancers put thongs through the flesh of their pectoral muscles and hung from the center pole of the lodge. At times the thongs would tear through the flesh. As gruesome as this sounds, it apparently inflicted no permanent injury.

Religious Leadership

Native American religions were remarkably free of a priesthood. Although there were those in every tribe who had a special connection with the spirit world, basic religious functions were performed by every member of the group. In a sense, the religion of the American Indians was a very personal religion, one that encouraged the individual to get in contact with the spirit world, alone. Prayers, dances, songs, and visions were all to be done by every member of the tribe, according to each person's need, not by the specialist in religion. Since there was a very limited use of sacrifice, there was little need for the trained professional to perform the ritual on behalf of the untrained layperson—the procedure so common to many religions of the world. Nevertheless, among Native Americans there were several categories of religious specialists who were used occasionally in encounters with the spirit world.

The specialist most often connected with American Indian religions is the so-called medicine man. The designation *medicine man* was given to this functionary by early white settlers because they

Navajo medicine man. (*Courtesy of Laura Adams Armer, Southwest Museum, Los Angeles, Calif.*)

recognized him as one who specialized in healing. To the Indian, sickness was caused by the invasion of the body by a foreign object, and healing came about when the foreign body was removed. It was the work of the medicine man to remove such objects. The person designated as the medicine man for his tribe received his power over the forces that caused sickness through visions from the spirit world. The spirits might appear to the medicine man after a period of fasting and prayer, or they might appear without any preparation. They usually took the form of some special animal, such as the bear or the badger, since these two animals were connected with healing in Indian mythology. The spirits did not take possession of the medicine man; they only appeared to, and instructed him on a frequent basis, perhaps giving him a song or instructing him in taboos.

Because of his special contacts with the spirit world the medicine man was empowered to heal, but he could also curse and bring sickness and even death to those who incurred his wrath. This brought a great responsibility to those who were recognized as medicine men. If the medicine man encountered a sickness too serious for him to heal, he could claim that it was the work of a more powerful medicine man. But if a number of his patients were dying, he might have been held responsible for the deaths and might even have been put to death himself.

The healing process the medicine man conducted frequently consisted of a sucking ritual. If sickness were caused by the intrusion of a foreign object into the body, it was the healer's job to remove the object. Thus the medicine man would attempt to literally suck the offensive object or spirit from the body of the sick person. This ritual was often accompanied by songs, dancing, or incantations. At other times, the medicine man would give the patient various herbs and teas to alleviate pain and induce healing.[7]

Among American Indians tribes whose lives revolved directly around a settled life and an agricultural community, ceremonies were maintained from one generation to the next, and a form of priesthood was needed to preserve and pass on these rituals. These religious leaders did not claim a vision from the spirits; instead, they were individuals who memorized and carried on prayers and ceremonies for the fertility of the soil and for the general welfare of the tribe.

Other Means of Contact with the Spirit World

One of the most common elements of all American Indian religions was the use of tobacco and the sacred pipe in religious ceremonies. Tobacco was one of the forms of incense used in Native American religions; it was a part of nearly every ceremony. It was smoked when people gathered to talk of peace, war, or the hunt. It was smoked by the medicine man as he performed the healing ceremonies. Tobacco smoke was a link with the spirit world.

Tobacco was apparently grown and used only for religious purposes by the Native Americans. There is no indication that it was used as a daily narcotic, in the fashion of twentieth-century civilization. One of the reasons tobacco was reserved for special religious occasions was that it was far too strong to be used more frequently. The tobacco used in religious ceremonies was *Nicotiana rustica*, which is far stronger than tobacco used in cigarettes and pipes. The fumes of this tobacco were so strong as to be intoxicating. Smokers who have tried

[7]During colonial times, if a person had a choice between white and Indian healing he would be well-advised to go to the Indian. The medicine man might go through his rituals and give the patient herbs. His work may or may not have been effective, but it was essentially harmless. The white healer, on the other hand, often resorted to bleeding the patient. This practice frequently weakened the sick person and hastened death.

Dakota tobacco pipe and pouch. The practice of smoking tobacco in decorated pipes was one of the means of contact with the spirit world in some American Indian religions. (*Courtesy of the Department of Library Services, American Museum of Natural History.*)

Indian tobacco marvel that anyone was ever able to smoke the six puffs usually required in ceremonies.

The ritual tobacco was occasionally smoked in cigarettes rolled from corn husks, but it was more frequently smoked in pipes. The bowls of these pipes were made from either clay or stone and the stems from reeds. Sometimes the most ceremonial of the pipes had stems up to four feet in length. They were often decorated with paints and feathers and were carried into battle or the hunt as talismans of the tribes.

The use of peyote in American Indian religions has received a great deal of attention in recent years. Peyote has been used in religious ceremonies for over four hundred years by the Indians of Mexico. The practice has spread to North American tribes over the last one hundred years. The peyote plant itself is described in the following manner:

> Peyote (Nahuatl, peyotl) or *Lophophora williamsii* Lemaire, is a small, spineless, carrot-shaped cactus growing in the Rio Grande Valley and southward. It contains nine narcotic alkaloids of the isoquiniline series, some of them strychnine-like in physiological action, the rest morphine-

like. In pre-Columbian times the Aztec, Huichol, and other Mexican Indians ate the plant ceremonially either in the dried or green state. This produces profound sensory and psychic derangements lasting twenty-four hours, a property which led the natives to value and use it religiously.[8]

One of the active morphine-like alkaloids found in peyote is mescaline. After a certain quantity of peyote is eaten or ingested in a tea, mescaline produces hallucinations and visions, and it is because of these colorful visions that peyote has been made a part of some Indian religious ceremonies.

With the defeats that the Native Americans suffered at the hands of the United States government at the end of the nineteenth century, Indians began to turn to the use of peyote ceremonies. Previously, the vision was sought only occasionally in Indian religions—at the rite of passage at puberty, prior to a great hunt or battle, or by the medicine man at crucial points in his life. However, when so little was left to the American Indians, and when they had been defeated and crowded into reservations, many felt the need of the visions more frequently. Therefore the peyote cult grew and developed rituals. Some scholars in the field of American Indian religions say the peyote cult continues to grow.[9]

In the early part of the twentieth century there developed an amalgamation of the peyote cult and a form of Christianity. Many American Indians has been taught the principles of the Christian religion, but they also appreciated the values of their own religion and peyote. Some reasoned thus: The Christians used wine and a wafer in celebrating communion, and Indians used the peyote button and tea in communing with the spirit world. Therefore, in 1918, a group that blended Christianity and the peyote cult, called The Native American Church, was legally organized in Oklahoma. In 1944 the movement became nationwide and was called "The Native American Church of the United States." In 1950 it expanded to include Canadian Indians, and was called "The Native American Church of North America." Currently it is estimated that perhaps 225,000 people are members of this religious movement.

The use of peyote in American Indian religions has had a running battle with the various courts of the United States. In the early part of this century peyote was outlawed by many states because it was considered a "narcotic." However, it has been proven that peyote is not habit-forming and produces no ill-effects. There is no current fed-

[8] Weston La Barre, *The Peyote Cult* (New York: Schocken Books, 1969), p. 7.
[9] See Hultkrantz, *Belief and Worship in Native North America*, p. 283.

eral legislation against its use in the religious ceremonies of American Indians.

DEATH AND LIFE AFTER DEATH

In discussing the beliefs of the American Indian about death and life after death, we must be reminded again that we are discussing a great variety of people who lived in various climates and had a variety of cultural systems. Therefore, attitudes toward death and practices regarding death varied widely. Furthermore, American Indians have been exposed to Christian eschatology for more than four hundred years. It is difficult to distinguish the true Native American view of the dead from the view that evolved in response to Christianity. Therefore, one can no more speak of *the* American Indian concept of life after death than one can speak of *the* American Indian religion; one can only generalize.

As we have noted, Native Americans tended to fear the dead and handled them with great care, lest they return and somehow trouble the living. Many of the most serious taboos of American Indian life were built around the treatment of the dead. Yet, in spite of the fear and dread of the dead, there was apparently little fear of death itself. Missionaries, anthropologists, and other white observers have noted again and again the remarkable lack of fear demonstrated by Indians when they were facing death.

Generally, American Indians seem to have believed in the existence of two souls, neither of which could be considered immortal in any sense. One soul was the life, or breath, that accompanies the body. When the body died, or at least when it decayed, this soul also died. The second soul was what might be called a free soul. This soul wandered about during dreams, or left the body during sickness. After death this free soul went to the land of the dead. Little is said about this land of the dead among Indians. Sometimes it is considered a happy place and sometimes it is a place of sadness. Often the land of the dead seems to be a continuation of this current life, but on another plane of existence. Most Indian descriptions of the land of the dead seem to indicate that all went to this land. There was no heaven for those who had been righteous and no hell for those who had been evil.

Some American Indians attempted to aid the deceased in the journey to the land of the dead by burying food and drink with the body. Occasionally this was carried further when an important person died, and an attempt was made to send along a guide to aid the deceased

Picture writing on a buffalo skin, depicting the principal events in the life of a Pawnee chief. (*Courtesy of Smithsonian Institution National Anthropological Archives.*)

in finding the land of the dead. Sometimes an animal was killed to act as guide, and on other occasions an enemy was killed for the same purpose. Among the Natchez Indians of Mississippi, when a great chieftain died, large numbers of wives, children, friends, and animals were sacrificed to accompany the dead.

When the free soul reached the land of the dead it did not live forever. Perhaps like the Hebrews' concept of *Sheol* or the Greeks' idea of *Hades*, the American Indian believed that the soul existed in the land of the dead only so long as the person was remembered by the living. When the person began to be forgotten, the free soul began to fade and would eventually disappear.

Occasionally, among American Indians, there are references to some beliefs in reincarnation. Sometimes an infant might resemble a deceased relative in some fashion and it was believed that the dead might have returned to live again. However, this feature is missing from most Native American religions. There seems to be no widespread belief in reincarnation. Neither is there an emphasis on the ancestors, after the manner of the Chinese.

American Indian Religions Today

With the coming of the European settlers and their religions, Native American cultures have undergone severe stress. One of the first activities of the whites was to seek to convert Indians to Christianity. This movement has continued for more than four centuries. The structure of Christianity is such that it insists on an all-or-nothing-at-all conversion. For an Indian to become a Christian meant that he had to turn his back on his former religion. The influence of Christianity has been so strong that today most Indians would consider themselves Christians.

Christianity among Native Americans has been tempered by two movements. The first, which we have discussed, is the Native American Church. In this church Indians attempt to combine Christianity with some aspects of their own religion, specifically the religious use of peyote. The Native American Church is seen as a viable alternative to white Christianity and continues to grow today.

The second factor that has involved traditional Indian religion is a revived interest in Native American culture. In the past two decades various groups have reasserted the values of Indian culture, including religion. These groups have taught that Indian ways and Indian religion are better for Native Americans than those of white culture. Therefore there is a renewed interest in studying and practicing traditional Indian religion.

STUDY QUESTIONS

1. Are Native American religions best described as monotheistic or polytheistic?

2. Give several examples of Indian animism as it relates to hunting and agriculture.

3. List some of the major taboos of Indian society.

4. What was the purpose of the Sun Dance?

5. In American Indian thinking, what is the primary cause of sickness? How is it to be cured?

6. Discuss the use of peyote in religious ceremonies. How is peyote involved in the Christian communion ritual in the Native American Church?

7. Distinguish the view of death in Native American religions from that of the traditional Judaeo-Christian position.

SUGGESTED READING

Deloria, Vine. *God is Red.* New York: Grosset & Dunlap, 1973.

Hultkrantz, Ake. *Belief and Worship in Native North America.* Syracuse, N.Y.: Syracuse University Press, 1981.

La Barre, Weston. *The Peyote Cult.* New York: Schocken Books, 1969.

McLuhan, T. C. *Touch the Earth.* New York: Outerbridge & Dienstfrey, 1971.

Underhill, Ruth M. *Red Man's Religion.* Chicago: The University of Chicago Press, 1965.

American Indian Myths

The following materials demonstrate the perspective on nature that is held by some American Indian religions. The first
is the story of a divine visitor to a Sioux tribe and shows the
reverence for nature which was an integral part of these religions. The second section contains the Zuñi creation story.[10]

Sioux Legend of the Buffalo Maiden

Braided sweet grass was dipped into a buffalo horn containing rain water
and was offered to the Maiden. The chief said, "Sister, we are now ready
to hear the good message you have brought." The pipe, which was in the
hands of the Maiden, was lowered and placed on the rack. Then the Maiden
sipped the water from the sweet grass.

Then, taking up the pipe again, she arose and said: "My relatives, brothers and sisters: Wakantanka has looked down, and smiles upon us this day
because we have met as belonging to one family. The best thing in a family
is good feeling towards every member of the family. I am proud to become
a member of your family—a sister to you all. The sun is your grandfather,
and he is the same to me. Your tribe has the distinction of being always
very faithful to promises, and of possessing great respect and reverence
towards sacred things. It is known also that nothing but good feeling pre-
vails in the tribe, and that whenever any member has been found guilty of
committing any wrong, that member has been cast out and not allowed to
mingle with the other members of the tribe. For all these good qualities in
the tribe you have been chosen as worthy and deserving of all good gifts.
I represent the Buffalo tribe, who have sent you this pipe. You are to receive this pipe in the name of all the common people (Indians). Take it,
and use it according to my directions. The bowl of the pipe is red stone—
a stone not very common and found only at a certain place. This pipe shall
be used as a peacemaker. The time will come when you shall cease hostilities against other nations. Whenever peace is agreed upon between two
tribes or parties this pipe shall be a binding instrument. By this pipe the
medicine-men shall be called to administer help to the sick."

Turning to the women, she said:

"My dear sisters, the women: You have a hard life to live in this world,
yet without you this life would not be what it is. Wakantanka intends that
you shall bear much sorrow—comfort others in time of sorrow. By your
hands the family moves. You have been given the knowledge of making

[10] Frances Densmore, *Teton Sioux Music* (Bureau of American Ethnology, Bulletin 61, 1918),
    pp, 65, 66.

49

clothes and of feeding the family. Wakantanka is with you in your sorrows and joins you in your griefs. He has given you the great gift of kindness toward every living creature on earth. You he has chosen to have a feeling for the dead who are gone. He knows that you remember the dead longer than do the men. He knows that you love your children dearly."

Then turning to the children:

"My little brothers and sisters. Your parents were once little children like you, but in the course of time they became men and women. All living creatures were once small, but if no one took care of them they would never grow up. Your parents love you and have made many sacrifices for your sake in order that Wakantanka may listen to them, and that nothing but good may come to you as you grow up. I have brought this pipe for them, and you shall reap some benefit from it. Learn to respect and reverence this pipe, and above all, lead pure lives. Wakantanka is your great grandfather."

Turning to the men:

"Now my dear brothers: In giving you this pipe you are expected to use it for nothing but good purposes. The tribe as a whole shall depend upon it for their necessary needs. You realize that all your necessities of life come from the earth below, the sky above, and the four winds. Whenever you do anything wrong against these elements they will always take some revenge upon you. You should reverence them. Offer sacrifices through this pipe. When you are in need of buffalo meat, smoke this pipe and ask for what you need and it shall be granted you. On you it depends to be a strong help to the women in the raising of children. Share the women's sorrow. Wakantanka smiles on the man who has a kind feeling for a woman, because the woman is weak. Take this pipe, and offer it to Wakantanka daily. Be good and kind to the little children."

Turning to the chief:

"My older brother: You have been chosen by these people to receive this pipe in the name of the whole Sioux tribe. Wakantanka is pleased and glad this day because you have done what is required and expected that every good leader should do. By this pipe the tribe shall live. It is your duty to see that this pipe is respected and reverenced. I am proud to be called a sister. May Wakantanka look down on us and take pity on us and provide us with what we need. Now we shall smoke the pipe."

Then she took the buffalo chip which lay on the ground, lighted the pipe, and pointing to the sky with the stem of the pipe, she said, "I offer this to Wakantanka for all the good that comes from above." (Pointing to the earth:) "I offer this to the earth, whence come all good gifts." (Pointing to the cardinal points:) "I offer this to the four winds, whence come all good things." Then she took a puff of the pipe, passed it to the chief, and said, "Now my dear brothers and sisters, I have done the work for which

I was sent here and now I will go, but I do not wish any escort. I only ask that the way be cleared before me."

Then, rising, she started, leaving the pipe with the chief, who ordered that the people be quiet until their sister was out of sight. She came out of the tent on the left side, walking very slowly; as soon as she was outside the entrance she turned into a white buffalo calf.

Zuñi Genesis: The Creation and Emergence of Man[11]

A Myth from the Zuñi Indians of New Mexico

Before the beginning of the new-making, Awonawilona (The Maker and Container of all, the All-father Father), solely had being. There was nothing else whatsoever throughout the great space of the ages save everywhere black darkness in it, and everywhere void desolation.

In the beginning of the new-made, Awonawilona conceived within himself and thought outward in space, whereby mists of increase, steams potent of growth, were evolved and uplifted. Thus, by means of his innate knowledge, the All-container made himself in person and form of the Sun whom we hold to be our father and who thus came to exist and appear. With his appearance came the brightening of the spaces with light, and with the brightening of the spaces the great mist-clouds were thickened together and fell, whereby was evolved water in water; yea, and the world-holding sea.

With his substance of flesh outdrawn from the surface of his person, the Sun-father formed the seed-stuff of twain worlds, impregnating therewith the great waters, and lo! in the heat of his light these waters of the sea grew green and scums rose upon them, waxing wide and weighty until, behold! they became Awitelin Tsita, the "Four-fold containing Mother-earth," and Apoyan Tä'chu, the "All-covering Father-sky."

The Genesis of Men and the Creatures

From the lying together of these twain upon the great world-waters, so vitalizing, terrestrial life was conceived; whence began all beings of earth, men and the creatures, in the Four-fold womb of the world.

Thereupon the Earth-mother repulsed the Sky-father, growing big and sinking deep into the embrace of the waters below, thus separating from the Sky-father in the embrace of the waters above. As a woman forebodes evil for her first-born ere born, even so did the Earth-mother forebode, long withholding from birth her myriad progeny and meantime seeking counsel with the Sky-father. "How," said they to one another, "shall our children,

---

[11] F. H. Cushing, *Outlines of Zuñi Creation Myths* (Bureau of American Ethnology, Thirteenth Annual Report, 1896), pp. 379–383.

when brought forth, know one place from another, even by the white light of the Sun-father?"

Now like all the surpassing beings the Earth-mother and the Sky-father were 'hlimna (changeable), even as smoke in the wind; transmutable at thought, manifesting themselves in any form at will, like as dancers may by mask-making.

Thus, as a man and woman, spake they, one to the other. "Behold!" said the Earth-mother as a great terraced bowl appeared at hand and within it water, "this is as upon me the homes of my tiny children shall be. On the rim of each world-country they wander in, terraced mountains shall stand, making in one region many, whereby country shall be known from country, and within each, place from place. Behold, again!" said she as she spat on the water and rapidly smote and stirred it with her fingers. Foam formed, gathering about the terraced rim, mounting higher and higher. "Yea," said she, "and from my bosom they shall draw nourishment, for in such as this shall they find the substance of life whence we were ourselves sustained, for see!" Then with her warm breath she blew across the terraces; white flecks of the foam broke away, and, floating over above the water, were shattered by the cold breath of the Sky-father attending, and forthwith shed downward abundantly fine mist and spray! "Even so, shall white clouds float up from the great waters at the borders of the world, and clustering about the mountain terraces of the horizons be borne aloft and abroad by the breaths of the surpassing of soul-beings, and of the children, and shall hardened and broken be by the cold, shedding downward, in rain spray, the water of life, even into the hollow places of my lap! For therein chiefly shall nestle our children mankind and creature-kind, for warmth in thy coldness."

Lo! even the trees on high mountains near the clouds and the Sky-father crouch low toward the Earth-mother for warmth and protection! Warm is the Earth-mother, cold the Sky-father, even as woman is the warm, man the cold being!

"Even so!" said the Sky-father; "Yet not alone shalt thou helpful be unto our children, for behold!" and he spread his hand abroad with the palm downward and into all the wrinkles and crevices thereof he set the semblance of shining yellow corn grains; in the dark of the early world-dawn they gleamed like sparks of fire, and moved as his hand was moved over the bowl, shining up from and also moving in the depths of the water therein. "See!" said he, pointing to the seven grains clasped by his thumb and four fingers, "by such shall our children be guided; for behold, when the Sun-father is not nigh, and thy terraces are as the dark itself (being all hidden therein), then shall our children be guided by lights—like to these lights of all the six regions turning round the midmost one—as in and around the midmost place, where these our children shall abide, lie all the other regions of space! Yea! and even as these grains gleam up from the water, so shall seed-grains like to them, yet numberless, spring up from thy bosom when touched by my waters, to nourish our children." Thus and in other ways many devised they for their offspring.

Anon in the nethermost of the four cave-wombs of the world, the seed of men and the creatures took form and increased; even as within eggs in warm places worms speedily appear, which growing, presently burst their shells and become as may happen, birds, tadpoles or serpents, so did men and all creatures grow manifoldly and multiply in many kinds. [But these are still imperfect beings: heaped and crowded together in the darkness, they crawl over one another like reptiles, grumbling, lamenting, spitting, and using indecent and insulting language. A few among them try to escape, however. One above all, distinguished from all the others as the most intelligent is the all-sacred master, Poshaiyankya, who somehow participates in the divine condition. He emerges all alone into the light after having traversed all the four telluric cave-wombs one after another. He arrives on the surface of the Earth, which has the appearance of a vast island, wet and unstable; and he makes his way towards the Sun-father to implore him to deliver mankind and the creatures there below. The sun then repeats the process of the creation, but this time it is creation of another order. The Sun wishes to produce intelligent, free and powerful beings. He again impregnates the foam of the Earth-mother, and from this foam twins are born. The Sun endows them with every kind of magical power and orders them to be the ancestors and lords of men.] Well instructed of the Sun-father, they lifted the Sky-father with their great cloud-bow into the vault of the high zenith, that the earth might become warm and thus fitter for their children, men and the creatures. Then along the trail of the sun-seeking Poshaiyankya they sped backward swiftly on their floating fog-shield, westward to the Mountain of Generation. With the magic knives of the thunderbolt they spread open the uncleft depths of the mountain, and still on their cloud-shield—even as a spider in her web descendeth—so descend they, unerringly, into the dark of the under-world. There they abode with men and the creatures, attending them, coming to know them, and becoming known of them as masters and fathers, thus seeking the ways for leading them forth.

The Birth and Delivery of Men and the Creatures

Now there were growing things in the depths, like grasses and crawling vines. So now the Beloved Twain breathed on the stems of these grasses (growing tall, as grass is wont to do toward the light, under the opening they had cleft and whereby they had descended), causing them to increase vastly and rapidly by grasping and walking round and round them, twisting them upward until lo! they reach forth even into the light. And where successively they grasped the stems ridges were formed and thumb-marks whence sprang branching leaf-stems. Therewith the two formed a great ladder whereon men and the creatures might ascend to the second cave-floor, and thus not be violently ejected in after-time by the throes of the Earth-mother, and thereby be made demoniac and deformed.

Up this ladder, into the second cave-world, men and the beings crowded, following closely the Two Little but Mighty Ones. Yet many fell back and, lost in the darkness, peopled the under-world, whence they were delivered in after-time amid terrible earth shakings, becoming the monsters and fearfully strange beings of olden time. Lo! in this second womb it was dark as is the night of a stormy season, but larger of space and higher than had been the first, because it was nearer the navel of the Earth-mother, hence named K'olin tebuli (the Umbilical-womb, or the Place of Gestation). Here again men and the beings increased, and the clamour of their complainings grew loud and beseeching. Again the two, augmenting the growth of the great ladder, guided them upward, this time not all at once, but in successive bands to become in time the fathers of the six kinds of men (the yellow, the tawny grey, the red, the white, the mingled, and the black races), and with them the gods and creatures of them all. Yet this time also, as before, multitudes were lost or left behind. The third great cave-world, where unto men and the creatures had now ascended, being larger than the second and higher, was lighter, like a valley in starlight, and named Awisho tehuli—the Vaginal-womb, or the Place of Sex-generation or Gestation. For here the various peoples and beings began to multiply apart in kind one from another; and as the nations and tribes of men and the creatures thus waxed numerous as before, here, too, it became overfilled. As before, generations of nations now were led out successively (yet many lost, also as hitherto) into the next and last world-cave, Tepahaian tehuli, the Ultimate-uncoverable, or the Womb of Parturition.

Here it was light like the dawning, and men began to perceive and to learn variously according to their natures, wherefore the Twain taught them to seek first of all our Sun-father, who would, they said, reveal to them wisdom and knowledge of the ways of life—wherein also they were instructing them as we do little children. Yet like the other cave worlds, this too became, after long time, filled with progeny; and finally, at periods, the Two led forth the nations of men and the kinds of being, into this great upper world, which is called Tek'ohaian ulahnane, or the World of Disseminated Light and Knowledge or Seeing.

CHAPTER 3

African Religions

Mask worn in a ritual dance by the women's society of the Mende tribe of Sierre Leone. (*Courtesy of Mrs. William Bascom.*)

We worship the Orisha.
If we worship the Orisha
We will always have money,
We will always have children.
                —*Yoruba Song*

During the past forty years, Europe's control over its former empires has declined, and many of the countries that were once members of these empires have become independent. Much of this activity has taken place on the vast continent of Africa. Today these new African nations have become a vocal and active segment of the so-called Third World. Many of them control raw materials that are essential to the industrialized nations of the world. The leaders of today and of the future must learn to deal with Africans on both political and business levels if there is to be peace and prosperity in the world.

Essential to understanding the leaders of black Africa is a knowledge of their culture. A major step in understanding customs and values is a basic knowledge of religion. As it is in the case of nearly every other people in the world, religion is one of the keystones of African culture. A basic understanding of African religions will provide an awareness of African customs, the African approach to the family, the African appreciation of land, and, of course, the African view of death and life beyond death.

Perhaps no religions have been so confused in the minds of Western audiences as the religions of Africa. The images of these religions as presented in films and popular literature depict the black African as a hopeless savage and African religion as ugly superstition. Most people associate African religions with the image of a missionary in the cannibal's pot, about to be boiled and eaten. Or people remember the many, many motion pictures in which the evil witch doctor in a horrible mask tries to put a voodoo curse upon a victim. Even supposedly factual sources are likely to contain images of blood sacrifice, fetishes, shrunken heads, and babies sacrificed to crocodile gods. All these are distorted images drawn from half truths and fertile imaginations. Nevertheless, they have left their impression on most Westerners. As with American Indian religions, the full truth about African religions cannot be told in such a brief and general text as this because the topic is simply too broad. There is no "African religion" as such, and beliefs and practices vary widely throughout the African continent. However, general truths, concepts, and trends about certain areas of African religions can be highlighted and some of the popular misconceptions dispelled.

NON-NATIVE AFRICAN RELIGIONS

The emphasis of this chapter will be on the basic concepts of native African religions. However, we cannot overlook several non-native religions that have had enormous influence upon the continent in the past, and which may influence it even more in the future. Today approximately one-half of the African population is estimated to adhere to non-native religions.

Christianity

Christianity has had a long and illustrious history in Africa. Indeed, Africa may have been one of the first locations for Christianity outside of Palestine. The earliest known fragment of the New Testament is a section from the Gospel of John that was found in Egypt. This fragment is dated approximately 125 A.D. It is reasonable to assume that Christian missionaries took the trade routes by land and sea to North Africa early in the first Christian centuries.

Regardless of the date that Christianity entered Africa, it found fertile ground there. Some of the finest minds and leaders of early Christianity were from this region. Leaders such as Augustine, Origen, Arius, Athanasius, Tertullian, and Cyprian came from North Africa. The libraries, universities, and fine scholarly traditions found in such communities as Alexandria contributed much to early Christian thought.

In the seventh and eighth centuries the new religion of Islam swept across northern Africa and eventually became the religion of most of the African people. The only African nations that remained Christian after the Muslim conquest were Ethiopia and Nubia. In Egypt, a minority sect of Christians, called *Copts,* remains to this day.

It was not until the fifteenth century that any part of Africa south of the Sahara was exposed to Christianity. Portugese traders of that era were the first Europeans to venture along the west and east coasts of Africa, bringing their religion and its missionaries with them. They succeeded in converting many Africans all over the continent to Christianity. The period from the seventeenth through the nineteenth centuries was the era of the slave trade, so the encounter between Christian Europeans and black Africans was not pleasant. With the end of the slave trade in the nineteenth century and the eventual rise of the colonial empires, Christian missionaries made a serious effort to convert black Africans. Because these missionaries were representatives of the dominant European and American cultures, and because they brought with them modernity, medicine, and education, in many cases they were successful. It is estimated that of a total population of approximately 537 million, today there are 147 million Christians in Africa.[1]

In addition to the traditional Catholic and Protestant groups in Africa, many independent Christian sects developed there. In many cases the sects are amalgamations of Christian doctrines and native African religious concepts. In other cases these sects are Christian groups that have developed around the charismatic leadership of a prophet or a faith healer. It is estimated that there may be as many as six thousand independent Christian churches in Africa.[2] In the 1980s, Christianity is the fastest growing religion on the African continent.

Islam

As it moved out of the Arabian desert, Islam spread over nearly all of northern Africa within a century of the death of the prophet Muhammad. However, like Christianity before it, Islam seemed restricted or bounded by the Sahara desert, and with rare exception, did not move southward for many centuries.

In the eleventh and twelfth centuries Muslim traders began to spread Islam southward. Several of the large African empires of that era, such as Ghana, Mali, and Songhai, were converted to Islam. During the centuries that followed, Islam continued to grow in black Africa. However, it too was impeded by the slave trade, because many of the agents of the slave trade were Arab. Because Islam is a religion that stresses the brotherhood and equality of all Muslims before Allah, it was difficult for Muslims to convert those whom they might later enslave. With the end of the slave trade in the nineteenth century, and with the travel advantages of the colonial period, Muslim missionary activity enjoyed a tremendous upsurge.

In the twentieth century Islam has had a great entree into black Africa, for several reasons. First, Islam is widely identified as the religion of Third World nations, and many Africans find this appealing. Second, Islam can be more easily adapted to native African customs and beliefs than other world religions. Islam speaks of the one true High God, Allah, and this is a concept shared with many native African religions. Finally, Islam allows polygamy under certain conditions, and this too has been a regular feature of African life. Today it is estimated that there are approximately 153 million Muslims in Africa.[3]

---

[1] *1985 Encyclopedia Britannica Book of the Year* (Chicago: Encyclopedia Britannica Inc., 1985), p. 365.

[2] Benjamin C. Ray, *African Religions* (Englewood Cliffs, N.J.: Prentice-Hall, 1976), p. 194.

[3] *1985 Encyclopedia Britannica Book of the Year*, p. 365.

A minaret in Agadez, Niger shows Muslim influence in Africa. (*Courtesy of the United Nations. Photo by S. Jackson.*)

Other Religions

Christianity and Islam are the two largest non-native religions in Africa, but there are elements of several other religions of the world to be found on the continent. A distinct branch of Judaism is found in

Ethiopia among a group of people called the Falashas. The Falashas trace their ancestry back to the Queen of Sheba in the tenth century B.C. They practice a form of Judaism that is influenced by the Penta-teuch but which does not seem to be aware of the Talmud.

On the east coast of Africa there are settlements of people from India. Here live one-half million Hindus and small groups of Bud-dhists and Confucianists. Although there is speculation that some of these Indian religions may have influenced certain aspects of African Islam, they seem to offer little attraction for the native African. The major choice seems to be among native African religions, Christian-ity, and Islam.

NATIVE RELIGIONS

When we speak of native African religions, we cannot speak with authority about a single religion, theology, world view, or cult. Africa is a huge continent that has supported millions of people for many centuries. Since most of the religions of Africa have existed in pre-literate times, the modern student of religion must realize that only the tip of the iceberg can be known. What *is* known about African religions has been gathered by modern anthropologists or has been remembered from the past by Africans. Furthermore, religious beliefs and practices of any one group of Africans are not necessarily shared by other groups. Therefore, when we speak of basic concepts within these religions we must keep in mind that these ideas do not always apply universally; there is a great variety of beliefs.

The High God

A belief that above all local deities there is one supreme High God who created the world and then withdrew from active participation is frequently found among many of the polytheistic religions of the world. This belief is also found among some African peoples. Al-though most of the native religions of Africa are basically polytheistic in their day-to-day practices, there is an overriding belief that beyond all the minor gods, spirits, and ancestors, one High God exists. When this became known among early anthropologists some of them con-cluded that Africans had originally been monotheistic but had lapsed into polytheism.[4] There are few, if any, authorities on African reli-gions who advocate this position today, however.

---

[4]The best known advocate of this position was Father Wilhelm Schmidt, in his book *Der Ursprung der Gottesidee.*

In many African religions the High God seems to have been a creator god who did his work and then retired to some distant place. It is currently believed that this god has little contact with the world and its daily operations. Typical of the African understanding of the High God is the Yoruba story of Olorun. The Yoruba are native to the central west Africa territory now governed by Nigeria. In their mythology the High God, Olorun, gave the job of creating the world to his eldest son, Obatala. This son failed to complete the task, so it was passed on to the younger son, Odudua, but he too failed. Therefore Olorun had to complete the work of creation himself. He assigned the other tasks of creation to various *orisha*, who are regarded as lesser deities. After the work of creation was done. Olorun seems to have retired to the heavens with little interest or control over his universe. While various Yoruba villages have special *orisha* who have saved them or helped them in times of trouble, there is no record that the Olorun ever has been of direct assistance. He remains detached from the problems of the world and allows the *orisha* to intervene when necessary.

A legend from the people of Upper Zambezi reveals the retiring nature of the High God even more clearly.

In the beginning Nyambi made all things. He made animals, fishes, birds. At that time he lived on earth with his wife, Nasilele. One of Nyambi's creatures was different from all the others. His name was Kamonu. Kamonu imitated Nyambi in everything Nyambi did. When Nyambi worked in wood, Kamonu worked in wood; when Nyambi forged iron, Kamonu forged iron.

After awhile Nyambi began to fear Kamonu.

Then one day Kamonu forged a spear and killed a male antelope, and he went on killing. Nyambi grew very angry at this.

"Man, you are acting badly," he said to Kamonu. "These are your brothers. Do not kill them."

Nyambi drove Kamonu out into another land. But after awhile Kamonu returned. Nyambi allowed him to stay and gave him a garden to cultivate.

It happened that at night buffaloes wandered into Kamonu's garden and he speared them; after that some elands, and he killed one. After some time Kamonu's dog died; then his pot broke; then his child died. When Kamonu went to Nyambi to tell him what had happened he found his dog and his pot and his child at Nyambi's.

Then Kamonu said to Nyambi, "Give me medicine so that I may keep my things." But Nyambi refused to give him medicine. After this, Nyambi met with his two counselors and said, "How shall we live since Kamonu knows too well the road hither?"

Nyambi tried various means to flee Kamonu. He removed himself and his court to an island across the river. But Kamonu made a raft of reeds and crossed over to Nyambi's island. Then Nyambi piled up a huge mountain and went to live on its peak. Still Nyambi could not get away from man. Kamonu found his way to him. In the meantime men were multiplying and spreading all over the earth.

Finally Nyambi sent birds to go look for a place for Litoma, god's town. But the birds failed to find a place. Nyambi sought council from a diviner. The diviner said, "Your life depends on Spider." And Spider went and found an abode for Nyambi and his court in the sky. Then Spider spun a thread from earth to the sky and Nyambi climbed up on the thread. Then the diviner advised Nyambi to put out Spider's eyes so that he could never see the way to heaven again and Nyambi did so.

After Nyambi disappeared into the sky Kamonu gathered some men around him and said, "Let us build a high tower and climb up to Nyambi." They cut down trees and put log on log, higher and higher toward the sky. But the weight was too great and the tower collapsed. So that Kamonu never found his way to Nyambi's home.

But every morning when the sun appeared, Kamonu greeted it saying, "Here is our king. He has come." And all the other people greeted him shouting and clapping. At the time of the new moon men call on Nasilele, Nyambi's wife.[5]

Occasionally the High God is an object of worship, and some communities have temples and priests dedicated to him. Apparently, however, most Africans regard the High God as too high, too distant, and too great to pay much attention to his worship. It is the lesser spirits and the ancestors that receive the greatest attention in African religions.

The Lesser Spirits

When we get beyond the stories of the High God that are found in many African religions, we encounter true animism. Like many other people of the world, the Africans tend to people the universe with spirits. All the earth, the seas, and the skies are believed to contain a spiritual or life force similar to that in humankind. These forces can be beneficial or harmful; they are subject to flattery and sacrifice. Therefore it behooves humans to be aware of these spirits and to seek their favor.

Africans recognize the life force in mountains, forests, pools, streams, trees, and animals. They are aware of it in the sun and the moon. Not only is it found in these objects, but Africans also see it in storms, thunder, and lightning. In fact, in some west African villages there are temples, priests, and cults established to worship the storm gods. The earth, too, is worshiped. As in ancient Europe and nearly every

[5] Susan Feldmann, ed., *African Myths and Tales* (New York: Dell, 1963), pp. 36–37.

Serpent temple, Dahomey. *(Courtesy of Dr. Boniface Obicheri.)*

other ancient culture, the earth is often pictured as a goddess and receives worship by some Africans. Among the Ashanti people there are regular ceremonies to the Earth Mother in which the following lines are recited:

> Earth, while I am yet alive,
> It is upon you that I put my trust,
> Earth who receives my body . . .
> We are addressing you,
> And you will understand.[6]

Among native Africans water is frequently recognized as a sacred element. Water is used in religious rituals the world over and is particularly important and sacred in many of the basic religions. When the life of a people is dependent upon rainfall, rivers, and streams, or when water appears to have a life of its own, its religious significance is accentuated. When Africans use water for an essentially religious ritual such as bathing a new-born baby, the water must come from a source of *living water* (for instance, a spring or a river), and must not be boiled because that would kill the spirit or power in it. Throughout Africa, rivers, streams, lakes, springs, and the seas are venerated

[6] Geoffrey Parrinder, *African Traditional Religion* (London: Hutchinson House, 1954), p. 48.

for the spiritual powers that abide in them. Because serpents are often connected with bodies of water, they too are often regarded with awe, and cults are sometimes developed for their worship.

Although the nature gods and lesser spirits of the universe are seldom a major aspect of African worship, they are recognized and do receive veneration. Worship may vary from fully established cults, complete with temples, priests, and rituals, to less formal types of worship. Perhaps the most common form of worship of these lesser spirits is the simple libation or offering. The African wishing to acknowledge the spirits may pour out a bit of water, wine, beer, or milk upon the ground or may offer a bit of foodstuff to these gods at each meal.

Ancestors

The most commonly recognized spiritual forces in African religions are departed ancestors. In perhaps no other part of the world except China and Japan is such high regard and concern for the dead apparent. Africans believe that departed members of the family exist in a spirit world and yet maintain an interest in the lives of those who continue to live. They are regarded as a great *cloud of witnesses* who watch the spectacle of life. More important, the dead are believed to be able to interfere in the affairs of the living. They can help a person, a family, or an entire nation if they wish. Therefore ancestors are often consulted before a battle, before an agricultural season, or before the birth of a child. In some areas no one may eat the first fruits of a harvest until proper sacrifice has been made to the ancestors.

It is the ancestor's ability to do harm that makes ancestor veneration such a potent force in Africa. Africans' fear of any god is of no consequence when compared to the dread Africans feel toward their ancestors. While the Chinese attitude toward their ancestors may be described as one of respect and reverence, the attitude of Africans toward their ancestors can only be described as one of awe and dread. Ancestors are believed to be capricious and unpredictable. In spite of all offerings and reverence, ancestors may turn on one person or an entire group and cause great damage. Ancestors are believed to be the cause of droughts, famines, and earthquakes. They are held responsible for many forms of sickness and even death. One of the most terrible misfortunes that can befall any African couple is childlessness, and this curse if often attributed to the wrath of offended ancestors.

Because of the tremendous respect for the ancestors that is a part of the African consciousness, it is the spirits of the ancestors, rather than of the recognized deities, who enforce the social and moral codes of the people.

Because of this great concern for the ancestors, Africans frequently offer sacrifices and libations to them. It is believed that the ancestors are in control of the land and its produce. Therefore, before anyone enjoys this produce, a bit of it must be offered to the ancestors. At harvest time there are larger offerings to them. When new animals are born to the flocks, some must be slaughtered and their blood spilled to the ancestors in order to insure continued blessings in the future.

Ancestors are believed to communicate with the living from time to time. One of the most common forms of this communication is the dream. Sometimes the message in the dream is direct and needs no interpretation, but at other times the message is not clear, and the dreamer must seek the help of a diviner to understand it.

Sometimes the ancestors use a more direct means to communicate with the living. Among the Tallensi there is a story of a young man named Pu-eng-yii who left his family and settled with a rival family because he felt he could earn greater wealth with them. In this manner he effectively cut himself off from his family and offended his ancestors. In his pursuit of wealth Pu-eng-yii suffered a serious leg injury in an auto accident. He consulted a diviner as to the cause of the accident. The diviner told him that his ancestors were angry with him and had caused his injury. Actually they had intended to kill him but had failed to carry through their plans. The diviner told Pu-eng-yii that he must make restitution to his family and his ancestors and give up his association with the other family. The hapless man gave in to the demands of his ancestors and returned to his family, offering the proper sacrifices, and making full restitution because he feared death.[7]

Diviners who can contact the departed ones are also in demand to gain knowledge about the future. Not only do the dead know what is happening among the living at the present, but they also know what the future will bring. Therefore, before special events such as battles, Africans often will consult the ancestors through a medium, in order to predict the outcome.

Sacrifice

African religions have developed a series of rituals that seek to appease the gods and the ancestors and provide proper transition through the various stages of life. At many points of contact between Africans and the spirit world, various forms of sacrifice are used to smooth the way and provide a point of communion between humankind and the spirit world.

[7] Ray, *African Religions*, p. 149.

Perhaps the most common rituals in African religions are the daily libations offered to the gods and the ancestors. As a display of recognition to the deities and the ancestors, those who are living in this world pour out a bit of their drink or toss away bits of their food.

On more serious occasions, there is animal sacrifice. The blood of such animals as dogs, birds, sheep, goats, and cattle is ritually poured out upon the ground to placate the gods or to assure their support in some trying and difficult period. Blood sacrifice may be offered when a group is preparing for battle or when there has been a long drought or in times of illness. A person who is engaged in the dangerous business of hunting may wish to offer a sacrifice to one of the deities before the hunt begins. In modern times the Yoruba god, Ogun, for centuries considered the god of iron, has become known as the god of automobiles and trucks. Therefore drivers engaged in the deadly business of operating automobiles will offer a dog to him and will decorate their cars with his symbols. His protection is sought for other objects of iron as well, as is illustrated in this sacrifice song:

Ogun, here are Ebun's kola nuts:
He rides a bicycle,
He cultivates with a matchet,
He fells trees with the axe.

Do not let Ebun meet your anger this year,
Take care of him.
He comes this year,
Enable him to come next season.[8]

On many occasions of African animal sacrifice the worshiper partakes of the sacrificed flesh with the deity or ancestor. After the blood has been poured out of the animal onto the altar or the ground, the flesh is roasted or boiled. A portion of it is given to the deity upon the altar, and a portion is eaten by the person who brought the sacrifice and that person's family. In this way a communion is established between the living and the spirits; it is almost universally believed that eating together forms a bond.

On rare occasions in the past human sacrifice has ben a part of native African religions. This aspect has been grossly exaggerated by the movies and by nineteenth century tales of cannibalism and great stacks of human skulls. While it is true that in the past Africans did sacrifice humans to their gods, such sacrifices were rare and occurred only on the most serious occasions. An Akikuyu legend tells of a time when there was a great drought in the land. A diviner deter-

[8] Ray, *African Religions*, p. 80.

mined that only when a certain maiden was sacrificed would it rain. The girl was placed in the center of the village where she gradually sank into the ground. When she had sunk to the depth of her nose, rain began to fall. Her family allowed her to sink completely out of sight as the rain continued. It was only the action of a lover who followed her into the earth that spared her life. Eventually he was able to find her and bring her back to the surface again.[9]

The most common form of human sacrifice occurred when a great king died and it was believed that he needed servants in the next life. At such times certain persons were sacrificed to accompany their leader into the world of the dead. Apparently human sacrifice was practiced only under the most severe circumstances and was never intended to establish a communion with the spirit world. The flesh of the victim was almost never eaten after the sacrifice. Cannibalism in any form seems to have been restricted to only a few tribes.

Rites of Passage

As in every other society, certain points along the pathway of life are marked by the African community and religion with rituals. These passage points are usually birth, puberty, marriage, and death. In societies where there is no clear distinction between the secular and the religious, these rites of passage are often regulated by religious practices and functionaries.

The birth of children is an event of great rejoicing among African people. Children are regarded as great blessings from the world of the spirits, and conversely childlessness is considered to be a curse. A childless woman will go to great lengths to determine the reason for her plight and to alleviate it. Not all childbirths are welcomed however. For example, African people tend to regard the birth of twins as something unusual and evil. Sometimes twins are regarded as a sign that the woman has been unfaithful to her husband and that each of the babies has a different father. Occasionally one or both of the twins is killed. Sometimes the twins and their mother are forced to live apart from the rest of the community. Among other African people the taboo against twins is reversed, and they are considered to be extremely lucky to the community into which they were born.

In many African societies, such as the Ashanti, children are not named or given much consideration for the first week of life. Because of the high infant mortality rate, it is considered unwise for a family to become attached to what may be a ghost child who has come to deceive them into loving it. If the child lives through the first week

9 Feldmann, *African Myths and Tales*, pp. 278–280.

of life then it is considered a true human baby and attention and joy may be lavished upon it. At this point the baby is named. In some cases a lengthy process of divination may be invoked in order to choose the proper name for the child. Other peoples recite the names of ancestors until the child makes some motion or gesture of recognition. In this manner the names of the ancestors are kept alive.

The ceremony of naming is often followed by the practice of showing the child to the moon. The Gu people of Dahomey throw their children gently up into the air several times, instructing them to look at the moon. The Basuto people of South Africa lift their children toward the moon and say, "There is your father's sister."[10] Some African people practice circumcision at the time of birth, but the majority wait until puberty.

During childhood young Africans receive instruction in their roles in society. As they approach puberty, instruction becomes more intensive. Special classes are established separately for the boys and girls. In these groups they are instructed in the adult roles expected of them, and they are prepared for initiatory rites. For the boys, these rites may invoke whippings and harsh trials designed to test their courage and resourcefulness. During these rituals they learn tribal religion, myths, and morality. Among some tribes the girls may be shut away in a fattening house where they will be encouraged to eat a great deal and grow plump in order to make them more attractive brides. Both boys and girls receive special training in sexual behavior and conduct. These puberty rites and instructions may take anywhere from a few days to several years, depending upon the tribe. However, their length and severity has declined in recent years because of the opposition of certain governments and the decline in power of village life.

Puberty rites for boys often culminate in the ritual of circumcision. No one seems to know where or how circumcision began among African people, but it is widely practiced. It may be, as Freud suggested, the final domination by the older males of the community over the young. Because circumcision is performed at puberty without any form of anesthetic, it is often regarded as a test of courage. The initiate is expected to accept the operation without flinching or crying out. Among some African people the operation is performed by a man wearing a mask, who represents the ancestors of the tribe.

Female circumcision is still practiced among some African peoples, but there is a growing sentiment against it. Sometimes this circumcision is a clitoridectomy, while at other times the labia is mutilated. Like male circumcision, there seems to be no clear reason for the practice.

---

[10] Parringer, *African Traditional Religion*, p. 94.

After puberty rituals and instruction, the young person is considered to be an adult and is expected to partake in the privileges and responsibilities of adult life. One of the first of these adult roles is marriage. There is little of a religious nature about African tribal marriage. It is often more of a secular contract between the families involved. Virginity is highly prized at the time of marriage, particularly among the young women. Chastity after marriage is also strongly encouraged by tribal customs and mores. Often one finds polygamy in African societies, especially polygyny. Frequently a husband is forbidden sexual contact with his wife during her pregnancy and for as long as she is nursing her infants. Since this can often be two years or more, it is considered wise for a husband to have several wives living in separate houses. There also have been rare instances of polyandry, where one woman is the wife of several brothers.

As in many societies, African religion tends to surround death with a great deal of ritual. The purpose of death rituals in these religions is to make the spirits of the newly dead as comfortable as possible with their new existence so they will not return to the living and haunt them. Many steps are taken during and after the burial of the dead to prevent them from returning to their villages, homes, and families. Women fear that their husband's ghosts will return and cause their wombs to die and so become unproductive.

Because of the warm climate of much of Africa, the dead are buried as quickly as possible. On rare occasions there are attempts to embalm or mummify the corpses of outstanding people such as kings. There are also a few examples of corpses regularly being turned over to the hyenas for disposal, but burial seems to be the most common practice. Buried with the dead are money, trinkets, tools, and weapons to make life in the next world as pleasant as possible. As has been mentioned before, a notable king might be buried with some servants to aid him in the life beyond.

Some African societies believe that no illness, no misfortune, and no death "just happens." These things must have been caused by witchcraft or foul play of some kind. In the past the dead sometimes were allowed to identify the individuals who caused their deaths. Often the couple would be seen to point out the house of the person that was responsible. Sometimes the corpse would fall from the backs of the bearers as it passed the guilty party. A person accused this way had to find some way to prove his or her innocence.

African religions generally have no system of eschatology, with a scheme of judgment and retribution after death. The dead simply move into the world of the spirits but continue to be interested in and effective among the living. An exception to this is the belief of the LaDagaa people of Ghana. According to their religion, the departed

Priestess' dance, Ghana. (*Courtesy of Yoram Lehmann, Peter Arnold, Inc.*)

person takes a long journey toward the land of the ancestors. Just before this land is reached, there is a river. There waits a ferryman who must be paid to take the deceased across the river. If the deceased has had a good life, the crossing will be easy. If the person has been wicked, he or she must swim across the river, and this will take three years. Individuals who owe anything to people who are still living must wait at the edge of the river until these creditors arrive so they can be paid. Once the deceased is in the land of the dead there are further tests and ordeals in which the person's lifetime deeds play a great part. Those who are judged to have been evil and suffer for it question the great God:

> "Why do you make us suffer?" . . . God replies, "Because you sinned on earth." And they ask, "Who created us?" To which God replies, "I did." And they ask, "If you created us, did we know evil when we came or did you give it to us?" God replies, "I gave it to you." Then the people ask God, "Why was it that you knew it was evil and gave it to us?" God replies, "Stop, let me think and find the answer."[11]

[11] Ray, *African Religions*, p. 146.

Religious Leaders

Since a great deal of native African religion is based upon rituals that are performed regularly by individuals without the aid of priests, such as the pouring out of libations to the ancestors, the need for religious functionaries is not as great as it is in religions that rely on complex theology and rituals. Nevertheless, African religions do have leaders who are essential at special times or places.

African religions generally do not require a priesthood. In western Africa, however, some communities maintain temples and altars to their deities. The existence of a temple virtually requires a priesthood to maintain and control it, and so in these areas priests, and occasionally priestesses, exist. Priests are required to go through a lengthy training period before they are allowed to serve. They must be trained in rituals, mythology, dances, and taboos connected with their religion.

One of the more common religious functionaries in Africa is the so-called witch doctor. Since the term *witch doctor* has a negative connotation, a better choice of names might be "doctor to the bewitched." As has been previously mentioned, the African world view does not include the idea of "natural" causes of death and disease. There is always a spiritual cause for these misfortunes. Someone has cast a spell or placed a curse on the one who is stricken, or the stricken person may have in some way offended the ancestors or one of the deities. Therefore it is the task of the witch doctor to ascertain the cause of the illness and prescribe a cure. The doctor will use some form of divination to determine the nature of the curse and who is responsible for it. Once that has been done it is the doctor's duty to use magic and herbs to drive away the witchcraft and dispel the curse. Often the doctor is called upon to clear a house of witches and curses before an owner will live in it.

Among the Acholi people of Uganda the evil spirits that cause a person to become ill are called *jok.* The healer is called *ajwaka.* When the *ajwaka* enters the presence of the sick person he will attempt to draw the *jok* up into the head of the patient by the use of music and song. When this is accomplished the *ajwaka* enters into conversation with the *jok.* "Why have you come? What do you want? What is your name?" Finally the evil spirit is driven out of the sick person by the *ajwaka,* captured in a gourd, and buried in the ground.[12]

Obviously the doctor to the bewitched is part religious functionary, part herbalist, and part psychologist. The skills this doctor has are highly valued and are sometimes imported into modern hospitals by Africans who don't want to leave anything to chance. When a young

[12] Noel Q. King, *Religions of Africa* (New York: Harper & Row, 1970), p. 30.

person decides on a life as a healer the youth must be apprenticed to an established doctor for several years to learn the many skills and secrets involved.

Closely allied to the healer in many African communities is the diviner. It is the diviner's task to utilize magic and divine the causes of present misfortune, past secrets, and things to come. This individual can also ferret out witches and sorcerers. In some African communities the diviner is primarily one who investigates the causes of trouble, while in other communities the function of prediction is more important.

Among the Ndembu people of northwestern Zambia individuals are chosen as diviners by being inhabited by a spirit. The spirit Kayong'u seeks out those whom he will have become diviners, and it is believed that he first makes them ill. The deity thus shows people what he wants. A person so selected then goes through an elaborate initiation ritual and a long period of training.

The tools that African diviners use are widely different. Most commonly they cast the shells of nuts to form a pattern and then read the pattern to find the answer they seek. Among the Yoruba people, a diviner shakes sixteen palm nuts out into a pattern. This allows for as many as 256 different patterns. Each pattern is associated with several poems, each of which contains a message. Even the beginning diviner is supposed to know from memory a minimum of four poems for each pattern. This means that a person must memorize at least 1,024 poems to be a diviner; an experienced diviner will know many more. When the pattern has been cast and the poems recited, the person who has sought divination will select the poem that he or she believes to be the most meaningful.[13] Other methods of divination include casting dice and gazing into a bowl of water. At one time, among many African people, trials by ordeal were used to determine the guilt or innocence of a person accused of some crime. The person being tried was given a poisonous substance to drink. If the person did not die, innocence was proven. In more recent times a fowl has been substituted. When the fowl dies from the poison, guilt or innocence is determined by the way in which it falls.

Another religious functionary found from time to time in many parts of Africa is the prophet. Like the biblical prophet, this person is seen as one who speaks the words of the gods. When there is a political upheaval or an impending religious revival, charismatic leaders may arise and proclaim the words of the gods to their people. In the late nineteenth century there were several prophets who led African people in resistance to the Arab slave trade and to the European co-

[13]Ray, *African Religions*, pp. 106–108.

lonial efforts. One of these was a man named Ngundeng, who arose among the Neur people of the southern Sudan and who spoke in the name of the sky god, Dengkur. Usually the prophetic figures in Africa gain their authority by the power of their personalities and their message. Therefore, they seldom leave successors.

One of the most enduring of the religious figures in Africa is the chief-king. While there are some societies in Africa without monarchs, those that have kings and queens look upon them with great awe and reverence. These rulers are regarded as the tribal connection to the world of the ancestors and are revered as the living symbol of the tribe. Because of this, they are the objects of many taboos. In some societies they are considered to be so sacred that commoners may not look upon their faces. In other societies it is regarded as certain death to eat food that has been prepared for the monarch. Some peoples, such as the Bantus, actually look upon their rulers as gods incarnate.

Since the rulers represent the community, their health must be good at all times. A sick monarch means a sick land. Therefore, any infirmity of the ruler must be dealt with quickly. In some societies, rulers are required to take their own lives when ill health or old age begin to weaken them. The queen of the Lovedu people of South Africa carries poison with her at all times and is expected to use it to prevent her death by other means. In other areas and at other times there have been stories indicating that the people felt it was necessary for them to kill an aged or infirm king. In some cases a substitute king is chosen to rule for a few days, and then be ritually killed in order to spare the true king.

Once the monarch is dead, the death often is kept secret until a successor can be chosen and enthroned. It is believed that the former king or queen fully becomes a god as he or she enters the land of the ancestors.

AFRICAN RELIGIONS TODAY

The past one hundred years have been extremely difficult for African religions. The European colonial empires on the continent worked to break up traditional tribal units and to enforce other forms of authority. With the end of colonialism following World War II, Africa was divided into more than forty separate nation-states. These nations also tended to break up tribal life. The recent pressure of modernization, urbanization, and a rapidly increasing population all further served to change African life. Christian and Muslim missionary work continues to grow in Africa. Christianity is attractive because it is the religion of the industrialized Western nations. Islam is popular because it is the religion of many of the third world countries with which Africans identify. Both religions have grown rapidly over the past two decades as thousands of Africans have left their native religions. It is probable that if current trends continue, by the end of this century few Africans would be practicing their traditional religions. However, the values of these religions will continue: The Christianity and Islam that is emerging in Africa has distinctive African qualities.

STUDY QUESTIONS

1. List four of the major religions of the world that have a significant following in Africa.

2. Compare and contrast the African idea of a high God with that of American Indian religions.

3. Why are the spirits of African ancestors regarded with dread?

4. What is the most common form of sacrifice in African religion?

5. Discuss African puberty rites for both male and female. How do these rituals prepare the young person for life as an adult?

6. What is divination? List several forms of divination in African religions.

SUGGESTED READING

Courlander, Harold. *Tales of Yoruba Gods and Heroes.* Greenwich, Conn.: Fawcett Publications, 1973.

Idowu, E. Bolaji. *African Traditional Religion.* Maryknoll, N.Y.: Orbis Books, 1973.

King, Noel Q. *Religions of Africa.* New York: Harper & Row, 1970.

Parrinder, Geoffrey. *African Traditional Religion.* London: Hutchinson House, 1954.

Ranger, T. O. and I. N. Kimambo. *The Historical Study of African Religion.* Berkeley: University of California Press, 1972.

Ray, Benjamin C. *African Religions: Symbol, Ritual and Community.* Englewood Cliffs, N.J.: Prentice-Hall, Inc., 1976.

An African Divine King

There are divine kings in many cultures. A careful look into
this office and the religious concept that surrounds it often
gives the reader an understanding of the supporting culture.
The following is a brief description of the life (and death) of
the divine king of the people of Nyasaland.[14]

Mbande is a hill on the plain of north Nyasaland with a commanding view
of the surrounding country and well suited to defence. The west side is
precipitous and below the scarp edge there used to be a marsh; to the
north the hill is protected by a wide reach of the Lukulu river. It is a sacred
place and for many generations was the home of the "divine king," the
Kyungu. Like the Lwembe he was the living representative of a hero, and
was selected by a group of hereditary nobles from one of two related lin-
eages, the office alternating (if suitable candidates were available) between
the two. They sought a big man, one who had begotten children and whose
sons were already married, not a young man for, the nobles said, "young
men always want war, and destroy the country." He must be a man of
wisdom (*gwa mahala*) and generous in feeding his people.

The kyungu's life was governed by taboos even more rigorous than those
surrounding the Lwembe. He must not fall ill, or suffer a wound, or even
scratch himself and bleed a little, for his ill health, or his blood falling on
the earth would bring sickness to the whole country. "Men feared when
Kyungu's blood fell on the ground, they said, 'It is his life.' " "If he had a
headache his wives (if they loved him) told him not to mention it, they hid
his illness; but if the nobles entered and found him ill they dug the grave
and put him in it, saying, 'He is the ruler (*ntemi*), it's taboo for him to be
ill.' Then he thought: 'Perhaps it is so' (with a gesture of resignation)."

Great precautions were taken to preserve his health. He lived in a separate house with his powerful medicines. His food was prepared by boys
below the age of puberty lest a menstruating woman, or a youth who had
laid with a woman, should touch it and so bring sickness upon him; and
his numerous wives were immured in the royal enclosure—a great stock-
ade—and jealously guarded, for any infidelity on their part was thought to
make their husband ill, and with him the whole country.

When the Kyungu did fall ill he was smothered by the nobles who lived
around him at Mbande, and buried in great secrecy, with a score or more
of living persons—slaves—in the grave beneath him, and one or two wives
and the sons of commoners above. And in the midst of all this slaughter

[14] Monica Wilson, *Communal Rituals of the Nyakyusa* (International African Institute, 1959),
    pp. 40–46.

the nobles brought a sheep to look into the grave that the dead Kyungu might be gentle (*milolo*) like the sheep!

The living Kyungu was thought to create food and rain, and his breath and the growing parts of his body—his hair and nails and the constantly replaced mucus of his nose—were believed to be magically connected with the fertility of the Ngonde plain. When he was killed his nostrils were stopped so that he was buried "with the breath in his body"; while portions of his hair and nails and of his nasal mucus were taken from him beforehand and buried by the nobles of Ngonde in the black mud near the river. This was "to defend the country against hunger, to close up the land, to keep it rich and heavy and fertile as it was when he himself lived in it."

His death was kept secret—a relatively easy matter since he lived in seclusion—and one of the nobles (Ngosi) impersonated him wearing his clothes. After a month of two when the nobles had decided whom to choose as the new Kyungu, the luckless man was summoned to Mbanbe: "Your father calls you." Then he came with his companions and entered the house to make obeisance; they seized him and put the sacred cloth on him and set him on the stool "Kisumbi," saying, "Thou Kyungu, thou art he," and he became the Kyungu. Then they struck the drum, Mwenkelwa, and everyone knew that the Kyungu had died and another had been installed. Men feared greatly to be seized as the Kyungu, just as they feared to be seized as the Lwembe, because the life of a divine king was short. Ngonde historians quote a number of cases of sons of the Kyungu who fled to escape being set on the stool; once they had sat on it they dared not flee lest they die.

In time of drought the nobles of Ngonde would go to a diviner to inquire who it was who was angry; they would mention all the names of the sacred groves of the Kyngus in turn and he would tell them it was so and so. They would inform the living Kyungu and he would give them a bull or a sheep, together with some beer—they would take one of the pots of beer from his own house, brought by his people as tribute. And he would give them some flour and cloths also. Then they would go with them into the grove and build a miniature hut. Next they would kill the beast and hang some of the meat up on a tree—the rest they would eat later outside the grove. Then they would tear up the cloths and fasten some of the pieces on to the hut in the grove—an action they would explain as "giving him cloths." And finally, they would pour out some of the beer and the flour. Nearly always, in time of drought, they would thus build a hut and make an offering in the grove of the Kyungu whom the diviner had mentioned.

But occasionally, if one of the chiefs had recently insulted the Kyungu, they concluded that it was the living Kyungu himself who was angry. They would go to a diviner and mention all the names of the dead Kyungus, but he would refuse to accept any of them: "No . . . no." And at length he would tell them that it was the living Kyungu who was angry because so-and-so had insulted him. Then there would be no sacrifice at the grove at all, but the nobles of Ngonde would go to the one who had insulted the Kyungu and charge him with it, asking him what he meant by thus killing them all, would not the whole land starve? And so the wrongdoer would take a cow to the Kyungu who, thereupon, would address the nobles of Ngonde, saying: "If it was my anger which brought the drought then it will rain (for I am no longer angry). But if the rain does not come then it cannot have been my anger, it must have been someone (of the dead Kyungus) whom you forgot to ask about it." And if, after that, the rain came soon, then it was not likely that anyone would insult the Kyungu again.

Thus to insult Kyungu was not only treasonable, it was blasphemous, and the whole plain was believed to be cursed with drought or disease in reply. An "insult" might mean any neglect of the obligations of the chiefs and nobles and commoners of the plain to their lord.

The majesty (ubusisya) of the Kyungu was cultivated in a variety of ways. He smeared himself with ointment made from lion fat, and his bed was built up with elephant tusks and lion pelts. He was enthroned on the sacred iron stool called Kisumbi, he had a spear, and Mulima, a porous piece of iron "like a mouth organ" used to make rain, all handed down from the first Kyungu. His zebra tails, set with medicines in horn handles, were waved in war and during prayer to the shades, and he also had the famous drum on which the blood of a child was poured.

But the majority of their subjects only worshipped from afar in fear and trembling. At Mbande no ordinary commoner was ever conducted into the sacred enclosure, but only the territorial nobles and the elder chiefs, and they only occasionally; while when the Kyungu travelled through his country all men save the very oldest fled from his approach. Even in speech fearful circumlocutions were used to refer to his journeyings—"The country is on the move"—"the great hill is moving"—"the mystery is coming." It was taboo both for the old men who stayed to see him, and for those who entered the sacred enclosure, ever to greet him in the usual way. Falling down and clapping the hands was the only greeting for the Kyungu.

From the wives of the Kyungu also men fled in terror, fearing lest they be compromised and thrown over the cliff of Mbande, and this both added to the atmosphere of terror which surrounded him and was an expression of it.

An African Creation Story

The following is the creation story of the Boshongo, who are a Bantu people.[15]

In the beginning, in the dark, there was nothing but water, and Bumba was alone.

[15]Maria Leach, The Beginning (New York: Krishna Press, 1956), pp. 145–147.

One day Bumba was in terrible pain. He retched and strained and vomited up the sun. After that light spread over everything. The heat of the sun dried up the water until the black edges of the world began to show. Black sandbanks and reefs could be seen. But there were no living things.

Bumba vomited up the moon and then the stars, and after that the night had its light also.

Still Bumba was in pain. He strained again and nine living creatures came forth; the leopard named Koy Bumba, and Pongo Bumba the crested eagle, the crocodile, Ganda bumba, and one little fish named Yo; next, old Kono Bumba, the tortoise, and Tsetse, the lightning, swift, deadly, beautiful like the leopard, then the white heron, Nyanyi Bumba, also one beetle, and the goat named Budi.

Last of all came forth men. There were many men, but only one was white like Bumba. His name was Loko Yima.

The creatures themselves then created all the creatures. The heron created all the birds of the air except the kite. He did not make the kite. The crocodile made serpents and the iguana. The goat produced every beast with horns. Yo, the small fish, brought forth all the fish of all the seas and waters. The beetle created insects.

Then the serpents in their turn made grasshoppers, and the iguana made the creatures without horns.

Then the three sons of Bumba said they would finish the world. The first, Nyonye Ngana, made the white ants; but he was not equal to the task, and died of it. The ants, however, thankful for life and being, went searching for black earth in the depths of the world and covered the barren sands to bury and honour their creator.

Chonganda, the second son, brought forth a marvellous living plant from which all the trees and grasses and flowers and plants in the world have sprung. The third son, Chedi Bumba, wanted something different, but for all his trying made only a bird called the kite.

Of all the creatures, Tsetse, lightning, was the only troublemaker. She stirred up so much trouble that Bumba chased her into the sky. Then mankind was without fire until Bumba showed the people how to draw fire out of trees. "There is fire in every tree," he told them, and showed them how to make the firedrill and liberate it. Sometimes today Tsetse still leaps down and strikes the earth and causes damage.

When at last the work of creation was finished, Bumba walked through the peaceful villages and said to the people, "Behold these wonders. They belong to you." Thus from Bumba, the Creator, the First Ancestor, came forth all the wonders that we see and hold and use, and all the brotherhood of beasts and man.

Religions Originating in India

*T*o the modern student of religions no series of religions is so fascinating as those that began in India. The great depth and variety of religious teaching and experience one finds in Hinduism, Jainism, Buddhism, and Sikhism are indeed awesome. Today the beauty of the Bhagavada Gita, the complexity of Vedanta, the simple mysteries of Zen Buddhism, and the concept of *ahimsa* taught by the Jains are appreciated by students in Western nations as never before. An understanding of the basic literature, history, and doctrines of these religions is essential for the person who would understand modern Asia.

Hinduism

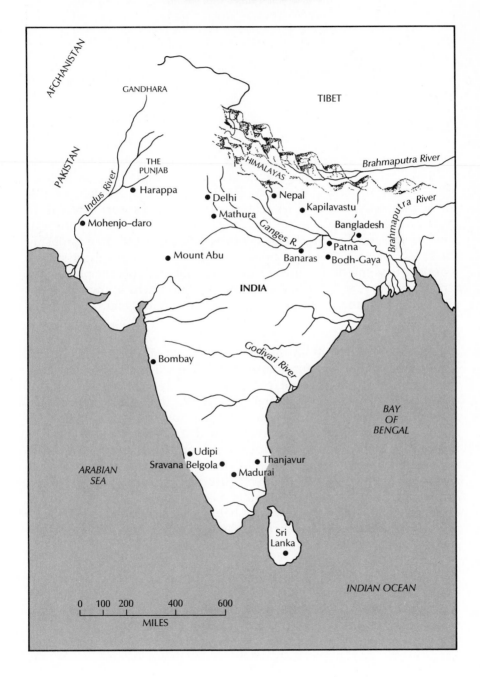

I am proud to belong to a religion which has taught the world both tolerance and universal acceptance. We believe not only in universal tolerance, but we accept all religions as true. As different streams having different sources all mingle their waters in the sea, so different paths which men take through different tendencies, various though they appear, crooked or straight, all lead to God
—*Swami Vivekananda*

Perhaps the oldest and most complex of all the religions of the world is Hinduism. Whereas most of today's active religions seem to have begun sometime around the sixth century B.C. or later, Hinduism traces the beginnings of some of its religious themes and forms to the third millennium B.C. One can find within Hinduism almost any form or style of religion that has been conceived or practiced. It is probably the most tolerant of all religions, and its scope ranges from simple animism to some of the most exalted and elaborate philosophical systems ever devised. In this vast tolerance, Hinduism allows for literally millions of major and minor gods, their temples, and their priests. Therefore, for the Hindu, the possible religious views are virtually infinite.

Hinduism has also been the source for three other religions. In the sixth century B.C. two reform movements, Jainism and Buddhism, arose from within Hinduism and challenged traditional Indian religious concepts. For a time it appeared that both movements might even replace Hinduism. Within a few centuries, however, their distinctive features were absorbed by Hinduism, which reemerged as the major religion of India. Today Jainism is a minority religion in India and Buddhism, while having great influence in other Asian nations, has almost no following in India. In the fifteenth century A.D., after Muslim invasions of India, Sikhism arose as a combination of the features of Islam and Hinduism. However, it has never become more than a minority religion. Hinduism overwhelmed these challengers by absorbing them and adopting their distinctive features into the mainstream of Hindu thought.

Unlike most of the other major religions of the world, Hinduism had no one identifiable founder. While there have been many great teachers and leaders in its history, there has never been one whose teachings became the wellspring of all later Hindu thought.

The word *Hindu* comes from the Sanskrit name for the river Indus,

Sindhu. While the designation *Hindu* may refer to a great variety of religious beliefs and practices, it generally applies to the religion of the people of India. To be Indian is, in a sense, to be Hindu and vice versa. While there have been many converts to Hinduism throughout its history, it has never been an active missionary religion like Buddhism, Christianity, or Islam.

THE ORIGINS OF HINDUISM

Pre-Aryan India

The history of Hinduism begins with the migratory waves of Aryan conquerors of the people of India during the second millennium B.C. The religion that these conquerors brought with them mingled with the religion of the native people, and the culture that developed between them became classical Hinduism.

However, before we can speak of the Aryan religion we must first take notice of the pre-Aryan natives of India. Actually very little is known about these people. Prior to the 1920s the only source that spoke of the pre-Aryan people was the Vedic literature of early Hinduism. Since this was the religious literature of the Aryans, references to the natives of India and their religions were mainly negative, and the people were presented as uncivilized and barbarian. However, in the 1920s archaeological excavations were carried out in the Indus valley and at least two pre-Aryan cities were uncovered. Contrary to the image presented in the Vedas, these excavations revealed that as early as 2500 B.C. there was a fairly high advanced civilization in the Indus valley. The cities had well-planned streets with drainage systems; they were supported by rather advanced agricultural communities which surrounded them; and these pre-Aryan people had a written language. Unfortunately this language has not yet been translated, and the great amount of information that it could supply regarding the life and religion of these people remains hidden.

What we do know of the religion of the pre-Aryan people is revealed by numerous statues and amulets that have been found by archaeologists. Many of these bear the image of what have been interpreted as fertility gods and goddesses. Some of the figures sit in the lotus position that was later adopted by Yoga Hinduism and other meditative sects. It is therefore assumed that far from being barbarian, the pre-Aryan people were highly civilized city dwellers and that later Hinduism took some of its gods and practices from this early period.

The Coming of the Aryans

To the modern student the word *Aryan* usually connotes the various meanings that the twentieth-century Nazi movement gave it. Hitler, in his attempt to depict his own people as the master race, called the large, blond, blue-eyed people of the world "the Aryan race." To the Nazis these people were the superior race who had historically given the world its strength and civilization. Other "races," such as the Semitic Jews and the blacks, were decidedly inferior to these "Aryans." This of course has no anthropological or historical foundation. The true Aryans were not a race and probably possessed none of the physical characteristics that the Nazis ascribed to them.

The term *Aryan* is a Sanskrit word that means "the noble ones"; this word was applied to a group of migrants who moved into the Indus valley in the second millennium B.C. from the regions of Persia. The Aryans are believed to have been the people who first tamed horses on a wide scale and used them to pull war chariots. They were related to the Hyksos people who invaded Egypt in the second millenium B.C. and ruled it for two hundred years. They were also related to the Celtic people of the British isles. The Aryans who did not migrate into India became the founders of Zoroastrianism. There are many similarities between the religion revealed in the Indian Vedic literature and the Gathas of Zoroastrianism. These same people later founded the Persian Empire, which ruled the Middle East from the sixth to the fourth centuries B.C. When the modern Persian people sought a name for their nation they called it Iran, that is, the land of the Aryans.

During the period between 1750 and 1200 B.C. the Aryans came in migratory waves into the Indus valley. Presumably the highly civilized city cultures of this region had declined because they were easily conquered by the Aryans and assimilated into their culture. Of the early Aryans little is known. Scattered references in the Vedic literature indicate that they were basically wandering nomads following their flocks from place to place. They apparently had no permanent bases or cities. The Aryans of this period were organized along tribal lines, being led by chieftains who were called *rajahs*. The Aryans spoke an Indo-European language which became the basis for Sanskrit and which has many cognates with European languages. It was not until about the sixth century B.C. that these people began to settle into cities in the Indus valley and some of the rajahs began to collect and build minor kingdoms for themselves.

According to early sources, Aryan society began to develop into three basic categories called *varnas*. The highly regarded priests who served the cults of the various Aryan deities were called Brahmins.

The chieftains and their warriors, also considered to be near the apex of society, were called Kshatriyas. The commoners and merchants, regarded as subservient to the two upper classes, were called Vaishyas. A fourth group was made up of those conquered pre-Aryan people who were called Shudras. Shudras were not considered full members of the society and generally held the position of slaves or servants to the Aryans. These divisions were maintained in Indian society for centuries and were later subdivided into the multiple classes that became the basis of the so-called caste system.

Aryan Religion

The best source of knowledge about the religion of the Aryan invaders is the Vedic literature, but this literature was mainly composed after the Aryans had been settled in India for a time and had intermingled with the native people and with their religions. What is truly Aryan and what is truly pre-Aryan in the Vedas is therefore difficult to delineate. Nevertheless, certain basic assumptions about Aryan religion can be made.

It seems clear that the Aryan invaders of India brought with them a polytheistic religion similar to that of other Indo-European peoples. There have been considerable attempts to identify Aryan deities with those of the Graeco-Roman pantheon.[1] The collection of gods that the Aryans worshiped seem to have been personifications of various natural forces, such as the storm, the sun, the moon, and the fertility of the soil.

The chief manner of worship of the Aryan gods was apparently sacrifice. Since the Aryans were primarily nomadic people in the early days of their occupation of India, they built no temples to their gods, but rather offered sacrifices to them on altars built in open places. These offerings were frequently animal sacrifices, but they also included offerings of dairy products, such as butter and libations of milk, which were poured out to the gods. Another liquid apparently used as a libation was the juice of the sacred soma plant. The exact identification of the soma plant is lost to the modern world.[2] The ancient texts describe it as a sacred plant that was sent to earth by the god Indra. Its juice was described as delicious and invigorating to the worshiper who drank it and shared it with the gods. The plant that modern Indians identify as soma is not delicious and invigorating but produces nausea in those who drink it. Naturally there are those who

[1] The most common identifications are of the Indian god Varuna with Uranus and Dyaus Pitar with the Greek Zeus and the Roman Jupiter.

[2] *Soma* is frequently identified with the haoma plant, which is used in the ancient Persian religions, but that too is not easily identified by modern students of religion.

Entrance to Temple of Sangsit, Bali. The elaborate carvings at this entrancce depict many scenes from the lives of the gods. (*Courtesy of Burton Holmes Collection; Stockmarket, Los Angeles.*)

suggest that the original soma may have been some form of mushroom or other plant that produced hallucinations.[3]

Perhaps the most expensive and elaborate sacrifice ever used in any religion is said to have originated among the Aryans. This was the so-called horse sacrifice. Because of the expense and incredible detail involved, the horse sacrifice was limited to the Aryan rulers. This was a sacrifice that supposedly had extraordinary effects in atoning for a great sin or in giving great religious power to those who participated in it. The horse sacrifice was also helpful to rulers who wished to expand their territory, and this, of course, was its major attraction to Indian rulers. A young male horse chosen for this sacrifice was set loose to roam the countryside for one year. The attendants of the ruler who supported the sacrifice followed the horse wherever he went. If the horse covered any territory that was not in the domain of the

---

[3]It is noteworthy that Aldous Huxley named the happiness-producing drug of the future *soma*, in his book *Brave New World*.

ruler, that rajah had the right to claim that land as his own. After one year the horse was returned. At that time a great many other animals were sacrificed to the gods. This great holocaust included animals of all types, ranging from the bee to the elephant, and sometimes involved more than six hundred animals. Next, the sacred horse was strangled, and the wives of the rajah participated in fertility rites with the body of the horse. Finally the carcass was ritually butchered and eaten by the ruler and his family. According to legend, if one man could perform one hundred horse sacrifices he would become master over all the gods and the universe. Unfortunately for those who aspired to this, such an act would have required over one hundred years and incredible wealth. Consequently there is no record of a ruler who could or would perform it one hundred times. The horse sacrifice was last performed by an Indian ruler in the eighteenth century A.D.

THE VEDIC ERA

The Vedas

The basic sacred scripture of Hinduism is the Vedic literature. These books are the source of the Hindu understanding of the universe, and all later material refers back to them and is seen as mere commentary upon them. The Vedas were developed as the Aryans came into India, settled there, and mingled their religion with that of the native peoples. There is dispute over the exact period in which the Vedas were written. Some scholars believe that the earliest of the Vedic hymns may have developed prior to the coming of the Aryans, before 2000 B.C., and that they were still developing as late as the sixth century A.D. Others contend that the bulk of the Vedic material came into being between 1500 and 400 B.C. Like much other ancient religious literature, there is no sure way of knowing the exact time of the origin and development of these books. Undoubtedly they were first composed and transmitted orally for many generations before they were committed to writing; thus centuries may have passed between their origin and completion.

There are four basic Vedic books. The first and most important is the Rig-Veda. (The word *Veda* basically means "knowledge" or "sacred lore.") This is a collection of over one thousand hymns to the gods of the Aryan pantheon as well as various other materials. It contains the basic mythology of these gods. The other Vedic books are made up of much of the material that was originally contained in the Rig-Veda.

The second book is the Yajur-Veda ("knowledge of rites"). This is a collection of materials to be recited during sacrifice to the gods. The third book, the Sama-Veda ("knowledge of chants"), is a collection of verses from the basic hymns recited at sacrifices by the priests. The fourth book, second in importance only to the Rig-Veda, is the Atharva-Veda ("knowledge given by the sage Atharva"). It contains rituals to be used in the home and popular prayers to the gods, along with spells and incantations to ward off evil.

Each of the Vedic[4] books is made up of four parts. Each contains a section of hymns to the gods (*mantras*). As is the case in many ancient religions, hymns and religious poetry are to be regarded as the most ancient of all religious literature since they reflect the period when statements about and to the gods were memorized, chanted, and passed from one generation to the next without benefit of the written word. Each Vedic book also contains a section of ritual materials (Brahmanas) in which the worshiper is given instruction in the proper way to perform his sacrifices, and so on. The Brahmanas are considered to be later than the mantra sections. A third section in each of the Vedas is the so-called Forest Treatises (Aranyakas), which are materials for hermits in their religious pursuits. The fourth sections are called Upanishads, and are made up of philosophical materials. The mantra and Brahmana sections are considered to be the oldest material in the Vedas, with the Aranyakas and the Upanishads having been added later. The Vedas in their final form are written in a language called Vedic, which is a predecessor of early Sanskrit.

Within the Vedas are basic descriptions and mythology of the various Aryan and pre-Aryan gods. The god who receives the most attention in terms of numbers of hymns is Indra, the god of the thunderbolt, of clouds and rain, and the ruler of heaven. Indra is especially important because he is remembered as the conqueror of Vitra, the personification of evil. Within the Rig-Veda alone there are over 250 hymns specifically addressed to him. Following is one of these.

> That highest Indra power of thine is distant: that which is here sages possessed aforetime.
> This one is on the earth, in heaven the other, and both unite as flag with flag in battle.
> He spread the wide earth out and firmly fixed it, smote with his thunderbolt and loosed the waters.
> Maghavan with his puissannce struck down Ahi, rent Rauhina to death and slaughtered Vyansa.

[4]The word *Veda* is used in two ways. Generally, the word refers to only the ancient collection of hymns to the Aryan gods. However, in another sense the word refers to an entire collection of sacred literature which includes the hymns and the later additions: the Brahmanas, the Aranyakas, and the Upanishads. In this text we shall use the word in the latter sense.

Armed with his bolt and trusting in his prowess he wandered shattering the forts of Dasas.

Cast thy dart, knowing, Thunderer, at the Daysu: increase the Arya's might and glory, Indra.

For him who thus hath taught these human races, Maghavan, bearing a fame-worthy title.

Thunderer, drawing nigh to slay the Dasyus, hath given himself the name of Son for glory.

See this abundant wealth that he possesses, and put your trust in Indra's hero vigor.

He found the cattle, and he found the horses, he found the plants, the forests and the waters.

To him the truly strong, whose deeds are many, to him the strong bull let us pour the Soma.

The Hero, watching like a thief in ambush, goes parting the possessions of the godless.

Well didst thou do that hero deed, O Indra, in waking with thy bolt the slumbering Ahi.

In thee, delighted, Dames divine rejoiced them, the flying Maruts and all Gods were joyful.

As thou hast smitten Sushna, Pipru, Vritra and Kuyava, and Sambara's forts, O Indra.

This prayer of ours may Varuna grant, and Mitra, and Aditi, and Sindhu, Earth and Heaven.[5]

Many other Aryan gods are also mentioned in the Vedic literature. Agni, the god of fire, is mentioned in over two hundred hymns. He is basically regarded as the god of the priests and the priests of the gods. He leads the gods in proper sacrifice, and as the god of fire it is he who brings the burnt sacrifices to the other gods. The god Varuna receives his share of hymns in the Vedic material also. He is seen as the god over the order of the universe and the one who gives forgiveness to those who have sinned.

May we be in thy keeping, O thou Leader, wide-ruling Varuna, Lord of many heroes.

O sons of Aditi, forever faithful, pardon us, Gods, admit us to your friendship.[6]

Vishnu is mentioned briefly in the Vedas, but at the time they were composed he was not the important deity he was to become in later Hinduism. Another of the gods whose function and name was to change in later Hinduism was Rudra, later known as Shiva, the god of death and destruction. In later times Shiva, Vishnu, and Brah-

[5] *The Hymns of the Rig-Veda*, Ralph T. H. Griffith, trans. vol. I (Benares: E. J. Lazarus and Co., 1920), pp. 133, 134.
[6] Ibid., p. 294.

man became the three most important gods in Hinduism. The god of the dead who receives attention in the Vedas is Yama, who was supposed to have been the first man to die.

> Honor the King with thine oblations, Yama, Vivasvan's Son, who gathers
>   men together,
> Who travelled to the lofty heights above us, who searches out and shows
>   the path to many.
> Yama first found for us a place to dwell in: this pasture never can be taken
>   from us.
> Men born on earth tread their own paths that lead them whither our an-
>   cient Fathers have departed.[7]

In addition to hymns to the many gods of the Aryan pantheon, the Vedas also contain legendary and mythological material from early Indian life. One of the most interesting of these is the story of Manu.

> They brought water to Manu for washing, as it is now usual to bring it for washing hands. When he was washing, a fish came into his hands.
>
> It said to him in words, "Bring me up, I shall save you." "From what will you save me?" "A flood will carry away all the creatures. I shall save you from that flood." "How can I bring you up?"
>
> "Fish swallow fish. So long as we remain small, destruction awaits us. Keep me first in a jar. When I outgrow it, dig a pond and keep me in it. When I outgrow that also, take me to the sea. Then I shall be beyond danger."
>
> It quickly became a Jhasa, which become the largest. Then it said, "The flood will come in such and such a year. Take my advice then, and build a ship. Enter it when the flood rises, and I shall save you from the flood."
>
> After rearing the fish thus, Manu took it to the sea. In the year indicated to him by the fish, he acted according to the advice of the fish and built a ship. When the flood rose, he entered it. The fish then swam to him. He tied the rope of the ship to the horn of the fish and thus reached swiftly the Northern Mountain there.
>
> The fish then said, "I have saved you. Tie the ship to a tree and do not let the water leave you stranded when you are on the mountain. Descend as the water subsides." Thus gradually he descended, hence that slope of the Northern Mountain is called "Manu's Descent." The flood carried off all the creatures, Manu alone survived.
>
> Wishing for a progeny, he began to worship and do penance. Then he performed a sacrifice of cooked meal. In the waters he offered melted butter, buttermilk, whey, and curd as oblations. In a year, a woman was created out of them. She rose dripping, melted butter collected at her footprints.
>
> Wishing for progeny, he continued to worship and perform penance along

[7] Ibid., p. 398.

North gateway, Sanchi Stupa, India. (*Courtesy of the Government of India Tourist Office.*)

with her. Through her this race was generated by him. This is the race of Manu. Whatever blessings he desired through her were all conferred on him.[8]

The Upanishads

As noted earlier, the fourth section of each of the Vedas is called the Upanishads.[9] Within these materials one finds the early philosophical statements that became the basis for all later Hindu philosophy. Although there originally may have been more of these treatises, there are currently about two hundred Upanishads. They vary in length from one page to over fifty pages. Of these, fourteen are called the principal Upanishads. Scholarly research indicates that the earliest of the Upanishads probably originated in the ninth century B.C. and the most recent in the sixth century A.D.

Some scholars contend that the Upanishads are an integral part of the Vedas and that they are a natural commentary upon the early hymns and ritual texts. These persons tend to see the Upanishads as the philosophical expression of what one finds in the rest of the Vedas. Others disagree and point out the basic disharmony between the two. Whereas the hymns, chants, legends, and rituals in the rest of the Vedic material are clearly polytheistic, giving instruction on the proper worship of myriad gods, the Upanishads operate from a monistic presupposition. They assume that there is only one reality, the impersonal god-being called Brahman. All other beings are but an expression of Brahman. All that is not Brahman is an illusion (maya). Not only is there this basic distinction between the Upanishads and the rest of the Vedic material, but the Upanishads also seem to have been written as a reaction to the priestly form of worship that was prescribed by the other Vedic books. Whereas most of the Vedas seem to teach that the proper way to worship is by sacrifice to the various Aryan gods, the Upanishads emphasize meditation as a means of worship. They teach that people's real problem is ignorance (avidya) of their plight and that only when people realize this ignorance and come to true knowledge will they find salvation. Those scholars who point to these essential differences between the Upanishads and other portions of the Vedas believe that the Upanishads may have had a different point of origin and may have become attached to the Vedic literature at a later time. It is probably fair to say that while the Upanishads

---

[8] Satopoda Brahmana, 1:8.

[9] The basic meaning of the word *Upanishad* seems to be "near sitting," indicating that these are materials that were developed in the discussions between teachers *(gurus)* and their students as they sat together and spoke of the philosophical implications of the Vedas.

have been tremendously influential as the basis for later Hindu philosophy, they have never been extremely popular with the common people. They are complicated and difficult discussions, and they require the acceptance of a world view that is not easily understood. The Upanishads have been popular with a relative handful of Indian intellectuals.

As we have indicated, the fundamental assumption of the Upanishads is that there is but one true reality in the universe; that reality is known as Brahman. Brahman is eternal, infinite, unknowable, sexless,[10] without a past, present, or a future, and totally impersonal.

> Verily, in the beginning this world was Brahman, the limitless One—limitless to the east, limitless to the north, . . . limitless in every direction. . . . Incomprehensible is that supreme Soul, unlimited, unborn, not to be reasoned about, unthinkable—He whose soul is space![11]

The living beings that inhabit our world are really only expressions of the Brahman. They are souls that are a part of the great ocean of souls that make up the Brahman. Therefore, all phenomenal existence is illusion arising from ignorance of the true nature of reality. A person's individuality apart from the Brahman—the world in which one lives, that which one sees, hears, touches, and feels—is all an illusion, a dream.

> This whole world the illusion-maker projects out of this [Brahman].
> And in it by illusion the other is confined.
> Now, one should know that Nature is illusion,
> And that the Mighty Lord is the illusion-maker.[12]

The plight of human beings is that they are bound up in this world of illusion and ignorance, thinking that it is real, unaware of their true identification with Brahman. "Those who worship ignorance *(avidya)* enter blinding darkness."[13] This ignorance is often illustrated by the parable of the tiger who was reared by a goat. All his life he believed that he was a goat, and he ate grass. One day he met another tiger who took him to a pool where the first tiger saw his true image. The second tiger then forced him to eat meat for the first time and he slowly came to realize his tiger nature. In like manner humans are deceived about their true nature. It is the task of religion to reveal the divine within us and to show us how to live on the new plane.

Those who continue in ignorance are bound to life by karma, which

---

[10] The word, Brahman is neuter. Basically it means "ever growing."
[11] Maitri Upanishad, VI. 17.
[12] Svetashvatara Upanishad, 4, 9–10.
[13] Isavasya Upanishad, 9.

keeps them endlessly in the cycle of birth, life, death, rebirth *(sam-sara)*. Salvation from this cycle and release from life comes when there is true knowledge of the illusion of life. "By knowing God man is freed from all bonds."[14] When true knowledge of the illusion of life is realized, one can be freed from the bondage of life and achieve unity with the Brahman. This is difficult. It comes only after much study. "Arise, awake, go to the sages and learn. The wise say that the path is sharp like the edge of a razor, hard to walk on, and difficult to obtain."[15]

Within the Upanishads one finds a collection of materials similar to that found in the Jewish Talmud. Various legends and tales are used to illustrate the philosophical material of these books. They are frequently cast in the form of a student's discussion with a guru, and apparently have been collected over centuries of use. The Chandogya Upanishad records a conversation between a son and his father. The father instructs his son in the following manner:

> "Put this piece of salt in the water and come to me tomorrow morning."
> [Svetaketu] did as he was told. [Then his father] said to him: "[Do you remember] that piece of salt you put in the water yesterday evening? Would you be good enough to bring it here?"
> He groped for it but could not find it. It had completely dissolved.
> "Would you please sip it at this end? What is it like?" he said.
> "Salt."
> "Sip it in the middle. What is it like?"
> "Salt."
> "Sip it at the far end. What is it like?"
> "Salt."
> "Throw it away, and then come to me."
> He did as he was told but [that did not stop the salt from] remaining ever the same.
> [His father] said to him: "My dear child, it is true that you cannot perceive Being here, but it is equally true that it *is* here.
> "This finest essence, the whole universe has as its Self; That is the Real: That is the Self: That *you* are, Svetaketu!"
> "Good sir, will you kindly instruct me further?"
> "I will, my dear child," said he.[16]

The Code of Manu

Another piece of traditional Indian literature produced during the classical era is the ethical Code of Manu. This code, which was probably written sometime between 300 B.C. and 300 A.D., is of value not

[14] Svetashvatara Upanishad, 4:6.
[15] Katha Upanishad, 1, 14.
[16] Chandogya Upanishad, VI. 13.

Pilgrims travel from all over India to bathe in the sacred Ganges River at Benares.
(*Courtesy of Lejeune; Stockmarket, Los Angeles.*)

because of its great religious or philosophical teachings but because of what it reveals about Indian life during the period. Within this book the student finds the ethical and social standards that were held up as ideals during the classical era of Indian history and the effects that the religious and philosophical teachings of the Vedas had upon Indian society. Furthermore, one finds here the roots of many of the social and religious traditions that were to characterize Hinduism into modern times.

One of the basic assumptions of the Code of Manu is the *varna* system, which had apparently developed from the early Aryan divisions of society. In the Code of Manu the divisions are seen as divinely ordained.

> For the growth of the worlds, (Brahman) created Brahmanas (Brahmins), Kshatriyas (warriors), Vaishyas (traders) and Shudras (manual workers) from his face, arms, thighs and feet respectively.[17]

[17] The Code of Manu, 1:31

The first three are called "twice born" and the fourth, the Shudras, the "once born." Members of each group have certain specified duties *(dharma)* and opportunities, and must obey them only.

> For the Brahmanas (Brahmins), he created teaching, studying, sacrifice, officiating at sacrifice, giving gifts, and accepting gifts.
> For the Kshatriya, he created in short the protection of people, giving gifts, performing sacrifices, studying, and nonattachment to sense pleasures.
> For the Vaishya, he created the protection of cattle, charity, performance of sacrifices, studying, trading, lending on interest, and agriculture.
> The Lord created only one profession for the Shudra: service without envy of the above three castes.[18]

Apparently, people were expected to begin life as Shudras, serve willingly and obediently, and gradually move from life to life through the system until they came to the exalted rank of Brahmin. Thus, even at this early stage the Indian society was stratified into fixed classes, and the only mobility through these classes was by the means of reincarnation.

The Code of Manu also demonstrates the state of the understanding of reincarnation at this period.

> Man obtains the life of motionlessness (of plants, and so on) as a result of the evil committed by the body, the life of birds and beasts because of the evil committed by speech, and the life of the lowest born because of the evil committed by mind.
> If a man performs only good actions, he will be born a god; if he performs mixed actions, he will be born a man; and if he performs only evil actions, he will be born a bird or an animal. The result of evil speech is the destruction of knowledge; that of evil mind is the loss of the supreme destiny; and that of the evil body is the loss of the worlds. So let one protect the three in every way. The punishment prescribed for evil speech is silence; that for evil mind is fasting; and that for evil action is breath control.[19]

Another of the central teachings of the Code of Manu is the various stages through which a man was expected to pass in a successful life. In the first stage of life the typical Indian gentleman is supposed to be a student, studying the Vedas and giving careful attention to his teacher. In the second stage of life one is to become a householder and marry a proper girl from his own caste. In the ideal marriage described in the Code of Manu the man is to be considerably older than

[18] Ibid., 1:88–91.
[19] Ibid., 12:9.

his wife. "A man, when he enters the stage of the householder, if he is thirty years of age, should marry a girl of twelve whom he likes. A man of twenty-four may marry a girl of eight."[20] The role of householder and provider is one of the most important, for it is the householder who is seen as one of the cornerstone of society. When a man's duties as a householder are completed and when he is aged, he is to retreat to the forest and live there for some years as a hermit, meditating and offering sacrifices. Finally, when his days as a hermit are completed, the Indian gentleman should become a wandering beggar (sannyasin). These four stages are only the ideals of the twice born (the three higher castes); the complete role of the shudra is to serve the higher castes all his life.

The four stages of life are also only for the men of the society. The women are supposed to stay in the home under the control and protection of the chief male of the household.

> Even at home nothing should be done independently by a woman, whether she is a young girl, a youthful maiden, or an old lady.
> When young, she should be in the control of her father and in her youth of her husband. When the husband dies, she should be in the protection of her sons. She should not love independence.
> She should never desire separation from her father, husband, or children. Separated from them, she brings bad name to both the families.[21]
> Women are meant for children. They are for the good and light of home. They are to be worshiped. In a home there is no difference between a woman on the one side and wealth, beauty, and splendor on the other.[22]

The Code of Manu is mainly a statement of the moral and ethical ideals of the period. It contains the prohibitions that one would expect against murder, theft, and sexual immorality. The moral aims of the era are summed up in the following ten characteristics: pleasantness, patience, control of mind, nonstealing, purity, control of the senses, intelligence, knowledge, truthfulness, and nonirritability.[23]

It is notable that even at this early date, Indian society placed a premium upon the life of cattle and imposed penalties upon those who slaughtered them. "The Vaishya, having gone through the sacraments, and having accepted a wife, should engage himself in trade and in the protection of cattle."[24] Among the greatest of sins is listed "the killing of cows."[25] For those who have committed great sins the

[20] Ibid., 9:94.
[21] Ibid., 5:147–149.
[22] Ibid., 9:26.
[23] Ibid., 6:92.
[24] Ibid., 9:326.
[25] Ibid., 11:59.

remedy is to: "Live with cows for a year controlling his mind, studying sacred texts. . . ."[26]

The Code of Manu is also helpful in giving an understanding of the Indian conception of divine time, which is virtually endless.

> Eighteen movements of the eyelid are called Kashta, Kala is thirty Kashtas, thirty Kalas constitute a Muhurta, and thirty Muhurtas make a day and night.
>
> The night and day are divided by the sun for men and gods. The night is meant for the sleep of beings and the day for their work.
>
> The night and day off ancestors is one month of men. Its black fortnight is meant for their action and the white for their sleep.
>
> The night and day of gods is the year of men. Its division again is into the summer solstice as the day and the winter solstice as the night.
>
> Now, understand the night and day of Brahman and their duration, and also of each of the aeons in succession.
>
> The Krita aeon consists of 4,000 years. Four hundred years before and four hundred after are the intervening times for this aeon.
>
> In the case of the other three aeons with their prior and posterior twilights, the number of thousands and hundreds is to be less and less by one.
>
> The aeon of the gods is said to be 12,000 times the four aeons counted previously.
>
> One thousand times the aeon of the gods is the day Brahman. His night also is as long.
>
> The knowers of day and night call the day of Brahman, which is 1,000 aeons long, the auspicious day. His night also is such.[27]

In general, Indian philosophy saw time as moving endlessly through various cycles. When one cycle of time is completed the world dissolves and all souls depart into suspended being. After a period of repose the world begins again and the souls take up new bodies.

Jainism and Buddhism

In the sixth century B.C. there arose in India two new religions that offered alternative salvation schemes within the Indian world view. They will be discussed in detail in later chapters, but it is worth noting at this point in our discussion of classical Hinduism that they did arise as serious challenges to the mother religion.

Both Jainism and Buddhism rejected the sacrificial system as a means of salvation from life, taught in the Vedas. They both taught that one achieved release from life not by offering sacrifices to the gods or by any form of worship but through accomplishments in one's own life.

[26]Ibid., 11:257.
[27]Ibid., 1:64–73.

They both rejected the Vedas as sacred scripture, and they both taught that anyone of any caste who lived properly might find salvation.

Jainism taught that one found release from life through asceticism. The more one denied pleasures and satisfactions to the body, the more likely that person was to achieve freedom from the endless cycle of birth and rebirth. In addition, the founders of Jainism enlarged upon the traditional Indian concern for cattle and taught that all forms of life were sacred and were to be loved and preserved whenever possible (*ahimsa*). While Jainism had its moments of popularity, it tended to demand too much of the average person for it to have ever become a mass movement. In the centuries following Jainism's orgin, Hinduism absorbed its concern for asceticism and *ahimsa*, and today Jainism has two million followers in India.

Buddhism grew out of many of the same longings and beliefs that formed the basis for Jainism. However, it taught that while one could find release from life without priests and a sacrificial system, the extremes of asceticism were not necessary. For a time Buddhism, with its more moderate ways, appeared to have become the religion of India; it even became a missionary religion, sending its preachers to other Asian nations. However, Hinduism eventually reasserted itself and absorbed the distinctive features of Buddhism. Gautama Buddha, founder of Buddhism, was made a member of the Hindu pantheon, and many of his teachings became a part of Hinduism. By the fifteenth century A.D. there were few Buddhists left in India. (Buddhism did, however, become the dominant religion of many other Asian nations and survives in them today.) The rise and popularity of Jainism and Buddhism in the sixth century B.C. in India nevertheless demonstrates that not all Indians found satisfaction in the teachings of classical Hinduism.

Bhagavad-Gita

Perhaps the concluding statement on classical Hinduism is the great epic poem of Indian culture and religion, the Bhagavad-Gita. This poem is to Hinduism what the Homeric epic poems are to Greek and Hellenstic culture. Like the Homeric poems, the Bhagavad-Gita is about a great battle; it relates the stories of the struggles of great heroes and gods and contains much of the basic philosophy of the culture.

The Bhagavad-Gita is found within the text of an even longer poem called the Mahabharata.[28] The Mahabharata is the story of the struggles between the two leading families from the beginning of Indian

---

[28] While the Bhagavad-Gita is a massive epic in itself, it pales to insignificance beside the Mahabharata, which contains 110,000 couplets or 220,000 lines.

history. Finally these two families come together in the battle of Kurukshetra, which historians roughly place between 850 and 650 B.C. Just before this battle one of the warriors, Arjuna, contemplates his fate and the struggle before him. His charioteer, Krishna, enters into the dialogue with him. Their conversation, found between chapters 25 and 42 of the Mahabharata, makes up the Bhagavad-Gita.

While the Mahabharata is believed to have been composed over a very long period of time, beginning perhaps as early as the ninth or eighth century B.C., the Bhagavad-Gita itself is believed to have been composed sometime between the second century B.C. and the third century A.D. The eighteen chapters that make up the Bhagavad-Gita are divided into three sections of six chapters each. In the first section, Arjuna, the young warrior, looks out upon the battlefield and contemplates the coming war and his part in it.

> Standing there, Partha (Arjuna) saw his fathers, grandfathers, teachers, maternal uncles, brothers, sons, grandsons, friends, paternal uncles, well-wishers in both armies. He, a son of Kunti, saw closely all of them, his relations.[29]
>
> He was overcome by sorrow, felt dejected, and said, "Seeing my own men gathered and ready for battle, my limbs give way and mouth dries up, my body trembles and hairs stand on end. My Gandiva [bow] slips from my hand, and my skin burns. I am unable to stand and my mind whirls."
>
> "Even if they whose minds are struck by greed, do not see the sin in destroying the family and in being unfaithful to friends, why should it be not known by us that we should avoid this sin?"[30]
>
> If the sons of Dhritarashtra, with weapons in their hands, kill me who am without weapons in hand and who do not retaliate in this battle, it will be better for me."[31]

Thus, like other warriors in all ages, Arjuna ponders the folly of war, particularly interfamily war, and contemplates going into battle unarmed and thus committing suicide. Arjuna's contemplation is answered by his charioteer, Krishna. The remainder of the poem is the conversation between Arjuna and Krishna about the nature of life and one's duties in life. In the second section of the poem Krishna reveals that he is the incarnation of the god Vishnu. As such he has come to earth to help mortals who are struggling with their problems. In the third section Krishma and Arjuna continue to discuss the problems of life that confront mortals.

Much of the advice and teaching that Krishna gives Arjuna is a reflection of the philosophy of the Upanishads, which says that most of what mortals see as life and its problems is merely illusion. The

[29] Bhagavad-Gita, II. 26–30.
[30] Ibid., II. 35–39.
[31] Ibid., I. 46.

Vishnu, the preserver, one of the three most important gods of Hinduism, is depicted with his consort, Lakshmi, on a panel from the temple at Khajuraho, ca. 1000 A.D. (*Courtesy of the Government of India Tourist Office.*)

most direct teaching that Krishna gives to Arjuna is that he should not dread going into battle because he is a member of the Kshatriya class and as such it is his duty (*dharma*) to be a warrior and to kill. If Arjuna were a member of another class, such as the Brahmin, he might have reason to reject the battlefield. However, battle is the *dharma* of the Kshatriya, and Arjuna has an obligation to obey that duty.

Not by leaving works undone
Does a man win freedom from the [bond of] work,
Nor by renunciation alone
Can he win perfection ['s prize].

Not for a moment can a man
Stand still and do no work;
For every man is powerless and forced to work
By the "constituents" born of Nature.[32]

[32] Ibid., III. 4–5.

The basic teachings and religious implications of the Bhagavad-Gita are many. The obvious teaching is that individuals should perform the duty of their caste and thus avoid *karma*, the force that binds people to the endless cycle of birth, death, and rebirth.[33] The obligations that are placed upon each caste are raised to the level of religious duties.

A second feature of Indian religion apparent in the Gita is its openness to a variety of means of personal salvation. People can achieve release from life (Nirvana), through asceticism, through meditation, through devotion to and worship of the gods, or through obedience to the rules of his caste. Thus Hinduism is regarded as the most open of all the world religions, and Bhagavad-Gita makes this clear.

Perhaps the most lasting teaching of the Gita is its revelation of Vishnu as a god who loves and is concerned about human beings. His concern is such that he takes various forms and comes to earth at certain times to aid mortals in their struggles. As Krishna says, "Whenever there is a decline of faith and an upsurge of irreligion," Vishnu makes his appearance in the world.[34]

In postclassical Hinduism, Vishnu became one of the most popular gods. The Bhagavad-Gita makes clear that one of the legitimate means of salvation is through devotion (*bhakti*) to gods like Vishnu.

> Arjuna, of this be sure:
> None who pays me worship of loyalty and love is ever lost.
> For whosoever makes Me his haven,
> Base-born though he may be,
> Yes, women too, and artisans, even serfs,—
> Theirs it is to tread the highest Way. . . .
>
> On Me thy mind, for Me thy loving service,
> For Me thy sacrifice, and to Me be thy prostrations:
> Let self be integrated, and then
> Shalt thou come to Me, thy striving bent on Me.[35]

POSTCLASSICAL HINDUISM

With the completion of the Bhagavad-Gita the classical era in Indian religion came to a close. This period began with the coming of the Aryans to India. It included the development of the Vedas and other

---

[33] The word *karma* literally means "deed" or "act." In Indian religions it usually refers to those deeds or actions that have effects upon future lives.

[34] Bhagavad-Gita, III. 12:6.

[35] Ibid., IX. 31, 32, 34.

religious literature, such as the Code of Manu and the Bhagavad-Gita. This material, its philosophy, and the pantheon of gods that it presented, became the basis for later Hinduism.

Some scholars distinguish between the religion of the classical era and that of the postclassical period by referring to the earlier religion as Brahminism and the later as Hinduism. Within Brahminism the religion of the Indian people was much like that of the Graeco-Roman world. Gods were worshiped with sacrifices offered on altars built in the open. Priests, who were expert in rituals and methods of sacrifice, were very important.

One of the earliest gods to be recognized in Hinduism is Brahma the creator. This small bronze statue depicts Brahma with four arms. (*Courtesy of The Asia Society, New York: Mr. and Mrs. John D. Rockefeller 3rd Collection. Photography by Otto E. Nelson.*)

After the close of the classical period subtle changes gradually were introduced into the religion of India. While the existence of many gods was still acknowledged, interest tended to center on the worship of a few major deities. Worship came to be love and devotion to those gods. Temples were built to them, and hymns were composed about their outstanding qualities. Whereas the literature of the classical period tended to deal with the great epics of Indian history, the literature of the postclassical era tended to center on these gods. The major gods were seen as taking various forms and becoming involved in the affairs of humankind. Of special interest in the postclassical literature were the various wives and consorts of the gods. A number of these goddesses became as popular as their mates, and many of the people of India became devotees of these goddesses, developed cults about them, and built temples for their worship of them.

Some scholars also point to the change that occurred in the basic attitude toward life in India between the classical and the postclassical eras. When the Aryans came to India they were an aggressive and optimistic people. Pessimistic and passive peoples do not migrate thousands of miles from their homes, conquer a land, and establish themselves as its rulers. However, by the beginning of modern Hinduism one sees certain negative and life-denying forces emerging. If the basic world view of Hinduism is that life is an endless cycle of birth, life, death, and rebirth, and that the goal of religion is to cease living, then this is essentially a negative and world-denying religion. The ascetic who refuses the pleasures and comforts of this life becomes the religious and cultural hero rather than the warrior.

None of these changes occurred overnight or even over one century. Their roots appear even in the Vedas. However, by the beginning of the Christian era certain changes in the basic religious structure did appear.

Devotion to Three Major Gods

As we have observed repeatedly, Hinduism offers its devotees many paths to salvation. Individuals may find release from life by devotion to one or more of the Indian gods. They may give full religious attention to each of these gods or goddesses by worshiping at their temples, offering sacrifices, praying, supporting the priests of the temple, and so on. In this manner the gods or goddesses may look with favor upon the devotee, support the believer in life, and help in the struggle for salvation. This path to salvation is called *Bhakti Marga* ("the way of devotion").

Brahman, who is ultimate reality, is at the core of Hindu thought. He is one and undivided. Yet postclassical Hinduism sees him in terms of three forms or functions. These three, called the Trimurti, are creation, preservation, and destruction. Each of these three functions of Brahman is expressed by a god from the classical literature: Brahma, the creator; Vishnu, the preserver; and Shiva, the destroyer. Devotees of any of these three gods tend to see all of the functions of Brahman in their chosen deity.

Brahma. Of the three leading deities of the Hindu pantheon, Brahma[36] receives the least attention. Although Brahma is widely respected and recognized as the creator of the world, there are only two temples specifically dedicated to him in all of India, and he has no cult of devotees. When Brahma is depicted in Indian art he is shown as red in color, with four bearded faces and four arms. His chief wife, Sarasvati, is the goddess of science and wisdom. Although Brahma is not mentioned in the Vedas, considerable mythology has grown up about him and his work of creation in the post-Vedic era.

Shiva. By far the most popular god in postclassical Hinduism is Shiva, who is known as "the destroyer." Shiva is the god of death, destruction, and disease. Like Brahma, Shiva does not appear in the Vedic literature, but he is believed to have been developed from the Aryan god Rudra.

The functions of Shiva are many. Not only is he the god of death, disease, and destruction, but he is also the god of the dance. In the mythology connected with Shiva there is frequently some statement about his dancing. He is a special god to Hindu ascetics, probably because in the process of tormenting and destroying their flesh this terrible deity is the one who is closest to reality for them. One of the most common symbols of Shiva is the trident. Frequently ascetics will be seen carrying a trident or will have the form of a trident painted upon their faces.

Perhaps the most important reason for Shiva's popularity is the fact that he is also the god of vegetable, animal, and human reproduction. In Indian thought death is but the prelude to rebirth. Therefore it follows that the god of death will also be a god of reproduction and sexuality. In the mythology of Shiva he is described as having a constantly erect penis and being sexually alert at all times. Other symbols that depict Shiva are the *lingam* and the *yoni*, the male and female sexual organs. Thus Shiva becomes the special deity of those who seek fertility or who utilize sex as a basic for religion.

---

[36] The god Brahma is to be distinguished from the all-pervading god-force of the Upanishads, Brahman. The word *Brahman* is neuter. The word *Brahma* is masculine and refers to a distinct entity.

Devotees of Shiva are known as Shaivites. There are several sects of Shaivism in Hinduism today. All regard the Vedas and special Shavite texts as scriptures. Their philosophical stance is that Shiva is ultimate reality; he is creator, preserver, and destroyer. Humans are thought to be separated from Shiva because of ignorance, karma, and illusion. In order to achieve union with Shiva, people must follow a prescribed path, worship Shiva, and attend him in his temples. They must also meditate and study under the direction of a guru. Some Shaivites require the repetition of a special *mantra*. All of these acts culminate in a union between Shiva and the worshiper and ultimately result in *moksha* (release from the death-rebirth cycle).

Fully as popular as Shiva are his various consorts. Numerous goddesses are associated with him, but the most important and most popular is Kali or, as she is sometimes called, Durga. Kali is, if anything, more terrible than Shiva. She is frequently depicted as wearing a necklace of human skulls, of tearing away the flesh of sacrificed victims, and drinking blood. Mythology connects her with the founding of the modern city of Calcutta.

> When Kali died, Shiva was both grief-stricken and angry. He placed her corpse on his shoulders and went stamping round the world in a dervish dance of mourning which became more furious the longer it lasted. The other gods realized that unless Shiva was stopped the whole world would be destroyed by his rage, which was unlikely to end as long as he had his wife's body on his shoulders. So Vishnu took up a knife and flung it at the corpse, dismembering it into fifty-two pieces which were scattered across the face of the earth. By the side of a great river in Bengal the little toe of the right foot landed, and a temple was built there, with an attendant village, and the people called this place Kalikata.[37]

Among the many sects dedicated to Kali was a group known as Thugs. The chief function of this group of devotees was to offer freshly strangled victims to their goddess. Thus they would waylay and slowly strangle some lonely victim while calling for Kali to come and be present in the death struggle. Strangely enough, the cult of the Thugs attracted Indian Muslims as well as Hindus, after the eleventh and twelfth centuries. The organization was outlawed by the British in the nineteenth century.

Vishnu. The third god of the postclassical Hindu triad is Vishnu, the preserver. In contrast to Shiva, Vishnu is known as a god of love, benevolence, and forgiveness. The chief feature of Vishnu is his concern for humanity, which he expresses by appearing on earth a num-

[37] Geoffrey Moorhouse, *Calcutta* (New York: Harcourt Brace Jovanovich, 1971), p. 6.

Shiva, the Hindu god of death and reproduction, is often shown with one of his wives or consorts. Here he is seated with Parvati. (*Courtesy of the Asia Society, New York: Mr. and Mrs. John D. Rockefeller 3rd Collection. Photography by Otto E. Nelson.*)

ber of times in various forms (*avatars*). According to mythology, Vishnu has appeared on earth in nine forms and will come a tenth time to close this era (*kalpa*) and bring the world to an end. In some incarnations he has come as a man. According to the Bhagavad-Gita he has appeared as Krishna. As Hinduism absorbed the distinctive features of Buddhism it was taught that Vishnu had appeared as Gautama, the Buddha. He has purportedly also come to earth as various animals and creatures involved in helping people. For example, it is believed that Vishnu appeared as Matsya, the fish who acted to save Manu from the great flood. In every case he has come to aid humankind because he is the preserver and the restorer.

Devotees of Vishnu are known as Vaishnavites. In India they are noted for their deep love of God and the poems and songs that they write in his praise. Kabir and Nanak, the founders of Sikhism, were poets in this tradition. Like the Shaivites, the worshipers of Vishnu regard their god as ultimate reality. Generally they see salvation coming not from the actions of the devotees but through the love and grace of Vishnu.

An extreme example of devotion to one god has become familiar in many major American cities in the past few years—the so-called Hare Krishna movement. This group of devotees of the god Krishna traces its origin back to the appearance of Krishna in human form, as recorded in the Bhagavad-Gita. From that time onward there has been a group of people in India who have devoted themselves totally to the worship and adoration of Krishna.

Devotion to Knowledge

In postclassical Hinduism people could choose one or more of the gods and find salvation through devotion to those gods and their temples. This was probably the most acceptable and convenient way to salvation for the majority of the people. However, an equally acceptable way to salvation for those who could follow it was the so-called way of knowledge *(Jnana Marga)*. For the wealthy or the intellectual who had the time to spend studying the various philosophical implications of sacred writings, the way of knowledge had merit.

Generally when people speak of the way of knowledge as a means to salvation in Hinduism, they refer to the various systems of philosophy that offer paths to salvation. These systems are Samkhya, Yoga, Mimansa, Vaisheshika, Nyana, and Vedanta. All claim to be based upon the Vedas, all aim at salvation, and all believe in rebirth and preexistence. While the number of philosophical systems is usually limited to these six, there are many other lesser systems and variations within the six.

The Samkhya System.   The Samkhya system of philosophy is said to have been founded by the sage Kapila, who lived during the sixth century B.C. The Samkhya system arose during the era of the founding of Jainism and Buddhism; it apparently influenced both these religions and was in turn influenced by them. Like Jainism and early Buddhism, the Samkhhya system recognizes no personal gods and may be viewed as an atheistic approach to life. Like Jainism, it sees the universe as a dualism with the forces of spirit *(purusha)* and matter *(prakriti)*. All that exists is these two forces, and from them springs all that we know in the world.

The Yoga System.   Of all the Hindu philosophies Yoga is the best known to Westerners, although they tend to think only of physical, or Hatha Yoga, or of the various extremes of asceticism that the Yogin may achieve. The word *Yoga* is derived from the root *yuj*, which means

Sadhu holy man. This Hindu has entered the final stage of life, and has given himself totally to meditation and acts of devotion. (*Courtesy of Diane M. Lowe.*)

"to yoke" or "to join." Yoga basically follows the philosophical views of the Samkhya system, viewing the world as a dualism and teaching that one should attempt to yoke or join his individual spirit to God.

Statues depicting persons in various yogic positions have been found in the remains of the pre-Aryan cities dating back to the third millennium B.C. However, the philosophy of Yoga as it is known today was developed by the sage Patanjal. He lived in the second century B.C. and codified the teachings of Yoga in his *Yoga Sutra.*

The main feature of all Yoga is meditation. Meditation is necessary even for the gods if they are to find release from the cycle of birth, death, and rebirth.

There are several forms of Yoga, each having several features and each emphasizing a different one. Rajah Yoga stresses mental and spiritual development. In this form of yogic discipline one works through various stages in order to free the mind from anger, lust, hatred, greed, and so on. According to the *Yoga Sutra* there are eight steps one must take in order to achieve trance or the super-conscious level in Rajah Yoga.

1. Before one can progress, one must take certain vows of restraint (*yama*). These are vows against harming living creatures, and unchastity.
2. At this stage one attempts to achieve internal control, calmness, and equanimity (*niyama*).
3. In the third stage one learns and practices certain bodily postures (*asana*) that designed to help one achieve the aims of Yoga.[38]
4. Once the postures have been mastered, one works on breath control (*pranayama*).
5. The fifth stage is control of the senses (*pratyahara*), in which one seeks to shut out the outside world.
6. The sixth stage is extreme concentration on a single object (*dharana*).
7. Then one seeks to achieve meditation (*dhyana*).
8. Finally the Yogin seeks a trance (*samadhi*), in which the Yogin becomes one with the Brahman.

Those who work through these steps achieve great physical powers and remarkable abilities of concentration. The ascetics who master Yoga are those who perform the outstanding feats of asceticism that have come to be identified with Yoga in the Western mind.

The Mimansa System.   Purva Mimansa, the full name of the Mimansa system of philosophy, means "early examination'" of the Vedas. The primary scriptures for the advocates of this system are the Vedas and the Mimansa Sutra, which was written about 200 B.C. The leading advocates of the Mimansa philosophy were Kumarila and Prabhakara, who lived in the eighth century A.D.

The primary concern of Mimansa is the avoidance of rebirth. This is accomplished by obeying the laws laid down in the Vedas and by performing the rites established in them. Early advocates rejected the existence of gods, but by the eighth century A.D. some philosophers of this system were known to offer prayers to Shiva.

The Vaisheshika System.   The root meaning of *Vaisheshika* is "particularity." The Vaisheshika system of philosophy probably arose in the sixth century B.C., at the time of the founding of Buddhism and Jainism. The founder of Vaisheshika was Kanada, who wrote the primary document, the Vaisheshika Sutra. In contrast to the philosophies that teach that there is no reality except Brahman, the Vaish-

---

[38] The most common posture used in meditation is the so-called lotus position, in which one sits with his right foot upon his left thigh, his left foot upon his right thigh, and his back erect. In this extremely balanced position concentration is easier than it is in most other seated positions.

eshika teaches that the universe is made up of nine distinct elements: earth, water, air, fire, soul, mind, ether, time, and space. Since these elements are eternal and uncreated, no gods are needed in the universe. Later philosophers in this system adopted the idea of a supreme being who guides the universe.

The Nyaya System. The Nyaya philosophical system has adopted the metaphysical scheme of the Vaisheshika system and is often paired with it by those who classify Indian philosophies. Nyaya was founded by a man named Guatama who lived in the third century B.C. and who wrote the Nyaya Sutra. This Gautama has been called "the Aristotle of India" by some students of philosophy. Like the advocates of Vaisheshika, he was essentially atheistic and believed in the reality of the world. He therefore reasoned that individuals can have a real knowledge of the world. Thus the Nyaya system is primarily concerned with logical analysis as a means of arriving at truth about the world.

The Vedanta System. Another system or set of systems of Hindu philosophy is the Vedanta. The term *Vedanta* is usually translated as "the end of the Vedas," indicating that the major materials in these systems are taken from the Upanishads, which are placed at the end of the Vedic literature. (Contrast this with "Mimansa.") The term is also translated as "the acme of the Vedas," indicating that the Vedanta philosophy is the very peak of the religious teaching found in the Vedas. Regardless of the interpretation, the Vedanta philosophy is based upon the Upanishadic writings and their outlook on life. It is believed that the Vedanta philosophy was first formulated by a sage named Badarayan, who lived sometime between 250 B.C. and 450 A.D. and wrote the *Vedanta Sutra.*

In contrast to the Samkhya system, the Vedanta is monistic and assumes only one true essence in the universe. This essence may be called God, or Brahman. Nothing else exists but Brahman. The world of humankind, its bodies, souls, and material substances do not really exist. Therefore, humankind's basic problem is not its wickedness but its ignorance. People are ignorant of the true nature of reality and believe that they are separated from Brahman. This ignorance thus binds them endlessly to the cycle of birth and rebirth until they can achieve liberation through knowledge.

One branch of Vedanta that developed in the ninth century A.D. is called "Advaita." The word means "non-dual" and indicates its monistic viewpoint. Its founder was Shankara (788–838 A.D., who was perhaps the most outstanding scholar of medieval Hinduism. Although this man was a very famous ascetic and teacher in his time, he is best known for the philosophical approach he took in interpreting the Vedas. His abilities and reputation as a philosopher have prompted some Western readers to refer to Shankara as the Aquinas of Hinduism. His most outstanding literary contribution is a commentary he wrote on the *Vedanta Sutra*. This commentary has become such a classic in Hindu literature that it has been the object of several commentaries itself. In his commentary Shankara asserted the absolute oneness of Brahman, in the classic manner of the Upanishads. Brahman is all there is. All else in the universe is an illusion, and people are bound up in endless reincarnations until they rip aside the veil of this illusion. Shankara himself was a devotee of Shiva because he believed that Shiva was the best representation of the true nature of Brahman.

Shankara is also remembered for his fierce opposition to Buddhism. It is believed that his leadership against Buddhism was a major factor in destroying this religion in India and restoring Hindiusm to the dominant position.

According to one story, Shankara did not die; he simply disappeared. This has caused some Shaivites to believe that the great scholar was actually an avatar of Shiva.

A second philosopher of the medieval period in Hinduism, and who represents a side in the debate over the true meaning of the Vedas, was Ramanuja. Ramanuja lived in the twelfth century A.D. and was a teacher who believed that devotion to the gods was extremely important. He was himself devoted to the worship of Vishnu. He reasoned that if Shankara were correct and if each person were merely a part of the God Brahman, then devotion to God would not be possible, for how can one be devoted to oneself? While he could not move away from the traditional Vedanta position of the oneness of God, Ramanuja taught a qualified dualism, in which he asserted that the human soul and the divine soul were united and yet somehow separate. The analogy that he used to explain this was the human body and spirit. One cannot exist without the other, but they are separate entities.

The third point of view in this debate was presented by the philosopher Madhva, who lived in the thirteenth century. Madhva was also devoted to the god Vishnu and believed strongly in devotion to the gods as the only proper religious expression. He was willing to go farther than Ramanuja, however. He took the side of dualism even though he remained in the general school of Vedanta. However, he abandoned completely the notion that God was all and that all else was illusion. To him the world and individual souls were completely separate from Brahman and separate from one another. Thus each individual and separate soul is able to worship properly the separate nature of God.

Muslim Influences in India

In the seventh century A.D. a new and vital religion sprang from the deserts of Arabia. Within a few decades the religion of Islam had spread, through conquest and conversion, across the entire Middle Eastern world. By the eighth century it was on the verge of moving into Europe. Islam also moved eastward and by the eighth century had conquered Persia and Afghanistan and made occasional raids into India.

Portions of northwest India were conquered by Muslim leaders as early as 712 A.D. In the eleventh century the Turkish general Mahmud of Ghazni invaded India seventeen times and brought back vast treasure to his headquarters in Afghanistan. By the thirteenth century Islam was so well entrenched in India that there was a Sultanate of Delhi. In the sixteenth century a dynasty of Turkish rulers, known as the Moghuls, established an empire and ruled most of the subcontinent of India. However, by the eighteenth century this empire had run its course and had decayed into many small warring states which became easy prey for the invading British armies. Today, though Hinduism is the majority religion of India, there are more Muslims on the subcontinent than there are in any other nation in the world.

Relations between Hindus and Muslims have always been touchy. Indeed, it would be difficult to find two religions more different than Hinduism and Islam. Whereas Muslims are staunchly monotheistic, Hindus tend to be limitlessly polytheistic; whereas Muslims disdain the representation of Allah in any form, Hindus have richly decorated temples with statuary portraying their many gods; whereas Muslims have been known to occasionally offer a cow as a blood sacrifice to Allah, Hindus tend to regard the cow as a sacred animal and seek to protect it from any harm; and whereas Muslims regard every man as equal before Allah, Hindus have traditionally followed a caste system that divides society into classes, with the upper classes having more religious privileges than the lower.

In spite of these vast differences Hindus and Muslims have managed to live side by side for more than one thousand years. Hinduism has not altered its basic theology in light of its contacts with Islam, but Indian society has adopted many of the elements of the Muslim world. Particularly during the years of the Moghul empire Indian society was influenced by the art, architecture, sciences, and even the dress styles of the Muslim world.

In the fifteenth century there arose the most notable attempt at reconciliation between Islam and Hinduism: the religion of Sikhism. Sikhism will be discussed in detail in a later chapter. However, it must be said at this point that Sikhism managed to attain a harmony between the uncompromising monotheism of Islam and the doctrines of illusion and reincarnation of Hinduism. It must also be said that, whereas Hindus and Muslims have somehow managed to live together in India, the religious and political differences between the two peoples are one of the major problems facing India.

MODERN HINDUISM

Hinduism, like all major religions, has had to face the rigors of the modern age, with its nationalistic movements, its social reforms, its encounters between religions, and its scientific revolutions. The last four hundred years have been difficult for a religion that is as tied to tradition as is Hinduism.

Of all the factors of the modern era that have affected Hinduism, one of the most important has been Hinduism's encounter with Christianity and its European and American representatives. According to tradition, Christianity was brought to India by the disciple Thomas and has been an active religion there since the first century A.D.[39] However, Christianity probably had little effect upon the Indian people until more recent times.

The first serious encounter between India and the modern European nations came in 1510, when the Portuguese conquered Goa. In the seventeenth century the British invaded India and established the British East India Company. This began three centuries of British rule in India. Though the British were present in India as merchants and soldiers, it was not until the nineteenth century that they allowed missionaries to enter the country to try to convert the Indians. One of the reasons for this late entry was that many Protestant denominations did not actively seek to send missionaries earlier.

One of the British missionaries to enter India was the Baptist William Carey (1761–1834). Like many other missionaries of the nineteenth century Carey was concerned not only with preaching the gospel of his faith but also with raising the living and educational standards of the people he ministered to. He was the first to begin modern printing in India, and he also initiated many new educational programs for the Indian people. Carey, along with other missionaries, was alarmed at several practices—which he felt were inhuman and harmful—within Indian social life. One of these was the *suttee,* in which an Indian widow was expected to throw herself upon the funeral pyre or into the grave of her dead husband and be destroyed

---

[39] Some scholars believe that Christianity was a factor in the development of devotion to one god *(bhakti marga)* as a means of salvation in the postclassical period, and that it was also a factor in the development of the Bhagavad-Gita.

with him. Another practice that was abhorrent to the European missionary was that of child marriages. It had become common in India for parents to betroth their young children in order to insure a suitable marriage.[40] Frequently, this meant the betrothal of very young children, and the marriage of nine- and ten-year-olds. This was particularly harsh in the case of girls who might have been promised by their parents to men twenty or thirty years their senior. This practice tended to ensure that when a husband died he left behind a fairly young widow who was expected to destroy herself. The missionaries put pressure upon the British rulers, and eventually both the practices of child marriage and the *suttee* were officially outlawed in India.

The late nineteenth and twentieth centuries saw several reform movements in Hinduism. One of the earliest reformers was Ram Mohan Roy (1774–1833), who was called "the Father of Modern India." Roy tended to agree with the missionaries and supported them in their attempts to suppress the *suttee* and child marriages. He also saw in Christianity many elements that he appreciated although he did not accept the divinity of Jesus. Ram Mohan Roy tended to be a monotheist and sought to suppress the polytheism and idolatry of Hinduism. In order to continue his work after his death, Roy organized the *Brahmo Samaj* (The Society of God), which became a major force in the renewal of India in the nineteenth and twentieth centuries.

Perhaps the greatest religious reformer of the nineteenth century was Sri Ramakrishna (1834–1886). Once a priest of Kali in Calcutta, Ramakrishna was philosophically a follower of nondualistic Vedanta. He later became convinced that behind all religions there was a single reality which might be called God. Although Ramakrishna was illiterate, his contacts with Christians and Muslims as well as Hindus convinced him that truth was essentially one.

The teachings of Ramakrishna might have died with him in India had it not been for one of his disciples, Narendranath Dutt (1863–1902), who was later known as Vivekananda. Vivekananda became a member of the *Brahmo Samaj* early in his life. Later he met Ramakrishna and became his apostle. After a period of several years of retreat in the Himalayas he set forth to be the first Hindu missionary to the modern world. Vivekananda traveled widely, lecturing on the virtues of Vedanta Hinduism, which he described as "the mother of all other religions." He made his greatest impression at the Parliament of Religions in Chicago in 1893, as the spokesman for Hinduism. Wherever he went, this spokesman for the oneness of God captivated audiences and made converts.

---

[40] It is estimated that in modern India approximately 96 percent of all marriages are arranged by parents.

Mohandas K. Gandhi was one of the most outstanding Hindu leaders of the modern era. His work reforming Hindu society and ultimately bringing independence to India through nonviolent means brought him world-wide attention. (*Courtesy of Information Service of India, New York.*)

The best-known Indian reformer of the twentieth century was Mohandas K. Gandhi (1869–1948). Gandhi is chiefly remembered for his work in bringing political and social benefits to the Indian people near the end of the British rule, through a combination of religious idealism and civil disobedience. Gandhi was originally trained as a lawyer in England, where he came into contact with many of the social and political ideas of the nineteenth century. He was also introduced to Christianity, especially to Jesus' Sermon on the Mount. These factors, along with the ideals of his Hindu heritage, molded Gandhi into the figure that he became. As the leader of the Indian people in their struggle for freedom from British rule, he personally led many fasts and strikes against various British policies and was usually victorious. In addition to espousing civil disobedience and nonviolence, Gandhi was also influenced by the Jain teaching of noninjury of life. Thus he was a vegetarian and stoutly defended the Indian practice of cow protection. Gandhi also read and remembered the works of the American Thoreau, works that advocated passive resistance to civil authority. In turn Gandhi became one of the models for the political thinking of Martin Luther King, Jr., who led American blacks in their struggles for civil rights in the 1960s. Gandhi, who advocated nonviolence, died by an assassin's bullet in 1948, just a few months after his people had won their independence.

An object of special concern for both internal and external reformers was the caste system. Although the ancient Hindu literature spoke of society divided into four *varnas* (colors), the full-blown caste system is a relatively modern development. In early Hinduism there is evidence of social intercourse between the classes.

Sometime after 700 A.D. the modern caste system began to develop. The four basic social groups began to divide into literally thousands of castes. Sometimes these castes were based upon vocations. For example there may have been castes of metal workers and castes of weavers. Other castes developed along racial lines. Ultimately there came to be more than 3,000 separate castes in Indian society. When the Portuguese came to India in the sixteenth century they gave their word, *casta* (breed, race) to these divisions.

The multiple castes dominated every aspect of the lives of their members. One entered a caste by being born to parents of that caste. One's caste dictated diet, vocation, place of residence, and choice of mate. Rigid rules forbade much social intercourse between members of differing castes.

Most pitiful were those at the lowest end of the social scale. Those possessing no caste were called "outcastes," and because the higher castes could have nothing to do with them, this group was often called "untouchable." To them fell the lowest occupations. They were the street sweepers, the latrine cleaners, the handlers of the dead, and the tanners of leather. With these vocations came the lowest wages, the worst living conditions, and little hope of improvement..

The religion of Hinduism seemed to justify the status of the outcastes. Since the untouchables were in this situation in life, it must be because their karma from a previous life had dictated it. If the outcastes accepted the dharma of this life and did not rebel against it, they might have hope for a better caste in the next life.

As a result of the efforts of reformers like Gandhi, discrimination against the outcastes was officially forbidden in the 1948 constitution of the Republic of India. However, the long-standing and firmly entrenched rules of caste seem to die slowly in modern India.

HINDUISM TODAY

Like all religions, Hinduism today has to struggle with the issue of modernity. Its primary home, India, is the world's largest democracy and therefore the demands of its people must be heard. Perhaps for the first time in its history Hinduism must deal with issues such as social justice, birth control, and the problems raised by urbanization. In the past, one was taught to accept his or her lot in life and not complain. Perhaps the next life would be better. If problems became so severe that one simply could not endure them, there was always the alternative of life as an ascetic.

The ancient conflicts between Hindu and Muslim in India are also still an issue. Further complication has arisen in the 1980s with the strident demands of the Sikhs. The bloodshed that occurred in the past wars between religions seems likely to continue into the future.

However, Hinduism is an ancient religion and has absorbed many challenges over the centuries. New religions have arisen and been absorbed by Hinduism. Social changes have come and gone and Hinduism continues to be a viable force in the lives of millions. Its temples, gods, festivals, and so on, continue to fulfill a need in the lives of Indians.

STUDY QUESTIONS

1. Outline the early history of Hinduism. How did the gods and rituals brought by the Aryans blend with native religions to produce classical Hinduism?

2. Define the Rig-Veda, the Upanishads, and the code of Manu. Show how these three bodies of literature demonstrate basic Hindu religious concepts.

3. Discuss Jainism and Buddhism as heresies of Hinduism. What was the fate of these two religions in India? In Asia?

4. What is the central lesson which Arjuna must learn from the conversations with Krishna in the Bhagavad Gita?

5. List the three major gods of modern Hinduism and give a brief description of each.

6. Contrast Hinduism with Islam. Show Sikhism as an attempt to blend the major features of these religions.

SUGGESTED READING

Bolle, Kees W. (Trans.). *The Bhagavadgita.* Berkeley: University of California Press, 1979.

Chaudhuri, Nirad C. *Hinduism.* New York: Oxford University Press, 1979.

Hinnells, John R. and Eric J. Sharpe. *Hinduism.* Newcastle, England: Oriel Press, 1972.

Hopkins, Thomas J. *The Hindu Religious Tradition.* Encino, Calif.: Dickenson Publishing Co. Inc., 1971.

Nikhilanada, Swami, (Trans.). *The Upanishads.* 4 vols. New York: Harper & Row, 1949–1959.

Renou, Louis, ed. *Hinduism.* New York: George Braziller, 1961.

SOURCE MATERIAL

Selections from the Rig-Veda

The basis of all later Hindu scripture is the ancient collection of hymns to the Aryan gods called the Rig-Veda. The following are representative selections from this book.

Varuna and Indra

(Rig-Veda, IV, 42, 1–7, 10)

1. I am the royal Ruler, mine is empire, as mine who sway all life are all the Immortals.
   Varuna's will the Gods obey and follow. I am the King of men's most lofty cover.

2. I am King Varuna. To me was given these first existing high celestial powers.
   Varuna's will the Gods obey and follow. I am the King of Men's most lofty cover.

3. I Varuna am Indra: in their greatness, these the two wide deep fairly-fashioned regions,
   These the two world-halves have I, even as Tvashtar knowing all beings, joined and held together.

4. I made to flow the moisture shedding waters, and set the heaven firm in the seat of Order.
   By Law, the son of Aditi, Law-Observer, hath spread abroad the world in threefold measure.

5. Heroes with noble horses, fain for battle, selected warriors, call on men in combat.
   I Indra Maghavan, excite the conflict; I stir the dust, Lord of surpassing vigour.

6. All this I did. The god's own conquering power never impedeth me to whom none opposeth.
   When lauds and Soma juice have made me joyful, both the unbounded regions are affrighted.

7. All beings know these deeds of thine: thou tellest this unto Varuna, thou great Disposer!
   Thou art renowned as having slain the Vritras. Thou madest flow the floods that were obstructed. . . .

10. May we, possessing much, delight in riches, Gods in oblations and the kine in pasture;
And that Milch-cow who shrinks not from the milking, O Indra-Varuna, give to us daily.[41]

"What God Shall We Adore With Our Oblation?"

(Rig-Veda, X, 121, 1–10)

1. In the beginning rose Hiranyagarbha, born Only Lord of all created beings.
He fixed and holdeth up this earth and heaven. What god shall we adore with our oblation?

2. Giver of vital breath, of power and vigour, he whose commandments all the gods acknowledge;
The Lord of death, whose shade is life immortal. What God shall we adore with our oblation?

3. Who by his grandeur hath become Sole Ruler of all the moving world that breathes and slumbers;
He who is Lord of men and Lord of cattle. What God shall we adore with our oblations?

4. His, through his might, are these snow-covered mountains, and men call sea and Rasa his possession;
His arms are these, his are these heavenly regions. What God shall we adore with our oblation?

5. By him the heavens are strong and earth is steadfast, by him light's realm and sky-vault are supported;
By him the regions in mid-air were measured. What God shall we adore with our oblation?

6. To him, supported by his help, two armies embattled look while trembling in their spirit,
When over them the risen Sun is shining. What God shall we adore with our oblation?

7. What time the mighty waters came, containing the universal germ, producing Agni,
Then sprang the Gods' one spirit into being. What God shall we adore with our oblation?

[41] *The Hymns of the Rig-Veda,* Ralph T. H. Griffith, trans., I (Benares: E. J. Lazarus and Co., 1920), pp. 448, 449.

8. He in his might surveyed the floods containing productive force and
   generating Worship.
   He is the God of gods, and none beside him. What God shall we
   adore with our oblation?

9. Ne'er may he harm us who is earth's Begetter, nor he whose laws are
   sure, the heaven's creator,
   he who brought forth the great and lucid waters. What God shall we
   adore with our oblation?

10. Prajapati! thou only comprehendest all these created things, and none
    beside thee.
    Grant us our heart's desire when we invoke thee; may we have store
    in riches in possession.[42]

Selections from the Bhagavad-Gita

The Bhagavad-Gita, "the song of the blessed lord," is the
classic poem of India. In this massive poem about a great
battle the gods take human forms and talk with mortals. In
the following sections the god Krishna speaks with the poem's
hero, Arjuna, about the nature of life, death, and the gods.[43]

II, 16–26

16. Of what is not, no coming to be occurs;
       No coming not to be occurs of what is;
    But the dividing-line of both is seen,
       Of these two, by those who see the truth.

17. But know that that is indestructible,
       By which this all is pervaded;
    Destruction of this imperishable one
       No one can cause.

18. These bodies come to an end,
       It is declared, of the eternal embodied (soul),
    Which is indestructible and unfathomable.
       Therefore fight, son of Bharata!

---

[42] Ibid., II. 566, 567.

[43] *Bhagavad Gita*, trans., Franklin Edgerton, Vol. I, Oriental Series, Vol. 38 (Cambridge, Mass.:
Harvard University Press, 1944).

19. Who believes him a slayer,
       And who thinks him slain,
    Both these understand not:
       He slays not, is not slain.

20. He is not born, nor does he ever die;
       Nor, having come to be, will he ever more come not to be.
    Unborn, eternal, everlasting, this ancient one
       Is not slain when the body is slain.

21. He knows as indestructible and eternal
       This unborn, imperishable one,
    That man, son of Pritha, how
       Can he slay or cause to slay—whom?

22. As leaving aside worn-out garments
       A man takes other, new ones,
    So leaving aside worn-out bodies
       To other, new ones goes the embodied (soul).

23. Swords cut him not,
       Fire burns him not,
    Water wets him not,
       Wind dries him not.

24. Not to be cut is he, not to be burnt is he,
       Not to be wet nor yet dried;
    Eternal, omnipresent, fixed,
       Immovable, everlasting is he.

25. Unmanifest he, unthinkable he,
       Unchangeable he is declared to be;
    Therefore knowing him thus
       Thou shouldst not mourn him.

26. Moreover, even if constantly born
       Or constantly dying thou considered him,
    Even so, great-armed one, thou
       Shouldst not mourn him. . . .

XI, 15–21, 24, 25, 31–34

Arjuna said:
15. I see the gods in Thy body, O God,
       All of the hosts of various kinds of beings too,

Lord Brahma sitting on the lotus-seat,
    And the seers all, and the divine serpents.

16. With many arms, bellies, mouths, and eyes,
    I see Thee, infinite in form on all sides;
No end nor middle nor yet beginning of Thee
    Do I see, O All-God, All-formed!

17. With diadem, club, and disc,
    A mass of radiance, glowing on all sides,
I see Thee, hard to look at, on every side
    With the glory of flaming fire and sun, immeasurable.

18. Thou art the Imperishable, the supreme Object of Knowledge;
    thou art the ultimate resting-place of this universe;
Thou art the immortal guardian of the eternal right.
    Thou are the everlasting Spirit, I hold.

19. Without the beginning, middle, or end, of infinite power,
    Of infinite arms, whose eyes are the moon and sun,
I see Thee, whose face is flaming fire,
    Burning this whole universe with Thy radiance.

20. For this region between heaven and earth
    Is pervaded by Thee alone, and all the directions;
Seeing this Thy wondrous, terrible form,
    The triple world trembles, O exalted one!

21. For into Thee are entering yonder throngs of gods;
    Some, affrighted, praise Thee with reverent gestures;
Crying "Hail!" the throngs of the great seers and perfected ones
    Praise Thee with abundant laudations.

24. Touching the sky, aflame, of many colours,
    With yawning mouths and flaming enormous eyes,
Verily seeing Thee (so), my inmost soul is shaken,
    And I find no steadiness nor peace, O Vishnu!

25. And Thy mouths, terrible with great tusks,
    No sooner do I see them, like the fire of dissolution (of the world),
Than I know not the directions of the sky, and I find no refuge;
    Have mercy, Lord of Gods, thou in whom the world dwells!

31. Tell me, who art Thou, of awful form?
    Homage be to Thee: Best of Gods, be merciful!

I desire to understand Thee, the primal one;
  For I do not comprehend what Thou hast set out to do.

The Blessed One said:
32. I am Time (Death), cause of destruction of the worlds, matured
    And set out to gather in the worlds here.
  Even without thee (thy action), all shall cease to exist,
    The warriors that are drawn up in the opposing ranks.

33. Therefore arise thou, win glory,
    Conquer thine enemies and enjoy prospered kingship;
  By Me Myself they have already been slain long ago;
    Be thou the mere instrument, left-handed archer!

34. Drona and Bhisma and Jayadratha,
    Karna too, and the other warrior-heroes as well,
  Do thou slay, (since) they are already slain by Me; do not hesitate!
    Fight! Thou shalt conquer thy rivals in battle.

The Upanishads

> The Upanishads are a collection of philosophical writings from
> the classical teachers of Hinduism. The following is a de-
> scription of the moment of death, found in the Upani-
> shads.[44]

When this self gets to weakness, gets to confusedness, as it were, then the
breaths gather round him. He takes to himself those particles of light and
descends into the heart. When the person in the eye turns away, then he
becomes non-knowing of forms.

(When his body grows weak and he becomes apparently unconscious,
the dying man gathers his senses about him, completely withdraws their
powers, and descends into the heart. *Radhakrishnan.*)

He is becoming one, he does not see, they say; he is becoming one, he
does not smell, they say; he is becoming one, he does not taste, they say;
he is becoming one, he does not speak, they say; he is becoming one, he
does not hear, they say; he is becoming one, he does not think, they say;
he is becoming one, he does not touch, they say; he is becoming one, he
does not know, they say. The point of his heart becomes lighted up and
by that light the self departs either through the eye or through the head or
through other apertures of the body. And when he thus departs, life departs
after him. And when life thus departs, all the vital breaths depart after him.

[44]S. Radhakrishnan, ed. and trans., *The Principal Upanishads* (London: Allen & Unwin, 1953),
  pp. 269, 270, 296.

He becomes one with intelligence. What has intelligence departs with him. His knowledge and his work take hold of him as also his past experience. (*Brihad-aranyaka Upanishad,* IV, 4, 1, 2.)

Verily, when a person departs from this world, he goes to the air. It opens out there for him like the hole of a chariot wheel. Through that he goes upwards. He goes to the sun. It opens out there for him like the hole of a *lambara.* Through that he goes upwards. He reaches the moon. It opens out there for him like the hole of a drum. Through that he goes upwards. He goes to the world free from grief, free from snow. There he dwells eternal years. (Ibid, V. 11,1.)

The Laws of Manu

Asceticism has been associated with forms of Hinduism from its beginning. The following is a description of the life of an ascetic, from the Laws of Manu, VI, 33–36, 41–43, 45–49, 60–65.[45]

33. But having thus passed the third part of (a man's natural term of) life in the forest, he may live as an ascetic during the fourth part of his existence, after abandoning all attachments to worldly objects.

34. He who after passing from order to order, after offering sacrifices and subduing his senses, becomes, tired with (giving) alms and offerings of food, an ascetic, gains bliss after death.

35. When he has paid the three debts, let him apply his mind to (the attainment of) final liberation; he who seeks it without having paid (his debts) sinks downwards.

36. Having studied the Vedas in accordance with the rule, having begat sons according to the sacred law, and having offered sacrifices according to his ability, he may direct his mind to (the attainment of) final liberation.

41. Departing from his house fully provided with the means of purification (Pavitra), let him wander about absolutely silent, and caring nothing for enjoyments that may be offered (to him).

42. Let him always wander alone, without any companion, in order to attain (final liberation), fully understanding that the solitary (man, who) neither forsakes nor is forsaken, gains his end.

43. He shall neither pososess a fire, nor a dwelling, he may go to a village for his food, (he shall be) indifferent to everything, firm of purpose, mediating (and) concentrating his mind on Brahman.

45. Let him not desire to die, let him not desire to live; let him wait for (his appointed) time, as a servant (waits) for the payment of his wages.

[45] G. Buhler, trans., *Sacred Books of the East,* vol. XXV (Oxford: 1886), pp. 204–210.

46. Let him put down his foot purified by his sight, let him drink water purified by (straining with) a cloth, let him utter speech purified by truth, let him keep his heart pure.

47. Let him patiently bear hard words, let him not insult anybody, and let him not become anybody's enemy for the sake of this (perishable) body.

48. Against an angry man let him not in return show anger, let him bless when he is cursed, and let him not utter speech, devoid of truth, scattered at the seven gates.

49. Delighting in what refers to the Soul, sitting (in the postures prescribed by the Yoga), independent (of external help), entirely abstaining from sensual enjoyments, with himself for his only companion, he shall live in this world, desiring the bliss (of final liberation).

60. By the restraint of his senses, by the destruction of love and hatred, and by the abstention from injuring the creatures, he becomes fit for immortality.

61. Let him reflect on the transmigrations of men, caused by their sinful deeds, on their falling into hell, and on the torments in the world of Yama,

62. On the separation from their dear ones, on their union with hated men, on their being overpowered by age and being tormented with diseases,

63. On the departure of the individual soul from this body and its new birth in (another) womb, and on its wanderings through ten thousand millions of existences,

64. On the infliction of pain on embodied (spirits), which is caused by demerit, and the gain of eternal bliss, which is caused by the attainment of their highest aim, (gained through) spiritual merit.

65. By deep meditations, let him recognize the subtle nature of the supreme Soul, and its presence in all organisms, both the highest and the lowest.

Shankara on the Nature of the Brahman

> Shankara, an Indian philosopher of the ninth century A.D., was one of the founders of the nondualistic schools of Hindu thought. His understanding of the nature of the world and of God is based upon the Upanishads.[46]

But, it may be asked, is Brahman known or not known (previously to the enquiry into its nature)? If it is known we need not enter on an enquiry concerning it; if it is not known we can not enter on such an enquiry.

We reply that Brahman is known. Brahman, which is all-knowing and

---

[46] Shankara, *Commentary on Vedanta Sutra,* trans., George Thibaut, Vol. I, *Sacred Books of the East,* XXXIV (Oxford: Clarendon Press, 1890), *passim.*

endowed with all powers, whose essential nature is eternal purity, intelligence, and freedom, exists. For if we consider the derivation of the word "Brahman," from the root *brih,* "to the great," we at once understand that eternal purity, and so on, belong to Brahman. Moreover the existence of Brahman is known on the ground of its being the Self of every one. For every one is conscious of the existence of (his) Self, never thinks "I am not." If the existence of the Self were not known, everyone would think "I am not." And this Self (of whose existence all are conscious) is Brahman. But if Brahman is generally known as the Self, there is no room for an enquiry into it! Not so, we reply; for there is a conflict of opinions as to its special nature. Unlearned people and the Lokayatikas are of opinion that the mere body endowed with the quality of intelligence is the Self; others that the organs endowed with intelligence are the Self; others maintain that the internal organ is the Self; others, again, that the Self is a mere momentary idea; others, again, that it is the Void. Others, again (to proceed to the opinion of such as acknowledge the authority of the Veda), maintain that there is a transmigrating being different from the body, and so on, which is both agent and enjoyer (of the fruits of action); others teach that being is enjoying only, not acting; others believe that in addition to the individual souls, there is an all-knowing, all-powerful Lord. Others, finally (i.e., the Vedantins), maintain that the Lord is the Self of the enjoyer (i.e., of the individual soul whose individual existence is apparent only, the produce of Nescience).

Thus there are many various opinions, basing part of them on sound arguments and scriptureal texts, part of them on fallacious arguments and scriptureal texts, part of them on fallacious arguments and scriptural texts misunderstood. If therefore a man would embrace some one of these opinions without previous consideration, he would bar himself from the highest beatitude and incur grevious loss.

That same highest Brahman constitutes—as we know from passages such as "that art thou"—the real nature of the individual soul (i.e., *atman*), while its second nature, i.e., that aspect of it which depends on fictitious limiting conditions, is not its real nature. For as long as the individual soul does not free itself from Nescience in the form of duality—which Nescience may be compared to the mistake of him who in the twilight mistakes a post for a man—and who does not rise to the knowledge of the Self, whose nature is unchangeable, eternal Cognition—which expresses itself in the form "I am Brahman"—so long it remains the individual soul. But when, discarding the aggregate of body, sense-organs and mind, it arrives, by means of Scripture, at the knowledge that it is not itself that aggregate, that it does not form part of transmigratory existence, but it is the True, the Real, the Self, whose nature is pure intelligence; then knowing itself to be of the nature of unchangeable, eternal Cognition, it lifts itself above the vain conceit of being one with this body, and itself becomes the Self, whose nature is unchanging, eternal Cognition. As is declared in such scriptural passages "He who knows the highest Brahman becomes even Brahman" (*Mundaka Upanishad,* III, 2, 9). And this is the real nature of the individual soul by means of which it arises from the body and appears in its own form.

There is only one highest Lord ever unchanging, whose substance is cognition (i.e., of whom cognition is not a mere attribute), and who by means of Nescience, manifests himself in various ways, just as a thaumaturg appears in different shapes by means of his magical power. . . . To the highest Self which is eternally pure, intelligent and free, which is never changing, one only, not in contact with anything, devoid of form, the opposite characteristics of the individual soul are erroneously ascribed; just as ignorant men ascribe blue color to the colorless ether.

A man may, in the dark, mistake a piece of rope lying on the ground for a snake and run away from it, frightened and trembling; thereon another man may tell him, "Do not be afraid, it is only a rope, not a snake"; and he may then dismiss the fear caused by the imagined snake, and stop running. But all the while the presence and subsequent absence of his erroneous notion, as to the rope being a snake, make no difference whatever in the rope itself. Exactly analogous is the case of the individual soul which is in reality one with the highest soul, although Nescience makes it appear different.

As therefore the individual soul and the highest Self differ in name only, it being a settled matter that perfect knowledge has for its object the absolute oneness of the two; it is senseless to insist (as some do) on a plurality of Selfs, and to maintain that the individual soul is different from the highest Self, and the highest Self from the individual soul. For the Self is indeed called by many different names, but it is one only. Nor does the passage, "He knows Brahman which is real, knowledge, infinite, as hidden in the cave" (*Taittiriya Upanishad,* II, 1), refer to some one cave (different from the abode of the individual soul). And that nobody else but Brahman is hidden in the cave we know from a subsequent passage, viz., "Having sent forth he entered into it" (*Taittiriya Upanishad,* II, 6) according to which the creator only entered into the created beings.—Those who insist on the distinction of the individual and the highest Self oppose themselves to the true sense of the Vedanta-texts, stand thereby in the way of perfect knowledge, which is the door to perfect beatitude, and groundlessly assume release to be something effected, and therefore non-eternal. (And if they attempt to show that *moksha,* although effected, is eternal) they involve themselves in a conflict with sound logic.

That Brahman is at the same time the operative cause of the world, we have to conclude from the circumstance that there is no other guiding being. Ordinarily material causes, indeed, such as lumps of clay and pieces of gold, are dependent, in order to shape themselves into vessels and ornaments, on extraneous operative causes such as potters and goldsmiths; but outside Brahman as material cause there is no other operative cause to which the material cause could look; for Scripture says that previously to creation Brahman was one without a second.—The absence of a guiding principle other than the material cause can moreover be established by means of the argument made use of in the Sutra, viz., accordance with the promissory statements and the illustrative examples. If there were admitted a guiding principle different from the material cause, it would follow that everything cannot be known through one thing, and thereby the promissory statements as well as the illustrative instances would be stultified.— The Self is thus the operative cause, because there is no other ruling principle, and the material cause because there is no other substance from which the world could originate.

The entire complex of phenomenal existence is considered as true as long as the knowledge of Brahman being the Self of all has not arisen; just as the phantoms of a dream are considered to be true until the sleeper wakes. For as long as a person has not reached the true knowledge of the unity of the Self, so long as it does not enter his mind that the world of effects with its means and objects of right knowledge and its results of actions is untrue; he rather, in consequence of his ignorance, looks on mere effects (such as body, offspring, wealth, etc.) as forming part of and belonging to his Self, forgetful of Brahman being in reality the Self of all. Hence, as long as true knowledge does not present itself, there is no reason why the ordinary course of secular and religious activity should not hold on undisturbed. The case is analogous to that of a dreaming man who in his dream sees manifold things, and, up to the moment of waking, is convinced that his ideas are produced by real perception without suspecting the perception to be merely an apparent one.

Jainism

Ceiling of the Jain temple on Mount Abu. (*Courtesy of the Government of India Tourist Office.*)

The essence of right conduct is not to injure anyone; one should know only this, that non-injury is religion.
—Naladiyar, 14, 15

In the sixth century B.C. two protests arose in India against Hinduism. These two heresies were Jainism and Buddhism, and they each offered alternate means of salvation to that presented in the Vedic literature and taught by the Brahmin gurus. Both Jainism and Buddhism denied the validity of the Vedas as inspired scripture, and both rejected the religious implications of the Indian caste system. Of these two new religions (or new forms of Hinduism) Jainism was probably the first.

THE LIFE OF MAHAVIRA

It is difficult to determine precisely the origin of Jainism, although Nataputta Vardhamana, who became known to his followers as Mahavira ("great hero"), has traditionally been identified as its founder. The story of Mahavira's life, however, obviously has been covered with legend. Actually, in orthodox Jainism, Mahavira was only the last in a long line of founders. There are twenty-three figures who preceded Mahavira in the establishment of Jainism. These people, together with Mahavira, are called Tirthankaras, which means "crossing builders." They are believed to be those ideal persons who forged a bridge between this life and Nirvana. A total of twenty-four Tirthankaras receive the veneration of Jains in their temples.

Most sources suggest that Mahavira lived between 599 and 527 B.C., although some authorities place his death as late as 467 B.C. This means that he was contemporary with Siddhartha Gautama, Confucius, Lao-tzu, and the great Hebrew prophets of the sixth century B.C., Jeremiah, Ezekiel, and the anonymous author of Isaiah 40–66.

The reported details of the life of Mahavira are similar in many respects to those of the life of the Buddha, and some suggest that these details are taken from Buddhism. Like the Buddha, Mahavira was born in the sixth century B.C. to parents of the Kshatriya caste, and his father was a minor ruler. Mahavira was the second of two sons. According to legend, the family possessed great wealth and lived in luxury. They lived in Vesali, the capital city of the region of Mogadah in north India. At the proper age Mahavira married and had a daughter. Despite his position and wealth, he was not happy and sought a religious answer to this unhappiness. When a group of wandering ascetics came to dwell in his village Mahavira became interested in them and longed to join their order. However, being a dutiful son, he waited until his parents died[1] and the business affairs of the family had been taken over successfully by his older brother. Then he bade farewell to his family and his wife and child, turned his back upon his wealth and luxury, tore out his hair and beard by the handfuls, and went off to join the ascetics in their pursuit of salvation.

Mahavira did not find his salvation among this group of ascetics, as he had hoped. He came to believe instead that one must practice a more severe asceticism than they practiced in order to find release of the soul from this life. In addition to his concern for extreme asceticism, Mahavira eventually felt that one must also practice *ahimsa* (noninjury to life) in order to find release. Therefore he went forth on his own path.

The legends concerning this period of Mahavira's life emphasize the extreme measures of asceticism that he imposed upon himself. Since he did not wish to become attached to people or things he never stayed more than one night in any place when he traveled. During the rainy season he stayed off the roads to avoid walking where he might inadvertently step upon an insect. During the dry season he swept the road before him as he walked to avoid crushing insects. He strained all the water that he drank in order to prevent swallowing any creature that might be in it. Like any true ascetic, he begged for his food. But he refused to eat raw food and preferred to eat only that which had been left over from the meal of some other person, in order that he might not be the cause of death. In order to better torment his body he sought out the coldest spots in the winter months and the hottest climates in the summer and went about naked always. Whenever angry or vile persons sent their dogs after Mahavira he allowed himself to be bitten by them rather than resist. Legend also tells of a time when Mahavira was meditating and some people built a fire beneath him to see if he would resist; he did not. After twelve years of the harshest forms of asceticism he achieved release (*moksha*) from the bounds that tie one's soul to the endless cycle of birth, death, and rebirth. Thus he became known to his followers as a Jain ("conqueror") because he had heroically conquered the forces of life. Though he had achieved *moksha*, Mahavira lived for another thirty years and died at the age of seventy-two.

---

[1] According to some Jain legends, the parents of Mahavira died of self-imposed starvation. Since Jainism places such high value on asceticism, this form of death becomes ideal.

Jain temple, Khajuraho, India. (*Courtesy of Diane M. Lowe.*)

THE TEACHINGS OF JAINISM

Like the other Indian religions, Jainism views life in terms of endless reincarnation. People are born, live out their lives, die, and are born again. This is the religious problem around which Indian religions revolve. How does a person get off the wheel of lives and cease to live? Hinduism offers a variety of answers, as do Buddhism and Sikhism. Jainism views people as bound to life because of the karma that they acquire.

> All living beings owe their present form of existence to their own Karman; timid, wicked, suffering latent misery, they err about (in the Circle of Births), subject to birth, old age and death.[2]

[2] *Gaina Sutras*, Herman Jacobi, trans., *The Sacred Books of the East*, vol. XL (Oxford: Clarendon Press, 1895), Sutrakritanga, pp. 1, 2, 3, 18.

Apparently, Mahavira taught that karma was built up on an individual as the result of activity of any sort. Thus the ideal life for a Jain might simply be to do as little as possible and thereby escape karma and be freed from life.

> Liberation is absolute freedom from the totality of actions through the absence of the causes of bondage and exhaustion (of past karmas).[3]

The philosophical world view of Jainism is dualistic. According to Jainism the world essentially is made up of two substances, soul (*jiva*) and matter (*ajiva*). Soul is life; it is eternal and valuable. Matter is lifeless, material, and evil. The entire universe can be identified as either soul or matter. All persons are seen as soul encased in matter. As long as soul is enmeshed in matter it can never be free and is bound to remain in the endless cycle of lives. Thus it is the goal of Jainism to liberate the soul from matter. This philosophical basis sees the flesh as an evil since it traps the spirit. If the flesh is evil, then the ascetic answer is to release the soul by tormenting the flesh in some manner. This answer to human sinfulness is found in some form in Hinduism, Buddhism, Christianity, Islam, and nearly every other major religion in the world. Whereas these religions also have other solutions to the problem of human king's plight, Jainism is consistent. It views the world as a dualism. Its answer to the dualistic nature of the world is severe asceticism. Whereas not all Jains can be free from the responsibilities of life and dedicate themselves to the ascetic life, it is believed that the Jains who do are closest to salvation. Mahavira set the pattern by turning his back upon the wealth and pleasures of his home and submitting his body to the rigors of asceticism. Thus he found release.

Jainism maintains that the salvation of the soul must be accomplished by the individual. Soul can only be freed from matter by the action of the person involved, and that person cannot and does not receive help from outside. Therefore, the gods are of little consequence in Jainism. Jains have no need for a creator god since they believe that matter is eternal. Thus there never was a creation of the world. It has been here forever and will continue to exist forever. If Jainism has any awareness of gods it is that they are simply creatures living on a different plane from humankind and are trying to work out their own salvation. These gods cannot help humans in their search for salvation. Therefore prayer and worship are worthless. While Jainism may acknowledge the existence of gods it does not rely upon them, and for that reason it may be called an essentially atheistic religion.

[3] Tattvartha Sutra, 10, 2.

In regard to the practice of their religion, Jains tend to divide themselves into two distinct groups: the majority, who cannot afford to leave their homes and accept the rigors of the ascetic life, and the minority, who can and do become monks. The latter represent the ideal life for a Jain. Jain monks take five vows that are to guide their lives:

1. They vow noninjury of life (*ahimsa*). According to Jain tradition Mahavira taught:

> He who injures these (animals) does not comprehend and renounce the sinful acts; he who does not injure these, comprehends and renounces the sinful acts. Knowing them, a wise man should not act sinfully toward animals, nor cause others to act so, nor allow others to act so. He who knows these causes of sin relating to animals, is called a reward-knowing sage. Thus I say.[4]

This vow has become the most dominant characteristic of all Jains and the mark by which they are known to the world. A Jain will go to great lengths to avoid harming any living creature. They are of course vegetarian and avoid the use of products such as leather, which require the death or suffering of life. Jain monks, following Mahavira's example, sweep the path before them when they walk to avoid treading on insects, and they strain the water they drink in order to protect whatever life may have been in it. In certain extreme cases Jains have been known to establish hospitals for sick rats. Thus some have noted jokingly that Jains are those "who deny God, worship man, and nourish vermin." The Jain principle of not injuring life has had widespread influence among non-Jains, such as Mohandas Gandhi and Albert Schweitzer.

2. Jain monks vow always to speak the truth, and because of this vow they are widely respected for their truthfulness. However, in its search for truth, Jainism has tended to view truth as relative rather than absolute.[5]

3. Jain monks vow to refrain from taking anything that is not given to them. This too has added to the Jain's reputation for honesty.

---

[4] Ayaranya Sutra, 1, 1, 6, 6

[5] The well-known story of the blind men and the elephant is said to have been of Jain origin and illustrates the relativity of truth. In this tale, several blind men are asked to describe an elephant. Each touches a different part of the elephant's body and thus each describes the animal in a different way. To one man the elephant is like a stone wall, since he has touched the side; to another the elephant is like a rope, since he touched the tail; and to another the elephant is like a fan, since he touched the ear. Each man truthfully described the animal, but since each had contacted it from a different perspective, their descriptions varied tremendously.

All life, but especially animal life, is sacred to Jains. (*Courtesy of Diane M. Lowe.*)

4. The monks' fourth vow is to renounce sexual pleasures. This is in keeping with traditional asceticism, which views the pleasures of the flesh as evil; since sex is one of the greatest pleasures of the flesh it must be forsaken. (Mahavira went even further, by not only renouncing sexual pleasures but by also renouncing women in general. He is said to have declared that "women are the greatest temptation in the world." Thus the very conservative Jain sects today will not allow a woman even to seek salvation in a monastery.)

5. The final vow is to renounce all attachments. Attachments to and love for other persons or things is one of the elements that keep

humans bound to life. (It was for this reason that Mahavira renounced his family and possessions and refused to stay in any place longer than one day lest he build new attachments.)

Generally, all Jains seek to follow the first three vows as much as possible, while those who enter the monastic life will keep all five. Thus a Jain layperson may marry and have a family and possessions, with the understanding that he is not leading the ideal life and may not expect salvation in this life.

The scriptures of the Jains are called Agamas, which means "precepts," or Siddhantas, which means "treatises." Orthodox Jains believe that these Agamas are the actual sermons or teachings that Mahavira gave to his disciples. The various Jain sects differ as to the number of Agamas that are genuine and authoritative. Many of the lesser known Agamas have not yet been translated into English.

JAIN SECTS

By 80 A.D. the Jains were severely divided over what was to be the true meaning of Jainism, and they split into two sects that still exist today. The sect that takes the more liberal view in the interpretation of Jain teachings is the Svetambara (literally, "the white clad"). Today this group is located mainly in the northern part of India. They are liberal in their interpretation of Mahavira's teachings regarding the wearing of clothing and are called "white clad" because they reject the necessity of nudity and allow their monks to wear a white garment. They are also liberal in that they allow the admission of women to the religion and to their monasteries, and even accept the possibility that a woman may find salvation. Of the two sects, the Svetambara is the more popular.

The second sect, the Digambara (literally, "the sky clad"), is the more conservative of the two, and its members live mainly in the southern portion of India. The Digambaras adhere to the old ideals and require their monks to go about nearly nude; total nudity is reserved only for those of greatest holiness. In addition, they believe that women have no chance of achieving salvation and are to be regarded as the greatest of all temptations to a man. Therefore women are prohibited from entering the monasteries and the temples. The Digambaras even refuse to believe that Mahavira was ever married.

In 1473 a third sect arose as a splinter group from Svetambara. This group is known as the Sthanakavasi and is distinguished by its opposition to temples and idols. It also differs from other Jain sects in that it accepts only thirty-three Agamas as authoritative, while others accept as many as eighty-four.

JAINISM TODAY

Hinduism was affected by Jain teaching and was moved to accept its emphasis upon asceticism and *ahimsa* as regular parts of Indian religion. However, while Jainism and its ascetic movement may have been very popular in India at one time, today it is considered a minority sect of Hinduism. In its purest form it appeals to less than two million people, mainly in the Bombay region of India.

Because of their overwhelming concern for the sacredness of life the Jains are forbidden from entering certain occupations. No Jain can belong to any profession that takes life or profits from slaughter. For example, they cannot be soldiers, butchers, leather workers, exterminators, or even farmers, since farmers regularly plow the soil and might be a party to the death of worms and insects that live in the soil. These prohibitions have forced the Jains to enter the commercial professions. This fact, along with their reputation for honesty and morality, have made the Jains excellent businessmen. It is paradoxical that a sect that began with the intention of asceticism and poverty has become, by virtue of its respect for life, one of the wealthiest classes of India.

Though Jains have no need for gods they do venerate the twenty-four Tirthankaras, Jains have erected over forty thousand temples in India for the worship of these figures. Many of these temples are renowned for their beauty, and the one on Mount Abu is considered to be one of the seven wonders of India.

Apart from adoring the Tirthankaras in temples, Jain worship includes many rituals in the home. This worship may include reciting the names of the Jinas, bathing idols, and offering flowers and perfumes to them. Worship may also include the chanting of Jain hymns, prayers, and formulas. Many Jains also include meditation and the observance of vows in their worship.

STUDY QUESTIONS

1. Describe the movement begun by Mahavira as a reaction to classical Hinduism.

2. According to Jainism, how is one able to free oneself from the cycle of endless lives?

3. Define *ahimsa* and give examples of this teaching in the life of Mahavira.

4. What is the greatest contribution of Jainism to world religions?

SUGGESTED READING

Fenton, John Y. et al. *Religions of Asia.* New York: St. Martin's Press, 1983. (See section on Jainism.)

Frost, S. E., ed. *The Sacred Writings of the World's Great Religions.* New York: McGraw-Hill Book Company, 1972.

Jaini, Jagmanderlal. *Outlines of Jainism.* Cambridge, Mass.: Cambridge University Press, 1916.

Stevenson, Margaret. *The Heart of Jainism.* London: Oxford University Press, 1915.

SOURCE MATERIAL

A Jain Parable and "The Example of Mahavira"

Jainism, along with many other Indian religions, has historically taught that there are few "Yes" or "No" answers to
the problems of life. This is never better illustrated than in
the Jain parable of the man in the well. The story is also
found in many other cultures and literatures.[6]

A Jain Parable: The Man in the Well

Haribhadra, 'Samarādityakathā,' II, 55–88

A certain man, much oppressed by the woes of poverty,
Left his own home, and set out for another country.
He passed through the land, with its villages, cities, and harbors,
And after a few days he lost his way.

And he came to a forest, thick with trees . . . and full of wild beasts.
There, while he was stumbling over the rugged paths, . . . a prey to thirst
and hunger, he saw a mad elephant, fiercely trumpeting, charging him
with upraised trunk. At the same time there appeared before him a most
evil demoness, holding a sharp sword, dreadful in face and form, and
laughing with loud and shrill laughter. Seeing them he trembled in all his
limbs with deathly fear, and looked in all directions. There, to the east of
him, he saw a great banyan tree. . . .

And he ran quickly, and reached the mighty tree.
But his spirits fell, for it was so high that even the birds could not fly over it,
And he could not climb its high unscalable trunk. . . .
All his limbs trembled with terrible fear,
Until, looking round, he saw nearby an old well covered with grass.
Afraid of death, craving to live if only a moment longer,
He flung himself into the well at the foot of the banyan tree.
A clump of reeds grew from its deep wall, and to this he clung,
While below him he saw terrible snakes, enraged at the sound of his falling;
And at the very bottom, known from the hiss of its breath, was a black and
    mighty python
With mouth agape, its body thick as the trunk of a heavenly elephant, with
    terrible red eyes.
He thought, "My life will only last as long as these reeds hold fast,"
And he raised his head; and there, on the clump of reeds, he saw two large
    mice,

[6] Translated by A. L. Basham, in William T. de Bary, ed., *Sources of Indian Tradition* (New
York: Columbia University Press, 1958), pp. 56–58.

One white, one black, their sharp teeth ever gnawing at the roots of the reed-
   clump.
Then up came the wild elephant, and, enraged the more at not catching him,
Charged time and again at the trunk of the banyan tree.
At the shock of his charge a honeycomb on a large branch
Which hung over the old well, shook loose and fell.
The man's whole body was stung by a swarm of angry bees,
But, just by chance, a drop of honey fell on his head,
Rolled down his brow, and somehow reached his lips,
And gave him a moment's sweetness. He longed for other drops,
And he thought nothing of the python, the snakes, the elephant, the mice, the
   well, or the bees,
In his excited craving for yet more drops of honey.
This parable is powerful to clear the minds of those on the way to freedom.
Now hear its sure interpretation.
The man is the soul, his wandering in the forest the four types of existence.
The wild elephant is death, the demoness old age.
The banyan tree is salvation, where there is no fear of death, the elephant,
But which no sensual man can climb.
The well is human life, the snakes are passions,
Which so overcome a man that he does not know what he should do.
The tuft of reed is man's allotted span, during which the soul exists embodied;
The mice which steadily gnaw it are the dark and bright fortnights.
The stinging bees are manifold diseases,
Which torment a man until he has not a moment's joy.
The awful python is hell, seizing the man bemused by sensual pleasure,
Fallen in which the soul suffers pains by the thousand.
The drops of honey are trivial pleasures, terrible at the last.
How can a wise man want them, in the midst of such peril and hardship?

Jain Respect for Life

Ahimsa (the vow of noninjury to life) is one of the primary
doctrines of Jainism and may be its chief contribution to other
religions. The selection from the *Akaranga-sutra* details Jain
respect for all life.[7]

Akaranga-sutra, I, 1

Earth is afflicted and wretched, it is hard to teach, it has no discrimination.
Unenlightened men, who suffer from the effect of past deeds, cause great
pain in a world full of pain already, for in earth souls are individually
embodied. If, thinking to gain praise, honour, or respect . . . or to achieve

[7] Translated by A. L. Basham, in William T. de Bary, ed., *Sources of Indian Tradition* (New
   York: Columbia University Press, 1958), pp. 62, 63.

a good rebirth . . . or to win salvation, or to escape pain, a man sins against earth or causes or permits others to do so, . . . he will not gain joy or wisdom. . . . Injury to the earth is like striking, cutting, maiming, or killing a blind man . . . Knowing this man should not sin against earth or cause or permit others to do so. He who understands the nature of sin against earth is called a true sage who understands karma.

And there are many souls embodied in water. Truly water . . . is alive. . . . He who injures the lives in water does not understand the nature of sin or renounce it. . . . Knowing this, a man should not sin against water, or cause or permit others to do so. He who understands the nature of sin against water is called a true sage who understands karma.

By wicked or careless acts one may destroy fire-beings, and moreover, harm other beings by means of fire. . . . For there are creatures living in earth, grass, leaves, wood, cowdung, or dustheaps, and jumping creatures which . . . fall into a fire if they come near it. If touched by fire, they shrivel up . . . lose their senses and die. . . . He who understands the nature of sin in respect of fire is called a true sage who understands karma.

And just as it is the nature of a man to be born and grow old, so is it the nature of a plant to be born and grow old. . . . One is endowed with reason, and so is the other; one is sick, if injured, and so is the other; one grows larger, and so does the other; one changes with time, and so does the other. . . . He who understands the nature of sin against plants is called a true sage who understands karma.

All beings with two, three, four, or five senses, . . . in fact all creation, know individually pleasure and displeasure, pain, terror, and sorrow. All are full of fears which come from all directions. And yet there exist people who would cause greater pain to them. . . . Some kill animals for sacrifice, some for their skin, flesh, blood, . . . feathers, teeth, or tusks; . . . some kill them intentionally and some unintentionally; some kill because they have been previously injured by them, . . . and some because they expect to be injured. He who harms animals has not understood or renounced deeds of sin. . . . He who understands the nature of sin against animals is called a true sage who understands karma.

A man who is averse from harming even the wind knows the sorrow of all things living. . . . He who knows what is bad for himself knows what is bad for others, and he who knows what is bad for others knows what is bad for himself. This reciprocity should always be borne in mind. Those whose minds are at peace and who are free from passions do not desire to live (at the expense of others). . . . He who understands the nature of sin against wind is called a true sage who understands karma.

In short he who understands the nature of sin in respect of all the six types of living beings is called a true sage who understands karma.

CHAPTER 6

Buddhism

This unusual statue from the marble temple in Uruvela, Thailand, shows an emaciated Buddha during his ascetic period. (*Courtesy of Lejeune; Stock-market, Los Angeles.*)

Let, therefore, no man love anything; loss of the beloved is evil. Those who love nothing and hate nothing, have no fetters.

—*Dhammapada, 211*

Buddhism began in India in the sixth century B.C. as another interpretation of the Hindu religious system. As such, it had great appeal in India for several centuries. However, by the third century B.C. it developed something unusual for any version of Hinduism: a missionary imperative. The rulers of India, who were enamored of this new religion, sent Buddhist missionaries into neighboring Asian countries. At the same time, Buddhism was developing new theologies that became more and more attractive to the Asian people. This combination of missionary thrust and new theologies made it a sweeping success in countries such as China, Japan, Korea, and Indochina. Yet, while Buddhism was becoming a success in foreign missions, it was slowly being pushed aside in India by a resurging Hinduism. The Muslim conquest of India crushed the final remains of Buddhism there, and today one must look to other Asian nations to find its adherents.

THE LIFE OF GAUTAMA

The founder of Buddhism was a man named Siddhartha, who was a member of the Gautama clan. The dates usually given for his life are 560–480 B.C. However, the life of Gautama, as he has come to be known, is surrounded by legend and his exact dates are subject to question. Nevertheless he probably lived during the sixth century B.C. and was a contemporary of Mahavira.

Gautama was the son of a Kshatriya rajah called Suddhodana and his wife, Maya. The legends say that the birth of the child was surrounded by extraordinary events and portents. According to one story, a soothsayer predicted that the child would either become a great king, who would rule India, or a great Buddha ("Enlightened One"). Gautama's mother died soon after his birth, and he was reared by his maternal aunt, who became his father's second wife.

When Gautama was a child it was predicted that if he ever saw the sights of human misery or the tranquility of a monk, he would grow to be a religious leader. Since his father did not wish this he sought to protect him from seeing the ugliness and distress of humanity. The rajah specifically sought to keep the young prince from seeing four sights: a dead body, an aged person, a diseased person, and an ascetic monk. Thus Gautama grew up surrounded by youth, beauty, and health. He received a normal education for a prince of that era. He studied the arts and warfare and received some education in philosophy. When he was nineteen he married his cousin and they shared a happy home together. They had one child, a son.

As Gautama neared his thirtieth birthday he gradually became aware of the ugliness of the real world. According to some of the legends, the gods, wishing to awaken the future Buddha from the wasteful life he was leading, conspired to break through the walls of youth and beauty that had been erected about him. One by one he began to see the things his father had forbidden him to see. He saw a rotting corpse, a wrinkled and bent elderly person, a man with a loathsome disease, and a peaceful monk who had renounced the world for asceticism. Gautama, reaching his mature years, became aware that the life most people led was one of suffering and pain. It is said that he once entered his father's harem room where there were some of the most beautiful young women in the kingdom. There he received a vision that these women would soon become wrinkled, bent, gray, and stooped. These revelations made it impossible for the sensitive young prince to continue to live in his palace surrounded by ease and plenty, and one night he decided to leave his home. He crept into his wife's bedroom and said farewell to her and their infant son.[1] Then he took his best horse and rode off into the night. After going a certain distance he clipped off his hair and beard and sent back his horse. He changed clothes with a beggar and began a period of searching for answers to life's misery.

At first Gautama thought the answers to the questions that troubled him were to be found in the various schools of philosophy. Therefore he attached himself to a guru and studied with him for some time, but he received no satisfaction in his studies. A second avenue Gautama tried was that of asceticism. As a solution to the problems of life, asceticism was an acceptable pursuit in the sixth century B.C., as can be seen from the life of Mahavira and his followers. Gautama joined five other monks and with them began a life of severe asceticism that lasted for six years. The ascetic measures Gautama took were as severe as any recorded in the history of religion. According to legend, he became something of a champion ascetic. Gautama sought out anything that was unpleasant, painful, or disagreeable as a means by which he might find release. He is supposed

---

[1] According to one story, the son was named Rahula, which means "fetter," indicating that at the time of the child's birth, Gautama was at the point of considering that all things, even a beautiful child, could bind one to life like a fetter.

to have practiced fasting until he reached the point of living on a single grain of rice per day. When most Westerners think of Buddha they tend to think of a fat, jolly person because they have been influenced by the Japanese statuary that depicts plump figures as "Buddhas." However, these are not an attempt to depict the historical Buddha. At this time in his life Gautama reportedly became so thin that when he grasped his stomach he touched his backbone. In addition to eating very little food he ate nauseating food, and at one point is even supposed to have eaten his feces. He wore irritating garments and sat in awkward and painful positions for hours. He sat on thorns, and for a time slept in a graveyard among the rotting flesh of corpses. In the tradition of many ascetics, Gautama allowed filth and vermin to accumulate on his body. However, in spite of these heroic efforts at asceticism, he did not find the salvation he was seeking.

Apparently the turning point in Gautama's quest came one day when he was walking near a stream. Because he had been terribly weakened by his ordeals, he fainted and fell into the stream. The cold water revived him and when he was able to contemplate his situation he realized that, while he had done everything that could be expected of an ascetic, he still had not found satisfaction. He therefore arose, went to a nearby tavern, and had a meal. His five friends happened to pass by and when they saw him eating and drinking and enjoying himself, they spurned him as a traitor. When Gautama had finished his meal he went to the banks of a river and sat down under the shade of a fig tree and began to meditate.[2] He decided to sit and meditate until he received enlightenment. At last, after a period of meditation, Gautama was enlightened, and from then on he was known as the Buddha ("Enlightened One"). In his meditation the Buddha had a vision of the endless cycle of birth and death that is the lot of humankind. It was revealed to him that people were bound to this cycle because of *tanha* (desire, thirst, craving). It is desire that causes karma and thus fetters people. The Buddha had desired salvation and had sought it through asceticism and knowledge, but it had eluded him. When he had ceased to desire he found enlightenment and thus salvation.

The first step the Buddha took after his enlightenment was to go to the holy city of Benares and locate the five ascetic friends who had spurned him. He found them in the Deer Park, and, though at first they had contempt for him, they listened as he preached. In this first sermon the Buddha taught that neither the extreme of indulgence nor the extreme of asceticism was acceptable as a way of life and that one

[2]Because he found enlightenment under this tree, it has become known as the bo or bodhi tree.

Buddha's first sermon at Deer Park, Nagarjunakonda, India. (*Courtesy of the Government of Andhra.*)

should avoid extremes and seek to live in the middle way. The five ascetics noted the change that had come over the Buddha, and they accepted his teachings. These five formed the first *Sangha* (Buddhist monastic order).

The Buddha was enlightened when he was about thirty-five years of age. He spent the remaining years of his life teaching his growing band of disciples. Unlike orthodox Hindus, he taught that any person of any caste or sex could find salvation. Therefore his followers included a wide variety of persons. When women asked to join his group, the Buddha was at first reluctant, but he eventually relented and allowed them to form an order of nuns. According to legend, the Buddha's former wife was among the first women to seek admission to this group. Those persons who seriously joined the Buddha as monks shaved their heads and wore coarse yellow robes. Their only possession was a bowl that they carried when they begged for food. Their creed is said to have been, "I take refuge in the Buddha; I take refuge in the *Dharma* ("law"); and I take refuge in the Sangha."

In addition, the monks sought to observe the following rules of conduct as described in the Pali Sermons.

And How, O king, is a monk accomplished in morality?

Herein a monk abandons the killing of living things and refrains from killing; laying aside the use of a stick or a knife he dwells modest, full of kindliness, and compassionate for the welfare of all living things. This is his behavior in morality.

Abandoning the taking of what is not given he refrains from taking what is not given; he takes and expects only what is given, he dwells purely and without stealing.

Abandoning incontinence he practises continence and lives apart, avoiding the village practice of sex intercourse.

Abandoning falsehood he refrains from falsehood; he speaks truth, he is truthful, trustworthy, and reliable, not deceiving people.

Abandoning slanderous speech he refrains from slanderous speech; what he has heard from one place he does not tell in another to cause dissension. He is even a healer of dissensions and a producer of union, delighting and rejoicing in concord, eager for concord, and an utterer of speech that produces concord.

Abandoning harsh speech he refrains from harsh speech; the speech that is harmless, pleasant to the ear, kind, reaching the heart, urbane, amiable, and attractive to the multitude, that kind of speech does he utter.

Abandoning frivolous speech he refrains from frivolous speech; he speaks of the good, the real, the profitable, of the doctrine and the discipline; he is an utterer of speech worth hoarding, with timely reasons and purpose and meaning.

He refrains from injuring seeds and plants.

He eats only within one meal time, abstaining from food at night and avoiding untimely food.

He refrains from seeing dancing, singing, music, and shows.

He refrains from the use of garlands, scents, unguents, and objects of adornment; from a high or large bed; from accepting gold and silver; from accepting raw grain and raw meat.

He refrains from accepting women, girls, male and female slaves, goats and rams, fowls and pigs, elephants, oxen, horses, mares and farm-lands.

He refrains from going on messages and errands; from buying and selling; from cheating in weighing, false metal, and measuring; from practices of cheating, trickery, deception, and fraud; from cutting, killing, binding, robbery, pillage, and violence. . . .[3]

The Buddha reportedly died at the age of eighty after eating some bad mushrooms. According to tradition, his final words were, "Subject to decay are all component things. Strive earnestly to work out your own salvation."

[3] Pali Sermons, *Morality* (1). *Samannaphala-sutta, Digha* i, 47, E. J. Thomas, trans. (London: Kegan Paul, Trench, Trubner & Co. Ltd., 1935), pp. 54–69.

THE TEACHINGS OF THE BUDDHA

There is nothing in the life and teachings of the Buddha to indicate that he intended to found a new religion or even to reform Hinduism. His teachings are more concerned with ethics and self-understanding than with anything that might be called religion. Apparently he was opposed to the various existing forms of religious worship, and he was certainly opposed to the Brahmin system of animal sacrifice. In addition, he rejected the authority of the Vedas. The Buddha tended to be agnostic and sometimes atheistic in his teachings regarding the gods. He was much more concerned that people work out their own salvation than that they appeal to the gods for help and support. Yet the teachings of the Buddha came to be regarded by Hindus as a reformation of their religion and also as the basis for a vast family of religions in Asia outside of India.

Among the most unique teachings of the Buddha was that the soul did not exist. According to Buddha, people live in a state of *anatman* (nonsoulness). What is called a soul is actually a combination of five mental or physical aggregates: the physical body, feelings, understanding, will and consciousness. This combination, which makes up the human personality, is bound up in the endless cycle of birth, death, and rebirth that is typical in Indian religions. The Buddha's understanding of humankind's plight is presented in the classic Buddhist statement of the Four Noble Truths:

> And what, monks, is the Middle Path, of which the Tathagata has gained enlightenment, which produces insight and knowledge, and tends to calm, to higher knowledge, enlightenment, Nirvana? This is the noble Eightfold Way, namely right view, right intention, right speech, right action, right livelihood, right effort, right mindfulness, right concentration. This, monks, is the Middle Path, of which the Tathagata has gained enlightenment, which produces insight and knowledge, and tends to calm, to higher knowledge, enlightenment, Nirvana.
>
> Now this, monks, is the noble truth of pain: birth is painful, old age is painful, sickness is painful, death is painful, sorrow, lamentation, dejection, and despair are painful. Contact with unpleasant things is painful, not getting what one wishes is painful. In short the five groups of grasping are painful.
>
> Now this, monks, is the noble truth of the cause of pain: the craving, which tends to rebirth, combined with pleasure and lust, finding pleasure here and there, namely the craving for passion, the craving for existence, the craving for nonexistence.
>
> Now this, monks, is the noble truth of the cessation of pain, the cessation without a remainder of craving, the abandonment, forsaking, release, non-attachment.

Now this, monks, is the noble truth of the way that leads to the cessation of pain: this is the noble Eightfold Way, namely, right views, right intention, right speech, right action, right livelihood, right effort, right mindfulness, right concentration.[4]

The person who follows the Eightfold Path will break the bonds that tie him to life and achieve release from the cycle. The word used to describe this release is Nirvana, which basically means "extinguished" or "put out like a candle." Thus the goal of basic Buddhist thought is not the achievement of some state of bliss in some heaven but the extinguishing of the self and its desire. Those who have followed the Eightfold Path and arrived at the point of achieving Nirvana are called *arhat*, or "saint."

The teachings of the Buddha became the basis for an organization that took on many of the components of a religion. His followers organized themselves into a monastic order, or Sangha. His teachings became codified in the laws of that order and in various forms of scripture. The Buddha himself came to be regarded as the chief of beings. The rules under which early Buddhist monks were expected to live are noteworthy since they demonstrate the practical outworkings of the Buddha's teachings.

THE DEVELOPMENT OF BUDDHISM

When the Buddha died in the fifth century B.C. his teachings could scarcely be called a religion. They denied the relevance of the gods, they denied the necessity of worship or sacrifice, and salvation was seen as totally dependent upon the works of the individual. Those persons attracted to the teachings of the Buddha during his life must have been a special group of very intelligent people who were dissatisfied with life and had the capacity to discipline themselves. Had Buddhism remained as it was in the beginning, it is doubtful whether more than a mere handful of people in the history of the world would have been interested in it. However, in the twentieth century Buddhism is one of the major religions of the world. Its devotees are to be found in nearly every Asian nation. The path by which Buddhism was transformed from a world-denying, god-denying sect into one of the largest of the world's religions is a fascinating one indeed.

As in the case of almost every other founder of a religion, before the Buddha had been dead very long his followers were fighting over the real meaning of his teachings. According to one tradition, a schism

[4] Pali Sermons, the first sermon. *Samyutta*, V, 420, E. J. Thomas, trans. (London: Kegan Paul, Trench, Trubner & Co., Ltd., 1935), pp. 29–33.

A bust of Buddha from the second century. The top knot and the elongated ear lobes are added to show the extraordinary wisdom of the Buddha. (*Courtesy of The Asia Society, New York: Mr. and Mrs. John D. Rockefeller 3rd Collection. Photography by Otto E. Nelson.*)

occurred between the disciples the day after his death. Within the year of his death his followers were forced to call together a council to try to determine the true meaning of his teachings. This council failed to bring unity, and within a very short period of time there were four major Buddhist factions. During the next ten years the number increased to more than sixteen.

In 390 B.C. a second council was called, and an orthodox minority declared the majority of Buddhists to be heretics. From this point onward Buddhism has been divided into these two major camps, which have in turn been subdivided into numerous sects. The smaller and more orthodox wing of Buddhism is known by its adherents as *Ther-*

avada ("the tradition of the elders") and by its enemies as *Hinayana* ("the smaller vehicle"). The larger and more liberal segment is known primarily as *Mahayana* ("the larger vehicle"). The basic theological differences between these two sects will be discussed in a later section of this chapter.

Buddhism received its greatest impetus when a man who was to become the emperor of India, Asoka, was converted to the new religion. It is said that Asoka was to Buddhism what Constantine was to Christianity. In both cases these rulers of large empires were converted to what had previously been small struggling religions. Both emperors then threw the power of their thrones behind their new faiths, and from that point onward these religions grew rapidly. Asoka was converted in 297 B.C., and he became convinced that, unlike other religions of India, Buddhism was potentially the religion for all the peoples of the world. Thus he was the first Buddhist to send out missionaries, carrying the teachings of Gautama and urging non-Indians to accept them. According to some, Asoka's missionaries went as far west as Syria and Greece. While this may be an exaggeration, we are reasonably certain that he sent representatives to Ceylon (present-day Sri Lanka), where the king and his court were converted. Today Sri Lanka boasts the longest history of Buddhism of any Asian nation. Whatever Asoka's motives may have been in sending out these missionaries, the decision proved to be the salvation of Buddhism, since this religion ceased to exist in India as it was there absorbed by Hinduism. Asoka also called the third council of Buddhism in 247 B.C. The purpose of this council was to determine the authoritative list of Buddhist scriptures.

In spite of the enormous unifying work of Asoka and others, by the first century A.D. there were many major and minor sects within Buddhism. Some estimate that by this time there may have been as many as five hundred. However, the most distinct split was along the lines of the differences between Theravada and Mahayana.

THERAVADA BUDDHISM

As mentioned earlier, Hinayana or Theravada Buddhism is the more conservative of the two major divisions within this religion. As such, it believed itself to be closer to the original teachings of the Buddha. The major locations of Theravada Buddhism today are Sri Lanka, Burma, and the nations of Southeast Asia. Sri Lanka seems to be the model for early Buddhism since it was the object of Asoka's missionary efforts in the third century B.C. and has had a relatively peaceful and untroubled history, escaping the conquests and turmoil that have been the lot of India. Because of this rather peaceful history, the Buddhism of Sri Lanka had remained relatively unchanged.

According to Theravada Buddhism, people must work out their own salvation without reliance upon the gods or any force beyond themselves. For this reason the monk is the ideal figure. It is he who shaves his head, puts on the coarse yellow robe, takes up a begging bowl, and goes forth to seek release from life. His home is the Sangha, just as it was in the days of the Buddha. When a monk achieves the goal he is seeking he becomes a saint, and it only remains for him to die before he attains Nirvana and release from the cycle of birth, death, and rebirth, which is the common lot of humankind.

> There is no suffering for him who has finished his journey, and abandoned grief, who has freed himself on all sides, and thrown off all fetters.
>
> They exert themselves with their thoughts well-collected, they do not tarry in their abode; like swans who have left their lake, they leave their house and home.
>
> Men who have no riches, who live on recognized food, who have perceived void and unconditioned freedom [Nirvana], their path is difficult to understand, like that of the birds of the air.
>
> He whose appetites are stilled, who is not absorbed in enjoyment. . . .
>
> The gods even envy him whose senses, like horses well broken in by the driver, have been subdued, who is free from pride, and free from appetites;
>
> In a hamlet or in a forest, on sea or on dry land, wherever venerable persons [Arahanta] dwell, that place is delightful.[5]

If a Theravada Buddhist cannot or will not join the Sangha and become a monk, then he must content himself with living the life of a layperson, supporting the needs of the monks, and hoping that in another life he will be in a better position to seek to become a saint. The scriptures of Theravada Buddhism are relatively few in number.

Thus Theravada Buddhism, like the Buddhism that Gautama himself taught, contains little that might be called a religion. The gods, sacrifice, and prayer are of minor consequence. However, certain religious elements have evolved. For example, relics of the life of the Buddha have become important to Theravadins. His bones and possessions have become objects of veneration at many of the important sites of Theravadin life. One of the early missionaries reportedly took a branch from the sacred bo tree under which the Buddha found enlightenment and planted it in Sri Lanka. The resultant tree is supposed to be the world's oldest living tree. Some Theravadins even teach that the Buddha was actually a divine, omniscient, and sinless

[5] Dhammapada, 90–94, 98.

being who lived many lives before he became Gautama and that another Buddha is waiting now to be born and to give further light to the world through another incarnation.

The characteristic physical structure of Theravada Buddhism is a complex of buildings called a *wat*.[6] The most important building in the wat is the *bot*, a hall used for teaching, preaching, and meditation. Usually this hall contains a statue of the Buddha, with attending altars, candles, and incense. In another portion of the hall there may be a raised seat for lecturing teachers and preachers. Other buildings within the wat include the living quarters for the monks and a number of graceful towers known as *stupas* or pagodas. Some speculate that the pagodas may have begun as relic mounds, but today they serve as worship or festival centers for the Buddhist community.

Although Theravada Buddhism has had appeal for the peoples of Southeast Asia, its nonreligious attitude of expecting each individual to work out his own salvation as a monk never had the wide appeal that would have made it an international religion. It was necessary for Buddhism to change and develop. If it had not developed a greater religious appeal, as it did in Mahayana, it might have died in India or remained a minor religion of the Southeast Asian nations.

MAHAYANA BUDDHISM

The Principles of Mahayana

In the third century B.C., while King Asoka was spreading the gospel of Buddhism by means of his missionary efforts, certain subtle changes began to occur in the religion itself. When these new principles solidified they produced a Buddhism so different from that which Gautama taught and which was accepted by the Theravada Buddhists that it was virtually a new religion.

One of the basic assumptions underlying these new developments was that, in addition to what the Buddha had taught his disciples openly, there were many other principles that he had taught in secret and which were only for the elect who could properly interpret them. A favorite story of the Mahayanists is that, as the Buddha was teaching, he took a handful of leaves from the floor of the forest and explained to his disciples that as the leaves in his hand were less than the total leaves of the forest, so were the teachings that he had given them openly less than the total amount of truth that could be given in secret. Mahayana Buddhism simply picked up a few more leaves.

[6]The word *wat* is a Thai word. In Burma, similar clusters are called *phongyi chaung*.

This brass statue portrays the Bodhisattva, Manjushri-kumara. The develoment of these compassionate beings was one of the steps that made Mahayana Buddhism popular. (*Courtesy of The Asia Society, New York: Mr. and Mrs. John D. Rockefeller 3rd Collection. Photography by Otto E. Nelson.*)

Once this assumption was accepted, then all manner of new teachings could be added to Buddhism.

A second principle that began to develop in Mahayana Buddhism between the third century B.C. and the first century A.D. was that Gautama was really more than a man. In contrast to the original teachings of the Buddha and those of the Theravada school, the Mahayanists began to teach that the Buddha was really a compassionate divine being who came to earth in the form of a man because he loved humankind and wished to be of assistance.

The third principle of the Mahayanists put forth was that Gautama was not the only Buddha. If Gautama were a divine being who had come to earth to help people, the Mahayanists maintained that there must have been other such beings. Some of these beings had come before Gautama, some had come after him, and some were yet to come. This new idea did more than anything else to broaden the appeal of Buddhism. If there are many divine beings who are compassionate and have come to earth to help suffering people, then these beings are worthy of worship. Whereas Gautama had been unconcerned about the gods, and worship had meant nothing in his scheme of things, the Mahayana Buddhists could now develop worship around these many divine beings. They could study the lives of these new gods and build temples to them. Priests could be trained in worshipping these gods, and cultic systems of ritual, sacrifice, hymns, and so on, could be raised in their behalf. The discovery of many compassionate Buddhas was the most religious step ever taken in Buddhism. What had essentially been a philosophy based upon self-help now was free to become a religion in every sense of the word.

This development was also essential to the Buddhist missionary movement. Now when Buddhist missionaries entered a new country they did not have to ask the natives to give up their old gods; these gods were seen as various incarnations of the Buddha, and their cults could continue. In the same way that Hinduism absorbed Buddhism by saying that Gautama was really an avatar of Vishnu, Buddhism absorbed many other religions by saying that their gods were really incarnations of the Buddha.

In addition to these new principles, Mahayana Buddhists developed a path of salvation for the common person. It was taught that certain beings had taken vows to become *bodhisattvas* ("enlightened beings") at some point during their lifetimes. Then, by living exemplary lives they could acquire merit. Following death, these bodhisattvas postponed their achievement of Nirvana and shared their merit with humankind. The bodhisattvas are pictured as sitting in heaven answering the prayers of those who need their help. In this manner the polytheism that Mahayana developed continued to grow.

The Spread of Mahayana Buddhism

Whereas the original teachings of the Buddha and the more orthodox interpretations of Hinayana Buddhism had limited appeal to a rather select group, Mahayana, with its openness to more traditional religious concepts, developed wide appeal. The attractiveness of Maha-

yana Buddhism was so great that it eventually became one of the world's most successful missionary religions.

The teachings of the Buddha probably were carried into China as soon as they became popular in India. Surely Asoka must have sent his missionaries into that great land to the north and east of India in the third century B.C. There is some evidence that Hinayana Buddhism had been introduced and had achieved a minor foothold in China by the first century A.D. However, it was not until the third century, when Mahayana was introduced, that Buddhism really began to take hold there. From that era onward Buddhism became the major religion of China, with the native Confucianism and Taoism offering cultural values but taking a secondary position as religions.

From China Mahayana Buddhism spread to other east Asian nations. Because of its close ties to China, Korea was brought under the influence of Buddhism as early as the fourth century A.D. The spread to the East continued in the sixth century, when Buddhism entered Japan. The Japanese at first refused to accept this new religion, but after a short period of time they embraced it to the point that it came to share religious leadership with the native Shinto. In the ensuing centuries other Asian nations, such as Mongolia and Tibet, also accepted versions of Buddhism. Because of the remote nature of these countries, the religion developed along slightly different lines than it had in other places, and remains today an unusual variation.

While Buddhism was becoming a great success as a missionary religion in the East Asian nations, it was gradually dying in the land of its birth, India. Waves of invasions by various peoples caused the destruction of many Indian centers of Buddhist strength. This was particularly true of the Islamic invasions, in which Buddhists were forced to convert to Islam and Buddhist temples and images were destroyed by the iconoclastic Muslims. Whereas Hinduism, which also suffered at the hands of the Muslims, somehow had the resiliency to recover, Buddhism—in India—did not. In addition to the destruction encountered from the invaders of India, Buddhism suffered from absorption by Hinduism. Since Hinduism has the capacity for openness and toleration of other religions, it was able to absorb the distinctive qualities of the major challenging religions, Jainism and Buddhism. By the seventh century it had absorbed many Buddhist features, simply by stating that Gautama was an avatar of Vishnu. Therefore anything new, important, or distinctive about Buddhism came to be understood as an expression of Vishnu within the Hindu scheme of things. In this way Buddhism eventually ceased to be a distinctive religion in India, and today only a tiny minority of Indians are truly Buddhists.

Mahayanist Sects

Mahayana Buddhism began as a religion open to innovation and change. As it moved and grew in the various Asian nations it acquired many new concepts from these peoples. Therefore, when we speak of Buddhism today, we are not speaking of a single religion but of a whole family of religions; and within this family nearly every form of religious expression may be found.

The Pure Land Sect (Ching-t'u, Jodo).   One of the most popular and widespread branches of Mahayana Buddhism is the so-called Pure Land sect. The goal of its adherents is to achieve salvation when they die and live in a paradise called "the pure land of the west." As we mentioned earlier, the Mahayanists believe that there have been many Buddhas and other forms of divine beings, one of which is the Bodhisattvas. Another form of deity is a group called *Dhyani Buddhas*, who, unlike the Bodhisattvas, were never humans but deities who dwell in heaven and can help humans. One of the most popular of these is known as *Amitabha.*[7] Amitabha is viewed as the god who presides over a western paradise called "the pure land."

> This world Sukhavati, Ananda, which is the world system of the Lord Amitabha, is rich and prosperous, comfortable, fertile, delightful and crowded with many Gods and men. And in this world system, Ananda, there are no hells, no animals, no ghosts, no Asuras and none of the inauspicious places of rebirth. And in this our world no jewels make their appearance like those which exist in the world system Sukhavati.
>
> And that world system Sukhavati, Ananda, emits many fragrant odours, it is rich in a great variety of flowers and fruits, adorned with jewel trees, which are frequented by flocks of various birds with sweet voices, which the Tathagata's miraculous power has conjured up. And these jewel trees, Ananda, have various colors, many colors, many hundreds of thousands of colors. They are variously composed of the seven precious things, in varying combinations, i.e., of gold, silver, beryl, crystal, coral, red pearls or emerald. Such jewel trees, and clusters of banana trees and rows of palm trees, all made of precious things, grow everywhere in the Buddha-field.[8]

To the Pure Land Buddhist, salvation comes through faith in Amitabha. Some members of this sect believe that simply uttering the name of Amitabha many times during the day is an aid to salvation.

With faith in Amitabha as its central premise, and eternity in the

---

[7] In China this Buddha is known as O-mi-to, and in Japan is called Amida.

[8] The Pure Land, 15, 16. *Sukhavativyuha*, Edward Conze, trans. (Oxford, England: Bruno Cassirer, Ltd., 1954), p. 202.

Pure Land as its goal, this version of Buddhism is something quite different from that originally taught by the Buddha. It is possible for the Pure Land priesthood to marry, have children, eat meat, and live in the world in a manner very similar to that of the layperson. Worship for the Pure Land devotee often occurs in what may be best described as "churches"; in fact some Pure Land congregations in Western nations use that title. Pure Land Buddhists may have "Sunday Schools" for the religious instruction of their children, meet for worship in congregations, hear sermons from their clergymen, and offer prayers to Amitabha.

The Intuitive Sects (Ch'an, Zen).   There always seems to have been a group within Buddhism that has emphasized that the truths of religion do not come through rational thought processes, study of scripture, or faith in a deity but rather through a sudden flash of insight. These groups usually trace their origin to the experience of the Buddha under the bodhi tree. As you will recall, here the Buddha realized that he had not found the truth he sought through study with the Brahmin gurus or after five years of extreme asceticism. He therefore resolved simply to sit and meditate. He sat under the bodhi tree for several weeks, and the truth came to him in a flash of inspiration. Advocates of this position maintain that intuition or inspiration that comes after a period of mediation is the key to Buddhist truth. These groups have been known throughout the Buddhist world as meditative or intuitive Buddhists. In India the word for meditation is *dhyana*, in China it is *ch'an*, and in Japan it is *zen*.

Although these Buddhists believe that the Buddha himself received his knowledge intuitively and taught his disciples in this manner, the actual founding of the intuitive sects did not take place until some time in the sixth century A.D., with the work of a monk named Bodhidharma. A great deal about the life of Bodhidharma is legendary, but it seems clear that in the late fifth or early sixth century the concepts of intuitive Buddhism entered China from India. From China they were carried to Korea and Japan, where this version of Buddhism reached its peak in the form of Zen. According to legend, at the invitation of the Chinese emperor, Bodhidharma went as a missionary from South India to Canton in 480 A.D. There he taught the emperor that his scripture, monasteries, philanthropy, and so on, availed him nothing; the truth of Buddhism is only found through meditation and sudden insight. Again, according to legend, when he had finished teaching the emperor, Bodhidharma retired to a cave in the mountains where he spent ten years meditating while facing a wall, and during this time his lower limbs withered and he was no longer able to walk.

A purely apocryphal story says that Bodhidharma wished to stay

Stone Garden of Tofukuji Temple, Kyoto. The beauty and simplicity of this garden reflects the teachings of Zen. (*Courtesy of the Japan National Tourist Organization.*)

awake for many hours and meditate but he kept falling asleep. In a fit of anger at his own inability to stay awake, the monk took a knife and cut off his eyelids. The eyelids fell to the ground and sprang up as the tea plant. Therefore whenever Bodhidharma is depicted he is shown with harsh staring eyes, and no eyelids. Legend also has it that Bodhidharma brought tea from India to China. It is true that about this time in history tea was introduced from India to China and later to Japan, and that the intuitive monks began to use heavily caffeinated tea as a means of staying awake in order to meditate longer.

The basic principle behind all of the intuitive sects of Buddhism is that salvation is an individual matter and therefore one cannot receive much help from other persons or institutions. Individuals find salvation when through an accident or through meditation they are "enlightened." Therefore, the externals of religion are unnecessary. Scripture is not necessary because all people must learn the real truth of religion and life for themselves. Temples are not important because individuals can become enlightened while sitting under a tree or sweeping a floor. Statues of the Buddha and other saints are nice to look at but are not essential for enlightenment.[9] The same disregard is shown toward prayer, asceticism, and rituals.

According to the intuitive sects, reason is to be distrusted more than anything else because it cannot possibly lead people to real truth. In fact, people must deliberately confuse reason before they can find the truth. Therefore Zen Buddhism utilizes riddles that are carefully constructed to go beyond reason or to confuse reason in order to lead the initiates into enlightenment. Such riddles of Zen are called *koans* (case studies). Entire books have been filled with these riddles, tales, and short statements which have been used by the Zen masters to aid their pupils. Perhaps the best known of all to Westerners is the simple statement "You have heard the sound of the clapping of two hands, but what is the sound of one hand clapping?" This question makes no sense, but it is designed to induce the initiate to go beyond sense or reason and to ponder. The pupil of Zen first meditates. When the pupil's mind is cleared of day-to-day matters and is ready to be released from reason, the master gives the student a riddle. It is hoped that while the novitiate meditates upon one of these nonsense statements a flash of enlightenment (*satori*) will come and will lead the initiate to the truth beyond reason.

In addition to the riddles, Zen masters utilize other devices to bring a student to insight. Generally any device that confuses the reasoning processes of the pupil will be used. A Zen master might suddenly shout at the pupil or even slap or kick the student in order to do this. Tales from Zen monasteries tell of masters striking their pupils with sticks or even cutting off one of their fingers in an attempt to cause the intuitive flash. The occasions of brutality are the exception rather than the rule, however.

It is in Japan that intuitive Buddhism has had its most profound effect upon the society. The Zen principles of beauty, simplicity, and profundity have deeply touched many areas of Japanese life. Because tea was introduced along with intuitive Buddhism, tea drinking and the rituals that surround it have been affected by Zen principles. The architecture of the teahouse, the pottery used in the tea ceremony,

---

[9] The best illustration of the attitude of intuitive sects toward the externals of religion is found in a Zen cartoon that shows a monk seeking to warm himself on a cold morning. He has chopped up a statue of the Buddha, set fire to it, and is depicted raising his robe and warming his buttocks by the fire.

the music that is played during the tea ceremony, the poetry that is recited, and the floral arrangements that decorate the teahouse, all reflect the principles of Zen. In Japanese art that which is valued most highly is called "the controlled accident." That is, art that is not purely planned or contrived is valued above that which is planned. A teapot that is accidentally broken and glued back together with gold-colored cement is more valued because of the beautiful "accidental" lines of the breakage than a teapot with a contrived design painted upon it. A drawing that is done upon very porous paper with pen and ink and cannot be erased and corrected is considered more beautiful than one that has been planned, worked out very carefully, and corrected by an artist. Thus the concepts of beauty in Japanese life are heavily influenced by the nonrational approach of Zen.

The Rationalist Sect (T'ien-t'ai, Tendai). Whereas the intuitive groups, Ch'an and Zen, tended to distrust the rational process and felt that they had little need for scripture in their search for enlightenment, another group arose in China in the sixth century and taught that in addition to meditation one should utilize reason and a study of the scriptures in order to find the truth of Buddhism. This sect, which was called T'ien-t'ai, was founded by a monk named Chih-i. According to Chih-i, the Buddha had used a variety of teaching methods during his lifetime in order to get across his truths. At one point he taught the Theravada doctrines; at another time he felt that he could communicate better by teaching the Mahayana doctrines; and at still another point he taught in a manner similar to that used by the intuitive sects. In reality there is only one true Buddhist teaching, and individuals must study the scriptures of Buddhism in order to know this truth. Therefore, whereas meditation may be helpful at certain times, it is not the only path, and rational thought and study should not be disregarded. In the ninth century, the teachings of Chih-i were introduced into Japan, where this sect became known as Tendai.

The Sociopolitical Sect (Nichiren). From time to time the various sects of Buddhism have come to have great effect upon the social and political dimensions of various nations. One such sect is the so-called *Nichiren* ("sun lotus") Buddhist group that is a purely Japanese phenomenon. The founder of Nichiren lived in Japan in the thirteenth century. He was the son of humble parents, and at the age of fifteen he entered a Tendai Buddhist monastery. During his ten years there he came to believe that all the current sects of Buddhism were a perversion of the true teachings of the Buddha. He also came to believe that the Lotus Sutra was the only scripture a person needed to study to be a correct Buddhist. While mediating upon this sutra this man underwent a conversion experience. He changed his name to Nichiren, took a vow to faithfully follow and teach the Lotus Sutra, and set forth on a career of preaching and polemics with a fervor that is reminiscent of many of the Jewish prophets. He preached that he alone understood the truth of pure Buddhism and that the other Japanese sects, Zen, Pure Land, and so on, were preaching falsehoods and leading people to hell. Because the majority of the Japanese people followed these false sects, the nation was suffering from internal and external woes. Naturally this kind of preaching aroused powerful enemies; Nichiren was twice deported and twice condemned to death.

Throughout its history Nichiren Buddhism has expressed hostility toward the rituals and teachings of other Buddhist sects. Consequently it has always been a small and persecuted minority.

The Nichiren sect has also stressed a simpler form of Buddhism and uncompromising patriotism and loyalty to Japan. It teaches that when Buddhism becomes purified in Japan it will reach out to the rest of the world. Although Nichiren has only slightly over two million followers today, it has been the source of another Buddhist sect, Soka Gakkai, which is much larger.

Tibetan Buddhism

Another aspect of Mahayana Buddhism is represented by sects that emphasize the use of magical words or formulae as means of achieving various goals. In Buddhism, as in nearly every other religion, there are those who believe that the recitation of certain phrases, names, or "magical" words has the effect of achieving certain ends. The largest and best known of these is the religion that was once a dominant force in Tibet.

The native religion of Tibet was known as *Bon*. The original meaning of this word has been lost, but it is suggested that it referred to priests who performed acts of magic and taught the Tibetan people various incantations and spells to protect themselves from the demons that lurked in the shadows and dark places of that harsh land. When Buddhism entered Tibet it apparently took this concern for magic and protection from demons as its major emphasis.

Buddhism was officially introduced into Tibet in the Seventh century, when King Songstan-Gampo came to the throne. He was interested in bringing the benefits of Indian and Chinese culture to his people. One of his wives was Chinese and another was Indian. Both were Buddhist. Therefore he sent them back to their respective homelands and asked them to return with Buddhist books and teachers. In the eighth century the spread of Buddhism was interrupted when the Bonists persuaded the Tibetans that a certain epidemic was the result of the native deities' anger. This interruption did not last long, however, and soon the Buddhists were allowed to return and continue their missionary activities.

The theology of Tibetan Buddhism is much like that found throughout the Mahayana world, but because of the isolation of this nation many unique features have developed and been maintained. The most important practical feature of Tibetan Buddhism is its concern for magic as a means of coping with the problems of life. Tibetan Buddhism is frequently referred to as *Tantric* Buddhism. This is because of its heavy use of manuals (*tantras*) that teach the various magical words and spells that help one to deal with the unknown. Tantric religion is found in several of the sects of both Hinduism and Buddhism. In original Indian thought it was believed that within each deity there were two elements: the male and the female. Sometimes these elements were separated in the minds of the devotee into a god and his consort, or wife, as in the case of Shiva and Kali. The awareness of these two divine elements led certain Hindus and, later, Buddhists, to seek a mystical union with them through sexual excesses. It was also believed that people could conquer passion with an excess of that passion. Therefore, in addition to bringing about a union between the devotee and the god/goddess, tantric religion sought enlightenment and conquest over the flesh by carrying passion to excessive lengths. It was also believed that people could conquer the desire for meat, wine, or other forbidden items by overindulging in them. This form of religion became popular in early medieval Tibet. Reform came under the direction of a monk named Marpa (1020–1097) and Tibetan tantric Buddhism was purged of much of its eroticism and given more spiritual meaning.

Another feature of Tibetan Buddhism is its use of the phrase *Om mani padmi hum*, which means, "Om, the jewel of the lotus, hum." Although the phrase has no special literal meaning, it is used as an all-purpose formula for warding off evil and bringing good fortune. Some Tibetans believe that if this phrase is repeated often enough, magical effects will occur.

Another feature of Tibetan Buddhism that seems to be unique is the use of the prayer wheel. No one knows the origin of this, but its major use has been among the Tibetans. One form of the prayer wheel is a cylinder that contains various prayers and ritual incantations. Within this cylinder is an agitator of some kind. It is believed that by turning the agitator and stirring the prayers, the prayers are somehow prayed. The most common form of the prayer wheel is a small model that can be carried on one's person and activated regularly. Other larger models are found in monasteries. Inventive Tibetan Buddhists have

One of the special features of Tibetan Buddhism is the prayer wheel. This small cylinder contains written prayers. They are activated when the wheel is turned. (*Courtesy of The Newark Museum Collection.*)

even been known to set up prayer wheels near streams, where they are turned by water power.

Still another distinctive feature of Tibetan Buddhism is its clergy, the *lamas*. The word *lama* basically means "the superior one." From earliest days, these men who have turned aside from the normal pursuits of life to enter monasteries have been unusually powerful. As early as the ninth century the kings of Tibet gave the lamas certain lands for their monasteries, and with these lands the power to gather funds from the people. By the fourteenth century the leaders of the monasteries had become more powerful than the kings. The kings disappeared and for all practical purposes the country was ruled by the Buddhist priests. Although the lamas had originally taken the vows of celibacy, by the fourteenth century they had rejected it and lived in lordly splendor with their wives and children. However, in that same century reform measures were introduced and celibacy again became their lot.

The lamas of Tibetan Buddhism have been divided basically into two orders: One is identified by Western scholars as the so-called Yellow Hat school and is the larger of the two; the other is identified as the Red Hat school. One of the most interesting contributions of the Red Hat school is their scriptural book, *Bardo Thodol* (*The Book of the Dead*). It is believed that this book came to written form sometime in the eighth century A.D., although it may contain materials that are centuries older. Of course, it contains teachings that are pre-Buddhist in nature. It essentially teaches that after death the human soul abides for forty-nine days in a dream-like state called the *Bardo*.

During this period the ultimate destiny of the soul is determined. Individuals who have lived virtuous lives will achieve Nirvana from the Bardo; if, on the other hand, a karmic pull has been built up during an individual's life, then that person will be drawn again to rebirth.[10] It is also believed that the immediate pre-death hours can influence the soul in its stay in the Bardo. Therefore Tibetan Buddhist monks are trained to help the dying through this experience. Western witnesses have sometimes observed the elaborate rituals and efforts of monks as they seek to help the dying.

The leader of the Yellow Hat group has been known for centuries

The Dalai Lama is the religious and secular head of Tibet. The current Dalai Lama has lived in exile since 1959. (*Courtesy of Brian Beresford, Manjushri Institute, Ulverston, UK.*)

[10]In a strange manner the *Bardo Thodol* seems to have anticipated Freud: it declares that people to be reborn as males will feel hostility toward their fathers and attraction to their mothers, and people to be females will feel hostility toward their mothers and attraction to their fathers.

as the Dalai Lama[11] and by virtue of his position essentially has been the ruler of Tibet. When one Dalai Lama dies an extensive search is made for his replacement. A group of monks scours Tibet for a child who seems to have the qualities and characteristics of the dead Dalai, since it is believed that following his death he will reincarnate himself in the body of his successor. When the group has found such a child and agrees that this is the new Dalai Lama, the boy begins a long period of training that prepares him for leadership of the nation.

By the twentieth century, Tibet had become a nation in which the clergy once again literally ruled the land. The Dalai Lama served as both spiritual and temporal leader, and the position of lama became so popular and so important that it was estimated in 1950 that almost 20 percent of the entire male population lived behind the walls of the monasteries.

This all came to an end in 1950, when Tibet was invaded by China. For centuries Tibet has been claimed by both China and India, but since neither nation pressed the claim, Tibet enjoyed a virtually independent existence. In 1950 China pressed its claim and set up a puppet government. In 1959, under the leadership of the young Dalai Lama, the Tibetans attempted to overthrow Chinese rule, but their revolution was crushed. The Dalai Lama and a few of his followers escaped to India. In exile, the Tibetan Buddhists maintained their identity and even carried on some missionary work. Recent changes in Chinese policy have given some hope that Buddhism in Tibet may be revived.

BUDDHISM TODAY

After the great missionary movements in the first millennium of its existence, and after Asian nations such as China, Japan, and Korea had been converted, Buddhism slipped into a state of quiescence. For centuries there were no great movements or changes. Within the twentieth century, however, Buddhism has begun to revive and grow again. There are several reasons for this revival.

Strangely enough, one of the factors in renewed interest in Buddhism has been the work of Christian missionaries. As Christians entered Asian nations in the nineteenth and twentieth centuries, they felt the need to know more about Buddhism. They therefore initiated translations of ancient Buddhist texts. This interest caused many native Buddhists to reread and appreciate anew their heritage.

---

[11] The word *dalai* literally means "the sea" and is used to indicate the vastness and depth of the person.

A second factor that has contributed to the revival of Buddhism, particularly Theravada Buddhism, has been the rise of Asian nationalism. With the collapse of the colonial empires after World War II, many new Asian nations began to take pride in being Buddhist. In the past it had been in vogue to be western, to speak a European language, and to study Christianity. After World War II, in nations such as Burma, Theravada Buddhism attracted renewed attention. It was discovered that Buddhism and Hinduism, with their theories of endless ages, were much more in tune with science than the Judaeo-Christian story of creation. Furthermore, Buddhism's message of peace and tolerance seemed to fit the needs of the nuclear age. Therefore some Buddhists have come to see their religion as *the* religious option for the modern world.

Historically, the chief locations for Mahayana Buddhism have been China, Japan, and Korea. Following World War II, Buddhism suffered severe losses in China. With the establishment of the People's Republic of China in 1949, Buddhism was suppressed. It suffered more serious losses with the Cultural Revolution, beginning in 1966. However, in the 1980s there seems to be renewed Buddhist activity in China.

In Japan and Korea Mahayana Buddhism remains a vital force in the lives of the people. In the past two decades, Japanese forms of Buddhism, such as Zen, Nichiren, and Pure Land, have attracted much attention in Western nations. Today Buddhist temples and shrines are found in many of these countries, and Buddhist literature is widely read. Buddhism is perhaps on the verge of another great missionary outreach. Its world population is estimated today at approximately 250 million.[12]

STUDY QUESTIONS

1. Compare the life of Gautama to that of Mahavira. Why are the details of their lives similar?

2. List the four passing sights that Gautama saw. Why did these sights cause him to enter a search for religious answers?

3. What is there in the teachings of Gautama that caused Buddhism to be called "the middle way?"

[12] *Encyclopedia Britannica Book of the Year* (Chicago: Encyclopedia Britannica Inc., 1985), p. 365.

4. According to the Buddha, what is the central problem with humanity, which keeps it bound to the endless cycle of life?

5. What is the significance of King Asoka in the development of Buddhism into a world religion?

6. List four basic differences between Mahayana and Theravada Buddhism.

7. Distinguish between the Pure Land and the Intuitive sects of Mahayana Buddhism.

SUGGESTED READING

Conze, Edward, ed. *Buddhist Texts Through the Ages.* Oxford: Bruno Cassirer, 1953.

Gard, Richard A., ed. *Buddhism.* New York: George Braziller, 1961.

Humphreys, Christmas. *Buddhism.* New York: Penguin Books, 1951.

Robinson, Richard H. and Willard L. Johnson. *The Buddhist Religion.* Belmont, Calif.: Wadsworth Publishing Company, 1982.

Suzuki, Daisetz T. *Zen and Japanese Buddhism.* Tokyo: Charles E. Tuttle, 1958.

Watts, Alan. *The Way of Zen.* New York: Pantheon Books, 1957.

─────────── SOURCE MATERIAL ───────────

Gautama Speaks of His Ascetic Practices

Before Gautama achieved enlightment under the Bo tree he
had struggled for many years to find his way to salvation.
One of his paths had led him to practice extreme asceticism.
In the following passage Gautama relates his experiences to
one of his disciples.[13]

Majjhima-nikaya. XII

Aye, Sariputta, I have lived the fourfold higher life;—I have been an ascetic
of ascetics; loathly have I been, foremost in loathliness, scrupulous have I
been, foremost in scrupulosity; solitary have I been, foremost in solitude.

(i) To such a pitch of asceticism have I gone that naked was I, flouting
life's decencies, licking my hands after meals, never heeding when folk
called to me to come or to stop, never accepting food brought to me before
my rounds or cooked expressly for me, never accepting an invitation, never
receiving food direct from pot or pan or within the threshold or among the
faggots or pestles, never from (one only of) two people messing together,
never from a pregnant woman or a nursing mother or a woman *in coitu*,
never from gleanings (in time of famine) nor from where a dog is ready at
hand or where (hungry) flies congregate, never touching flesh or spirits or
strong drink or brews of grain. I have visited only one house a day and
there take only one morsel; or I have visited but two or (up to not more
than) seven houses a day and taken at each only two or (up to not more
than) seven morsels; I have lived on a single saucer of food a day, or on
two, or (up to) seven saucers; I have had but one meal a day, or one every
two days, or (so on, up to) every seven days, or only once a fortnight, on
a rigid scale of rationing. My sole diet has been herbs gathered green, or
the grain of wild millets and paddy, or snippets of hide, or water-plants, or
the red powder round rice-grains within the husk, or the discarded scum
of rice on the boil, or the flour of oil-seeds, or grass, or cow-dung. I have
lived on wild roots and fruit, or on windfalls only. My raiment has been of
hemp or of hempen mixture, of cerements, of rags from the dust-heap, of
bark, of the black antelope's pelt either whole or split down the middle, or
grass, of strips of bark or wood, of hair of men or animals woven into a
blanket or of owl's wings. In fulfillment of my vows, I have plucked out
the hair of my head and the hair of my beard, have never quitted the
upright for the sitting posture, have squatted and never risen up, moving

[13] Lord Chalmers, trans., *Further Dialogues of the Buddha*, vol. I (New York: Krisha Press, 1926), pp. 53–57.

only a-squat, have couched on thorns, have gone down to the water punctually thrice before nightfall to wash (away the evil within). After this wise, in divers fashions, have I lived to torment and to torture my body—to such a length in asceticism have I gone.

(ii) To such a length have I gone in loathliness that on my body I have accumulated the dirt and filth of years till it dropped off of itself—even as the rank growths of years fall away from the stump of a tinduka-tree. But never once came the thought to me to clean it off with my own hands or to get others to clean it off for me;—to such a length in loathliness have I gone.

(iii) To such a length in scrupulosity have I gone that my footsteps out and in were always attended by a mindfulness so vigilant as to awake compassion within me over even a drop of water lest I might harm tiny creatures in crevices;—to such a length have I gone in scrupulosity.

(iv) To such a length have I gone as a solitary that when my abode was in the depths of the forest, the mere glimpse of a cowherd or neatherd or grasscutter, or of a man gathering firewood or edible roots in the forest, was enough to make me dart from wood to wood, from thicket to thicket, from dale to dale, and from hill to hill,—in order that they might not see me or I them. As a deer at the sight of man darts away over hill and dale, even so did I dart away at the mere glimpse of cowherd, neatherd, or what not, in order that they might not see me or I them;—to such a length have I gone as a solitary.

When the cowherds had driven their herds forth from the byres, up I came on all fours to find a subsistence on the drippings of the young milch-cows. So long as my own dung and urine held out, on that I have subsisted. So foul a filth-eater was I.

I took up my abode in the awesome depths of the forest, depths so awesome that it was reputed that none but the passionless could venture in without his hair standing on end. When the cold season brought chill wintry nights, then it was that, in the dark half of the months when snow was falling, I dwelt by night in the open air and in the dank thicket by day. But when there came the last broiling month of summer before the rains, I made my dwelling under the baking sun by day and in the stifling thicket by night. Then there flashed on me these verses, never till then uttered by any:

> Now scorched, now froze, in forest dread, alone.
> naked and fireless, set upon his quest.
> the hermit battles purity to win.

In a charnel ground I lay me down with charred bones for pillow. When the cowherds' boys came along, they spat and staled upon me, pelted me with dirt and stuck bits of wood into my ears. Yet I declare that never did

I let an evil mood against them arise within me. —So poised in equanimity was I.

(80) Some recluses and brahmins there are who say and hold that purity cometh by way of food, and accordingly proclaim that they live exclusively on jujube-fruits, which, in one form or other, constitute their sole meat and drink. Now I can claim to have lived on a single jujube-fruit a day. If this leads you to think that this fruit was larger in those days, you would err; for, it was precisely the same size then that it is today. When I was living on a single fruit a day, my body grew emaciated in the extreme; because I ate so little, my members, great and small, grew like the knotted joints of withered creepers; like a buffalo's hoof were my shrunken buttocks; like the twists in a rope were my spinal vertebrae; like the crazy rafters of a tumble-down roof, that start askew and aslant, were my gaunt ribs; like the starry gleams on water deep down and afar in the depths of a well, shone my gleaming eyes deep down and afar in the depths of their sockets; and as the rind of a cut gourd shrinks and shrivels in the heat, so shrank and shrivelled the scalp of my head,—and all because I ate so little. If I sought to feel my belly, it was my backbone which I found in my grasp; if I sought to feel my backbone, I found myself grasping my belly, so closely did my belly cleave to my backbone;—and all because I ate so little. If for ease of body I chafed my limbs, the hairs of my body fell away under my hand, rotted at their roots;—and all because I ate so little.

Other recluses and brahmins there are who, saying and holding that purity cometh by way of food, proclaim that they live exclusively on beans— or seasamum—or rice—as their sole meat and drink.

(81) Now I can claim to have lived on a single bean a day—on a single seasamum seed a day—or on a single grain of rice a day; and (the result was still the same). Never did this practice or these courses or these dire austerities bring me to the ennobling gifts of super-human knowledge and insight. And why?—Because none of them lead to that noble understanding which, when won, leads on to Deliverance and guides him who lives up to it onward to the utter extinction of all ill.

The Buddha Explains the Eightfold Path

> At the heart of Buddha's teaching about the nature of life
> and death and the proper way to live is the eightfold path.
> The following selection from the Samytta-nikaya V, 8, con-
> tains the Buddha's explanation of this path.[14]

"The Noble Eightfold Way, monks, I will expound and analyse to you. Listen to it, reflect on it well, I will speak." "Even so, Lord," the monks replied to the Lord.

[14] E. J. Thomas, trans. *Early Buddhist Scriptures* (New York: Krisha Press, 1935), pp. 94–96.

The Lord said, "What, monks, is the Noble Eightfold Way? It is namely right view, right intention, right speech, right action, right livelihood, right effort, right mindfulness, right concentration."

"And what, monks, is the right view? The knowledge of pain, knowledge of the cause of pain, knowledge of the cessation of pain, and knowledge of the way that leads to the cessation of pain: that, monks, is called right view."

"And what is right intention? The intention to renounce, the intention not to hurt, the intention not to injure: that, monks, is called right intention."

"And what is right speech? Refraining from falsehood, from malicious speech, from harsh speech, from frivolous speech: that, monks, is called right speech."

"And what is right action? Refraining from taking life, from taking what is not given, from sexual intercourse: that, monks, is called right action."

"And what is right livelihood? Here a noble disciple abandoning a false mode of livelihood gets his living by right livelihood: that, monks, is called right livelihood."

"And what is right effort? Here a monk with the nonproducing of bad and evil thoughts that have not yet arisen exercises will, puts forth effort, begins to make exertion, applies and exerts his mind; with the dispelling of bad and evil thoughts that had arisen he exercises will, puts forth effort, begins to make exertion, applies and exerts his mind; with the producing of good thoughts that had not arisen he exercises will, puts forth effort, begins to make exertion, applies and exerts his mind; with the fixing, freeing from confusion, increasing, enlarging, developing and filling up of good thoughts that had arisen he exercises will, puts forth effort, begins to make exertion, applies and exerts his mind: that, monks, is called right effort."

"And what is right mindfulness? Here (1) on the body: a monk abides contemplating the body, ardent, thoughtful, and mindful, dispelling his longing and dejection towards the world; (2) on feelings: he abides contemplating the feelings, ardent, thoughtful, and mindful, dispelling his longing and dejection towards the world; (4) on thoughts: he abides contemplating thoughts, ardent, thoughtful, and mindful, dispelling his longing and dejection towards the world. That, monks, is called right mindfulness."

"And what is right concentration? Here (1) a monk free from passions and evil thoughts attains and abides in the first trance of joy and pleasure, which is accompanied by reasoning and investigation and arises from seclusion. (2) With the ceasing of reasoning and investigation, in a state of internal serenity, with his mind fixed on one point, he attains and abides in the second trance of joy and pleasure arising from concentration, and free from reasoning and investigation. (3) With equanimity and indifference towards joy he abides mindful and self-possessed, and with his body experiences pleasure that the noble ones call 'Dwelling with equanimity, mindful and happy,' and attains and abides in the third trance. (4) Dispelling pleasure and pain, and even before the disappearance of elation and depression, he attains and abides in the fourth trance, which is without pleasure and pain, and with the purity of mindfulness and equanimity: that, monks, is called right concentration."

The Infinite Compassion of the Bodhisattva

One of the distinctive features of Mahayana Buddhism is the Bodhisattva. These figures who may have lives as humans have delayed their achievements of Nirvana because of their compassion for humankind. In this passage taken from *Shikshasamuccaya* (pages 280–282), there is a statement of the compassion of the Bodhisattva.[15]

A Bodhisattva resolves: I take upon myself the burden of suffering. I am resolved to do so, I will endure it. I do not turn or run away, do not tremble, am not terrified, nor afraid, do not turn back or despond.

And why? At all costs I must bear the burdens of all beings. In that I do not follow my own inclinations. I have made the vow to save all beings. All beings I must set free. The whole world of living beings I must rescue, from the terrors of birth, of old age, of sickness, of death and rebirth, of all kinds of moral offence, of all states of woe, of the whole cycle of birth-and-death, of the jungle of false views, of the loss of wholesome dharmas, of the concomitants of ignorance,—from all these terrors I must rescue all beings. . . . I walk so that the kingdom of unsurpassed cognition is built up for all beings. My endeavours do not merely aim at my own deliverance. For with the help of the boat of the thought of all-knowledge, I must rescue all these beings from the stream of Samsara, which is so difficult to cross, I must pull them back from the great precipice. I must free them from all calamities, I must ferry them across the stream of Samsara. I myself must grapple with the whole mass of suffering of all beings. To the limit of my endurance I will experience in all the states of woe, found in any world system, all the abodes of suffering. And I must not cheat all beings out of my store of merit, I am resolved to abide in each single state of woe for numberless aeons; and so I will help all beings to freedom, in all the states of woe that may be found in any world system whatsoever.

And why? Because it is surely better that I alone should be in pain than that all these beings should fall into the states of woe. There I must give myself away as a pawn through which the whole world is redeemed from the terrors of the hells, of animal birth, of the world of Yama, and with this my own body I must experience, for the sake of all beings, the whole mass

---

[15] Edward Conze, trans. Conze et al., *Buddhist Texts Through the Ages* (Oxford: Bruno Cassirer, 1954), pp. 131–132.

of all painful feelings. And on behalf of all beings I give surety for all beings, and in doing so I speak truthfully, am trustworthy, and do not go back on my word. I must not abandon all beings.

And why? There has arisen in me the will to win all-knowledge, with all beings for its object, that is to say, for the purpose of setting free the entire world of beings. And I have not set out for the supreme enlightenment from a desire for delights, not because I hope to experience the delights of the five-sense qualities, or because I wish to indulge in the pleasures of the senses. And I do not pursue the course of a Bodhisattva in order to achieve the array of delights that can be found in the various worlds of sense-desire.

And why? Truly no delights are all these delights of the world. All this indulging in the pleasure of the senses belongs to the sphere of Mara.

The Importance of Sitting

In that branch of Mahayana Buddhism which is known in Japan as Zen, meditation is the key to enlightenment. The following text from *Shobo Genzo Zuimonki* speaks of the importance of meditation in Zen.[16]

When I stayed at the Zen lodge in T'ien-t'ung (China), the venerable Ching used to stay up sitting until the small hours of the morning and then after only a little rest would rise early to start sitting again. In the meditation hall we went on sitting with the other elders, without letting up for even a single night. Meanwhile many of the monks went off to sleep. The elder would go around among them and hit the sleepers with his fist or a slipper, yelling at them to wake up. If their sleepiness persisted, he would go out to the hallway and ring the bell to summon the monks to a room apart, where he would lecture to them by the light of a candle.

"What use is there in your assembling together in the hall only to go to sleep? Is this all that you left the world and joined holy orders for? Even among laymen, whether they be emperors, princes, or officials, are there any who live a life of ease? The ruler must fulfill the duties of the sovereign, his ministers must serve with loyalty and devotion, and commoners must work to reclaim land and till the soil—no one lives a life of ease. To escape from such burdens and idly while away the time in a monastery— what does this accomplish? Great is the problem of life and death; fleeting indeed is our transitory existence. Upon these truths both the scriptural and meditation schools agree. What sort of illness awaits us tonight, what sort of death tomorrow? While we have life, not to practise Buddha's Law, but

[16]William T. de Bary, ed. and trans., *Sources of Japanese Tradition* (New York: Columbia University Press, 1958), pp. 253, 254.

to spend the time in sleep is the height of foolishness. Because of such foolishness Buddhism today is in a state of decline. When it was at its zenith monks devoted themselves to the practice of sitting in meditation (*zazen*), but nowadays sitting is not generally insisted upon and consequently Buddhism is losing ground."

Upon another occasion his attendants said to him, "The monks are getting overtired or falling ill, and some are thinking of leaving the monastery, all because they are required to sit too long in meditation. Shouldn't the length of the sitting period be shortened?" The master became highly indignant. "That would be quite wrong. A monk who is not really devoted to the religious life may very well fall asleep in a half hour or an hour. But one truly devoted to it who has resolved to persevere in his religious discipline will eventually come to enjoy the practice of sitting, no matter how long it lasts. When I was young I used to visit the heads of various monasteries, and one of them explained to me, 'Formerly I used to hit sleeping monks so hard that my fist just about broke. Now I am old and weak, so I can't hit them hard enough. Therefore it is difficult to produce good monks. In many monasteries today the superiors do not emphasize sitting strongly enough, and so Buddhism is declining. The more you hit them the better,' he advised me."

CHAPTER 7

Sikhism

A Sikh preacher addresses an audience in the Golden Temple in Amritsar, India. The Golden Temple houses the Holy Granth, and is the most sacred of all Sikh shrines. (*Courtesy of the United Nations.*)

There is no Muslim and there is no Hindu.
  —*Nanak*

One of the world's newest religions, Sikhism, originated in the sixteenth century A.D. Although some call it a new and independent religion, there are those who think of Sikhism primarily as just one more reform movement in Hinduism. Indeed, like Buddhism and Jainism, Sikhism does take its basic theology and world view from Hinduism and does seek to reform certain elements in Hinduism. However, unlike other reform movements in Hinduism, Sikhism endeavors to incorporate elements from another major world religion, Islam. Interestingly, Islam has an entirely different world view than Hinduism. This attempt to blend elements from two religions that are so diverse is a fascinating story.

The Sikhs have always been a minority among the other religions of India, and today they number only about sixteen million worldwide. Sikhs are found mainly in the Punjab region of northwest India, which has traditionally been their home.

THE LIFE OF NANAK

From the tenth century onward, various Muslim groups invaded India from their bases to the west. These invasions eventually resulted in the domination of India by the Moghul rulers. Although all of India faced Muslim conquest at one time or another, the northwest section was invaded most frequently. It was here that Islam made its greatest number of converts and established its strongest bases. Because Islam and Hinduism were basically so different in so many areas, the encounters between Muslims and Hindus were often hostile and frequently violent.

From the earliest days, however, there were teachers who did not believe that the two religions had to be hostile and thought that a synthesis could be reached. The reformer who is best remembered for attempting to bring Hinduism and Islam together was a man named Kabir (1440–1518). Kabir was born a Muslim but found it possible to worship with his Hindu neighbors. While worshiping the Hindu deities, he was also teaching that the true god was one. It is not clear how he was able to work this out, but he left a profound impression upon the Sikhs and their literature.

The actual founder of Sikhism was a man named Nanak (1469–

1538), who was a later contemporary of Kabir and was undoubtedly influenced by him. Nanak was born into a Hindu home in the Punjab region about forty miles from the city of Lahore. Because of the mixed nature of the region, Nanak's schoolmaster was a Muslim and surely had an influence on him.

Nanak is pictured as a dreamer who seems to have had little grasp of the day-to-day world of business or practicality. His interests and talents were more toward poetry and religion than the business of earning a living. His father tried to place him in a variety of occupations, but Nanak apparently was a failure at all of them. He was betrothed to a young woman when he was twelve, and their marriage was consummated when he was nineteen. Two sons were born of this marriage. Nanak eventually left his wife and sons and went to the city of Sultanpur to earn his living. Here he was a bit more successful in business pursuits.

During his stay in Sultanpur, when he was about thirty years of age, Nanak received a vision from God which was to change his life. According to some stories, God spoke to him while he was meditating in the forest. The message of the vision was that Nanak had been singled out as a prophet of a true religion. His message was to be, "There is no Muslim and there is no Hindu." Thus he was to become an evangelist, preaching a gospel of unity between these two religions. Along with his constant companion, Mardana, Nanak became a wandering preacher of this new message. The two traveled widely in India over the next decades, preaching the essential unity of Islam and Hinduism. To emphasize his message Nanak wore a mixed costume, made up of the clothing of both Hindus and Muslims. Wherever he went he sought to organize communities of people who accepted his teachings, and his followers became known as Sikh, a Punjabi word for "disciple." In his travels Nanak even made the pilgrimage to Mecca, although he aroused antagonism there because of his unwillingness to display proper respect for Muslim shrines.

After many years of wandering Nanak returned home to northwest India, where he continued to teach and form communities of Sikhs. According to a charming Sikh legend, as Nanak was about to die, his followers were still divided over their basic religious loyalties. Those who originally had been Hindus planned to cremate his remains, while those who originally had been Muslim wished to bury him. Nanak, aware of this dispute over his body, requested that each group place flowers beside him, and the group whose flowers were still fresh on the following day could have his body. When the two factions agreed and placed their flowers beside him, Nanak covered himself with a sheet and died. The next morning when the sheet was removed, the Sikhs found that both sets of flowers were still fresh, but that the body of Nanak was gone. Thus, according to this legend, the peaceful and loving Nanak, even in death, sought to bring harmony between Muslims and Hindus.[1]

THE TEACHINGS OF NANAK

Nanak, like Kabir and others, sought to synthesize the best elements of Islam and Hinduism. He took from each religion what he believed to be of most importance. From Islam he took the teaching that there is but one God. While Hindus may see this God at work in many ways and in various disguises, still God is basically one. Sikhs refer to this God as "The True Name."

Nanak also taught that "The True Name" is the creator of the entire universe and that human beings are God's supreme creation. Thus Nanak rejected the teaching of *ahimsa*, which is so important to many Indian religions. Since people are the primary creation they are free to kill and eat animals. Sikhs are among the few Indians who may legitimately eat meat.

Nanak did adopt several elements of Hinduism. He accepted the principle of reincarnation, which is basic to many Indian religions. Sikhs came to believe that the spirit of Nanak was reincarnated in the bodies of those gurus who succeeded him as the leaders of Sikhism. Nanak also taught the Indian principle of karma and believed that people continue to acquire karma and live again and again until they are freed from this cycle by "The True Name."

Nanak rejected the ceremonialism and rituals of both Hinduism and Islam. He taught a very plain and simple form of religion which distrusted and rejected ritual.

> The Musalmans praise the Sharia, read it, and reflect on it:
> But God's servants are they who employ themselves in His service in order to behold Him.
> The Hindus praise the Praised One whose appearance and form are incomparable;
> They bathe in holy streams, perform idol-worship and adoration, use copious incense of sandal.
> The Jogis meditate on God the Creator, whom they call the Unseen,
> Whose form is minute, whose name is the Bright One, and who is the image of their bodies.[2]

According to one story, Nanak was ejected from Muslim worship once because he laughed aloud during the sermon of the *imam*. When

---

[1] The same story is told about the death of Kabir.
[2] Asa Ki War, Slok VI. *The Sacred Writings of the World's Great Religions.* S. E. Frost, ed. (New York: McGraw-Hill, 1943), 362.

he was asked why he was so disrespectful to Muslim worship, he replied that he had perceived that the *imam* was not really thinking about God while he was preaching but was in fact thinking about his horse and worrying lest the horse fall into a well. This perception struck Nanak as being so ludicrous that he burst into laughter.

Another element in the religion of Nanak was his pacifism. This man, in all his travels and with all the rejection that he received, maintained the stance of a pacifist. He never struck out at his enemies, and apparently he taught his disciples to follow this pattern. In contrast to the teachings of Nanak, Sikhs, in their later history, became known as the most militant of warriors.

THE HISTORICAL DEVELOPMENT OF SIKHISM

Upon the death of Nanak the leadership of the new movement was taken over by a man named Angad, who ruled until 1552. Nanak and Angad were the first two in a series of ten gurus who led Sikhism until the eighteenth century. Usually the word *guru* in Indian religions has the connotation of "teacher," but to the Sikhs the word means "leader." The first four of the ten gurus of Sikhism tended to follow the teachings of Nanak and to be rather pacific toward their enemies. Angad is remembered because he devised a new script and began to compile the Sikh scriptures. Other gurus followed similar paths.

With the ascension of the fifth guru, Arjan Dev (1581–1606), both the office and the religion underwent significant changes. Arjan is remembered for beginning the compilation of the official scriptures of Sikhism, the *Granth*. The Granth has become increasingly important in Sikhism since the days of the gurus. Basically, it is a collection of hymns, a large portion of which came from Nanak. The remainder of the hymns that make up the Granth came from Kabir and other gurus. The Granth contains 3,384 hymns and is roughly three times the size of the Rig-Veda.

In addition to his contribution as the compiler of the Granth, Arjan is remembered for giving Sikhism its militant aspect, in direct contrast to the pacifism of Nanak and the earlier gurus. Between the time of Nanak and that of Arjan, the Sikh movement had grown and was beginning to be recognized as a threat by the Muslim authorities. The Muslim emperor ordered Arjan to remove from the Granth any doctrine that was contrary to the teachings of the Quran. When Arjan refused, he was put into jail and tortured to death. However, before his death he instructed his son Har Gobind, who was to become the sixth guru (1606–1645), to arm and surround himself with bodyguards. The advice of Arjan was accepted, and henceforth the Sikhs were more militant and aggressive in their attitude toward their enemies.

The last of the Sikh gurus was Gobind Singh (1675–1708). He was given the leadership of the Sikhs when he was only a boy because his father, the ninth guru, had been imprisoned and executed by the Muslims. It was Gobind Singh, more than any other guru, who organized and prepared the Sikhs for self-defense and war. He introduced into Sikhism the worship of the terrible Hindu goddess of death, Durga. He also established the Granth as the final word for Sikhs. Since Sikhs were to be governed by the Granth there were no more gurus after Gobind Singh's death. Because of his love of weapons he is said to have introduced, as a religious ritual, the baptism of the sword. In order to strengthen his people further and prepare them for war he developed an elite class of Sikhs who made unusually fine warriors. This corps was known as Singhs ("Lions"). They were distinguished in the following ways: They wore the *kes* or long hair on their heads and faces; they adorned their hair with the *kangha* (comb); they wore *kachk* (short trousers); they wore a *kara* (steel bracelet); and they were equipped with *kirpan* (steel dagger). The members of this corps were not allowed the use of wine, tobacco, or any other form of stimulant. They were encouraged to eat meat. The order of the Singhs was open to men of all castes. These factors, combined with the theology of reincarnation, made the Singhs incredible warriors.

Gobind Singh, the last of the gurus, was assassinated in 1708. From that time until the present the Sikhs have been governed by their

Parade for the ninth Sikh guru. (*Courtesy of Diane M. Lowe.*)

scripture, the Granth, and their history has been full of strife. At certain times the Sikhs have been the victims of violence, and at other times they have been the aggressors. By the early nineteenth century they controlled most of the Punjab region. When the British sought to enter that area the Sikhs fought bloody wars against them but were finally subdued. Because of their valor as warriors the British came to admire and utilize the Sikhs as soldiers and policemen throughout India. However, with the departure of the British in the 1940s and with the partition of India into Hindu and Muslim states by the United Nations in 1947, the Sikhs were located in the Indian state of Punjab. There their numbers were only slightly larger than the Hindus.

DIVISIONS WITHIN SIKHISM

Modern Sikhs are found mainly in India, although there are Sikh communities in many other parts of the world. Within the main body of modern Sikhism there are three divisions. Each of these divisions accepts the central teachings of Nanak, each accepts the Granth as sacred scripture, and each accepts the ten gurus as inspired leaders of the faith.

The first sect is called the Udasis and is basically an order of holy men. These Sikhs follow many of the same principles and rules that govern the ascetics of Hinduism, Buddhism, and Jainism. They are celibate, and they wear coarse yellow garments like the Buddhist monks or go naked like Jain monks. Their only possession is a begging bowl. Unlike other Sikhs, the Udasis frequently shave their heads and beards. Often they are active missionaries, seeking to convince nonbelievers of the merit of their religion.

The second sect of Sikhs are the Sahajdharis ("conservative" or "slow-going"). Their development as Sikhs seems to have stopped at some point before Gobind Singh. They reject the militant stance that has become characteristic of much of Sikhism and prefer to be clean shaven.

The third sect is the Singhs, who already have been described.

SIKH RELIGIOUS LIFE

The religious life of the modern Sikh tends to be simple, probably because of the distrust of elaborate ceremonies that moved the early founders of this religion. One joins the Sikhs not by being born into a Sikh family but by undergoing a ritual of baptism when one is mature enough to accept it. In this ritual a bowl of sweetened water is

Golden Temple of Amritsar. Devout Sikhs try to visit the temple at least once during their lives. (*Courtesy of the United Nations.*)

stirred by a dagger, and the water is sprinkled upon the initiate as the initiate is instructed in the truths and prohibitions of the faith. Just as the initiatory ceremony of Sikhism is simple, so are the ceremonies surrounding marriage and death.

Daily rituals for a Sikh include an early morning bath, which is followed by the reading of certain hymns and the recitation of prayers. At night there is another ritual involving hymns and prayers. When Sikhs gather for congregational worship they meet in temples called *gurdwaras*. In these temples the central object of worship is a copy of the sacred Granth. Congregational worship involves prayers to the Granth, various hymns, a sermon, and a communional meal. There are no Sikh priests and the group services may be led by any member of the community. Also, there are no caste or sexual differentiations in worship. Men and women of all castes worship side by side.

An object of special attention to Sikhs all over the world is the *Takht* ("throne") of Sikhism at Amritsar. Although there are three other such thrones throughout the Sikh world, the one at Amritsar, within the golden temple, is central. It is here that the authorities of the Sikh world make decisions regarding the worship and practice of their people. Although Nanak specifically prohibited pilgrimages as worthless for true religion, most Sikhs like to go to Amritsar and plan to visit there at least once in their lives.

SIKHISM TODAY

The life of Sikhs has become increasingly precarious in India in the mid-1980s. In the Punjab region, the growth of Hindus and other religious groups has made the Sikhs again a minority group. Since they are neither Hindu nor Muslim, Sikhs lack the political strength of the major religions of India. Therefore radical factions in Sikhism have begun to demand that the Punjab be declared an independent Sikh nation. These strong feelings have led to armed conflict at times. The assassination of Prime Minister Indira Ghandi was attributed to one of her Sikh bodyguards. Her death led to several days of rioting against the Sikh people. This religion, born of the conflict between Hindu and Muslim, seems destined to remain in conflict.

STUDY QUESTIONS

1. Discuss Sikhism as a syncretism between Hinduism and Islam. Which features has it taken from each religion?

2. What factors were working to turn the pacific movement of Nanak into the warrior caste of later Sikhism?

3. List the three major sects of Sikhism. What are the major characteristics of each?

SUGGESTED READING

Archer, John Clark. *The Sikhs*. Princeton: Princeton University Press, 1946.

Fenton, John Y. *et al. Religions of Asia*. New York: St. Martin's Press, 1983. (See section on Sikhism.)

Singh, Harbans. *The Heritage of the Sikhs*. New York: Asia Publishing House, 1964.

The Japji

The following material,[3] which is called the *Japji*, is extremely important to Sikhs. It is to be memorized and recited each day and is believed to be essential to the understanding of all scripture. According to tradition, the *Japji* was written by Nanak, the founder of Sikhism.

A Book of Psalms of Guru Nanak Nirankari

Unity, Active Om, True Name!
Actor, Pervader, Fearless, devoid of Enmity,
Whom Time and the Ages do not cumber,
Self-existent, perceptible Guru—
Praise!
Pre-eminent Truth, primordial Truth,
Truth that is, saith Nanak, and will abide forever.

1. Thinking comprehendeth him not, although there be thoughts by the thousands,
   Silence discovers him not, though it be continuous silence;
   Man is persistently hungry, though he eats of tasty abundance;
   Not one of a hundred thousand artful devices avails him!
   How may the truth be attained, the bonds of falsehood be broken?
   By obeying the will of God as surely recorded, saith Nanak.

2. Forms have come of his order, but his order goes still undetected;
   Life has come by his will, through which comes life's exaltation.
   High and low are his will, and joy and sorrow his pleasure;
   In his will alone is he blessed who runs the round of his nature.
   All are subject to him, not one beyond his jurisdiction.
   If any perceives his will, he humbles himself, saith Nanak.

3. Some sing his power who themselves are feeble,
   Some sing his gifts—such as they may know;
   Some sing his attributes, his glory and his precepts,
   Some sing the substance of his vital wisdom:

   Some sing his altering of bodies into ashes,
   Some sing his gift of vitality to matter,

---

[3] The source material is taken from *The Sacred Writings of the World's Great Religions*, S. E. Frost, ed. (New York: McGraw-Hill, 1943), pp. 357–360.

Some proclaim him manifest, albeit at a distance,
Some sing him present and immediately beholding;

There is no end of the multitude of sayings—
Sayings, sayings by the million millions;
He bestows and men grow weary getting,
And go on eating, eating through the ages;

He goes on ever willing his good pleasure,
Making progress undismayed, saith Nanak.

4. The Lord is true, plainly known, his loving kindness infinite:
To those who crave and seek he gives, gives with full abandon.
What indeed must he be offered to throw his court wide open?
What words must lips be uttering to make his love responsive?

At deathless dawn give Sat Nam thought and glory,
Put on the garb of deeds—and salvation's way is open!
Be sure that he himself is fully true, saith Nanak.

5. He is not fabrication, nor subject to man's making.
Intrinsically devoid is he of passion;
Who does him homage meets in turn with honor.
Whoever sings and listens, heart-felt praise retaining,
His sorrows fade and he will dwell in blessing.

The Guru has a voice, speaks wisdom, teaches patience,
Whether he be Shiva, Vishnu, Brahmā, Parbati—
If indeed I knew him, would I not describe him?

Words are vain, but teach me the mystery, O Guru,
Of him who giveth life—such wisdom may I cherish!

6. At the place of pilgrimage no bath avails without his favor,
The whole creation that I see, it came of his exertion,
Counsel glows like priceless gems, if one harkens to the Guru.
Teach me the mystery, O Guru,
Of the life thou givest—such wisdom may I cherish!

7. To live four ages or even ten times longer,
Winning ninefold fame with every man's devotion,
Winning a good name through the whole earth published—
Lacking God's good grace, none will care about him.

A worm is but a worm, and sin rests on the sinner,
But he forgives, saith Nanak, adds virtue unto virtue—
No man exists who needs not added virtue.

8. Responding to the Name come lords, gods, saints and masters,
   The white bull earth and sky are made by harkening,
   Worlds, nether regions, islands came by harkening,
   Death itself is overcome by harkening.

   > Devotion leads to happiness, saith Nanak,
   > Sins and sorrow are destroyed by harkening.

9. Brahmā, Shiva and Indra came by harkening,
   Which prompts their lips the Gayatri to utter,
   Yoga skill and mystery come by harkening,
   By harkening come Vedic praise and wisdom.

   > Devotion leads to happiness, saith Nanak,
   > Sins and sorrow are destroyed by harkening.

10. Truth, knowledge and contentment come by harkening
    By harkening comes the bathing places' merit,
    Honor and the art of reading come by harkening,
    And by it the last stage of meditation.

    > Devotion leads to happiness, saith Nanak,
    > Sins and sorrow are destroyed by harkening.

11. By harkening one knows the avataras,
    The role of prelates, saints and rulers come by harkening,
    The blind find their own paths by harkening,
    By harkening streams impassable are forded.

    > Devotion leads to happiness, saith Nanak,
    > Sins and sorrow are destroyed by harkening.

12. His state is indescribable who keeps the Name in mind,
    He repents it afterwards who undertakes description,
    No use of pen or paper is availing,—
    Let them think it in the prose of meditation.

    > The Name is such to him devoid of passion,
    > He knows him in his heart on due reflection.

13. Wisdom comes and understanding by reflection,
    By reflection comes the knowledge of creation,
    Slights and slaps are nothing by reflection,
    Death's ties are cut asunder by reflection.

    > The Name is such to him devoid of passion,
    > Who knows him in his heart by due reflection.

14. One's path is rid of hindrance through reflection,
    Through reflection one appears at last with honor,
    By reflection one may journey quite unshaken
    And find companionship at last with Dharma.

    The Name is such to him devoid of passion,
    Who knows him in his heart by due reflection.

15. Salvation's doors are opened by obedience,
    And one may save his family by obedience,
    Obedience to the Guru gets salvation,
    Who obeys, saith Nanak, is ne'er a lifelong beggar.

    The Name is such to him devoid of passion,
    Who knows him in his heart by due reflection.

16. Some saints are genuine and some impostors,
    Some receive their honor at the threshold,
    Some saints shine at the gateway of the ruler,
    And some think sincerely of the Guru.

    Though thought and speech be far extended,
    This measures not the works of the creator,
    Not by the bull but by the law of mercy
    Joy becomes man's guardian and guidance.

    Who comprehendeth this hath truth discovered,
    Nor rests his burden faithless on the bull,
    There are so many earths, another and another,
    A burden far beyond his power to uphold it.

    Creatures, castes, of many shades of color,
    Have ever been described in varied phrase,
    Many who have known the art of writing
    Have written many essays on such themes.

    Impressive are the varied forms of beauty,
    Who knows the generous bounty of the whole?
    How many issues out of one source flowing—
    A hundred thousand rivers from one spring.

    > What mighty power for man to fix his thought on!
    > No self-denial comprehends it all,
    > To please thee is a man's best aspiration,
    > O thou who art eternal, ever dwelling in repose.

17. Countless repetitions, countless salutations,
    Countless genuflections and numberless tabus,

Countless recitations of the Vedic writings,
Yogis beyond number all indifferent to the world;

Countless devotees with minds intent on virtue,
Countless the generous and those who are sincere,
Countless warriors with their steel unflinching,—
Incomparable the minds in their silent, fixed attention.

What mighty power for one to fix his mind on!
No self-denial comprehends it all,
To please thee is man's best aspiration,
O thou who art eternal, dwelling ever in repose.

18. Countless the fools who are devoid of vision,
Countless the thieves with their illicit gain,
Countless the rulers who dispense their judgments,
Countless the assassins inflicting wanton pain;

Countless the sinners living in their sin,
Countless the liars tangled in their lies,
Countless the outcastes groveling in dirt,
Countless the slanderers whom all good men despise.

Nanak very humbly undertakes expression,
Saying self-denial is of slight avail;
To please thee is man's best aspiration,
O thou who art eternal, dwelling ever in repose.

19. Countless names and countless places,
Regions too numerous to name,
Countless praises humbly uttered,
Names and praises couched in written signs.
Knowledge, songs and recitation,
Writing, speaking—all the while by signs.
In symbol also is the tale of final union.

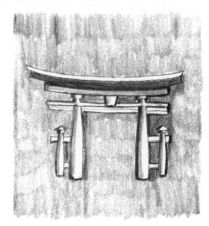

Religions Originating in China and Japan

*U*ntil fairly recent times the religions of China and Japan were relatively unknown to the Western world. However, the missionary movement and modern travel and communication technology have brought us the texts and traditions of Taoism, Confucianism, and Shinto. Within them are found a deep and very modern love for the beauty of nature and the family. Because of this, the Tao Tê Ching of Taoism has become one of the most read and quoted religious texts among college students in the late twentieth century. Today these religions seem to be in decline in the lands of their origin, and yet they have much to teach us.

CHAPTER 8

Chinese Religions

Portrait of Confucius. (*Courtesy of the Collection of the National Palace Museum, Taipei, Taiwan, Republic of China.*)

The Wise Man chooses to be last
And so becomes the first of all.
        —*Lao-Tzu*

It has been said that the Chinese people have no native religions; having been influenced by missionaries from Buddhism, Islam and Christianity, many Chinese have adopted these religions, giving them Chinese characteristics, but they have never developed a religion of their own. According to this argument, Taoism and Confucianism, which are native to China, are not truly religions but philosophies of life or systems of ethics. Indeed, Taoism and Confucianism lack many of the elements common to other religions of the world. In their purest forms they are more philosophy than religion. However, religious factors were added to them in later years, and therefore both Taoism and Confucianism deserve discussion in any text that describes the religions of the world.

Another aspect of Chinese religions the Western student may find puzzling is their syncretistic nature. The European or American finds it impossible to be an advocate of more than one religion at a time. The Christian may be tolerant of the views of a Jewish neighbor but could never say, "I am a Christian and I am a Jew," or "I am a Christian and I am a Muslim." The very nature of these religions makes it impossible to adhere to more than one of them at a time. This is not the case with Chinese religions. It is perfectly acceptable for the traditional Chinese to say that he or she is a Buddhist, a Taoist, and a Confucian. This is illustrated in the story of the emperor who asked a Buddhist scholar if he were a Buddhist. The scholar pointed to his Taoist cap. "Are you then a Taoist?" the emperor asked, and the scholar pointed to his Confucian shoes. "Are you then a Confucian?" he asked, and the scholar pointed to his Buddhist scarf. It is not at all unusual for a Buddhist priest to attend a Taoist temple and to memorize the teachings of Confucius. This willingness on the part of the Chinese to harmonize the teachings of widely diverse religions must have been maddening to Muslim and Christian missionaries.

Another element that makes the study of Chinese religions difficult for the modern student is that for the past forty years the government of China has been at best neutral and sometimes hostile to any form of religion. All missionaries have been excluded, and the teachings of Lao-tzu and Confucius have been suppressed as hostile to modern China. Therefore we are dealing with religions with which

196

we have had no direct contact for many years, and our sources are at least forty years old.

The history of religion in China falls into several broad categories. From earliest recorded history until the end of the Shang Dynasty in the eleventh century B.C., the Chinese people apparently followed a basically polytheistic religion intermingled with ancestor worship. From the development of the Chou Dynasty in the eleventh century B.C. until the beginning of the Christian era, the Chinese became aware of one supreme god above all other gods and spirits. The second period was also characterized by an emphasis upon morality, particularly the morality of the rulers. And this was the era that produced Lao-tzu, the legendary founder of Taoism, and Confucius. From the beginning of the Christian era until the eleventh century A.D. Buddhism and religious Taoism developed in China, and for the first time fully developed religious cults are to be found. The fourth general period of religious development extends from the eleventh century to the present. In this period we find an eclectic movement, bringing about a synthesis among Buddhism, Taoism, and Confucianism for most of the Chinese people.

BASIC CHINESE RELIGIOUS CONCEPTS

From earliest times the Chinese have held certain religious concepts and practices that later played a part in the development of the philosophies of Taoism and Confucianism. Although the ancient records are sketchy in their description of these concepts, we must examine them first in order to better understand Chinese religions.

The Recognition of Multiple Gods and Spirits

As already stated, the earliest religion of the Chinese people seems to have been based upon the recognition of many gods and spirits which controlled the universe. As it was in the case of many other basic religious groups, the ancient Chinese were apparently polytheistic and animistic in their understanding of the cosmos. The gods of the heavens and the earth received particular attention and sacrifice. In the spring and fall the emperors of ancient China performed elaborate and expensive sacrifices to the gods of the heavens and the earth. Many of these rituals were intended to incur the fertility of the soil and bountiful harvests. Lesser rulers and the common people also performed sacrifices to these spirits.

In addition to the major deities of heaven and earth, the Chinese also recognized several kinds of local deities and spirits. In general the beneficial spirits were known as *Shen*. They were to be found in the bright and lighted places of the earth and were associated with the sun and the spring. The evil spirits were known as *Kwei* and were associated with dark and gloomy places. Generally, the common people performed sacrifices and rituals that would put them on good terms with the Shen and keep them safe from the Kwei. Usually animals or grain were sacrificed, but there were occasional records of human sacrifice as the supreme offering to the deities. Archaeological investigations have revealed tombs of wealthy men that have contained the bodies of hundreds of servants and wives who were presumedly buried alive with their master. One record speaks of an emperor who was buried along with all of his wives who had failed to bear him children. One wonders if this was a matter of religious sacrifice or simple revenge. By the end of the Chou Dynasty in the pre-Christian era, this practice had ceased. Apparently, the practice of burying straw figures or paper likenesses of the victims was instituted as a substitute.

The Yin and the Yang

In searching for a principle to explain the true nature of the universe, the ancient Chinese philosophers developed the concept of the *yin* and the *yang*. What made the universe operate the way it did was understood to be a balance between these two forces. The yin was the negative force in nature. It was seen in darkness, coolness, femaleness, dampness, the earth itself, the moon, and the shadows. The yang was the positive force in nature. It was seen in lightness, brightness, warmth, maleness, dryness, and the sun. Traditionally, the yin and the yang were represented by this symbol:

No value judgment was placed upon the yin and the yang. No one said that *yin* was better than yang or vice versa. No philosopher said that *yang* was good and yin was evil. The interaction between yin and yang was simply the way the universe operated. Except for a few objects, such as the sun or the earth, which were clearly yin or yang, all the rest of nature, humankind, and even events were a combination of both forces. When these two forces were at work in harmony, life was what it should be.

Filial Piety and Ancestor Worship

A characteristic of the Chinese people throughout history has been their respect for and even veneration of aged members of the family. Perhaps the most difficult aspect of Chinese life for modern Western students to understand is this veneration of old age. The legendary founder of Taoism was named Li-poh-yang, but his disciples called him Lao-tzu, which means "Old Master" or "Old Boy." To the Chinese the term *old* or *aged* is not the sign of disrespect that it often is in many Western countries; rather it is the ultimate term of respect. To the Chinese, life may truly be said to begin at sixty, when a person reaches the age when he or she is respected. Historically, it is the aged father, mother, grandfather, or grandmother who dominates the Chinese home. It is the obligation of the children to support the elderly, to obey them, and to give them proper burial after their death. Even after the parents' death the child is obligated to maintain their grave site, to remember them and their deeds, and to offer sacrifices to them. Western students of Chinese life have often referred to this attitude as "ancestor worship." Indeed there is a religious aspect to these practices. Individuals revere their parents while they are alive and after they are dead. While they are alive the aged represent the wisdom of the family, and after their deaths they may be in a position to help the family further because of their contact with the spirit world. Therefore support of the dead ancestors with remembrance and sacrifices is essential. The Chinese who forget their ancestors are disgraces and will one day become homeless ghosts. Historically, the Chinese home is apt to have a small shrine or altar at which the names and deeds of many previous generations of the family are remembered and where small sacrifices of rice and wine may be offered.

Divination

Like many other basic religious groups, the early Chinese believed that the unity of the universe allowed future events to be predicted by some means. Whereas certain ancient religions sought out the future in the patterns of the flight of birds or in the entrails of sacrificed animals or in the ravings of various oracles, the ancient Chinese sought the future in the patterns of the shell of the tortoise or in the stalks of grain. The shell of the tortoise was thought to be especially in touch with the rhythms of the universe because of the long life of its inhabitant. Frequently the shell was heated, and the future was divined by the cracks that appeared in it. Divination among the ancient Chinese probably reached its peak in the development of a book called the *I Ching* (*The Book of Changes*), which was edited by Confucius and is still in use today. With the casting of coins or stalks of a plant, certain patterns emerge. By identifying these patterns among some sixty-four presented in the *I Ching,* a statement or prediction is evoked.

Development of Belief in the Shang Ti

Prior to the eleventh century B.C., the religious nature of the Chinese people was basically polytheistic, as previously described. In the eleventh century, however, certain political events affected the theology of the Chinese, perhaps for all time. In that century the Chou clans rebelled against the ruling Shang Dynasty. By the end of the century the Chou warriors had effectively completed the rebellion and began a new dynasty that was to rule China for several centuries. The Chou rulers began to assert that true rulership had to be based upon morality and religion. They further asserted that there was one supreme god who controlled the destinies of men and rulers. This god was Shang Ti, who had previously been regarded as the patron ancestor of the Shang Dynasty. The Chou rulers asserted that Shang Ti was more than an ancestor; he was the supreme god, and he had been responsible for the fall of the Shang Dynasty because of their immorality. Shang Ti was seen as the rewarder of good morality and the punisher of immorality, particularly among rulers. Therefore government had to be founded upon virtue. While Shang Ti might delight in elaborate sacrifice and ritual, he still loved morality more, and all the sacrifices in the world could not cover up evil. We read of his concern for morality in the ancient *Book of Documents* (*Shu Ching*).

> The capital of Shang was full of crime. [The king] was not distressed that the kingdom of Yin was ruined. Nor did he care that the fragrance of virtue should rise up from the sacrifices to plead with *T'ien* (*Shang Ti*). Instead the complaints of the people and the rank odour of drunken orgies were felt on high. Therefore *T'ien* determined to destroy Yin. It loved Yin no more, because of Yin's excesses. It is not *T'ien* that is cruel. It is people who bring evil on themselves.[1]
>
> His [King Wen] fame reached up to *Shang Ti* who blessed him. *T'ien* therefore bestowed its great command on King Wen to extirpate the dynasty of Yin, to receive the mandate, and take over its territories and people, that they might be well governed.[2]

[1] D. Howard Smith, *Chinese Religions* (New York: Holt, Rinehart and Winston, 1968), p. 15.
[2] Ibid.

Some scholars have suggested that the Chinese at this period were very close to developing an ethical monotheism similar to that enunciated by the Hebrew prophets in the eighth century B.C. However, the emphasis upon morality as a means of satisfying the high god remained in the hands of the rulers, and prophets never arose in this period of Chinese history. Nevertheless, the emperors of China held their thrones with one eye upon the heavens and a concern for personal morality and good government.

The Decline of the Feudal System

During the Chou Dynasty China had been organized and governed by a feudal system similar to that which existed in medieval Europe. The empire was divided into vassal states whose princes were subject to the emperor. The states in turn were subdivided into districts ruled by governors who were vassals to the princes. Each substate supported its lord financially while the lord in turn provided protection for the state. Society was then stratified into ranks. Members of the society knew their ranks and duties. They also knew who was above and below them.

In the five centuries between the eighth and third centuries B.C., the feudal system in China began to break down. Lords were no longer able to protect their vassals from invading armies. This led to the development of warlords who could provide protection and command respect. Serfs sometimes became landowners in these upsetting times. Merchant classes began to appear in the cities, and their economic power began to be felt. Old aristocratic families began to find themselves without either wealth or power. In general, the feudal world turned upside down. Into this era came the great Chinese schools, each with its own distinctive answer to the problems facing the nation. The Confucians dreamed of a restored idealized form of feudalism as the best government; the legalists wanted nothing to do with feudalism but wished for a strong centralized government; the Taoists wanted no government at all, or at least as little government as possible. It was out of this confused milieu that the great Chinese philosophy-religions were born.

TAOISM

Taoism is extremely difficult to define. It can be described in terms of its history and its effects upon the Chinese people, but it cannot be clearly delineated as a religion, with a certain body of doctrines and rituals, in the way Islam or Christianity can be described. Its origins are lost in the mists of Chinese antiquity. Little is known of its founder, and, indeed, there are those who even deny his existence. Its sacred book is more a brief poetical statement of philosophy than a scripture. The name *Taoism* is taken from the title of this book, *Tao Tê Ching*, and is probably best translated as "the way" or "the way of nature." In spite of this seemingly religious title the earliest teachers of Taoism were only vaguely theistic in their beliefs. By the early Christian centuries, however, Taoism had been converted into a religion complete with gods, priests, temples, and sacrifices. In modern China Taoism is mainly associated with charms, exorcisms, and magical attempts to prolong life. A philosophy of nature, a religion, a system of magical practices—Taoism is all of these.

The Life of Lao-tzu

Traditionally, the founder of Taoism is thought to be Lao-tzu, who lived in the sixth century B.C., although the basic philosophy of Taoism is probably much older. Little is known about Lao-tzu, and some scholars doubt that he was an historical figure. Legends about him state that he was born approximately fifty years before Confucius, and, according to Confucian materials, there was a meeting between the two. His original name was Li-poh-yang but he was given the title Lao-tzu ("Old Master" or "Old Boy") by his disciples as a title of respect. It is said that he was the keeper of royal archives in the court of the Chou Dynasty during the tumultuous period when order was breaking down. He tired of the artificial life in court and retired from his post. Journeying to the west, he reached a pass in the mountains at the northwest boundaries of China, where he sought to leave the country. The guard of the pass recognized the wise man and refused to allow him to leave until he had committed to writing the sum of his wisdom. Thereupon Lao-tzu sat down and wrote the Tao Tê Ching. When this was completed he was allowed to leave the country and was never seen again. The truth of this story has never been verified. Certainly we know less about the founder of Taoism than we know of any of the other founders of world religions.

The Tao Tê Ching

The book that Lao-tzu was supposed to have written in the sixth century B.C., the Tao Tê Ching, has become the most influential book in Chinese literature, except for the Analects of Confucius. The title literally means "The Classic of the Way and Its Power or Virtue." It is a small book, made up of slightly more than five thousand words contained in eighty-one chapters, and it is usually translated in poetical form. It has been the object of at least a thousand commentaries and has been translated into English more than forty times. In fact, it has been translated more times than any other book in the world except the Bible, and thus is probably the best known of all Chinese books.[3]

That the Tao Tê Ching was written by Lao-tzu in the sixth century B.C., as he waited to be allowed to leave China, has been the subject of much scholarly doubt for some time. It is generally agreed that the book was developed over many centuries and evolved into its present form sometime around the fourth century B.C. Arthur Waley suggests that the book was written in the third century B.C. as a polemic against the Confucians and Legalists who wished for either an idealized form of feudalism or some strong central government.[4] The theme of the Tao Tê Ching is that all of peoples' achievements are folly, especially elaborate government.

The Teachings of the Early Taoist Philosophers

The beliefs of the early Taoists are difficult to ascertain. Our two major sources for the Taoism of the pre-Christian era are of course the Tao Tê Ching and the writing of a fourth century B.C. disciple of Lao-tzu, Chuang-tzu. Chuang-tzu covered the field of Taoism as it was practiced by the early devotees. He collected this material into a book and used it to try to convince the Chinese to accept Lao-tzu instead of Confucius as their main teacher. The teachings of early Taoism as found in these books center around the following themes:

1. *The basic unity behind the universe is a mysterious and undefinable force called the Tao.* Usually the word *Tao* is defined as "the way," and it may best be understood in terms of "the way of the universe" or perhaps "nature's way." Yet the true Tao is impossible to define. The Tao Tê Ching begins with the following admonition:

> The Way (Tao) that can be told of is not an Unvarying Way (Tao);
> The names that can be named are not unvarying names.[5]

Nameless and undefinable though it may be, the Tao is the source of the universe.

> It was from the Nameless that Heaven and Earth sprang;
> The named is but the mother that rears the ten thousand creatures, each after its kind.[6]

---

[3] An exception to this may be the collected writings of Chairman Mao.
[4] Arthur Waley, *The Way and Its Power* (London: George Allen & Unwin, 1956), p. 86.
[5] Ibid., p. 141.
[6] Ibid.

Even the gods, along with all the rest of the universe, seem to have evolved from the flow of the Tao.

Though the Tao is defined as "the way," it is most often compared to a stream or a moving body of water as it progresses endlessly and inexorably. As water wears away the hardest stone or metal and carries off buildings in its path, it is useless to struggle against the Tao. Therefore, the ancient Taoist philosophers believed that all human-kind's accomplishments and monuments will sooner or later be destroyed by the Tao. Peoples' greatest buildings will fall into decay, their hard-won knowledge will be superseded, their wealth will fail, and even the sharpest sword will become dull. For this reason it behooved people not to struggle against the Tao but to seek to blend with it and be guided by it. True Taoists live quiet and simple lives. They avoid any achievement except that of seeking to understand the Tao.

2. *Life is the greatest of all possessions.* Because of their belief in the Tao as the source of all life and their belief in the folly of achievement, the early Taoist philosophers taught that life itself was the greatest of possessions; all others were doomed to decay. Fame, wealth, power, and education were mere flitting, transient illusions, literally here today and gone tomorrow. If people are not interested in the acquisition of goods, power, or education, then they can give their full attention to the enrichment of their own lives. This led the Taoists to search for a way whereby life might be lengthened, and eventually they employed various magical practices in an attempt to prolong and enrich life.

3. *Life is to be lived simply.* Believing that all life originated from the Tao, which would ultimately destroy peoples' achievements, the early Taoists turned their backs upon civilization with all its ills and benefits and sought to live as simply as possible. The Taoist philosophers may have carried this dream to its greatest extreme. They considered that education, wealth, power, family ties were all worthless and in fact impediments to living.

> Banish wisdom, discard knowledge,
> And the people will be benefited a hundredfold.
> Banish human kindness, discard morality,
> And the people will be dutiful and compassionate.
> Banish skill, discard profit,
> And thieves and robbers will disappear.
> If when these three things are done they find life too plain and unadorned,
> Then let them have accessories;
> Give them Simplicity to look at, the Uncarved Block to hold,
> Give them selflessness and fewness of desires.[7]

[7] Ibid., p. 166.

Ideally, individuals should turn their backs upon the advancements of civilization and live as simply and as quietly as possible. The word *innocence* characterizes the ideal state. Like the plants and the creatures of the earth, innocent human beings are content with what the Tao has ordained for them. According to early Taoist philosophers, there should be little government in the ideal state. In fact, it was an axiom of the Taoists that the least government is the best government. Lao-tzu is remembered for saying, "Govern a great nation as you would cook a small fish"—do not overdo it.[8] The small village is the ideal unit of society. The best ruler is the one who rules least and is virtually anonymous. If all this were the case, all strivings, quarrels, and wars would cease. Taoism is pacific, not out of any moral commitment to pacifism, but because warring is useless and wasteful. If a larger, stronger state wished the territory of the quiet Taoist village, the village should simply submit to the larger state. In the long run there will be no grief because of this decision, and the village ultimately will conquer the large state with its humility.

The early Taoists looked upon the innocence of the child as an ideal toward which all human beings should strive. The infant knows no craft; and has no ambitions but to live; yet the child is cared for, fed, and clothed. The weakness and softness of the infant are the ideals of Taoism.

4. *Pomp and glory are to be despised.* Because the Taoists were concerned with living according to the path of nature, i.e., as simply as possible, they despised the fame, pomp, and glory that most people seek. They saw such things as the cause of strife and discord in society. If each person were only content to live as the Tao intended, without seeking to rise above other people, then life would be as it was intended. This attitude also contained a condemnation of pride. It was a Chinese teaching, perhaps older than Taoism, that pride invited destruction, that the tree that stood taller than its neighbors would be the first felled by the woodsman. Therefore it is better to be humble, small, or imperfect than to stand out from all the rest.

> To remain whole, be twisted!
> To become straight, let yourself be bent.
> To become full, be hollow.
> Be tattered, that you may be renewed.
> Those that have little, may get more,
> Those that have much, are but perplexed.
> Therefore the Sage
> Clasps the Primal Unity,

---

[8] Herbert A. Giles, *Religions of Ancient China* (Freeport, N.Y.: Books for Libraries Press, 1969), p. 47.

Testing by it everything under heaven.
He does not show himself; therefore he is seen everywhere.
He does not define himself, therefore he is distinct.
He does not boast of what he will do, therefore he succeeds.
He is not proud of his work, and therefore it endures.
He does not contend,
And for that very reason no one under heaven can contend with him.
So then we see that the ancient saying "To remain whole, be twisted!"
    was no idle word; for true wholeness can only be achieved by return.[9]

Perhaps the best example of the Taoists' contempt for pomp, glory, rank, and wealth is the story of Chuang-tzu, the fourth century B.C. Taoist philosopher. Chuang-tzu was widely regarded for his wisdom and was offered the position of prime minister by Prince Wei of Ch'u. When the messengers of the prince brought this offer, Chuang is said to have replied in the following manner:

You offer me great wealth and a proud position indeed; but have you never seen the sacrificial ox? When after being fattened up for several years, it is decked with embroidered trappings and led to the altar, would it not willingly then change places with some uncaring pigling? . . . Begone! defile me not! I would rather disport myself to my own enjoyment in the mire than be a slave to a ruler of a state. I will never take office. Thus I shall remain free to follow my own inclinations.[10]

History does not record the response of the prince whose offer was spurned with such contempt.

There is little in this early form of Taoism that can be called religion. The Tao itself is a vague and impersonal force behind the universe and is more of a First Cause than a god, in any traditional sense of the word. In one translation of the Tao Tê Ching the word *god* is used only once,[11] and in many translations it does not appear at all. Only rarely does the term *heaven* appear. The Tao is not conceived of as a force to whom one can pray or sacrifice, and the early Taoists seem to have had no rituals for worship. In fact, they may have been rejecting religion and all its accoutrements as a part of their rejection of the Confucians, who placed a very high value upon rituals.

The early Taoists also seem to have had little concern for life after death. One of the most frequently remembered tales of Chuang-tzu

---

[9] Waley, *The Way and Its Power,* p. 177.
[10] D. Howard Smith, *Chinese Religions* (New York: Holt, Rinehart & Winston, 1968), p. 71.
[11] "How pure and still the Tao is. I do not know whose song it is. It might appear to have been before God." *The Sacred Books of the East,* James Legge, trans. vol. XXXIX (Oxford: Clarendon Press, 1891), p. 50.

此是老君爺手托八卦面放金
爐鐵行人供之

Watercolor of Lao-Chün. The inscription reads, "This is Lao-Chün, worshiped by ironsmiths." (*Courtesy of Philadelphia Museum of Art; Photography by A. J. Wyatt, Staff Photographer.*)

concerns an occasion following his wife's death. His disciples sought to comfort him in his time of mourning but found him singing and beating time on a wooden bowl.

> "To live with your wife," exclaimed Hui-tzu, "and see your eldest son grow up to be a man, and then not to shed a tear over her corpse—this would be bad enough. But to drum on a bowl and sing; surely this is going too far!" "Not at all," replied Chuang-tzu. "When she died I could not help being affected by her death. Soon, however, I remembered that she had already existed in a previous state before her birth, without form or even substance; that while in that unconditioned condition, substance was added

to spirit; that this substance then assumed form; and that the next state was birth. And now, by virtue of a further change, she is dead, passing from one phase to another like the sequence of spring, summer, autumn and winter. And while she is thus lying asleep in eternity, for me to go about weeping and wailing would be to proclaim myself ignorant of these natural laws. Therefore I refrain."[12]

In general, the Taoists were concerned about the quality of life as it is lived on a day-to-day basis, without much interest in the heavens, the gods, rituals, or life after death.

Schools that Rivaled the Early Taoists

The fourth and third centuries B.C. were eras of chaos in China. The old governmental structure of feudalism was breaking down; invaders regularly made inroads into the country; the social order was in a state of flux; and the ancient systems of values were seriously being questioned. The Taoist philosophers and their challenge to existing values and structures were, of course, a part of that era. Other philosophers, politicians, and teachers held other views of life and government and toured the nation. According to Arthur Waley,

> Every Court in China was infested by "journeying philosophers" each in turn pressing upon a bewildered ruler the claims of Activism, of Quietism, of morality, of non-morality, of force, of non-resistance, of individualism, of State supremacy. In one thing only were they united; each claimed to possess the secret "art of ruling" whereby the Ancestors had grown mighty in the past.[13]

In addition to the Taoists there were three major schools of thought that were dominant in those days. These were the Confucians, the Legalists, and the Mohists.

The Confucians.   More will be said about the school of Confucius in the following section. However, it must be noted here that its members were rivals to the Taoists, in the fourth and third centuries (B.C.) in advising the rulers of China on government. Whereas the Taoists believed that the least government was the best government, the disciples of Confucius believed that an idealized feudal system was the best form of government. Whereas the Taoists had little use for formal religion, the Confucians at least believed that the rites and rituals of religion served the function of uniting the people. Whereas the Taoists believed that the best society was one with little structure,

[12] Ibid., p. 73.
[13] Waley, *The Way and Its Power*, p. 70.

the Confucians taught that society needed an elaborate structure, reinforced by etiquette, to be effective.

The Legalists.   A second group that vied for the attention of the rulers of China during this period was a large one that followed no specific teacher; its members were known as "Legalists" or "Realists." These people believed that human nature and the condition of China at the time demanded strong, tough leadership. To them, human nature tended to be wicked and lazy. People followed the line of least resistance. If left to their own devices, people would make decisions that would be bad for society as a whole. Therefore government should be run under what Westerners might call Machiavellian principles. Government should not be affected by morality or pity. People do not need love or pity . . . they need food and houses. Thus leaders of government should determine what is best for the majority of society and take the hard steps necessary to achieve these ends. If this means hardship for the minority, it should not affect the decisions. In their scheme of things the Legalists had no room for religion. Money and time spent on sacrifices to the gods could be better spent on good government. Naturally, these teachers had little in common with the passive Taoist sages.

The Mohists.   The third group that sought to influence government during the fourth and third centuries were the Mohists. These teachers were disciples of Mo-tzŭ, who lived in the fifth century B.C. (ca. 468–390). Mo-tzu began his career as a Confucian but later broke away to form his own distinctive philosophy. He and his disciples believed that the best government operates under the direction of the traditional Chinese religions. Under these religions people are taught to love one another; thus, the government would operate from a position of love. The Mohists were pacifists, who despised warfare, yet they recognized the necessity of self-defense and allowed the possibility of building fortifications.

   Though there were probably many representatives of each of these distinct philosophies, it is doubtful that any of them had serious influence on the governors of China, except perhaps the Legalists. Nevertheless, the teachings of the Taoists, the Confucians, and the Mohists have been held up as ideals for the Chinese people—in a strange eclecticism—for thousands of years.

The Later Development of Taoism

Basically, Taoism as it is seen in the Tao Tê Ching and in the essays of Chuang-tzu was concerned with living life in harmony with the basic force behind nature, the Tao. As a pure philosophy this appealed to a small group of persons who were malcontent with the intricacies of society and government, but it probably never had wide appeal to the populace.

However, after the period of the early philosophers, Taoism did develop wide appeal for the masses and is frequently listed among the major religions of the world. This development from a philosophy for the few to a religion for the many is a fascinating story.

Following the period of the early Taoist philosophers, two kinds of Taoists seem to have developed. One group followed the philosophical writings of Lao-tzu and Chuang-tzu. The second group were searching for immortality, not in the sense of life after death as taught by many other religions, but in an endless extension of the present life through various devices. The philosophers had taught that life was the greatest of all possessions and that the person whose life was properly attuned to the Tao might have long life. This appealed to the Chinese people, who look forward to old age and the relative ease and honor that it has traditionally brought in Chinese culture. Taking up this aspect of Taoism, scholars, priests, and magicians began to seek the means whereby life could be extended indefinitely. They sought every possible means, including special dietary regulations. Some came to believe that all foods, particularly solid foods, were poisonous and tried to train their bodies to live on only a very little liquid food. Some claimed that eventually they were able to live on only saliva and air. Others practiced fasting and breath control, in a manner similar to that of the Indian Yogin.

Still another popular means of extending life was the use of alchemy. Some believed that since dead meat could be preserved from decay by salt, living flesh might be preserved by some other mineral, such as gold. One can only guess at the outcomes of some of these experiments in longevity. Nevertheless the hope that immortality might be achieved did not die among the Chinese. Regarding one of the leaders of these movements, it was said by a contemporary:

> He abstained from cereals, escaped old age, knew the method to avoid dying, and transmuted cinnabar. When he died, it was said that he had been transformed and, on opening the tomb several years later, they found no corpse there but only his cap and clothing.[14]

The Taoist alchemist seeking to work his magic soon became concerned with gods that might be involved in the process. Since the alchemists worked at the stove, they began to offer sacrifices to the god of the stove, Tsao Chun. Thus it is said that Tsao Chun, by the

[14]Smith, *Chinese Religions,* p. 100.

third century A.D., became the first god of Taoism. The process of apotheosis continued until there were many, many Taoist gods. And so a philosophy that began by essentially denying personal gods developed its own gods.

By the second century A.D., the Tao Tê Ching had been officially recognized as a Chinese classic and soon was on its way to becoming the Taoist scripture. Those who were seeking immortality came to believe that the only way they could achieve this was through the practice of morality and virtuous deeds toward their fellow human beings. Thus the elements found in most religions gradually began to creep into Taoism.

Also in the second century the Han Dynasty, which had ruled China for several centuries, began to break down. During this time of chaos there arose certain charismatic Taoist leaders. Several of these people not only led in the search for immortality but also gathered together great armies of followers and participated in wars in a most un-Taoist fashion. With the organization that these people brought, with the concern for faith healing, the search for immortality, and the other religious accoutrements of gods, morality, temples, priests, rituals, and so on, Taoism became one of the religions, if not *the* religion, of the masses of the Chinese people by the beginning of the third century A.D.

Since there were contacts between India and China from very early times, and since Buddhism under the influence of Asoka had become a missionary religion, doubtless there were Buddhist missionaries and traders in China as early as the third century B.C. However, the early contacts the Chinese had with Buddhism were with its Theravada branch. It is likely that this version of Buddhism, with its emphasis on individual salvation through a monastic life, was far too Indian for the Chinese, and therefore it made little headway in China. In later years there came the development of Mahayana Buddhism, with its rich rituals, its many gods, its heavens and hells, and its promise of salvation through more traditional religious means. There also came extraordinary missionaries, such as the legendary Bodhidharma, who brought the *dhyana* version of Mahayana Buddhism from India to China in the fifth century A.D. In China, as in most Asian nations, this version of the teachings of the Buddha appealed tremendously to the masses.

By the fourth century A.D. Mahayana Buddhism was a force to be reckoned with by the Taoists. At first, there seems to have been no rivalry between the two religions. The Taoists helped the Buddhists translate their texts into Chinese, and the Buddhists used Taoist terms to explain Buddhist concepts. However, as Buddhism became more popular among the Chinese people the Taoists began to recognize it as a threat. Fierce struggles arose between the two groups to determine who would have influence with the various rulers and thus control the provinces. In a most uncharacteristic fashion each religion became hostile to the other, and even persecution developed. In the ninth century the emperor Wu Tsung, who was greatly influenced by Taoist priests, ran a vast persecution of the Buddhists, destroying numerous temples. At other times Buddhists influenced the rulers to discriminate against the Taoists.

The struggle between the Buddhists and the Taoists was settled more by syncretism than by persecution. Each religion borrowed from the other until they both became associated, along with the teachings of Confucius, as the common religion of the Chinese people. Taoism borrowed widely from the Mahayana teachings of an afterlife with heavens and hells and judgment. The Buddhists followed their traditional pattern of accepting the native gods and heroes of the land as Buddhist bodhisattvas, and the Taoists sought to turn the tables by asserting that Lao-tzu and others were created before the foundations of the earth and were thus superior to the Buddha. All in all the Taoists seem to have copied the most. By the sixth century A.D., the Taoists had taken the Buddhist pattern of monasticism. Their priests could now live in monasteries and in some cases were commanded to be celibate. Nunneries were established for the Taoist women who wished the celibate life. By the tenth century the shape of Taoism was established, and it changed little during the next ten centuries.

Taoism, with its religious side fully developed and with its traditional emphasis upon magical means of extending life, continued to have its hold upon the common people of China into the twentieth century. The upper classes and the intellectuals of China continued to read the Tao Tê Ching and other classics of philosophical Taoism, but they tended to regard the religion itself as fit only for the ignorant masses.

CONFUCIANISM

Since Confuciansim is generally considered to be one of the major religions of the world, it might be appropriate to discuss it in a separate chapter rather than include it as a part of a general chapter on the religions of China. However, in its origins and development, Confucianism, like Taoism, is inextricably interwoven into the total philosophy of the Chinese people. Therefore, to lift Confucianism out and set it into a chapter apart from Taoism and Chinese religious thinking would be to present it in an unreal situation.

As in the case of Taoism we begin the discussion of Confucianism by asking if it is truly a religion. There are those who contend that the teachings of Confucius and his disciples were never intended to be a religion, that Confucius was probably an atheist who discouraged prayer to the gods as worthless, and whose main concern was the nature of human society. If Confucianism is a religion, it is a very different kind of religion. It has no priesthood; its sacred writings, although terribly important, have never been considered a revelation from the gods like the Vedas or the Quran; it has frowned upon asceticism and monasticism; and it has no doctrine of an afterlife. In spite of all of these nonreligious aspects there have been some cultic developments in the history of Confucianism, and its philosophy has deeply affected the Chinese character. Therefore Confucianism deserves at least to be inspected as a possible world religion.

The Life of Confucius

The man whom the West knows as Confucius was really named Kung. When he became a famous teacher his disciples referred to him as Kung, the master (Kung Fu-tse). As his teachings became known to Western missionaries and scholars, the name was Latinized to "Confucius."

Although Confucius was born in the sixth century B.C., because of the influence that he and his disciples had upon the Chinese people, the biographical material about him is extensive and fairly reliable. This is in marked contrast to the life of Lao-tzu, who also lived in the sixth century but about whom we know almost nothing. The earliest and most authentic material about Confucius is the Analects of Confucius, a collection of his teachings that was compiled about seventy years after his death. In addition to the biographical material in Confucian literature, Confucius is mentioned in the writings of the contemporary Taoists and Mohists. No one seriously doubts the historicity of Confucius.

Confucius was born in 551 B.C. in the state of Lu (now in modern Shantung). He was the child of an aristocratic family which had lost its wealth and position in the decline of the feudal states of China during that chaotic period. His father was said to have been a famous warrior, of gigantic size and strength, who was seventy years old when Confucius was conceived. The father died shortly before the birth of the child, and Confucius was reared in poverty by his widowed mother. Although his mother had to struggle for survival, she was determined to provide her son with an education. Therefore Confucius was allowed to study with the village tutor. The biographies say that he studied subjects that were the traditional fare of Chinese students of his time: poetry, the history of China, music, hunting, fishing, and archery. He seems to have been extremely interested in the inter-workings of society even as a youth; particularly in what constituted good government. This was to be his main theme for the rest of his life.

In his late teens he accepted a minor position in government, where he was to closely observe the ruling process. He married and fathered one son but the marriage ended in divorce. We know little about the wife or family of Confucius beyond these scanty facts. However, there are still Chinese today who claim to be the physical descendants of Confucius. While in his mid-twenties his mother died, and, being the devoted son that he was, Confucius mourned for her for three years.

Sometime during his twenties Confucius began his true career, that of a teacher. His reputation as a man of learning allowed him to es-tablish himself as a teacher of young people. In the following years his reputation spread widely and he attracted many students. They lived in his home and followed him in his journeys. He taught them history, the principles of good government, and divination.[15]

Legend has it that at the age of fifty Confucius was finally able to put some of his principles of good government into practice when he was asked to join the government of the Duke of Lu, as its prime minister. According to these pious Confucius legends, Confucius's government was ideal. During the period of his leadership the state was so well governed that the crime rate dropped to almost nothing. People stopped locking their doors and a wallet dropped on the street was left untouched for days. However, the enemies of Confucius be-came jealous of his success and conspired against him. Consequently he was forced to retire from government at the age of fifty-five.

During the next twelve years of his life Confucius was a man with-out a position. He wandered from place to place with a few of his faithful disciples. Sometimes he was accepted by the populace and treated hospitably. At other times he and his friends were jeered at and even placed in jail. Finally, when he was sixty-seven years of age, a position was found for him as an advisor to the Duke of Ai. While this was not as important as the position he had formerly held, it at least gave Confucius a home for himself and his disciples. During the next years he spent his time teaching and compiling some of the clas-sical Chinese texts. The master died in the year 479 B.C. and was widely mourned by his disciples. According to one tradition, his most faithful disciple built a hut beside the grave and stayed to mourn Confucius for three years.

---

[15] The principal form of divination taught by Confucius was probably the Chinese clas-sic, the *I Ching*. Current versions of the *I Ching* are believed to have been edited by Confucius.

Confucius' birthday ceremony at Taipei, Taiwan. (*Courtesy of the Chinese Government Information Service.*)

The Teachings of Confucius

Confucius's attitude toward religion has been a point of great debate; on the one hand, some regard him as the founder of one of the world's great religions, and on the other, there are those who believe that he was an agnostic, if not an atheist. The truth about Confucius's teachings on religion probably lies somewhere between the two extremes. Relative to his contemporaries he was somewhere in the middle of the spectrum, with Lao-tzu on the left, denying the validity of religions, and Mo-tzŭ on the right, advocating a return to the ancient religions of China.

Confucius seems to have believed that, while the gods existed and worship and rituals were of value in bringing people together, these things were of secondary importance when compared to an equitable social order. When praying to the spirits interfered with a person's proper social duties, prayer should be secondary. His attitude seems to have been that, ideally, one should respect the spirits but keep them at a distance.[16] Even though Confucius was not an atheist or antireligious, there is no evidence to suggest that he was interested in starting a religion. In the strictest sense of the word, Confucianism cannot be called a religion. Rather, it is a system of ethics, a theory of government, a set of personal and social goals that have deeply influenced the Chinese for almost twenty-five centuries.

The teachings of Confucius were based on certain central themes. One of these themes is represented by the word *li*. *Li* has been variously translated into English as "propriety," "rites," "ceremonies," and "courtesy." Originally it may have meant the grain found in wood or the pattern in jade. Basically, the word seems to mean "the course of life as it is intended to go," and of course it has religious and social connotations. When society lives by *li*, it moves smoothly. Men and women respect their elders and superiors. The proper rituals and ceremonies are preformed. Everything and everyone is in its proper place. Naturally the principle of *li* was most closely followed when an idealized form of feudalistic government existed. In such a state all people know their superiors and inferiors and are able to act in the genteel manner that Confucius believed was necessary for a smooth society. Furthermore, Confucius believed that China in his day was in a state of chaos because the people were no longer living according to the principles of *li*.

One of the Confucian classics, the *Li Chi*, whose primary subject is *li*, records the following conversation:

> Duke Ai asked Confucius, "What is the great *li?* Why is it that you talk about *li* as though it were such an important thing?"
>
> Confucius replied, "Your humble servant is really not worthy to understand *li*."
>
> "But you do constantly speak about it," said Duke Ai.
>
> Confucius: "What I have learned is this, that of all the things that people live by, *li* is the greatest. Without *li*, we do not know how to conduct a proper worship of the spirits of the universe; or how to establish the proper status of the king and the ministers, the ruler and the ruled, and the elders and the juniors; or how to establish the moral relationships between the sexes; between parents and children, and between brothers; or how to distinguish the different degrees of relationships in the family. That is why a gentleman holds *li* in such high regard.[17]

---

[16] *The Analects of Confucius*, Arthur Waley, trans. (London: Allen & Unwin, Ltd., 1938), 6:20.

[17] *Li Chi*, XXVII.

According to Confucius, there were five basic relationships in life. If *li* were present in these relationships throughout society, then the social order would be ideal. These five relationships are:

1. *Father to son.* There should be kindness in the father and filial piety in the son.
2. *Elder brother to younger brother.* There should be gentility in the elder brother and humility in the younger.
3. *Husband to wife.* There should be righteous behavior in the husband and obedience in the wife.
4. *Elder to junior.* There should be consideration among the elders and deference among the juniors.
5. *Ruler to subject.* There should be benevolence among the rulers and loyalty among the subjects.

In Confucian ideals the principle of *li* was the outward expression of the superior man toward others in his society. The inward expression of Confucian ideals was called *jen. Jen* is frequently translated into English with words such as "love," "goodness," and "humaneness." According to Confucius, only the great sages of antiquity truly possessed *jen,* but it was a quality that all men should seek to develop. The pursuit of this quality is mentioned many times in the Analects of Confucius.

Jen is of more importance to people than fire and water. I have seen men die through walking through water or fire, but I have never seen a man die through walking in *jen.*[18]

Jen is self-denial and a return to propriety (*li*). For by self-denial and a return to propriety the whole world would return to *jen.*[19]

Thus Confucius taught that people should love one another and practice respect and courtesy toward each other in their daily lives. He did not go so far as Jesus did and command that people should exchange good for evil, nor did he command, "So whatever you wish that men would do to you do so to them. . . ."[20] Rather Confucius taught that society was best served when people acted toward each other with reciprocity (*shu*).

[18] Analects 15:34.
[19] Ibid., 12:1.
[20] Matthew 7:12. This quotation and those that follow are from the *Revised Standard Version of the Bible* (New York: Thomas Nelson & Sons, 1952).

Tzu Kung asked: "Is there any one word that can serve as a principle for the conduct of life?"

Confucius said: "Perhaps the word, 'reciprocity': Do not do to others what you would not want others to do to you."[21]

If the principles of *li* and *jen* were present and operative in a person, the end product is the Confucian goal, the superior human being. Apparently Confucius believed in the natural goodness, or at least in the natural perfectibility, of humankind, although it is not so clear in his teachings as it is in the work of his disciple Mencius. This teaching places the Confucians in direct contrast to those philosophies—such as Christianity—that believe people's natural state is evil and needs divine intervention for salvation. Confucius apparently believed that under the proper circumstances it was possible for individuals to achieve goodness and to eventually achieve the status of the superior human being.

One of the circumstances necessary for persons to achieve goodness was a good government. Confucius believed that poor government with bad laws caused people to do evil, and that a generation of good rulership can cure most of the moral ills of a people. A good example set by the ruling classes will bring out the true morality of the people. Because of the natural morality of humanity, Confucius believed that it was not necessary to offer people rewards or punishments in order to induce them to good conduct. Good conduct is its own reward. Therefore, whatever Confucius might have believed about the gods, he never spoke of an afterlife in heaven or hell to reward good deeds or punish evil. Under the proper conditions, people simply grow and develop into what Confucius called the "Superior Man."

The Development of Confucianism

When Confucius died in 479 B.C., his teachings were remembered and followed by only a small group of disciples. He had not had the success as a ruler he had hoped for, and his teachings had not received widespread support. Nor did the rulers of China open their doors to his immediate disciples. However, in the next five hundred years the disciples of Confucius began to take a major part in training and advising the rulers of China, to such an extent that his teachings became an integral part of Chinese culture.

After the death of Confucius approximately seventy of his disciples scattered out across the empire. Some sought positions as advisor to rulers while others tried to begin schools of their own. They were not

[21] Analects 15:23.

spectacularly successful in either of these attempts, for at least two reasons. First, there was the opposition of the rival schools, the Taoists, the Legalists, and later the Mohists, who all claimed to have the key to good government for the official who would listen. Second, the disciples of Confucius taught that the best form of government was an idealized feudalism, and they were teaching this in a time when the feudal society was breaking down all over China. They were out of step with their time. Nevertheless the disciples did manage to reach a few attentive ears with both their teaching and their advising, and Confucius's teaching was perpetuated. In the fourth and third centuries B.C. there arose two of the most outstanding Confucians of all times, Mencius and Hsün Tzŭ, who did much to popularize and spread the teachings of Confucius.

In Chinese thought the sage of China second only to Confucius is Confucius' latter-day disciple, the man who is known to us as Mencius.[22] Mencius was born approximately one hundred years after the death of Confucius and lived from 372–289 B.C. We are not certain about a great many details in his life, but like many of the ancients there is an abundance of legend about him. Much of the legendary material about Mencius apparently is intended to draw parallels between him and Confucius. We are told that, like Confucius, Mencius was the only child of a poor widow who struggled to support her son and to provide him with education. Like Confucius, Mencius became a teacher and sought a position as a political advisor. Also, like his master, his advice was not wanted, and he too wandered about teaching his disciples. More substantial tradition says that Mencius studied under the disciples of Tzu Ssu, the grandson of Confucius, and was in fact an ineffective advisor to some of the Chinese rulers of his day.

The teachings of Mencius have been maintained in the Book of Mencius. From this text and others his contribution as a Confucian scholar can be learned. Like Confucius, Mencius was not terribly interested in religion. Little is said about the gods in his writings, and no attempt is made to influence people to return to the worship of the traditional Chinese gods. Mencius's major ethical position was a reinforcement of Confucius's teaching of the natural goodness of human beings. Whereas this teaching had not been terribly clear in Confucius, it become crystal clear in Mencius. The latter strongly asserted that human nature was basically good. He observed that all people did not act in a virtuous manner, but this is because of their environment. Given the proper environment, it is possible for all peo-

---

[22] His real name was Meng and his private name K'o, but his Chinese name has been Latinized by Western scholars to Mencius.

ple to be virtuous. Naturally, for a Confucian scholar the best environment is that which occurred in a government based upon paternalistic feudalism that was operated for the benefit of the people. Thus he distinguished between the feudal tyrant and the sage-king.

> He is a tyrant who uses force while making a show of benevolence. To be a tyrant, one must have a large kingdom at one's command. He is a true king who practises benevolence in a virtuous spirit. To be a true king, one need not wait for a large kingdom. T'ang ruled over seventy square *li*, and King Wen over a hundred. When men are subdued by force, it is not their hearts that are won but their strength that gives out. When men are won by goodness, their hearts are glad within them and their submission is sincere.[23]

Since war destroyed the possibility for the kind of just and honorable conditions under which human goodness could develop, Mencius was opposed to war. On the other hand, since people were the most important element in any state, if the government were oppressive Mencius believed that persons had the right to revolt against it. In many ways Mencius sharpened the focus of Confucius's teachings, and in other ways he added his own distinctive ideas to the Confucian canon.

The second most famous Confucian interpreter was Hsŭn Tzŭ, who lived in the generation after Mencius (298–238 B.C.). Whereas Mencius has come to be regarded as the orthodox interpreter of Confucius, Hsŭn Tzŭ is regarded as the heterodox interpreter; yet Hsŭn Tzŭ had a greater impact upon his times. Some authorities even give him credit for the development of Confucianism during the Han Dynasty (206 B.C.–220 A.D.).[24] He was a native of Chao and a widely respected and revered scholar. In his later years he served as a magistrate of the city of Lan-Ling. Beyond these bare facts we know little about the man.

Hsŭn Tzŭ is remembered for two major contributions to Confucian thought. First, he, even more than Confucius himself, believed in the worth of rites (*li*) as devices that would bring people together and educate them.

> What is the origin of rites? I say: Man is born with desires. If he does not get what he desires, he can but seek for it. If there are no degrees or limits to his seeking, he can but contend with others. Contention leads to disorder and disorder leads to exhaustion. As ancient kings hated such disorder, they established rites and moral principles to bring about the proper shares in order to nourish men's desires and meet their demands. They

[23] *The Sacred Writings of the World's Great Religions.* S. E. Frost, ed. (New York: McGraw-Hill, 1943), p. 114.
[24] D. Howard Smith, *Chinese Religions*, p. 54.

made it possible that men's desires did not exhaust the material supplies and the material supplies did not suppress the desires. Both desires and material supplies support each other and thus grew. This is how rites originated. . . .[25]

The second contribution of Hsŭn Tzŭ, and the one for which he is more famous, is his denial of the basic goodness of humankind. In direct contradiction to the teachings of Mencius, Hsŭn Tzŭ contended that people were basically evil in nature. He believed that goodness can only come through proper training. Therefore training, laws, and restraint are necessary in order that society might survive. This made rites all the more important, because it is through rites that people are trained in proper living. Added to this teaching was Hsŭn Tzŭ's belief that the spirits of the heavens were basically impersonal forces. For this reason Hsŭn Tzŭ appears as the most nonreligious of all the early Confucian scholars.

The rise of the Han Dynasty marked a new era in Chinese history. The period preceding it had been one of chaos and political upheaval. When the Han rulers came to power they needed great numbers of new administrators and advisors. This new market for political theorists attracted many scholars who had been trained by the disciples of Confucius. The Confucians' position was further strengthened when in 136 B.C. they were placed in charge of the education of Chinese youth, particularly those youth who would eventually govern. From that date until 1905 A.D. Chinese education included a study of the teachings of Confucius. Master Kung himself could not have devised a system in which his philosophy would have had more influence over the future of China.

In addition to the development of Confucianism as the leading educational theory of China, in the years of the Han Dynasty there developed a cult of Confucius himself. The ruler of the state of Lu is said to have mourned for Confucius after his death and built a shrine to him. However, with the coming of the Han rulers and the ascendancy of the Confucian scholars the reverence for him increased dramatically. In 195 B.C., the first of the Han emperors visited the grave of Confucius and offered a pig, a sheep, and an ox as sacrifices. Fifty years later a temple was built to Confucius in his native town. By 8 B.C. titles and land were given to his descendants. The practice of awarding posthumous titles to Confucius himself began, and he was given the title of Duke. Gradually the temples and the ceremonies increased in number all over China. By the sixth century A.D. every prefecture in China had a temple to Confucius, and some people came

---

[25] Hsŭn Tzŭ, Chapter 19.

to look upon him as a god. However, there never developed a popular religion about Confucius. He was generally regarded as the patron saint or ancestor of the Chinese scholar, and he was remembered and revered as one would remember any ancestor.

The growth of the Confucian cult was set back in 1503, when the images of Confucius were ordered removed from the temples and replaced with wooden tables upon which were inscribed his teachings. In addition, all the titles that had been given were removed, and he was known simply as "Master Kung, the perfect teacher of antiquity." In 1906 there was an attempt to restore the Confucian cult to some of its original glory, but with the birth of the People's Republic of China the sacrifices to Confucius, along with the other "great sacrifices," were abandoned.

TAOISM AND CONFUCIANISM TODAY

Prior to 1949, those religions and philosophies which might be called "native" to China, i.e., Taoism and Confucianism, had for all practical purposes ceased to be influential in Chinese life. The writings of Confucius and the *Tao Tê Ching* continued to be read by a few intellectuals, but the temples, altars, and priests of their cults had fallen into disuse and disrepair. Taoism maintained some kind of a foothold among the rural people by virtue of its magical properties and festivals. The dominant religions of China prior to 1949 were those that had been imported from outside. These were Buddhism, Christianity, and Islam.

In 1949 China underwent a revolution and became the People's Republic of China, under the direction of Marxist government. The official attitude of this government toward religion was that it was a vestige of the feudal past and would gradually fade away from a modern society. Theoretically at least, the government allowed freedom of religious belief. However, Taoism and Confucianism were regarded with great suspicion since Confucianism seemed so clearly tied to the feudalism of the past and Taoism was seen as superstition. Buddhism was viewed as a religion that had been brought in from outside nations and was therefore suspect. Christianity was clearly tied to the imperialistic Western nations. Therefore nearly all Christian missionaries were expelled from China by 1952. Islam was a more delicate matter for the new government. Most Muslims in China lived in the western part of the nation and were members of various minority ethnic groups. Even though Islam was clearly a religion that had been brought in from outside China, the government of the People's Republic could not afford to be too harsh in supressing it for fear of offending Muslims in the Middle East and in African nations.

In spite of the official government position, in the years following 1949 many temples, mosques, and churches were closed down or converted to other uses. Christians were required to join together in the so-called "Three-Self Movement"[26] to insure against foreign intervention or control. Generally, post-1949 China was not a healthy place for religions of any kind, although some adherents of all the five faiths maintained their practices.

It was during the so-called Cultural Revolution, which began in August 1966, that all religions in China were severely repressed. For three years the Red Guards moved actively against anything that represented the four "olds." These "olds" were: old ideas, old culture, old customs, and old habits. The remnants of religion were inviting targets. Temples and churches that had managed to survive until 1966 were closed. Buddhist temples were especially chosen to be painted and plastered with slogans. Their statues were smashed and dragged through the streets. Confucius was called, "the number one criminal of feudal thinking." His birthplace was raided and the temple there was destroyed. People who dared to celebrate Taoist festivals were arrested and accused of wrong thinking. Many Taoist shrines, tablets, altars, and relics were destroyed in the purge.

In 1977, after the death of Mao and with the thawing of relationships between China and Western nations, the government became more open to religions. Churches and temples were allowed to reopen and hold services. The University of Nanking established a Center for Religious Studies, in 1979. The Chinese government is paying the costs for a translation of the Bible and its publication. Even with this new and freer attitude toward all religions, the future of the specific Chinese religions of Taoism and Confucianism is not clear.

STUDY QUESTIONS

1. Are Taoism and Confucianism truly religions? Argue both sides.

2. Describe the Chinese concept of the *yin* and *yang* as a unifying explanation for the universe.

3. Study the hexagrams of the *I Ching*. How could these hexagrams be viewed as a means of divination? How could they be seen as having

[26] Self-government, self-support, and self-propagation.

personality and wisdom of their own? Note the editorial work of Confucius.

4. Why did the decline of the feudal system in ancient China set the stage for both Taoism and Confucianism?

5. Contrast the view of the best government as it is revealed in the *Tao Tê Ching* and in the teachings of Confucius.

6. By what process did Taoism become magic?

7. How would the current rulers of China regard Taoism? How would they regard the teachings of Confucius?

SUGGESTED READING

Bush, Richard C. *Religion in Communist China.* Nashville, Tenn.: Abingdon Press, 1970.

Giles, Herbert A. *Religions of Ancient China.* Freeport, N.Y.: Books for Libraries Press, 1969.

Smith, D. Howard, *Chinese Religions.* New York: Holt, Rinehart & Winston, 1968.

Thompson, Laurence G. *The Chinese Way in Religion.* Encino, Calif.: Dickenson Publishing Company, 1973.

Waley, Arthur. *The Way and its Power.* London: George Allen & Unwin, 1956.

Yang, Y. C. *China's Religious Heritage.* New York: Abingdon-Cokesbury Press, 1943.

Selections from Sacred Chinese Literature

The sourcebook for Taoism is the *Tao Tê Ching*. According to tradition, it was written by Lao-tzu as he sought an exit from China in the sixth century B.C. Modern scholarship believes that these poems were really compiled over a long period of time by many Taoist sages. One can gather a sense of the message of the *Tao Tê Ching* in the segment called "The Tao of Heaven."

Tao Tê Ching [27]

Chapter I

The Way that can be told of is not an Unvarying Way;
The names that can be named are not unvarying names.
It was from the Nameless that Heaven and Earth sprang;
The named is but the mother that rears the ten thousand creatures, each
    after its kind.
Truly, "Only he that rids himself forever of desire can see the Secret Es-
    sences";
He that has never rid himself of desire can see only the Outcomes.
These two things issued from the same mold, but nevertheless are different
    in name.
This "same mold" we can but call the Mystery,
Or rather the "Darker than any Mystery,"
The Doorway whence issued all Secret Essences.

Chapter II

It is because every one under Heaven recognizes beauty as
beauty, that the idea of ugliness exists.
And equally if every one recognized virtue as virtue, this
would merely create fresh conceptions of wickedness.
For truly "Being and Not-being grow out of one another;
Difficult and easy complete one another.
Long and easy complete one another.
Long and short test one another;
High and low determine one another.
Pitch and mode give harmony to one another.
Front and back give sequence to one another.
Therefore the Sage relies on actionless activity,

[27] *The Way and Its Power: The Tao Tê Ching and Its Place in Chinese Thought,* Arthur Waley,
    trans. (London: Allen & Unwin Ltd., 1977), pp. 141, 143, 159, 171, 238.

Carries on wordless teaching,
But the myriad creatures are worked upon by him; he does not disown
     them.
He rears them, but does not lay claim to them,
Controls them, but does not lean upon them,
Achieves his aim, but does not call attention to what he does;
And for the very reason that he does not call attention to what he does
He is not ejected from fruition of what he has done.

Chapter XIV

Because the eye gazes but can catch no glimpse of it,
It is called elusive.
Because the ear listens but cannot hear it,
It is called the rarefied.
Because the hand feels for it but cannot find it,
It is called the infinitesimal.
These three, because they cannot be further scrutinized,
Blend into one.
Its rising brings no light;
Its sinking, no darkness.
Endless the series of things without name
On the way back to where there is nothing.
They are called shapeless shapes;
Forms without form;
Are called vague semblances.
Go towards them, and you can see no front;
Go after them, and you see no rear.
Yet by seizing on the Way that was
You can ride the things that are now.
For to know what once there was in the Beginning,
This is called the essence of the Way.

Chapter XXII

"To remain whole, be twisted!"
To become straight, let yourself be bent.
To become full, be hollow.
Be tattered, that you may be renewed.
Those that have little, may get more,
Those that have much, are but perplexed.
Therefore the Sage
Clasps the Primal Unity,
Testing by it everything under heaven.
He does not show himself; therefore his is seen everywhere.
He does not define himself, therefore he is distinct.

He does not boast of what he will do, therefore he succeeds.
He is not proud of his work, and therefore it endures.
He does not contend,
And for that very reason no one under heaven can contend with him.
So then we see that the ancient saying "To remain whole,
be twisted" was no idle word; for true wholeness can only
be achieved by return.

Chapter XXVII

Perfect activity leaves no track behind it;
Perfect speech is like a jade-worker whose tool leaves no mark.
The perfect reckoner needs no counting-slips,
The perfect door has neither bolt nor bar,
Yet cannot be opened.
The perfect knot needs neither rope nor twine,
Yet cannot be untied.
Therefore the Sage
Is all the time in the most perfect way helping men,
He certainly does not turn his back on men;
Is all the time in the most perfect way helping creatures,
He certainly does not turn his back on creatures.
This is called resorting to the Light.
Truly, "the perfect man is the teacher of the imperfect;
But the imperfect is the stock-in-trade of the perfect man."
He who does not respect his teacher,
He who does not take care of his stock-in-trade,
Much learning though he may possess, is far astray.
This is the essential secret.

Chapter LVII

"Kingdoms can only be governed if rules are kept;
Battles can only be won if rules are broken."
But the adherence of all under heaven can only be won by letting-alone.
How do I know that it is so?
By this.
The more prohibitions there are, the more ritual avoidances,
The poorer the people will be.
The more "sharp weapons" there are,
The more benighted will the whole land grow.
The more cunning craftsmen there are,
The more pernicious contrivances will be invented.
The more laws are promulgated,
The more thieves and bandits there will be.
Therefore a sage has said:

So long as I "do nothing" the people will of themselves be transformed.
So long as I love quietude, the people will of themselves go straight.
So long as I act only by inactivity the people will of themselves become
     prosperous.
So long as I have no wants the people will of themselves return
to the "state of the Uncarved Block."

Chapter LXXVIII

Nothing under heaven is softer or more yielding than water; but when it
attacks things hard and resistant there is not one of them that can prevail.
For they can find no way of altering it. That the yielding conquers the
resistant and the soft conquers the hard is a fact known by all men, yet
utilized by none. Yet it is in reference to this that the Sage said "Only he
who has accepted the dirt of the country can be lord of its soil-shrines;
only he who takes upon himself the evils of the country can become a
king among those what dwell under heaven." Straightwords seem crooked.

The Analects

> *The Analects* are a collection of the sayings of Confucius
> and his disciples, dating from the fifth century B.C. The fol-
> lowing selections from *The Analects* are representative of its
> concern for a well-ordered society.[28]

Book III

1. Master K'ung said of the head of the Chi family when he had eight
teams of dancers performing in his courtyard, "If this man can be endured,
who cannot be endured!"

2. The Three Families used the *Yung Song* during the removal of the
sacrificial vessels. The Master said,

> "By rulers and lords attended,
> The Son of Heaven, mysterious————"

What possible application can such words have in the hall of the Three
Families?

3. The Master said, "A man who is not Good, what can he have to do
with ritual? A man who is not Good, what can he have to do with music?"

4. Lin Fang asked for some main principles in connection with ritual.
The Master said, "A very big question. In ritual at large it is a safe rule

---

[28] *The Analects of Confucius,* Arthur Waley, trans. (London: Allen & Unwin, Ltd., 1938), pp.
   94–106.

always to be too sparing rather than too lavish; and in the particular case of mourning-rites, they should be dictated by grief rather than fear."

5. The Master said, "The barbarians of the East and North have retained their princes. They are not in such a state of decay as we in China."

6. The head of the Chi family was going to make the offerings on Mount T'ai. The Master said to Jan Ch'iu, "Cannot you save him from this?" Jan Ch'iu replied, "I cannot." The Master said, "Alas, we can hardly suppose Mount T'ai to be ignorant of matters that even Lin Fang inquires into!"

7. The Master said, "Gentlemen never compete. You will say that in archery they do so. But even then they bow and make way for one another when they are going up to the archery-ground, when they are coming down and at the subsequent drinking-bout. Thus even when competing, they still remain gentlemen."

8. Tzu-hsia asked, saying, "What is the meaning of

Oh the sweet smile dimpling,
The lovely eyes so black and white!
Plain silk that you would take for colored stuff."

The Master said, "The painting comes after the plain groundwork." Tzu-hsia said, "Then ritual comes afterwards?" The Master said, "Shang it is who bears me up. At last I have someone with whom I can discuss the Songs!"

11. Someone asked for an explanation of the Ancestral Sacrifice. The Master said, "I do not know. Anyone who knew the explanation could deal with all things under Heaven as easily as I lay this here"; and he laid his finger upon the palm of his hand.

12. Of the saying, "The word 'sacrifice' is like the word 'present'; one should sacrifice to a spirit as though that spirit was present," the Master said, "If I am not present at the sacrifice, it is as though there were no sacrifice."

13. Wang-sun Chia asked about the meaning of the saying,

"Better pay court to the stove
Than pay court to the Shrine."

The Master said, "It is not true. He who has put himself in the wrong with Heaven has no means of expiation left."

14. The Master said, "Chou could survey the two preceding dynasties. How great a wealth of culture! And we follow upon Chou."

15. When the Master entered the Grand Temple he asked questions about everything there. Someone said, "Do not tell me that this son of a villager from Tsou is expert in matters of ritual. When he went to the Grand

Temple, he had to ask about everything." The Master hearing of this said, "Just so! such is the ritual."

16. The Master said, "the saying

In archery it is not the hide that counts,
For some men have more strength than others,

is the way of the Ancients."

17. Tzu-kung wanted to do away with the presentation of a sacrificial sheep at the announcement of each new moon. The Master said, "Ssu! You grudge sheep, but I grudge ritual."

18. The Master said, "Were anyone to-day to serve his prince according to the full prescriptions of ritual, he would be thought a sycophant."

23. When talking to the Grand Master of Lu about music, the Master said, "Their music in so far as one can find out about it began with a strict unison. Soon the musicians were given more liberty; but the tone remained harmonious, brilliant, consistent, right on till the close."

25. The Master spoke of the Succession Dance as being perfect beauty and at the same time perfect goodness; but of the War Dance as being perfect beauty, but not perfect goodness.

26. The Master said, "High office filled by men of narrow views, ritual performed without reverence, the forms of mourning observed without grief—these things I cannot bear to see!"

Book IV

1. The Master said, "It is Goodness that gives to a neighborhood its beauty. One who is free to choose, yet does not prefer to dwell among the Good—how can he be accorded the name of wise?"

2. The Masters said, "Without Goodness a man

Cannot for long endure adversity,
Cannot for long enjoy prosperity."

The Good Man rests content with Goodness; he that is merely wise pursues Goodness in the belief that it pays to do so.

3, 4. Of the adage "Only a Good Man knows how to like people, knows how to dislike them," the Master said, "He whose heart is in the smallest degree set upon Goodness will dislike no one."

5. "Wealth and rank are what every man desires, but if they can only be retained to the detriment of the Way he professes, he must relinquish them. Poverty and obscurity are what every man detests, but if they can only be avoided to the detriment of the Way he professes, he must accept

them. The gentleman who ever parts company with Goodness does not fulfill that name. Never for a moment does a gentleman quit the way of Goodness. He is never so harried but that he cleaves to this, never so tottering but that he cleaves to this."

6. The Master said, "I for my part have never yet seen one who really cared for Goodness, nor one who really abhorred wickedness. One who really cared for Goodness would never let any other consideration come first. One who abhorred wickedness would be so constantly doing Good that wickedness would never have a chance to get at him. Has anyone ever managed to do Good with his whole might even as long as the space of a single day? I think not. Yet I for my part have never seen anyone give up such an attempt because he had not the *strength* to go on. It may well have happened, but I for my part have never seen it."

7. The Master said, "Every man's faults belong to a set. If one looks out for faults, it is only as a means of recognizing Goodness."

8. The Master said, "In the morning, hear the Way; in the evening, die content!"

9. The Master said, "A Knight whose heart is set upon the Way, but who is ashamed of wearing shabby clothes and eating coarse food, is not worth calling into counsel."

10. The Master said, "A gentleman in his dealings with the world has neither enmities nor affections; but wherever he sees Right he ranges himself beside it."

11. The Master said, "Where gentlemen set their hearts upon moral force (*tê*), the commoners set theirs upon the soil. Where gentlemen think only of punishments, the commoners think only of exemptions."

12. The Master said, "Those whose measures are dictated by mere expediency will arouse continual discontent."

13. The Master said, "If it is really possible to govern countries by ritual and yielding, there is no more to be said. But if it is not really possible, of what use is ritual?"

14. The Master said, "He does not mind not being in office; all he minds about is whether he has qualities that entitle him to office. He does not mind failing to get recognition; he is too busy doing the things that entitle him to recognition."

15. The Master said, "Shên! My Way has one (thread) that runs right through it." Master Tsêng said, "Yes." When the Master had gone out, the disciples asked, saying "What did he mean?" Master Tsêng said, "Our Master's Way is simply this: Loyalty, consideration."

16. The Master said, "A gentleman takes as much trouble to discover what is right as lesser men take to discover what will pay."

17. The Master said, "In the presence of a good man, think all the time how you may learn to equal him. In the presence of a bad man, turn your gaze within!"

18. The Master said, "In serving his father and mother a man may gently remonstrate with them. But if he sees that he has failed to change their opinion, he should resume an attitude of deference and not thwart them; may feel discouraged, but not resentful."

19. The Master said, "While father and mother are alive, a good son does not wander far afield; or if he does so, goes only where he has said he was going."

20. The Master said, "If for the whole three years of mourning a son manages to carry on the household exactly as in his father's day, then he is a good son indeed."

21. The Master said, "It is always better for a man to know the age of his parents. In the one case such knowledge will be a comfort to him; in the other, it will fill him with a salutary dread."

22. The master said, "In old days a man kept a hold on his words, fearing the disgrace that would ensue should he himself fail to keep pace with them."

23. The Master said, "Those who err on the side of strictness are few indeed!"

24. The Master said, "A gentleman covets the reputation of being slow in word but prompt in deed."

25. The Master said, "Moral force (tê) never dwells in solitude; it will always bring neighbors."

26. Tzu-yu said, "In the service of one's prince repeated scolding can only lead to loss of favor; in friendship, it can only lead to estrangement."

The Meaning and Value of Rituals

> One of the greatest interpreters of Confucius was Hsŭn Tzŭ.
> In the following section Hsŭn Tzŭ states the Confucian view
> of the value rituals have for a society.[29]

Rites (li) rest on three bases: Heaven and earth, which are the source of all life; the ancestors, who are the source of the human race; sovereigns and teachers, who are the source of government. If there were no Heaven and earth, where would life come from? If there were no ancestors, where would the offspring come from? If there were no sovereigns and teachers, where would government come from? Should any of the three be missing, either there would be no men or men would be without peace. Hence rites are to serve Heaven on high and earth below, and to honour the ancestors and elevate the sovereigns and teachers. Herein lies the threefold basis for rites.

In general, rites begin with primitive practices, attain cultured forms,

[29] Y. P. Mei, trans., in William T. de Bary, ed., *Sources of Chinese Tradition* (New York: Columbia University Press, 1960), pp. 123, 124.

and finally achieve beauty and felicity. When rites are at their best, men's emotions and sense of beauty are both fully expressed. When they are at the next level, either the emotion or the sense of beauty oversteps the others. When they are at still the next level, emotion reverts to the state of primitivity.

It is through rites that Heaven and earth are harmonious and sun and moon are bright, that the four seasons are ordered and the stars are on their courses, that rivers flow and that things prosper, that love and hatred are tempered and joy and anger are in keeping. They cause the lowly to be obedient and those on high to be illustrious. He who holds to the rites is never confused in the midst of multifarious change; he who deviates therefrom is lost. Rites—are they not the culmination of culture?

Rites require us to treat both life and death with attentiveness. Life is the beginning of man, death is his end. When a man is well off both at the end and the beginning, the way of man is fulfilled. Hence the gentleman respects the beginning and is carefully attentive to the end. To pay equal attention to the end as well as to the beginning is the way of the gentleman and the beauty of rites and righteousness.

Rites serve to shorten that which is too long and lengthen that which is too short, reduce that which is too much and augment that which is too little, express the beauty of love and reverence and cultivate the elegance of righteous conduct. Therefore, beautiful adornment and course sackcloth, music and weeping, rejoicing and sorrow, though pairs of opposites, are in the rites equally utilized and alternately brought into play. Beautiful adornment, music, and rejoicing are appropriate on occasions of felicity; coarse sackcloth, weeping, and sorrow are appropriate on occasions of ill-fortune. Rites make room for beautiful adornment but not to the point of being fascinating, for coarse sackcloth but not to the point of deprivation or self-injury, for music and rejoicing but not to the point of being lewd and indolent, for weeping and sorrow but not to the point of being depressing and injurious. Such is the middle path of rites.

Funeral rites are those by which the living adorn the dead. The dead are accorded a send-off as though they were living. In this way the dead are served like the living, the absent like the present. Equal attention is thus paid to the end as well as to the beginning of life.

Now the rites used on the occasion of birth are to embellish joy, those used on the occasion of death are to embellish sorrow, those used at sacrifice are to embellish reverence, those used on millitary occasions are to embellish dignity. In this respect the rites of all kings are alike, antiquity and the present age agree, and no one knows whence they came.

Sacrifice is to express a person's feeling of remembrance and longing, for grief and affliction cannot be kept out of one's consciousness all the time. When men are enjoying the pleasure of good company, a loyal minister or a filial son may feel grief and affliction. Once such feelings arise, he is greatly excited and moved. If such feelings are not given proper expression, then his emotions and memories are disappointed and not satisfied, and the appropriate rite is lacking. Thereupon the ancient kings instituted rites, and henceforth the principle of expressing honour to the honoured and love to the beloved is fully realized. Hence I say: Sacrifice is to express a person's feeling of remembrance and longing. As to the fullness of the sense of loyalty and affection, the richness of ritual and beauty— these none but the sage can understand. Sacrifice is something that the sage clearly understands, the scholar-gentleman contentedly perform, the officials consider a duty, and the common people regard as established custom. Among gentlemen it is considered the way of man; among the common people it is considered as having to do with the spirits.

CHAPTER 9

Shinto

Mount Fuji, Japan. (*Courtesy of the Japan National Tourist Organization.*)

Think not God is something distant, but seek for him in your heart, for the heart is the abode of God. That which in Heaven begets all things is, in man, that which makes him love his neighbor, so doubt not that Heaven loves goodness of heart and hates its opposite. Reverence for Heaven and one's ancestors is the foundation of the Way of the sages.

—Muro-Kiuso

Shinto, a loosely organized native religion of the Japanese people, embraces a wide variety of beliefs and practices. Indeed this variety is so wide that it is as difficult to define Shinto as Hinduism. Therefore we can only list some of the areas that it covers. In its most basic sense Shinto is a fervent religious form of Japanese patriotism. Its mythology describes the formation of Japan as a land superior to all lands; its shrines commemorate the great heroes and events in the history of Japan. Historically, it has taught the Japanese people that their emperors were literally the descendants of the sun goddess. Commentators have frequently compared Japanese Shinto to Americans visiting Gettysburg, the Washington Monument, or the Alamo. Probably the closest comparison would be that which takes place in some American towns and villages on Memorial Day when graves of the war dead are visited by the community, the blessings of God are invoked upon the nation, and great events in the national history are remembered in the beauty of a late spring day.[1]

Shinto further involves the Japanese in a worshipful attitude toward the beauties of their land, particularly its mountains. As practiced by the common people, it may also include various aspects of animism and ancestor worship. In addition, it embraces the religious activity that takes place in the numerous shrines throughout Japan—which, prior to 1945, received the financial support of the government—the simple rituals that are carried out in shrines in Japanese homes, and the highly organized and active religious sects that have developed from basic Shinto. Thus the term *Shinto* may refer to a multitude of varying Japanese religious and national practices.

The word *Shinto* itself was not officially coined until the sixth century A.D. It was developed then to distinguish native Japanese religion from the newer religions being imported from China and Korea dur-

[1] For a discussion of Memorial Day as American Shinto see W. Lloyd Warner, *American Life, Dream, and Reality* (Chicago: The University of Chicago Press, 1953), pp. 1–12.

ing the period, Buddhism, Taoism, and Confucianism. The word *Shinto* actually comes from the Chinese words *shen* and *tao*, which may be roughly translated in this context as "the way of the gods." The preferred Japanese term that describes this native religion is *Kami-no-michi*, which also may be defined as "the way of the gods."

JAPANESE MYTHOLOGY

In order for us to understand Japanese religion prior to the sixth century, it is necessary to take a quick look at some of the traditional myths surrounding the origin of the nation of Japan, its native gods, and the early history of the country. In the beginning there were the *kami*. The term *kami* is usually defined as "gods," but that is inexact. Some scholars have chosen to define kami as *mana*.

> Kami in its original meaning is practically identical with *mana*, the name adopted by science from the language of the Melanesians to indicate the occult force which preliterate man found emanating from objects and experiences that aroused in him emotions of wonder and awe.[2]

Others have identified the kami with the Greek term *daimon*. However, this too is inadequate. Even the great Japanese Shinto scholar, Motoori Norinaga, in the eighteenth century confessed: "I do not yet understand the meaning of the term *kami*."[3] Kami certainly refers to the deities of heaven and earth worshiped by the Japanese people, but it can also refer to the spirit that is in human beings, animals, trees, plants, seas, and mountains. Any thing, any person, any force that possessed superior power or was awesome in any way was described by the ancient Japanese as kami. While kami may be defined in these broad terms, in ancient mythology it generally refers to gods or humans with godlike powers.

The major source for our knowledge of Japanese mythology is the Kojiki, "Chronicles of Ancient Events." These chronicles were collected in the seventh and eighth centuries A.D. as a response to the entrance of Chinese culture and religions. In these centuries the Japanese, while willing to accept the advanced culture of the Chinese, looked about for their own heritage. The results of this search yielded the chronicles, which contain a section called "The Age of the Gods." In this material one finds the mythological background of Japanese

---

[2] Daniel Clarence Holtom, "Shinto," in *Religion in the Twentieth Century*, Vergilius Ferm ed. (New York: The Philosophical Library, 1948), p. 147.

[3] William T. de Bary, ed., *Sources of the Japanese Tradition* (New York: Columbia University Press, 1958), p. 23.

culture. The Kojiki includes stories that describe the special creation of the Japanese islands by two kami, Izanagi and his consort, Izanami. These two become the divine parents of the other kami in Japanese mythology. The chief of these spirits is Amaterasu, who is the sun goddess. It is from the line of Amaterasu that all the future Japanese emperors are believed to have descended.

THE HISTORY OF SHINTO

Shinto Prior to 300 A.D.

According to the mythological tradition, the first Japanese emperor was enthroned in the seventh century B.C., but most modern scholars agree that the actual history of Japan does not begin until the third century A.D. At this point the Japanese people became known to other nations and began to keep historical records. Therefore the culture of Japan is one of the youngest of all the Asian nations. It is difficult to say what the exact worship of the Japanese was prior to this period. The coming of Buddhism in the sixth century A.D. caused the Japanese to collect their various myths and rituals under the title of *Kami-no-michi* to distinguish native religion from those brought in by the Chinese and Koreans. Prior to this, Japanese worship probably consisted of a loosely organized and widely varying collection of practices. The myths allowed for a limitless number of gods, goddesses, spirits, ancestor worship, and various forms of animism. Shrines were established all over the Japanese islands for the worship of the various kami, and shrines were built in individual homes for ancestor and kami worship. Amaterasu and Susa-No-O were probably the most popular gods and received more than their share of attention at the shrines built for them and in private homes. Beyond these very general statements it is difficult to say anything more about Japanese worship in its prehistoric period.

Chinese Influence upon Shinto

Early in its history Japan became an object of interest to Chinese and Korean merchants and missionaries. These persons brought with them much of the older culture of China, including its arts, its language and alphabet, and of course its various religions and ethical systems. After the fourth century A.D. the Japanese came under the influence of Buddhism, Taoism, and Confucianism. All of these had a lasting effect on Japanese civilization. The Kojiki records the entrance of Chinese culture into Japan.

The inner shrine of the temple of Ise, dedicated to the goddess Amatersu. (*Courtesy of Japan National Tourist Organization.*)

In the years that followed, intercourse between China and Japan greatly increased. Prior to this period the Japanese had no written language. They subsequently adopted the Chinese script and many other elements of the Chinese culture. Japan was organized and governed by a feudal system during this era and Confucian ethics were therefore welcomed. Ancestor worship had always been practiced in Japan and thus the Confucian and Taoist elements that emphasized filial piety were readily accepted by the Japanese. The Chinese arts, particularly those connected to Buddhist ritual, were also adopted. Altogether, the period between the fourth and the eighth centuries was one of dramatic change for Japan.

The entrance of Buddhism from China and Korea was extremely important in the development of the religious traditions of Japan. According to the Japanese chronicles, it was in the year 522 A.D. that Mahayana Buddhism was first introduced from China. In that year the emperor of Japan was presented with an image of Buddha and several volumes of Buddhist scripture. Though the emperor was delighted his advisors warned him that the introduction of a foreign god might arouse the anger of the native kamis. Shortly after the introduction of the Buddha a pestilence broke out in Japan. Fearing that it was the work of the vengeful kamis, the emperor had the statue thrown into a canal, and the temple that had been built for the Buddha was burned, whereupon the pestilence ceased.

Buddhism could not so easily be turned away from Japan, however. In succeeding generations other statues of the Buddha were introduced, along with prayers, rituals, and Buddhist magic. By the end of the sixth century Mahayana Buddhism had taken a firm foothold on Japan.

Japanese reaction to Buddhism was fourfold. First, there was the introduction of the name *Shinto* or *Kami-no-michi* to distinguish the native Japanese religion from the new foreign religion. As we have suggested before, this may have been the first point at which the Japanese actually began to think of their native worship as a distinct religion.

The second reaction was for the Japanese advocates of Shinto to recognize the many Buddhas and bodhisattvas of Buddhism, but to think of them as the revelation of the kamis to the Indian and Chinese people. Naturally the Buddhists tended to reverse this line of thinking and to identify the kamis as Japanese revelations of the Buddhas and bodhisattvas.

The third reaction was a syncretism between Shinto and Buddhism that developed in Japan between the sixth and the ninth centuries, and was called *Ryobu,* i.e., "Two Aspect" Shinto. There gradually developed an identification between the various Shinto kami and the Buddhist deities. Little by little the boundaries between the two religions were obliterated. The Shinto sanctuaries also came to serve Buddhist priests. The rituals performed in these sanctuaries made little distinction between the two religions. Buddhist architectural elements were added to Shinto temples. Generally, Japanese life began to be divided into two spheres. The concerns of day-to-day life became the domain of the Shinto side of the religion while the concerns for the afterlife were served by the Buddhists. Thus a traditional citizen of Japan might be said to have been born a Shintoist but to die a Buddhist. For ten centuries Shinto and Buddhism lived side by side in Japan, each serving a special need of the people.

The fourth reaction of the Japanese to Buddhism was the development of some distinctively Japanese forms of Buddhism. Mahayana Buddhism is an extremely elastic religion, allowing for many variations. This is true to such a degree that it may be considered a family of religions rather than a single branch of the religion of Buddhism. Within a few centuries of the time that Buddhism came to Japan new variations on the Buddhist theme began to develop. Buddhism had emphasized meditation (dhyana) as a means of insight into religious truth. The Chinese Buddhists had picked this up through the missionary work of Bodhidharma, and called it *Ch'an*, but it remained for the Japanese to develop meditative Buddhism to its fullest form, under the name of *Zen*. The Japanese also originated or developed other forms of Buddhism, such as Pure Land and Nichiren. (For a further discussion of these forms, see Chapter 6.) These and other forms of Buddhism became so popular in Japan that even though Shinto was intermingled with them, it was almost forgotten as a viable religion for the Japanese people.

The Revival of Shinto

From the eighth century onward, Shinto and Buddhism were submerged into a syncretistic form of religion, to the point that Shinto was almost obliterated. Nevertheless, there often arose reformers who wished to revise and revitalize the native religion of Japan. As early as the fourteenth century, various scholars tried to point out the strengths of Shinto and to restore it to its place of prominence with the people. However, it was not until the seventeenth century and the rise of the Tokugawa regime (1600–1867) that Shinto got the boost it needed. This was an era in which the Japanese people were unified by tough-minded military leaders who sought to isolate the nation from outside influences. Since religions such as Buddhism and Christianity were foreign-born they were pushed aside; since Shinto was native to Japan it was given new strength and support by the national government. A Japanese version of Confucianism was the only foreign system that was allowed support during this period because Confucian ethics were supportive of the militaristic regime of the Tokugawa rulers.

One of the most colorful aspects of Japanese life during the Tokugawa era was the feudal knights, called the *samurai*. Throughout the history of Japan individual warriors hired themselves as bodyguards or mercenary soldiers to lords, but it was in the Tokugawa era that the samurai was idealized and a code of conduct was established for him. In the seventeenth century the government set up the Shushi School of Confucianism as the orthodox model for the conduct of the upper classes. One of the leaders of this school was Yamaga Soko (1622–1685), who led in a combining of Shinto and Confucianism to develop the warrior code called *Bushido*, "the way of the fighting knight." The standard of conduct established for the Japanese feudal knight was similar in many respects to that of the idealized Christian knight of medieval Europe, except for the absence of any form of romantic love. Generally, Bushido may be summarized under the following categories:

1. The samurai is bound to be loyal to his master in the hierarchy of the feudal system. The extremes to which this loyalty was carried is best illustrated by one of the most famous stories in Japanese literature, the tale of the forty-seven ronin. Told very briefly, in 1702 a certain lord was insulted by a government official. He drew his sword and wounded the official. For this act the lord was required to commit suicide and his property was confiscated by the government. He had in his employ forty-seven samurai who, since their lord was dead, were officially known as *ronin* ("men without a master"). These knights took a vow of vengeance for the injustice brought against their master. In order to avoid suspicion they disbanded and acted publicly as if they had no concern for their master. When their enemies ceased to be watchful they gathered together, attacked the castle of the one who had humiliated their master, and killed him. Then they quietly waited for the government to order them to commit suicide. Thus the forty-seven ronin became the ideal example of the loyalty that samurai are to have toward their masters.

2. The samurai must have great courage in life, in battle, and in his willingness to lay down his life for his master.

3. Above all, the samurai is to be a man of honor. He prefers death to dishonor and is expected to take his own life rather than face a situation in which he is dishonored.

4. Like a true Confucian the samurai is expected to be polite to his master and to people in a position of authority above him. However, this politeness and gentility did not extend to everyone in society. There are stories of samurai who felt quite justified in trying out the edge of their swords on peasants if there were no battle at hand. The age-old story of the man who struck out at a peasant with his sword seven times and had no apparent effect until the peasant fell into eight pieces probably originated in samurai lore.

5. In spite of his attitude toward peasants the samurai is expected to be a gentleman in every sense of the word. He is supposed to be a man of benevolence, to right wrongs, and to bring justice to the victims of injustice. A popular Japanese movie, *The Seven Samurai*, is probably a good example of this sense of justice.

The willingness of the proper samurai to commit suicide before dishonor and the attitude of the Japanese people toward suicide as a whole have long amazed Westerners. Many European religious traditions teach directly against the practice of suicide, but in Japan sui-

The fighting skills of ancient Samurai warriors is being reenacted by a modern Japanese movie company. (*Courtesy of the Japan National Tourist Organization.*)

cide has often been encouraged as a means of avoiding dishonor, as a means of escaping a bad situation in life, as a means of protest, and in World War II as a very effective means of destroying enemy warships. Perhaps no other culture in the history of the world has had this attitude toward suicide.

In Bushido the warrior is expected to kill himself in a very slow, painful manner called *seppuku*. (Westerners prefer the term *hara-kari*,[4] which means "belly slitting.") This is a form of suicide by disembowelment. At the proper time the warrior is expected to slit open his abdomen in such a way that his intestines fall out. Thus he dies in a very slow and painful manner. In more recent times it became common for a friend to stand by and chop off the head once the necessary slitting had taken place. This form of death was reserved for warriors and nobility. Women and peasants were forbidden to commit *seppuku* and were expected to kill themselves in a quicker manner by stabbing themselves in the throat. A. B. Mitford, a secretary to the British consulate in Japan in the nineteenth century, was allowed to

[4]One frequently hears this term further corrupted to something that sounds like "harry karry."

witness a ritual suicide, and he recorded the incident in the following manner:

> The condemned man was Taki Zenzaburo, an officer of the Prince of Bizen, who gave the order to fire upon the foreign settlement at Hiogo in the month of February, 1868.
>
> The ceremony, which was ordered by the Mikado himself, took place at 10:30 at night in the temple of Seifukukji, the headquarters of the Satsuma troops at Hiogo. A witness was sent from each of the foreign legations. We were seven foreigners in all.
>
> After an interval of a few minutes of anxious suspense, Taki Zenzaburo, a stalwart man, thirty-two years of age, with a noble air, walked into the hall attired in his dress of ceremony, with the peculiar hempen-cloth wings which are worn on great occasions. He was accompanied by a *kaishaku* and three officers, who wore the *jimbaori* or war surcoat with gold-tissue facings. The word *kaishaku*, it should be observed, is one to which our word "executioner" is no equivalent term. The office is that of a gentleman: in many cases it is performed by a kinsman or friend of the condemned, and the relation between them is rather that of principal and second than that of a victim and executioner. In this instance the *kaishaku* was a pupil of Taki Zenzaburo, and was selected by the friends of the latter from among their number for his skill in swordsmanship.
>
> With the *kaishaku* on his left hand, Taki Zenzaburo advanced slowly towards the Japanese witnesses, and the two bowed before them, then drawing near to the foreigners they saluted us in the same way, perhaps even with more deference: in each case the salutation was ceremoniously returned. Slowly, and with great dignity, the condemned man mounted to the raised floor, prostrated himself before the high altar twice, and seated himself on the felt carpet with his back to the high altar, the *kaishaku* crouching on his left-hand side. One of the three attendant officers then came forward, bearing a stand of the kind used in temples for offerings, on which, wrapped in paper, lay the *wakizashi*, the short sword or dirk of the Japanese, nine inches and a half in length, with a point and an edge as sharp as a razor's. This he handed, prostrating himself, to the condemned man, who received it reverently, raising it to his head with both hands, and placed it in front of himself.
>
> After another profound obeisance, Taki Zenzaburo, in a voice which betrayed so much emotion and hesitation as might be expected from a man who is making a painful confession, but with no sign of either in his face or manner, spoke as follows: "I, and I alone, unwarrantably gave the order to fire on the foreigners at Kobe, and again as they tried to escape. For this crime I disembowel myself, and I beg you who are present to do me the honor of witnessing the act."
>
> Bowing once more, the speaker allowed his upper garments to slip down to his girdle, and remained naked to the waist. Carefully, according to custom, he tucked his sleeves under his knees to prevent himself from falling forwards. Deliberately, with a steady hand, he took the dirk that lay before him; he looked at it wistfully, almost affectionately; for a mo-

ment seemed to collect his thoughts for the last time, and then, stabbing himself deeply below the waist on the left-hand side, he drew the dirk slowly across to the right side, and, turning it in the wound, gave a slight cut upwards. During this sickeningly painful operation, he never moved a muscle of his face. When he drew out the dirk, he leaned forward and stretched out his neck; an expression of pain for the first time crossed his face, but he uttered no sound. At that moment the *kaishaku*, who, still crouching by his side, had been keenly watching his every movement, sprang to his feet, poised his sword for a second in the air; there was a flash, a heavy, ugly thud, a crashing fall; with one blow the head had been severed from the body.

A dead silence followed, broken only by the hideous noise of the blood throbbing out of the inert heap before us, which but a moment before had been a brave and chivalrous man. It was horrible.[5]

The willingness of warriors to die in such a manner for personal honor or for the good of the Japanese nation may seem out of place to the Westerner who has been trained in the sacredness of life and the evils of suicide, but in the coming together of the Shintoist's love of and worship for his nation and its heroic figures, and the Confucianist's high sense of honor, *seppuku* is considered to be very religious.

The Modern Era

During the Tokugawa era Japan did its best to avoid foreign influence in any form. It closed itself off from foreign trade, from tourism, and from any kind of foreign religion. During this period it attempted to draw only from its native resources. In the meantime the rest of the world, particularly the Western world, moved toward industrialization. In 1853 Japan was brought to a sudden confrontation with the modern world when Commodore Perry of the United States Navy appeared in Tokyo Bay and asked that the Japanese ports be opened and trade relations begun between the United States and Japan. In 1854 Perry appeared again with more ships, troops, and cannon, and the Japanese rulers were forced to open their nation to foreigners. Since that date Japan has been racing to catch up with and get ahead of the rest of the world in industrialization. This race toward modernity has of course had its effect upon the religions of Japan.

After a period of some confusion over what role religion was to play in the new Japan, it was decided, in the Constitution of 1889, that the nation would follow the pattern of many Western nations in that there would be a state-supported religion but all other religions

---

[5] A. B. Mitford, *Tales of Old Japan*, Vol. I (London: Macmillan, 1871), pp. 231–236.

would be allowed the freedom to exist and propagate. There would be state-supported Shinto that would essentially consist of patriotic rituals at certain shrines. In addition, those who wished could develop Shinto sects, which would be supported by their adherents. Further, Shinto could be carried on in every home around simple domestic shrines. Beyond these forms of Shinto any other religion, Buddhism, Christianity, and so on, was free to exist in Japan. However, only the patriotic rituals at the state shrines would receive financial support from the government of Japan.

THREE FORMS OF SHINTO

State Shinto

Following the Constitution of 1889, the state took over the support of some 110,000 Shinto shrines and approximately 16,000 priests who tended these shrines throughout the nation. This version of Shinto became known as *Jinja* (shrine) to distinguish it from the more religious *Skuha* (sectarian) versions.

Each shrine supported by the state was dedicated to some local deity, hero, or event; the grand imperial shrine at Ise was dedicated to the mother goddess of Japan, Amaterasu. The visitor approaches the shrine by way of a distinctive Japanese archway, called a *torii*, which was so inseparably connected to Shinto that it became known worldwide as its symbol.

The typical major shrine consists of two buildings, an inner and an outer shrine. Both are built of unpainted wood and must be torn down and rebuilt once every twenty years. Anyone may visit the outer shrine, but the inner one is reserved for priests and government officials. The inner shrine contains objects of importance to the deity or event it commemorates. For example, at the grand imperial shrine the sacred objects are a mirror, a sword, and a string of beads, all of which are important to the myth of Amaterasu. On certain occasions or holidays these relics are publicly displayed.

The visitor who enters the outer shrine meditates on the importance of the deity or the event celebrated there, offers a modest offering, and perhaps a brief prayer. No one is obligated to visit the shrine, but it is an unwritten assumption that every loyal Japanese will try to visit the shrine at Ise at least once during his lifetime.

State Shinto was established for the purpose of engendering patriotism and loyalty toward the nation of Japan; it was to have no religious functions. After the 1889 Constitution, the Japanese government forbade the priests who tended the state shrines and were supported by the state from performing any religious act, such as conducting funerals. The Constitution of 1889 began with these words: "The Empire of Japan shall be reigned over and governed by a line of Emperors unbroken for ages eternal. . . . The Emperor is sacred and inviolable."[6] This constitution also made the military leaders responsible to the emperor rather than to the parliament. State Shinto therefore became an instrument of support for the military leaders in the wars that Japan participated in during the last part of the nineteenth century and the first part of the twentieth. It was particularly supportive of the Japanese war effort during World War II. Shinto had become such an inseparable part of Japanese militarism that the American occupation forces felt it necessary to direct the abolition of state support for Shinto, in December of 1945. In January of 1946, the occupation forces directed the emperor to issue a statement declaring that he was not divine.

Since 1945, the shrines once supported by the Japanese government have continued to exist, but they are now sustained with the financial support of private citizens. Immediately following World War II, attendance at these shrines dropped off and many fell into disuse. However, in the ensuing years interest in them revived.

Sectarian Shinto

With the developments of the Meiji era (1868–1912), specifically when the government said that Shinto was not a religion but rather an institution which fostered patriotism, the religious side of Shinto was forced to identify itself separately and find its own support, as did all other religions in Japan. (The adherents to these religions are presently thought to number over eighteen million; however, statistics regarding any religion are always suspect, and this is especially true in Japan, where a person may in good conscience be a Buddhist, a Confucian, and a member of a Shinto sect all at the same time.)

The thirteen major sects of Shinto may be divided into three categories. First there are the sects whose primary emphasis is on mountain worship. The beautiful and graceful mountains of Japan have always been objects of reverence to its people. Somewhere it became popular for people to climb the mountains during seasonal pilgrimages, in a combination of nature worship and asceticism. Some made exhausting climbs from the valleys to the peaks while others took up temporary dwellings in the mountains for ascetic purposes. Moun-

---

[6]Floyd Ross, *Shinto: The Way of Japan* (Boston: Beacon Press, 1965), pp. 138, 139.

Torii at Mijajima, Hiroshima, Japan. The typical Shinto Torii is a refinement of the primitive symbolic design of vertical and horizontal tree trunks. (*Courtesy of the Japan National Tourist Organization.*)

tains Ontake and Fuji were the special favorites for these purposes. During the Meiji era three groups dedicated to nature worship and asceticism became established Shinto sects.

A second category developed from the basic practices of shamanism and divination of the Japanese peasants. The basic appeal of these sects in modern Japan is their promise of faith healing. Representative of such sects is *Tenri-kyo* ("Teaching of Heavenly Reason"). *Tenri-kyo* was founded in the nineteenth century by a peasant named Nakayama Miki (1798–1887). When she was forty-one years old this woman felt that she was possessed by the kami of Divine Reason. She believed that she had been miraculously healed from a serious illness and began to teach others as a result of this experience. Her religion emphasized various elements that had always been a part of the basic religion of the Japanese peasant, such as shamanism, ecstatic dance, and faith healing. Today this sect emphasizes volunteer labor for public charity and, of course, faith healing. Because of its teachings on healing and because it was established by a woman, *Tenri-kyo* is often referred to as "the Christian Science of Japan," but outside of these two common features the two religions are scarcely alike.

A third type of sectarian Shinto includes those sects that are classified as more or less pure Shinto. When the rulers of Japan took over the shrines of Shinto in the Meiji era and declared that it was not a religion, this left behind a basic residue of the religious tradition of Shinto, its mythology and its rituals. Three major sects developed to emphasize these religious elements. These sects revived the myths of the origin of Japan from the ancient chronicles. They believed that there was a religious and ethical dimension as well as a political aspect to Shinto. They emphasized purification of the body through fasting, breath control, bathing in cold water, chanting, and many other devices similar to the Yoga cults of Hinduism. Today, these sects seem to be losing ground among the people of Japan, while groups like *Tenri-kyo* are growing.

Domestic Shinto

Beyond the organized forms of state and sectarian Shinto there is another and more basic form. This is the very simple and common form of Shinto that takes place in many Japanese homes. The basic unit or symbol of domestic Shinto is the *kami-dana* (god shelf), which is found in many Japanese homes, particularly in rural areas. The *kami-dana*, whether it is elaborate or simple, contains the symbols of whatever may be of religious significance to the family. It usually contains the names of the ancestors of the family, since a part of the religion of the household is filial piety. The *kami-dana* might contain statues of the gods that have been beneficial to the family or are highly regarded. In the homes and shops of many Japanese artisans the images of the various patron deities are present, and the literature of Japan contains many stories of skilled workers creating masterpieces under the direction of an unseen patron god. The traditional *kami-dana* contains objects that have been bought at the great shrines, such as the one at Ise. Any object the family considers to be sacred is fit for veneration at the god shelf. There is a story that the *kami-dana* in one household contained the cast-off shoes of a man who had been a benefactor of the household when it was in trouble. The shoes were believed to be symbolic of the friend's goodness or to contain the mana or kami that prompted the good deeds. At any rate, they became objects of veneration.[7]

Worship at the *kami-dana* in the Japanese home is a very simple affair. Offerings of flowers, lanterns, incense, food, and drink may be placed before this altar daily. A simple daily service, in which the worshiper washes his hands, makes an offering, claps his hands as a

---

[7] It has been suggested that the closest parallel to the Japanese *kami-dana* in American life is the dashboard of the automobile, where in many cases objects that promise good fortune or bring back good memories are displayed.

symbol of communication with the spirits, and offers a brief prayer, may also be held here. On special occasions as holidays, weddings, or anniversaries, more elaborate ceremonies may be held at the *kami-dana*. However, if the occasion is decidedly religious—a funeral, for example—it is not to the Shinto deities or priest that the Japanese family turns but to the Buddhist priest. In the special religious syncretism of Japan, Shinto is for this life, but Buddhism is for the life beyond. Therefore, in addition to their *kami-dana*, many Japanese homes will have a *butsu-dan*, a Buddhist household altar, where worship to the Buddhist deities is also carried on.

As we have seen, Shinto, the native religion of Japan, is many things to many people. To some Japanese it is a set of myths and rituals that remind them of the special origin of their nation. They are occasionally reminded of these myths and rituals on national holidays or on visits to a national shrine. Religion in terms of more regular worship and a concern for the future life is likely to be Buddhism. To those who are members of specific Shinto religious sects, Shinto may be related to faith healing, ascetic practices, or purification of the body. To many rural families of Japan, Shinto includes the daily worship that is carried on in the home at the *kami-dana* and contains elements of ancestor worship and animism.

SHINTO TODAY

Following the defeat of Japan at the end of World War II, several things took place that made the future of Shinto uncertain. The most direct threat to this religion was the removal of official government support for state Shinto. The second threat to Shinto came from Japan's rapid industrialization. Within a few decades, Japanese industry and science caught up to that of most Western nations and, in some cases, surpassed it. In this environment of quick movement into the twentieth century it would seem that an ancient religion like Shinto would have little chance of survival. In addition to a struggle with the modern world, Shinto faced its old rival, Buddhism. Most Japanese would think of themselves primarily as Buddhists. Shinto would be thought of as a secondary, patriotic practice. Christianity provided even more competition. Therefore, one would think that Shinto, with its ancient myths, rituals, and shrines, would quickly fade away.

However, Shinto has not faded at all. It may be as strong today in Japan as ever. It has survived the withdrawal of support by the state and continues to exist on private donations. Furthermore, the new Shinto sects, which emphasize faith healing, positive thinking, and chanting, have been accepted by millions of Japanese. In some cases, adherents of these new forms of Shinto have entered politics, and have taken up the causes of certain labor unions. They have adapted to the struggles of postwar Japan and have made a place for themselves. Therefore, Shinto, in its many forms, still remains an important force in Japanese culture.

STUDY QUESTIONS

1. Discuss Shinto as a reverential form of Japanese patriotism. Discuss Shinto as religion. Can the two be clearly distinguished?

2. Review Japanese mythology and connect the imperial family to the *kami.*

3. What effect did the entrance of the Chinese and Buddhism have upon Shintoism?

4. What is the connection between Shinto and the Samurai class?

5. List the three forms of Shinto in modern Japan.

SUGGESTED READING

Anesaki, Masaharu. *Religious Life of the Japanese People.* Tokyo: The Society for International Cultural Relations, 1961.

de Barry, William T., ed. *Sources of Japanese Tradition.* New York: Columbia Universtiy Press, 1958.

Earhart, H. Byron. *Religion in the Japanese Experience.* Encino, Calif.: Dickenson Publishing Company, 1974.

Earhart, H. Byron. *Japanese Religion: Unity and Diversity.* Encino, Calif.: Dickenson Publishing Company, 1969.

Kitagawa, Joseph M. *Religion in Japanese History.* New York: Columbia University Press, 1966.

Ross, Floyd Hiatt. *Shinto, the Way of Japan.* Boston: Beacon Press, 1965.

SOURCE MATERIAL

Shinto Myths

The *Kojiki* (The Chronicles of Ancient Events) contain the myths of ancient Japan. These chronicles were compiled in the seventh and eighth centuries A.D., at a time when Japan was being deeply influenced by Chinese Buddhism. At that time, the Japanese felt a need to remember their own heritage.[8]

Myths Regarding the Plain of High Heaven

Birth of Kami

At the beginning of heaven and earth, there came into existence in the Plain of High Heaven the Heavenly Center Lord Kami, next, the Kami of High Generative Force, and then the Kami of Divine Generative Force.

Next, when the earth was young, not yet solid, there developed something like reedshoots from which the Male Kami of Excellent Reed Shoots and then Heavenly Eternal Standing Kami emerged.

The above five kami are the heavenly kami of special standing.

Then, there came into existence Earth Eternal Standing Kami, Kami of Abundant Clouds Field, male and female Kami of Clay, male and female Kami of Post, male and female Kami of Great Door, Kami of Complete Surface and his spouse, Kami of Awesomeness, Izanagi (kami-who-invites) and his spouse, Izanami (kami-who-is-invited).

Solidification of the Land and the Divine Marriage

The heavenly kami at this time gave the heavenly jeweled spear to Izanagi and Izanami and instructed them to complete and solidify the land. Thus, the two kami, standing on the floating bridge in Heaven, lowered the spear and stirred around, and as they lifted up the spear, the brine dripping from the tip of the spear piled up and formed an island. This was the island of Onogoro.

Descending from heaven to this island, Izanagi asked his spouse Izanami as to how her body was formed. She replied, "My body is formed in such a way that one spot is not filled." Then Izanagi said, "My body is formed in such a way that there is one spot which is filled in excess. How would it be if I insert the portion of my body which is formed to excess into that portion of your body which is not filled and give birth to the land?" Izanami replied, "That would be excellent." Then Izanagi said, "Let

---

[8]The following source material in an abridged translation of selections from the Kojiki, by Joseph M. Kitagawa in Wing-Tsit Chan et al., *The Great Asian Religions: An Anthology* (New York: Macmillan, 1969), pp. 231–236.

us then walk around the heavenly pillar and meet and have conjugal intercourse."

Birth of Other Kami

After giving birth to the land, they proceeded to bear kami [such as the kami of the wind, of the tree, of the mountain, and of the plains.] But Izanami died after giving birth to the kami of fire.

Izanagi, hoping to meet again with his spouse, went after her to the land of Hades. When Izanami came out to greet him, Izanagi said, "Oh my beloved, the land which you and I have been making has not yet been completed. Therefore, you must return with me." To which Izanami replied, "I greatly regret that you did not come here sooner, for I have already partaken of the hearth of the land of hades. But let me discuss with the kami of hades about my desire to return. You must, however, not look at me." As she was gone so long, Izanagi, being impatient, entered the hall to look for her and found maggots squirming around the body of Izanami.

Izanagi, seeing this, was afraid and ran away, saying, "Since I have been to an extremely horrible and unclean land, I must purify myself." Thus, arriving at [a river], he purified and exorcised himself. When he washed his left eye, there came into existence the Sun Goddess, or Heavenly Illuminating Great Kami (Amaterasu), and when he washed his right eye, there emerged the Moon Kami (Tsukiyomi). Finally, as he washed his nose there came into existence Valiant Male Kami (Susanoo).

Greatly rejoiced over this, Izanagi removed his necklace, and giving it to the Sun Goddess, he gave her the mission to rule the Plain of High Heaven. Next he entrusted to the Moon Kami the rule of the realms of the night. Finally, he gave Valiant Male Kami the mission to rule the ocean.

The Conflict Between Amaterasu and the Storm God Susa-No-O

The following selection from the *Nihongi*, I, 40–45 relates the tale of a struggle between Amaterasu and her kinsman, Susa-No-O. It explains some of the features of the cult of Amaterasu.[9]

After this Susa-no-o Mikoto's behavior was exceedingly rude. In what way? Amaterasu (the Heaven-shining Deity) had made august rice fields of Heavenly narrow rice fields and Heavenly long rice fields. Then Susa-no-o, when the seed was sown in spring, broke down the divisions between

[9]William T. de Bary, ed., *Sources of Japanese Tradition* (New York: Columbia University Press, 1958), pp. 29–31.

the plots of rice, and in autumn let loose the Heavenly piebald colts, and made them lie down in the midst of the rice fields. Again, when he saw that Amaterasu was about to celebrate the feast of first-fruits, he secretly voided excrement in the New Palace. Moreover, when he saw that Amaterasu was in her sacred weaving hall, engaged in weaving garments of the Gods, he flayed a piebald colt of Heaven, and breaking a hole in the roof-tiles of the hall, flung it in. Then Amaterasu started with alarm, and wounded herself with the shuttle. Indignant of this, she straightway entered the Rock-cave of Heaven, and having fastened the Rock-door, dwelt there in seclusion. Therefore constant darkness prevailed on all sides, and the alternation of night and day was unknown.

Then the eighty myriads of Gods met on the bank of the Tranquil River of Heaven, and considered in what manner they should supplicate her. Accordingly Omoio-kane no Kami, with profound device and far-reaching thought, at length gathered long-singing birds of the Eternal Land and made them utter their prolonged cry to one another. Moreover he made Ta-ji-kara-o to stand beside the Rock door. The Ame no Koyane no Mikoto, ancestor of the Nakatomi Deity Chieftains, and Futo-dama no Mikoto, ancestor of the Imibe Chieftains, dug up a five-hundred branched True Sakaki tree of the Heavenly Mount Kagu. On its upper branches they hung an august five-hundred string of Yasaka jewels. On the middle branches they hung an eight-hand mirror.

On its lower branches they hung blue soft offerings and white soft offerings. Then they recited their liturgy together.

Moreover Ama no Uzume no Mikoto, ancestress of the Sarume Chieftain, took in her hand a spear wreathed with Eulalia grass, and standing before the door of the Rock-cave of Heaven, skilfully performed a mimic dance. She took, moreover, the true Sakaki tree of the Heavenly Mount Kagu, and made of it a head-dress, she took club moss and made of it braces, she kindled fires, she placed a tub bottom upwards, and gave forth a divinely-inspired utterance.

Now Amaterasu heard this, and said: "Since I have shut myself up in the Rock-cave, there ought surely to be continual night in the Central Land of fertile reed-plains. How then can Ama no Uzume no Mikoto be so jolly?" So with her august hand, she opened for a narrow space the Rock-door and peeped out. Then Ta-jikara-o no Kami forthwith took Amaterasu by the hand and led her out. Upon this the Gods Nakatomi no Kami and Imibe no Kami at once drew a limit by means of a bottom-tied rope (also called a left-handed rope) and begged her not to return again (into the cave).

After this all the Gods put the blame on Susa-no-o, and imposed on him a fine of one thousand tables, and so at length chastised him. They also had his hair plucked out, and made him therewith expiate his guilt.

The Enshrinement of Amaterasu at Ise

The following material from *Nihongi*, I, 175, 176 relates how
the cult of Amaterasu became installed on the island of Ise.[10]

Third month, 10th day. The Great Goddess Amaterasu was taken from (the
princess) Toyo-suke-iri-hime, and entrusted to (the princess) Yamato-hime
no Mikoto. Now Yamato-hime sought for a place where she might en-
shrine the Great Goddess. So she proceeded to Sasahata in Uda. Then
turning back from thence, she entered the land of Omi, and went round
eastwards to Mino, whence she arrived in the province of Ise.

Now the Great Goddess Amaterasu instructed Yamato-hime saying: "The
province of Ise, of the divine wind, is the land whither repair the waves
from the eternal world, the successive waves. It is a secluded and pleasant
land. In this land I wish to dwell." In compliance, therefore, with the instruction of the Great Goddess, a shrine was erected to her in the province
of Ise. Accordingly an Abstinence Palace was built at Kawakami in Isuzu.
This was called the palace of Iso. It was there that the Great Goddess
Amaterasu first descended from Heaven.

[10] Ibid. pp. 34, 35.

Religions Originating in the Middle East

*I*n the twentieth century, Christianity and Islam have more adherents than any other religions in the world, sharing almost one-half of the world's population between them. Their influence upon the values and aspirations of humanity is therefore enormous, and a basic knowledge of them is essential. These two giant missionary religions arose from the milieu of the ancient Middle East, which first produced Zoroastrianism and Judaism. It was from these two religions that Christianity and Islam drew much of their world view, ethics, and especially their view of world history, beginning with a creation and ending with a divine judgment. Baha'i grew out of Islam in the nineteenth century. A study of these religions is essential for the student who would truly be aware of the past and future of many of the people of planet Earth.

CHAPTER 10

Zoroastrianism

Parsee girl being invested with the kusti, the sacred string worn around the waist, which is one of the symbols of Zoroastrian faith. (*Courtesy of Popperfoto/Paul Popper Ltd.*)

Make thy own self pure, O righteous man! Any one in the world here below can win purity for his own self, namely, when he cleanses his own self with good thoughts, words, and deeds.
—Vendidad, 10, 19

One of the world's oldest living religions is Zoroastrianism; depending upon the date accepted, it may be as much as three thousand years old. Unlike its kindred religions, Christianity and Islam, Zoroastrianism is today a minor religion, with adherents numbering approximately 250,000. Nevertheless, this religion cannot be overlooked in any study of the religions of the world because of its great contributions to Judaism, Christianity, and Islam. It should also be studied by the student of world history because it was the religion of the mighty Persian Empire, which once controlled the entire Middle East and attempted to conquer the Greek city-states in the fifth century B.C. Students of philosophy may be interested in the founder of this religion, Zarathustra,[1] who was chosen as the key figure in Friedrich Nietzsche's *Also Sprach Zarathustra.*

PRE-ZOROASTRIAN PERSIAN RELIGION

The origins of Zoroastrian religion are shrouded in great mystery. Existing literary sources are contradictory as to dates and events. Naturally, our knowledge of the pre-Zoroastrian Persians and their religion is also confused. The major literary sources that deal with this period are the Gathas or hymns of early Zoroastrianism. The Gathas are to the people of this religion what the Torah is to the Jews. These hymns are looked upon as the very words of the prophet Zoroaster, and all remaining scriptural books are based upon them. Naturally, these books present the preceding religious practices of the Persian people in a negative light, and for this reason the real truth is difficult to ascertain.

The ancient inhabitants of the land that later became the Persian Empire were a group of people who are generally known as Aryans

---

[1] The true name of the founder of this religion is probably "Zarathustra." The name has been Latinized into the more familiar form "Zoroaster" by Western writers.

("noble ones").[2] A portion of the Aryan population migrated into the Indus valley and laid the foundations for the Indian peoples and their religion. Other Aryans continued to live in the region east of Mesopotamia and became the basis of the Medo-Persian Empire. Originally, the Aryans who migrated to India and those who remained probably both worshiped the same deities.

The Gathas indicate that the Aryans were nature worshipers who venerated a series of deities. Many of these gods are also mentioned in the Indian Vedic literature. They were generically known as *daevas*, and were associated with the sun, moon, earth, fire, and water. Above this series of daevas there were higher gods, such as Intar, the god of war; Asha, the god of truth and justice; and Uruwana, a sky god. The most popular and most important of all these gods was Mithra, who was known as the giver and benefactor of cattle, a god of light, and the representative of loyalty and obedience. Although Zoroaster attempted to discount all gods but one, Mithra could not be displaced in the minds of the Aryan people. He reappears as a judge in the Zoroastrian judgment day; he is seen as Mitra in the Indian Vedic literature; and in the times of the Roman Empire, a religion based on the myth of Mithra became popular among Roman soldiers and merchants and rivaled Christianity in some parts of the Empire.

Above and beyond the local nature gods, there was one supreme lord who was recognized as the one reality and was called Ahura Mazda, "The Wise Lord." As in the case in many other basic religions, there was the recognition of one supreme deity, but the actual day-to-day worship seemed to revolve around the less important localized gods.

Since the predecessors of Zoroaster were nomadic people, it is likely that they worshiped the nature gods on altars, with blood sacrifices. They also favored the sacramental use of the juice of the sacred haoma plant. The actual reason for this is not clear, but some suggest that the juice may have been drunk by the worshiper for its psychedelic qualities.[3] The worship of fire and water may also have been a part of the religion of the ancient Aryans.

The pre-Zoroastrian Aryans also believed that whenever religious practices strayed from the truth, prophets or reformers, called Saoshyants ("those who benefit the community"), would come and restore the purity of the religion. They believed prior to Zoroaster there had been a series of Saoshyants who had restored pure religion, and some saw Zoroaster himself as one of the last and greatest of these reformers.

[2] It is suggested by some that the name of the modern nation, Iran, is actually a shortened version of a name that meant "the land of the Aryans."

[3] See Mary Boyce, *A History of Zoroastrianism*, 2 vols. (Leiden: E. J. Brill, 1975, 1982), I, pp. 157–160.

THE LIFE OF ZOROASTER

Several diverse sources provide information on the life of the prophet Zoroaster. There are, of course, the Gathas, which reveal many of the events of his life. In addition, there are the writings of many ancient Greek and Roman authorities, who showed a great interest in Zoroaster's life. Writers such as Plato, Pliny, and Plutarch made many references to Zoroaster. It is said that Plato attempted to go to Persia to study with the magi, the Zoroastrian priests, but was forbidden because of the outbreak of war between Greece and Persia. Some of the material in these sources is obviously legendary, but some bears the mark of authenticity.

Zoroaster's birth date is uncertain. Many of the ancient Greek writers placed it at various points between 1000 and 600 B.C. Others place it approximately three hundred years before the time of Alexander the Great. Modern investigation into the Gathas seems to indicate a date between 1400 and 1000 B.C.[4]

Since biographical data are scanty, and much of them are heavily laced with legendary material, it is difficult to know more about Zoroaster than the broad outline of his life. His name, Zarathustra Spitama, indicates that he was born into a warrior clan that was connected to the royal family of ancient Persia. The name Zarathustra may mean "possessor of camels" and is taken by some to indicate that he came from a nomadic family. Regarding his early life we know little. Legendary material states that demons attempted to kill the infant Zoroaster several times because they recognized him as a potential enemy.

> They rush away shouting, the wicked, evil-doing Daevas; they run away shouting, the wicked, evil-doing Daevas; "Let us gather together at the head of Aresura! For he is just born, the holy Zoroaster, in the house of Porushaspa. How can we procure his death? He is the weapon that fells the fiends; he is a Druj to the Druj!" Vanished are the Daeva-worshipers, the Nasu made by the Daevas, the false speaking lie.[5]

Each attempt on the infant's life was thwarted by the powers that looked over him. Regarding his childhood we have no information beyond the fact that at age fifteen he put on the *kusti*, the sacred string belt symbolic of his passage into manhood as a member of his religion. Later, Zoroaster became a priest in his religion. He was therefore the only founder of a world religion to be trained as a priest.

[4] Ibid., p. 190.
[5] *The Sacred Books of the East*, James Darmesteter, trans. vol. IV, (Oxford: Clarendon Press, 1880), Zend-Avesta, Vendidad, Fargard XIX, 45, 46, p. 218.

The literature on his life informs us that Zoroaster had three wives and was the father of six children.

At the age of thirty Zoroaster received a revelation from Ahura Mazda. At this most critical time in his life he was wandering about seeking answers to religious questions that troubled him. By the banks of a river he had a vision of the angel Vohu Mana, who appeared nine times the size of a man. In this meeting the angel told Zoroaster that there was only one true God, Ahura Mazda, and that he was to become the prophet of Ahura Mazda. During the next ten years Zoroaster had other visions in which each of the archangels of Ahura Mazda appeared and revealed further truth to him. He began to preach his new revelation at once but with absolutely no success. For ten years no one converted to the message of this new prophet. He was condemned by his people as a heretic and a sorcerer and tempted by evil spirits to cease his preaching. Finally he was able to convert his cousin Maidhyomah.

The turning point in the career of Zoroaster came when he and his cousin journeyed to Bactria to the court of a monarch named Vishtaspa. Zoroaster sought an audience with Vishtaspa in an attempt to convert him, but neither the audience nor the conversion was easy to attain. Although the stories of these events are mixed, it seems clear that Zoroaster stayed at the court of Vishtaspa for several years. During that time rival priests conspired against him and had him thrown into prison. Finally, however, he converted the prince to his new religion. Some of the legends say that the conversion was achieved when Zoroaster healed the favorite horse of Vishtashpa. At any rate, Vishtashpa and his entire court and kingdom became followers of the prophet. In the ensuing years Zoroastrianism spread rapidly in the lands of the Aryan people. Sometimes the conversion rates were speeded up by means of the holy wars. During a war with the Turanians, the city in which Zoroaster lived was invaded. An enemy soldier found the seventy-seven-year-old prophet tending the sacred flame in the fire temple, and killed him.

THE TEACHINGS OF ZOROASTER

The Nature of God

As it was with the life of Zoroaster, so it is with his original teachings: the sources are distant and confused. The problem is compounded by the fact that over the years other teachings and legends have been added to the original message of the prophet. However, the central teaching of Zoroaster seems clear: There is only one true God in all the world and his name is Ahura Mazda. It is he who created the world.

> This I ask Thee, tell it to me truly, Lord! Who set firmly earth below and kept the sky Sure from falling? Who the streams and trees did make? Who their swiftness to the winds and clouds hath yoked? Who, O Mazda, was the Founder of Good Thought?
>   This I ask Thee, tell it to me truly, Lord! Who, benignant, made the darkness and the light? Who, benignant, sleep and waking did create? Who the morning, noon and evening did decree As reminder, to the wise, of duty's call.[6]

It was with this point that Zoroaster began. All the many gods of nature (the daevas) that his people worshipped and the gods to whom they offered sacrificial animals were declared to be false gods. For its time, Zoroaster's monotheism must have been revolutionary. Prior to him there were few who believed that there was one and only one god. There was the monotheism of Aten, supported by Amenophis IV (Akhenaten), the Pharaoh of Egypt in the fourteenth century B.C., but apparently this religion survived less than twenty years, and then the Egyptians went back to their polytheism. Moses, living in the thirteenth century B.C., is said to have taught the Israelites that they were to have no other gods before Yahweh, but he never denied the existence of other gods. It is no wonder that Zoroaster's assertion that there was only one god was so controversial.

The one true god in Zoroaster's religion, Ahura Mazda, was the same god who had been worshiped by the Aryan people for centuries as the distant high god. Zoroaster simply declared that he was the only god. The name *Ahura* means "lord" and indicates one who created and governs the universe. The name *Mazda* means "all wisdom." Thus Ahura Mazda is usually translated as "Wise Lord." Zoroastrian scripture attributes another twenty names to this god, such as He of Whom Questions Are Asked, Giver of Herds, Strong One, Perfect Holiness, Understanding, Blessing, the Unconquerable, Healing, the Creator, and so on.[7] Ahura Mazda is understood to be the invisible and intangible creator and ruler of the universe.

In Zoroaster's understanding of his god, Ahura Mazda revealed himself to humankind through the agency of six modes. These are the *Amesha-Spenta* (usually translated as "Holy Immortals"). West-

---

[6] *The Sacred Books of the East*, L. H. Mills, trans. vol. XXXI (Oxford: Clarendon Press, 1887), Yasna 44:4, 5. pp. 113, 114.

[7] *The Sacred Books of the East*, James Darmesteter, trans. vol. XXIII (Oxford: Clarendon Press, 1883), Ormazd Yast 7, 8, pp. 24, 25.

ern scholars have tended to equate these six modes with the archangels found in Christian theology or with some form of secondary deity. The analogy is not exact, however. The six figures are really six outstanding attributes of Ahura Mazda. Since people cannot properly comprehend the nature of god, Ahura Mazda comes to them as one of these aspects of his total nature. Three of the immortals bear masculine names and carry masculine qualities, while the other three bear feminine names and represent feminine qualities. Thus the total nature of Ahura Mazda is an equal balance of the male and female. The three masculine or father types of these immortals are *Asha* ("Knowledge of the law of God and the law itself"), *Vohu-Mana* ("love"), and *Kshathra* ("loving service"). The three feminine immortals are *Armaiti* ("piety"), *Haurvatat* ("wholeness" or "perfection"), and *Ameretat* ("immortality"). Faithful Zoroastrians pray that these six immortals may come into their homes and bless them.

In addition to these expressions of the total nature of Ahura Mazda, there are other beings who serve him and who may be helpful to human beings. If the six immortals were the archangels of Zoroastrianism, the multiple *Yazata* ("Adorable Ones") would be the hosts of angels surrounding the throne of God. They are limitless in number, but only about forty are mentioned in the Zoroastrian texts and only three received any regular mention. These angels are *Sraosha*, the guardian of humanity who shows obedience to the law of God; his sister and feminine counterpart, *Ashi Vanguhi*, who is the rewarder of good deeds; and the ever-popular *Mithra*, the strongest of these beings and the ideal of soldiers.

The God of Evil

Perhaps Zoraster's greatest contribution to the religions of the world was in the area of the problem of evil. The world is full of both good and evil. It is easy enough to ascribe the good in the world to the good god who has created the world, but who is responsible for the evil? If the creator god is responsible for the evil of the world, then where is his goodness and justice? Many religions have their powers of darkness, their demons, but it remained for Zoroaster to systematize and delineate the forces behind the world's evil.

Zoroastrianism is often referred to as dualistic, that is, as a religion that sees two supreme forces contending with each other for control of the universe. The usual interpretation of Zoroastrianism is that it recognizes a good god and his angels, who are in charge of the good that happens in the world, and it recognizes an evil god and his demons, who are responsible for all of the world's evil. But if this were Zoroaster's understanding of the universe, then he would not be teaching a monotheism but a dualism. In the same vein, one might say that since Christianity recognizes a Satan figure, it too is not monotheistic. This is not the case in the teachings of Zoroaster. According to him, there are two spirits emanating from Ahura Mazda; one is Spenta Mainyu, the Beneficent Spirit; the other is Angra Mainyu, the Evil Spirit. These two have coexisted since the beginning of time.

> Now the two primal Spirits, who revealed themselves in vision as Twins, are the Better and the Bad in thought and word and action. And between these two the wise once chose aright, and the foolish not so.
> And when these twain spirits came together in the beginning, they established Life and Not-Life, and that at the last the Worst Existence shall be to the followers of the Lie, but the Best Thought to him that follows Right. . . .[8]

These two spirits do not exist independently but relate to one another and meet in unity of Ahura Mazda. In this sense they are much like the *yin* and *yang* of Taoism. Neither is free from the influence of the other and each is bound by the other. In the truest sense, Zoroastrianism remains a monotheism with the forces of both good and evil under the control of Ahura Mazda.

Angra Mainyu is also known by others names. He is sometimes known as Ahriman and at other times, as Shaitin or Satan. He is surrounded and abetted by a host of demons who do his bidding in tempting and tormenting human beings. Zorastrianism may have been the first religion to develop a full scheme of demonology. All of the daevas of pre-Zoroastrian Aryan religion came to be identified as demons in the corps of Angra Mainyu. One of the most frequently mentioned of these demons is Aeshma, the demon of wrath.[9] Aeshma is second in command to Angra Mainyu and stalks the earth, polluting it and spreading disease and death.

The Nature of Humankind

Zoroaster saw the forces of good struggling with the forces of evil in the world, and he taught that human beings played a part in this struggle by cooperating with either of the forces. To Zoroaster, men and women were born in a pure, sinless state and could choose to serve either good or evil. Their lives and ultimate destiny depended on the exercise of their free will. If they wished, individuals could serve the forces of evil—they could cooperate in lies, hate, corruption,

[8] Yasna 30:3,4.
[9] Some scholars have suggested that Aeshma is the demon Asmodeus, who tormented Sarah and killed her seven bridegrooms in the Apocryphal book of Tobit.

and every sort of evil—but they could also choose to be a part of good acts that would improve the world. The choice of conduct was entirely up to the individual. In this respect Zoroastrianism is markedly different from the various deterministic views of human conduct. Some religions see a deity controlling the choices that people make; others see human conduct determined by economic or social factors. Unlike these philosophies of human nature, Zoroastrianism taught that men and women were genuinely free to decide if they would do good or evil, and thus were to be held accountable for those choices.

> Hear with your ears the Highest Truths I preach,
> And with illumined minds weigh them with care,
> Before you choose which of Two Paths to tread,—
> Deciding man by man, each one for each;—
> Before the great New Age is ushered in
> Wake, up, alert to spread Ahura's Word.[10]

By exercising the reason with which they were endowed, it is possible for human beings to choose the path of righteousness and in fact achieve perfection in this life. Therefore a scheme of multiple lives, such as the of Hinduism, is not necessary for Zoroastrianism.

> Within the span of this life of Earth
> Perfection can be reached by fervent souls,
> Ardent in zeal, sincere in their toil.[11]

Thus we see that in Zoroastrianism, perhaps more than in any other religion, ethical conduct is urged. Ethical conduct is possible since people have a free choice, and ethical conduct is important since it will determine people's ultimate destiny.

The Destiny of Humankind

Because people have freedom of choice they must stand responsible for their choices. Each deed, either good or evil, will bear its own fruits. Therefore Zoroastrianism sees a law of retribution at work in this life. That which is called karma in Hinduism, and that which is stated by St. Paul as "whatsoever a man soweth, that shall he also reap" [12] is also taught in Zoroastrianism: "Evil to Evil, Good to Good." [13]

[10] Yasna 30:2.
[11] Yasna 51:12.
[12] Galatians 6:7.
[13] Yasna 43:5.

Sassanian period relief, Kermanshaw Province, Iran, 226 A.D. Zoroastrianism was proclaimed the official religion of Persia during this period. (*Courtesy of the Iran Government Tourist Office.*)

> Falsehood brings on age-long punishment,
> And Truth leads on to fuller, higher life.[14]

In this case, Zoroastrianism may be unique among all religions. Zoroastrians so firmly believe in the freedom of people to choose good or evil, and in the inevitability of retribution for those choices, that there is no means of atonement for evil deeds. There is no one to intercede for the sinner, there are no prayers that can change the results of the deed, and there are no offerings that can cover the sin. Human beings choose how they will live, and they are wholly responsible for that choice.

[14]Yasna 30:11.

Another of Zoroaster's gifts to the world of Western religions was his organized scheme of eschatology (belief concerning the end of the world). In religions prior to Zoroastrianism there were sometimes elaborate preparations for the life beyond the grave, as it was with the ancient Egyptians. However, in most religions it was simply assumed that with death, life essentially came to an end. The ancient Hebrews of the pre-exilic period (before 586 B.C.), for example, believed that the dead lived in a realm called Sheol for a time and then gradually faded into nothingness. Perhaps the Aryan kinsmen of Zoroaster living in India had begun to think in terms of reincarnation by this time, but that is not clear. Zoroaster and his followers developed a complete eschatology that was the consistent outworking of his theology of free choice and complete responsibility.

According to Zoroastrianism, upon the death of an individual the soul stays with the body for three days and meditates upon the deeds that were done in life. On the fourth day the soul journeys to the place of judgment. There Mithra judges the soul, based on the deeds performed during life. These deeds are balanced on a scale. If the preponderance of a person's life has been given over to evil, that person's soul will be sentenced to hell, but if the scale tips even slightly toward good, that person's soul will go to paradise. The soul on its way to paradise crosses the Chinvat bridge, which is a wide, easy path. The soul is greeted by beautiful maidens who escort it into heaven. Zoroastrian paradise is a place of beauty, light, pleasant scents, and noble souls who have lived life according to Zoroastrian ethics.

For the person whose balance is weighted down by evil deeds and thoughts, the Chinvat bridge becomes an entirely different experience. Once condemned, the soul is forced out upon this bridge, which turns up on its edge and becomes as hard to walk on as the edge of a sword. Moreover, the soul is tormented by an old hag and eventually falls off the bridge and into hell. Zoroastrian hell is one of the most terrible hells of all. It is vividly described in a work called the *Vision of Arda Viraf*, which was written sometime between 226–641 A.D. In this work the hero is allowed to travel to both heaven and hell, and there to see the miseries and delights of its inhabitants.

I saw the greedy jaws of hell: the most frightful pit, descending, in a very narrow, fearful crevice and in darkness so murky that I was forced to feel my way, amid such a stench that all whose nose inhaled that air, struggled, staggered, and fell, and in such confinement that existence seemed impossible. Each one thought, "I am alone"; and when a mere three days had elapsed supposed that the end of the nine thousand years of time had come, when time would cease and the resurrection of the body occur. "The nine thousand years are run," he would think, "yet, I am not released." In that place even the lesser noxious creatures are as high as mountains, and these so tear, seize, and worry the souls of the wicked as would be unworthy of a dog. But I passed easily thereby in the guidance of Obedience and Thought.

I saw the soul of man through whose fundament a snake went in, like a beam, and came forth out of the mouth; and many other snakes ever seized his limbs. "What sin," I inquired, "was committed by this body whose soul suffers so severe a punishment?" "This," I was told, "is the soul of a man who, in the world, committed sodomy."

A woman's soul I saw, to whom they gave to drink one cupful after another of the impurity and filth of men. I asked, "What sin was committed by the body whose souls thus suffers?" "Having failed to abstain," they replied, "this wicked woman approached water and fire during menstruation." I saw also, the soul of a man, the skin of whose head was being flayed . . . who, in the world, had slain a pious man. I saw the soul of a man into whose mouth they poured continually the menstrual discharge of women, while he cooked and ate his own child . . . "While in the world," I was told, "that wicked man had intercourse with a menstruating woman."[15]

The scene continues with all sorts of horrors. It seems the Zoroastrian hell is filled with men and women who have broken the laws of clean and unclean and who are being punished accordingly. Also there is a large category of men and women who have violated the sexual taboos of Zoroastrianism and who are being punished in a particularly horrible manner.

In the Zoroastrian scheme the souls of the dead abide in their heaven and hell until that point when time ends. The cycle of time will run out at a specified point in the future, and the world will come to its final consummation, as established by Ahura Mazda when he created the world. He will wipe out every tract of the evil work of Angra Mainyu. The souls from hell will be brought up and purified and will join the resurrected souls of the righteous. Then the world will enter a new cycle without the evil and misery of the past. The Saoshyant will restore the world, and in this restored world no one will ever grow old or decay. Angra Mainyu and his demons will be destroyed forever, and the will of Ahura Mazda will reign supreme.

Zoroastrian Ethics

Since the essence of Zoroastrian theology is that people are free to choose between good and evil in this life and will be held responsible for their choices in an afterlife, one would expect Zoroastrians to have a lengthy and involved code of ethics. This is in fact the case, and

[15] Joseph Campbell, *The Masks of God: Occidental Mythology* (New York: Viking, 1964), pp. 198, 199.

Zoroastrians as a people have long been noted in both the ancient world and the modern for their high ethical standards.[16]

The basis for much of Zoroastrian ethics and worship is the understanding of the sacredness of the elements of the earth, fire, water, and air. Whatever violates or pollutes these sacred elements is wicked. Thus, in the Zoroastrian hell those who have polluted the earth or the water with their excrement are subject to unusually harsh punishments. The concern for the elements is seen again and again in Zoroastrian life.

Zoroastrianism also teaches a concern for *Humata, Hukhta, and Hvarshta,* good thought, good word, and good deed. A prayer is "Henceforth let me stand firm for good thoughts, good words, and good deeds, which must be well thought, must be well spoken, and must be well done."[17] Based upon these rather general concerns are the specific demands of Zoroastrianism for righteousness as expressed in truthfulness, chastity, justice, compassion, care of the soil and cattle, charity, education, and service. The ancient Persians were known to the Greek historians for these virtues, particularly for the virtue of truthfulness. In modern India, where most contemporary Zoroastrians live, they are known for their purity of life, for their honesty as business people, and for their concern over the education of their children.

Zoroastrian Worship

Pre-Zoroastrian Aryan worship depended heavily upon blood sacrifices to the various deities, but Zoroaster drastically changed these patterns. Zoroastrian worship consists mainly of prayers offered to Ahura Mazda requesting assistance in living a righteous life and in avoiding temptations. The only form of sacrifice that currently exists is the offering of sandalwood to sacred flames that burn eternally in Zoroastrian fire temples. These fires are tended by priests who have been especially trained for their tasks and who wear surgical masks over their faces lest their breath contaminate the sacred flames. On special occasions during the year Zoroastrians visit the fire temple, offer bundles of sandalwood, and receive the ashes of the sacred flames.

In addition to these forms of worship there are Zoroastrian rituals for each of the points in life that are normally associated with rites of passage. There are ceremonies that attend the birth of a child. Zoroastrian scripture lays out very careful regulations regarding the state

---

[16] The Hebrew Bible pays tribute to the reliability of the Persians when it refers to "the law of the Medes and Persians which altereth not." Esther 1:19.

[17] Sir Rustom Masani, *Zoroastrianism: The Religion of the Good Life* (New York: Macmillan, 1968), p. 78.

of purification of the household and the mother at the time of the birth of a child.

At a certain age (seven years in India and ten years in Iran), young Zoroastrians are received into this religion with the investiture of a sacred shirt (*sadre*) and sacred thread (*kusti*). Except when bathing, they must wear these two items for the rest of their lives. The *kusti* is to be tied and untied on at least five occasions during each day, as a form of prayer. This sacred belt is made up of seventy-two threads which represent the seventy-two chapters of the Zoroastrian scripture, the Yasna.

There are, of course, Zoroastrian ceremonies at other important points in life, such as marriage, periods of purification, and initiation into the priesthood for those who choose it. The most distinctive ritual of all, however, is that which occurs at death. If one believes that earth, fire, water, and air are the most sacred elements in life, and if one believes that the corpse is the most contaminating element of all, then how is one to dispose of the dead? The body cannot be buried lest it contaminate the soil; it cannot be cremated lest it contaminate the sacred fire; and it cannot be buried at sea lest water be polluted. The Zoroastrian solution to this problem is one that has attracted widespread attention.

When a Zoroastrian dies, the corpse is washed, clean suit of clothes is placed upon it, and the *kusti* of the deceased is wrapped around the body. After certain purification ceremonies the body is carried out of the house by corpse bearers. The corpse bearers, along with the mourners, take the body to an enclosure called a *Dakhma*, or "tower of silence." This enclosure looks something like a small version of an American football stadium. It is a round structure, open to the sky. Inside the *Dakhma* there are open compartments and, in the center, a dry well. The body is placed in one of the compartments and its clothing is either removed or torn open. The mourners leave the site and within a few moments vultures descend upon the body and begin to strip it of its flesh. In an area where there are fairly frequent deaths, a large number of vultures usually stay near the *Dakhmas*, and within thirty minutes they are able to strip the body cleanly. After a time, when the bones are dried out by the sun, they are washed down into the central well of the *Dakhma*. Thus the body of the Zoroastrian is disposed of without risking contamination of the soil, fire, or water.

The principle of exposing the dead to birds and beasts of prey seems to have been a part of Zoroastrian life from earliest times. The Zend-Avesta commands the following procedure:

> And two men, strong and agile, having changed their garments, shall lift the body from the clay or the stones, or out of the plastered house, and

A modern Zoroastrian priest attends the sacred fire. (*Courtesy of Magnum Photos, Inc.*)

they shall lay it down at a place where they know that there are always corpse-eating dogs and corpse-eating birds.[18]

Zoroastrian disposal of the dead occasionally runs into problems when the community is small and deaths are so infrequent that there are not large numbers of vultures about the *Dakhmas*. On some oc-

---

[18] Vendidad Fargard VIII, II, 10.

casions there is protest against this procedure by non-Zoroastrian majorities. In such situations it is permissible to bury the body in a stone casket that has been lined with lead to prevent contamination of the soil. Modern Zoroastrians living in Western cities where the practice of exposing the dead may be frowned upon, have begun thinking in terms of cremation by means of an electrical oven, since the body might be burned in this fashion without exposing it to a flame.

THE HISTORICAL DEVELOPMENT
OF ZOROASTRIANISM

Apparently, Zoroastrianism was well established as the religion of the Persian people by the sixth century B.C. It was therefore the religion of Cyrus the Great when he founded the Medo-Persian empire and ruled from 558–530 B.C. Cyrus is mentioned in the Jewish Bible as the one who liberated the Jews from Babylonian captivity in 538 B.C. However, the Zoroastrian sources do not mention Cyrus or his contemporaries. The earliest sources of information on the religion of the Persian Empire are inscriptions from the time of Darius (522–486 B.C.). While they indicate that the people of that era worshipped Ahura Mazda, they do not mention Zoroaster.

> A great god is Ahuramazda, who created this excellent work which is seen, who created happiness for man, who bestowed wisdom and activity upon Darius the king.
>
> Says Darius the king: By the favor of Ahuramazda I am of such a sort that I am a friend to the right, I am not a friend to wrong; it is not my desire that the weak man should have wrong done to him by the mighty; nor is that my desire, that the mighty man should have wrong done him by the weak.
>
> What is right, that is my desire. I am not a friend to the man who is a Lie-follower. I am not hot-tempered. What things develop in my anger, I hold firmly under control by my willpower. I am firmly ruling over my own [impulses].[19]

Zoroastrian influence upon people and religions other than the Persians is also a matter of some speculation. Many of the ancient Greek and Roman writers were apparently enamored with Zoroaster and his thoughts, and he is featured in many of their writings. However, the Persian emperors of the fifth century B.C. failed in several attempts to conquer Greece. Consequently, Persian influence was never strong

---

[19] Jack Finegan. *The Archaeology of World Religions* (Princeton: Princeton University Press, 1952), p. 95.

there. Persia did conquer and hold the Middle East for two centuries, and its influence was very strong upon the peoples of that world. The Jews came under Persian control in 538 B.C. when Cyrus conquered Babylon, where many Jews lived in captivity. According to the Bible, Cyrus allowed the captive Jews to return to Jerusalem.[20] Apparently, a minority of the Jews returned, but most stayed in Mesopotamia and became a part of the culture there. If the book of Esther is correct, a Jewish woman even became the wife of the king of Persia.

How much influence did Zoroastrianism have upon Judaism during this period? We cannot be certain. However, there are certain changes in the theology of Judaism between the pre-exilic days of 586 B.C. and the postexilic period beginning in 538 B.C. Biblical books that reflect the period prior to 586 B.C. have no Satan figure. However, the literature that was written after the exile speaks of a Satan figure four times.[21] In the Intertestamental literature[22] Satan and his demons are mentioned frequently, and in the New Testament literature they are accepted as a regular part of life. Jesus is confronted by Satan as he begins his public ministry, and a large part of that ministry is devoted to exorcising demons. Pre-exilic biblical books have no mention of the resurrection of the body, little concern for life after death, in either a heaven or a hell, no mention of God's plan for bringing the earth to an end, only an occasional mention of angels, and no word about a day of judgment. Each of these themes, which were a part of the teachings of Zoroastrianism, developed in Judaism after the exile and had become vital parts of the religion by the time of Jesus.

The early Christians incorporated these items into their religion. In later years it was the eschatology of Judaism and Christianity that most deeply influenced the prophet Muhammad, and judgment day, resurrection, heaven, hell, Satan, demons, and angels all became a vital part of Islam. It may be that all of these major religions drew their eschatology from Zoroastrianism.

The Persian Empire was conquered by Alexander the Great in the fourth century B.C. In the years that followed, Zoroastrianism suffered a decline. The entire Persian culture was invaded by the pervasive Hellenistic culture. During the era of the Roman Empire Zoroastrianism was quiescent also. All that seems to have been active in this period was the cult of Mithra. The Roman Empire became ac-

---

[20] II Chronicles 36:22,23, Ezra 1:2–4.

[21] I Chronicles 21:1, Job, Zechariah 3, and Psalm 109.

[22] The so-called Intertestamental literature consists of books written between the conclusion of the Hebrew Bible (ca. 400 B.C.) and the beginning of the Christian New Testament (ca. 50 A.D.). Many of these books were written in the style of scripture and were popular, but for various reasons were never accepted into either the Jewish or Christian Bibles.

The Birth of Mithras. Mithras was believed to have been born from a rock. He holds his short sword and the torch, symbols of his obedience to the god Sol Invictus (the unconquered sun). Other symbols of events in his life surround his birth scene. (*Courtesy of the Museum of Antiquities of the University and Society of Antiquaries of Newcastle upon Tyne.*)

quainted with Mithra in the first century A.D. Mithra, the god of light and obedience, appealed especially to the Roman soldier, and so Mithraic cults were established over the entire Mediterranean world. The worship of Mithra became so popular that some suggest it was a major rival to early Christianity. However, when Christianity was declared to be the official religion of the Roman Empire, Mithraism was suppressed.

A revival of Zoroastrianism occurred in the third century A.D. under the Sassanid rulers of Persia. These rulers established official support for Zoroastrianism and had the ancient scriptures translated into contemporary language. The religion continued to flourish until the seventh century. At this time, Islam was arising out of the desert regions to the south of Persia. By 642 the Muslim warriors had, with three major battles, caused the collapse of the Sassanian empire. At first the Muslims were tolerant of the Zoroastrians. The latter were, after all, a people with a book (scripture) and they worshiped only one god. However, by the ninth century Muslim persecution of the Zoroastrians had grown to such a point that most Zoroastrians were forced to either convert to Islam or flee the country. Those who chose to flee followed the path of their ancient Aryan relatives and went to India. There they found tolerance by the Hindu majority and were known as the Parsees (that is, those who came from Persia). They remained an insignificant minority in India until the nineteenth century, when the British arrived. Because the Parsees were not encumbered with the caste system or intricate food taboos, and because they valued education, they quickly became favorites of the British. As a result of this favored position in British India, the modern Parsee community leads in fields such as education, business, and finance, in a far greater way than its minority status would indicate.

ZOROASTRIANISM TODAY

The Zoroastrianism is one of the smallest religions in the modern world. Approximately 11,000 Zoroastrians remain in the land of Iran. They have always been regarded with suspicion by the Shi'ite Muslims, who are the majority in Iran. The Zoroastrians who remained were called *Gabars* ("infidels") by the Muslims. Their situation became more difficult with the development of the Islamic Republic in Iran in 1979. At that time the Shah of Iran was overthrown and the country came under the strict Islamic rule of Ayatollah Khomeini. Since then, non-Muslim groups such as the Zoroastrians and the Baha'is have suffered much persecution.

The Parsee community in India is small but prosperous. It numbers perhaps 100,000. Its members tend to be leaders in many fields and are valued highly. However, the Parsee birthrate lags behind that of the rest of India, and, since it does not encourage conversion, Zoroastrianism is not a growing religion. Parsees are found in many other parts of the world including North America. The total population of Zoroastrian people in the world is estimated at 250,000.

STUDY QUESTIONS

1. Zoroastrianism is called a dualism. What does this mean? Contrast the dualism of Zoroastrianism with the monotheism of Judaism or Islam.

2. One of the great contributions of Zoroastrianism to Western religions is eschatology. Show how Zoroastrian eschatology influenced Judaism, Christianity, and Islam.

3. How does the Zoroastrian scheme of the afterlife effect the ethical teachings of this religion?

4. Why have Zoroastrians refused to bury or burn the bodies of the dead?

SUGGESTED READING

Boyce, Mary. *A History of Zoroastrianism.* 2 vols. Leiden: E. J. Brill, 1975, 1982.

Duchesne-Guillemin, Jacques. *Symbols and Values in Zoroastrianism.* New York: Harper & Row, 1966.

Masani, Rustom. *Zoroastrianism: The Religion of the Good Life.* New York: Macmillan, 1968.

Vermaseren, M. J. *Mithras, The Secret God.* Translated by Therese and Vincent Megaw. New York: Barnes & Noble, 1963.

Zaehner, R. C. *The Dawn and Twilight of Zoroastrianism.* New York: Putnam, 1961.

Zoroastrian Eschatology

One of the major contributions of Zoroastrianism to the religions of the world is its eschatology. The Zoroastrian understanding of the judgment of the soul after death, life
after death either in paradise or in Hell, and end of the world,
was paralleled in the eschatology of Judaism, Christianity,
and Islam. The following materials, taken from Zoroastrian
sources, illustrate some of these concepts.[23]

Roads to the Netherworld

Put not your trust in life, for at the last death must overtake you; and dog
and bird will rend your corpse and your bones will be tumbled on the
earth. For three days and nights the soul sits beside the pillow of the body.
And on the fourth day at dawn (the soul) accompanied by the blessed
Srōsh, the good Vāy, and the mighty Vahrām, and opposed by Astvihāt
(the demon of death), the evil Vāy, the demon Frēhzisht and the demon
Vizisht, and pursued by the active ill-will of Wrath, the evil-doer who bears
a bloody spear, (will reach) the lofty and awful Bridge of the Requiter to
which every man whose soul is saved and every man whose soul is damned
must come. Here does many an enemy lie in wait. Here (the soul will
suffer) from the ill-will of Wrath who wields a bloody spear and from Astvihāt who swallows all creation yet knows no sating, and it will (benefit
by) the mediation of Hihr, Srōsh, and Rashn, and will (needs submit) to the
weighing (of his deeds) by the righteous Rashn who lets the scales of the
spiritual gods incline to neither side, neither for the saved nor yet for the
damned, nor yet for kings and princes; not so much as a hair's breadth
does he allow (the scales) to tip, and he is no respecter (of persons), for he
deals out impartial justice both to kings and princes and to the humblest
of men.

And when the soul of the saved passes over that bridge, the breadth of
the bridge appears to be one parasang broad. And the soul of the saved
passes on accompanied by the blessed Srōsh. And his own good deeds
come to meet him in the form of a young girl, more beautiful and fair than
any girl on earth. And the soul of the saved says, "Who art thou, for I have
never seen a young girl on earth more beautiful or fair than thee." In answer the form of the young girl replies, "I am not girl but thy own good
deeds, O young man whose thoughts and words, deeds and religion were
good: for when on earth thou didst see one who offered sacrifice to the
demons, then didst thou sit (apart) and offer sacrifice to the gods. And

[23] R. C. Zaehner, *The Teachings of the Magi* (London: Allen & Unwin, 1956), pp. 133–138.

when thou didst see a man do violence and rapine, afflict good men and treat them with contumely, and hoard up goods wrongfully obtained, then didst thou refrain from visiting creatures with violence and rapine of thine own; (nay rather,) thou wast considerate to good men, didst entertain them and offer them hospitality, and give alms both to the man who came from near and to him who came from afar; and thou didst amass thy wealth in righteousness. And when thou didst see one who passed a false judgement or took bribes or bore false witness, thou didst sit thee down and speak witness right and true. I am thy good thoughts, good words, and good deeds which thou didst think and say and do. . . ."

And when the soul departs from thence, then is a fragrant breeze wafted towards him,—(a breeze) more fragrant than any perfume. Then does the soul of the saved ask Srōsh saying, "What breeze is this, the like of which in fragrance I never smelt on earth?" Then does the blessed Srōsh make answer to the soul of the saved, saying, "This is a wind (wafted) from Heaven; hence is it so fragrant."

Then with his first step he bestrides (the heaven of) good thoughts, with his second (the heaven of) good words, and with his third (the heaven of) good deeds; and with his fourth step he reaches the Endless Light where is all bliss. And all the gods and Amahraspands come to greet him and ask him how he has fared, saying, "How was thy passage from those transient, fearful worlds where there is much evil to these worlds which do not pass away and in which there is no adversary, O young man whose thoughts and words, deeds and religion are good?"

Then Ohrmazd, the Lord, speaks, saying, "Do not ask him how he has fared, for he has been separated from his beloved body and has traveled on a fearsome road." And they served him with the sweetest of all foods even with the butter of early spring so that his soul may take its ease after the three nights terror of the Bridge inflicted on him by Astvihāt and the other demons, and he is sat upon a throne everywhere bejeweled. . . . And for ever and ever he dwells with the spiritual gods in all bliss for evermore.

But when the man who is damned dies, for three days and nights does his soul hover near his head and weeps, saying, "Whither shall I go and in whom shall I now take refuge?" And during those three days and nights he sees with his eyes all the sins and wickedness that he committed on earth. On the fourth day the demon Vizarsh comes and binds the soul of the damned in most shameful wise, and despite the opposition of the blessed Srōsh drags it off to the Bridge of the Requiter. Then the righteous Rashn makes clear to the soul of the damned that it is damned (indeed).

Then the demon Vizarsh seizes upon the soul of the damned, smites it and ill-treats it without pity, urged on by Wrath. And the soul of the damned cries out with a loud voice, makes moan, and in supplication makes many a piteoous plea; much does he struggle though his life-breath endures no more. When all his struggling and his lamentations have proved of no avail, no help is proffered him by any of the gods nor yet by any of the demons, but the demon Vizarsh drags him off against his will into nethermost Hell.

Then a young girl who yet has no semblance of a young girl, comes to meet him. And the soul of the damned says to that ill-favored wench, "Who art thou? for I have never seen an ill-favored wench on earth more ill-favored and hideous than thee," And in reply that ill-favored wench says to him, "I am no wench, but I am thy deeds,—hideous deeds,—evil thoughts, evil words, evil deeds, and an evil religion. For when on earth thou didst see one who offered sacrifice to the gods, then didst thou sit (apart) and offer sacrifice to the demons. And when thou didst see one who entertained good men and offered them hospitality, and gave alms both to those who came from near and to those who came from afar, then didst thou treat good men with contumely and show them dishonour, thou gavest them no alms and didst shut thy door (upon them). And when thou didst see one who passed a just judgement or took no bribes or bore true witness or spoke up in righteousness, then didst thou sit down and pass false judgement, bear false witness, and speak unrighteously. . . ."

Then with his first step he goes to (the hell of) evil thoughts, with his second to (the hell of) evil words, and with his third to (the hell of) evil deeds. And with his fourth step he lurches into the presence of the accursed Destructive Spirit and the other demons. And the demons mock at him and hold him up to scorn, saying, "What grieved thee in Ohrmazd, the Lord, and the Amahraspands and in fragrant and delightful Heaven, and what grudge or complaint hadst thou of them that thou shouldst come to see Ahriman and the demons and murky Hell? for we will torment thee nor shall we have any mercy on thee, and for a long time shalt thou suffer torment."

And the Destructive Spirit cries out to the demons, saying, "Ask not concerning him, for he has been separated from his beloved body, and has come through that most evil passage-way; but serve him (rather) with the filthiest and most foul food that Hell can produce."

Then they bring him poison and venom, snakes and scorpions and other noxious reptiles (that flourish) in Hell, and they serve him with these to eat. And until the Resurrection and the Final Body he must remain in Hell, suffering much torment and many kinds of chastisement. And the food that he must for the most part eat there is all, as it were, putrid and like unto blood.

Zorastrian Dualism

One of the unique contributions of Zoroastrianism was its dualistic understanding of the world. Zoroaster saw the forces of good and the forces of evil struggling for control of the universe. The following section from the *Greater Bunda-hishn*, I, 18–26 speaks of this dualism.[24]

18. Ohrmazd, before the act of creation, was not Lord; after the act of creation he became Lord, eager for increase, wise, free from adversity, manifest, ever ordering aright, bounteous, all-perceiving.

19. (First he created the essence of the gods, fair movement, that genius by which he made his own body better) for he had conceived of the act of creation; from this act of creation was his lordship.

20. And by his clear vision Ohrmazd saw that the Destructive Spirit would never cease from aggression and that his aggression could only be made fruitless by the act of creation, and that creation could not move on except through Time and that when Time was fashioned, the creation of Ahriman too would begin to move.

21. And that he might reduce the Aggressor to a state of powerlessness, having no alternative he fashioned forth Time. And the reason was this, that the Destructive Spirit could not be made powerless unless he were brought to battle.

22. Then from Infinite Time he fashioned and made Time of the long Dominion: some call it finite Time. From Time of the long Dominion he brought forth permanence that the works of Ohrmazd might not pass away. From permanence discomfort was made manifest that comfort might not touch the demons. From discomfort the course of fate, the idea of chang-lessness, was made manifest, that those things which Ohrmazd created at the original creation might not change. From the idea of changlessness a perfect will (to create) material creation was made manifest, the concord of the righteous creation.

23. In his unrighteous creation Ahriman was without knowledge, with-out method. And the reason and interpretation thereof is this, that when Ahriman joined battle with Ohrmazd the majestic wisdom, renown, per-fection, and permanence of Ohrmazd and the powerlessness, self-will, im-perfection and slowness in knowledge of the Destructive Spirit were made manifest when creation was created.

24. For Time of the long Dominion was the first creature that he fash-ioned forth; for it was infinite before the contamination of the totality of Ohrmazd. From the infinite it was fashioned finite; for from the original creation when creation was created until the consummation when the De-structive Spirit is made powerless there is a term of twelve thousand years which is finite. Then it mingles with and returns to the Infinite so that the creation of Ohrmazd shall for ever be with Ohrmazd in purity.

25. As it is said in the Religion, "Time is mightier than both creations—

[24] R. C. Zaehner, trans., *Zurvan: A Zoroastrian Dilemma* (Oxford: Clarendon Press, 1955), pp. 314–316.

the creation of Ohrmazd and that of the Destructive Spirit. Time understands all action and order. Time understands more than those who understand. Time is better informed than the well-informed; for through Time must the decision be made. By Time are houses overturned—doom is through Time—and things graven shattered. From it no single mortal man escapes, not though he fly above, not though he dig a pit below and settle therein, not though he hide beneath a well of cold waters."

26. From his own essence which is material light Ohrmazd fashioned forth the form of his creatures—a form of fire—bright, white, round and manifest afar. From the material (form) of that Spirit which dispels aggression in the two worlds—be it Power or be it Time—he fashioned forth the form of Vāy, the Good, for Vāy was needed: some call it Vāy of the long Dominion. With the aid of Vāy of the long Dominion he fashioned forth creation; for when he created creation, Vāy was the instrument he needed for the deed.

CHAPTER 11

Judaism

Raising the ancient ram's horn. (*Courtesy of Israeli Government Tourist Office.*)

Hear, O Israel: The Lord our God is one; and you shall love the Lord your God with all your heart, and with all your soul, and with all your might.
—*Deuteronomy 6:4,5*

One of the most perplexing problems that arises in any discussion of Judaism is its definition. If we were to define Judaism as we define any other religion, we might say that a Jew is anyone who adheres to a certain set of Jewish religious beliefs or practices. Indeed, in many cases this may be a very effective definition. Unfortunately the issue has been clouded so that it not always so simple. Alan W. Miller, in his introduction to *The God of Daniel S.: In Search of the American Jew*, lists eight different types of persons who are called Jews in American society. These range all the way from the extremely orthodox Hasidic Jew to the person whose parents or grandparents happened to be born Jewish.

Judaism cannot be defined primarily in terms of religious beliefs because there are some people who are called Jews but consider themselves atheists. Adolph Hitler found it expedient to define Judaism in terms of race, but in modern Israel Jews display the physical characteristics of nearly every race. There are European Jews, African Jews, and Oriental Jews.

If we cannot define Judaism in terms of all people who might be called Jews, we can speak of those people who identify themselves with the religion of Judaism. Though religious practices among Jews differ widely, generally the unifying feature among all Jews is a belief in the oneness of a God who works in and through historical events and who has in some manner chosen the Jewish people as agents. Around this basic principle Judaism is built.

THE BIBLICAL PATRIARCHS

Since Judaism is concerned with God's activity in history, it is necessary to describe Jewish beliefs and practices historically. According to the Bible, God found it necessary to call out one man and his family from all the people on earth. This calling of Abraham is recorded in Genesis 12. It came after a series of disastrous dealings with all humankind (Adam and Eve, Cain and Abel, the flood, the tower of Babel, and so on). Because of these disasters, God chose to communicate with only one nation, the descendants of Abraham. Abraham was called to enter a convenant with God, in which Abraham was promised that he would become the father of a great nation, would possess a land, and would become a blessing to all people if he would be faithful to his part of the covenant. Abraham is succeeded in this convenant by his son Isaac, his grandson Jacob (or Israel), and Jacob's twelve sons. These figures are called the patriarchs of the Jewish people because they are the physical forebears of the nation, and their stories are found in Genesis 12–50. These tales were probably written by authors generations after the times of the patriarchs. Though some scholars doubt the historicity of these figures, their names and their ways of life fit into history of the Fertile Crescent at the beginning of the second millennium B.C.[1]

If there were people like Abraham and Isaac who were the forebears of the Jews, what was the nature of their lives and their religion? The biblical narratives present the patriarchs as nomads, following their flocks from place to place. Abraham is described as a citizen of the city of Ur of the Chaldees (Genesis 11:31) who left his home to follow the voice of God to the land of Canaan, on the western side of the Fertile Crescent. Historically, he could have been one of the waves of Amorites who flooded the Fertile Crescent between 2000–1750 B.C. The Mari letters from Mesopotamia in this era reveal the use of such names as Benjamin and Jacob, indicating the historical plausibility of the biblical narrative.

Though the Bible does not give the reader a systematic presentation of the religious beliefs and practices of the patriarchs, the narratives reveal a great deal about their theology. They worshiped one God who was guiding their destinies. The generic name for God among the Semites is *El*. This name is frequently used in various combinations in the patriarchal literature to refer to their God. He is called *El Shaddai* ("God of the mountains" or "God Almighty"); *El Elyon* ("God Most High"); *El Olam* ("God Everlasting") and most frequently, *Elohim* ("Gods").[2]

This God was worshiped by burning animal sacrifices on crude altars built in the open. The Israelites apparently did not worship their God in a building or a temple until the time of Solomon (961–922

---

[1] A collection of tablets unearthed at Ebla, in Syria, in the middle 1970s lists some patriarchal names and some biblical sites in an historical context as early as the mid-third millenium B.C. All the material from Ebla has not yet been translated, and archaeologists are far from agreement as to their true worth and significance.

[2] The use of the plural here is a mystery. While it might be tempting to assume that at one point the patriarchs may have been polytheists, there is nothing in the narratives to indicate worship to any but the one God, and the term is used only in a singular sense.

B.C. In the story of Abraham's attempt to offer his son Isaac upon the command of God (Genesis 22) there is a hint that the patriarchs may have practiced human sacrifices in previous times.

There are also indications of basic animistic practices in the worship of the patriarchs. Abraham made a covenant with Abimelech in Beersheba and called upon the name of God. To seal the covenant Abraham planted a grove in Beersheba (Genesis 21:32, 33). God appeared to Isaac and reaffirmed the convenant while Isaac was digging wells near Beersheba (Genesis 26:17–25). Jacob slept upon certain stones, and in his dreams God spoke to him and renewed the covenant (Genesis 28:11–16). The connection between the appearance of God, the reaffirmation of the covenant, and the typical animistic symbols of trees, wells, and stones may be significant.

From very early in the worship of the patriarchs, circumcision of the male was practiced. Genesis traces the ritual back to a commandment of God to Abraham (Genesis 17:10, 11). However, circumcision is a very ancient and widespread religious custom, which probably did not originate with Abraham. In addition, the practice of keeping a Sabbath may have been a part of the worship of the patriarchs. Genesis attaches the custom to the days of creation, when God rested on the seventh day after laboring for six days (Genesis 2:2) In the patriarchal stories, it is not clear what the practices of these figures were on the Sabbath.

THE EXODUS

Whatever their religious practices may have been, and whatever gods they may have worshiped, the stories of the patriarches are in Genesis to give the reader a reason for the most important event in Judaism, the Exodus. God promised Abraham that a great nation would spring from his seed, that this nation would have a homeland (Canaan), and that the entire world would be blessed by this nation. The book of Genesis closes with a great nation springing up from the descendants of Abraham, but they were not in Canaan. They were in Egypt where they were bound in slavery. Therefore, the Exodus from Egypt and their slavery, the journey back to Canaan, and the conquest of the land had to be accomplished before God's promise to Abraham could be fulfilled. The events and characters of the Exodus—in which God acted to save his chose people, the Israelites; in which he miraculously delivered them from slavery at the hands of the most powerful nation in the world at that time; in which he revealed his name and his laws to its leaders and finally brought the former slaves, as a conquering army, into Canaan—became the heart and soul of the Jewish religion. These events are remembered annually in the various major holidays of Judaism. The legal material, which is attributed to the Sinai experience, became the most important material in the Jewish Bible.

The book of Exodus opens with the descendants of Abraham, the Israelites, crying out for deliverance from their enslavement by the Egyptians. The key figure in this drama of salvation is Moses. Like many great figures in religion, Moses was endangered as an infant by the forces of evil and was miraculously delivered. He was rescued and reared by the daughter of the Pharaoh of Egypt. Since the name *Moses* is an Egyptian name, there may be a factual basis for the story. Recognizing his Israelite heritage, and killing an Egyptian in defense of a slave, Moses was exiled to the Sinai desert, where he lived for forty years as a shepherd. In the desert, the God of Abraham revealed himself to Moses, speaking through a bush that burned but was not consumed. The God revealed that his name was YHWH[3] and commanded Moses to lead the Israelites from their slavery. Moses returned to Egypt and, after a series of ten miraculous plagues upon the Egyptians, was able to gain the release of the Israelites. The final plague was death to the firstborn of every house in Egypt. Israelites who ate a sacred meal of roasted lamb, bitter herbs, and unleavened bread, and who smeared lamb's blood upon their doorposts, were passed over by the angel of death.

When the Israelites fled Egypt, they were pursued by the Pharaoh, who had changed his mind about their release. The waters of the Sea of Reeds[4] were parted by YHWH, and the Israelites crossed through on dry land. When the Egyptians attempted to follow them, the waters returned, and the Egyptians were trapped and drowned. This event, along with the Passover, became a part of Jewish history—an act in which God intervened to deliver his chosen people.

The next event of significance was the giving of the law on Mt. Sinai. After crossing the Sea of Reeds, the Israelites came to Mt. Sinai on their journey to Canaan. From this mountain, YHWH communicated his law to the Israelites through Moses. Ten absolute laws that are basic to Jewish life are found in Exodus 20:1–17 and Deuteronomy 5:6–21. They may be summarized as follows:

1. I am the Lord your God, who has brought you out of the land of Egypt, out of the house of bondage. You shall have no other gods before me.

---

[3] The vowels of this name have been lost because Jews preferred not to pronounce the divine name lest they take it in vain. Many modern scholars vocalize it as Yahweh.
[4] The usual reading of this as "Red Sea" is based upon an ancient mistranslation.

2. You shall not make any graven image.
3. You shall not take the name of the Lord your God in vain. . . .
4. Remember the sabbath day, to keep it holy.
5. Honor your father and your mother.
6. You shall not kill.
7. You shall not commit adultery.
8. You shall not steal.
9. You shall not bear false witness against your neighbor.
10. You shall not covet your neighbor's property.

Basically, these commandments stress obedience and loyalty to YHWH and decent behavior toward members of the community. The books of Exodus, Leviticus, and portions of Numbers and Deuteronomy, which follow, elaborate codes of law that regulate every area of life. These laws purport to have been given by God through Moses during the wilderness experience, but many of them reflect a community that has been established in agricultural life for centuries.

Whenever they may have been codified, the legal material in the Pentateuch (the first five books of the Bible) became the single most important part of the Bible for Judaism. It is to this material that Jews have turned for centuries, looking for inspiration and guidance. It is this material that became the basis for the later Mishnah and Talmud, which in turn became central for Judaism. It is at this point that Judaism is defined as a religion of the law, and Jews as a people primarily concerned with obedience to the laws of God.

In addition to the laws of God, the years in the Sinai wilderness gave the Israelites two other religious institutions. These were the Ark of the Covenant and the Tent of Meeting. The Ark of the Covenant was a coffinlike box that contained the sacred relics of the Exodus and may have been the portable throne of YHWH. This box was the most treasured sacred possession of the Israelites and was eventually placed in Solomon's temple in the tenth century B.C. It presumably remained there until the temple was destroyed by the Babylonians in 586 B.C. The Tent of Meeting was not so popular or long lived as the Ark. It was literally a tent that could be moved from place to place with the nomadic Israelites. It provided a place for the worship of YHWH and for sacrifice to him. After the Israelites entered Canaan, it is mentioned only once in connection with the cult at Shiloh.

After a period of wandering in the wilderness, the Bible records that the Israelites conquered the territories on the east bank of the Jordan River. Then, under the leadership of Joshua, Moses' successor, they crossed the Jordan and conquered the cities of Canaan. Two conflicting accounts are given. According to the book of Joshua, the Is-

The modern city of Jerusalem seen from the Mount of Olives. The Dome of the Rock located in the right center probably occupies the location of Solomon's temple. (*Courtesy of Israeli Government Tourist Office.*)

raelites swept across the country and destroyed the Canaanites. The book of Judges tells another story, however. Here we have a picture of the worshipers of YHWH living side by side with the native dwellers of Canaan, and sometimes even being subjected to them. Later events seem to support the second story.

When the Israelites settled in Canaan, they renewed their covenant with YHWH. The cult of YHWH, its ark, its priests, and its sacrifices was centered in Shiloh. Worship at this time seems to have been a rather informal matter. The cultic priests attended to those who came, on special days, to the sanctuary for special needs. They were in turn supported by the gifts of those who came to worship, and perhaps by the donations of the various tribal groups who surrounded the cult center.

THE RELIGION OF THE HEBREW MONARCHY

The religion of Israel took a more formal turn when David became the first truly effective king of the Israelites. David, who was from the southern portion of the country, needed a central capital and a cult to unify his nation, He captured Jerusalem in the central hill country and made it his capital. Jerusalem had little to recommend it except its location, its easily defended hills, and perhaps a history as a sacred site. David and later historical events parlayed these features into making Jerusalem one of the most important, most disputed cities in the world. David's abilities as a military leader and administrator helped Israel to develop into a fairly powerful and wealthy small nation of the ancient Middle East. The Bible tells us that David wished to build a magnificent temple for YHWH in Jerusalem but was forbidden.

The Temple

It remained for Solomon, David's son and successor, to build the temple. With all the wealth that his father had amassed, Solomon built a palace for himself and a temple for his God. Strangely enough, the temple was designed by Tyrian builders who were worshipers of the Baalim, the gods of the Canaanites and Phoenicians, condemned in the Bible. The temple naturally took the form of other Canaanite temples built for the Baalim. The Ark of the Covenant was placed in the temple, and a class of priests were attached to the temple. Worship of YHWH thus took on a more formal status. The main form of worship remained the animal sacrifice, with its flesh burned in the courtyard. In the temple, prayers were offered to YHWH, and, if the example of David is typical, there may also have been sacred dancing before the Ark (II Samuel 6:14).

The Prophetic Movement

With the development of the temple cult another aspect was introduced into the worship of Israel. Other ancient religions, including that of the worship of the Baalim, had developed bodies of religious leaders called prophets. In their earlier forms, the prophetic figures were persons involved in the ecstatic aspects of worship. Unlike the priests, whose duties involved the proper offerings of sacrifices, the prophets of ancient religions danced, sang, breathed incense, and worked themselves into an ecsatic state in order to hear the voices of their gods. The prophets of Israel may have begun in this fashion.[5] Occasionally they performed the function of the witch doctors of other religions. They healed the sick, cursed, blessed, produced food for their followers, and worked other miracles.[6]

Eventually, a portion of the Israelite prophetic movement became attached to the royal household. The first of these prophets to be in-

---

[5] I Samuel 19:24.
[6] The prophet about whom there is the most information in the Bible, and who fits this pattern, is Elisha. See II Kings 2:1–13, 13:21.

volved with the palace was Nathan, who was part of the court of David. It was Nathan who accused David after David had murdered Uriah and taken Uriah's wife, but it was also Nathan who was instrumental in placing Solomon on the throne at the death of David. Others who were more or less attached to the royal houses, or at least had the ear of the kings, were Elijah, Isaiah, and Jeremiah. Still other prophets were common men who preached fiery denunciations against wickedness among peasants and royalty. Outstanding in this group were men like Amos and Micah. These prophets must have been but a few of many who preached in troubled times. Their messages were remembered and preserved by their disciples, and eventually written into the Bible.

In contemporary English, the word *prophet* has the connotation of prediction, but to label all the works of the prophets of Israel as predictions is to do them injustice. In the social and political upheavals of the eighth century B.C., the prophetic movement produced four classic figures—Amos, Hosea, Isaiah, and Micah—who are remembered not so much for their predictions as for the boldness with which they denounced the social injustices of their times, and for the beautiful, poetic language with which they bade the Israelites to return to their God.

> Thus says the Lord:
> "For three transgressions of Israel,
>   and for four, I will not revoke the punishment;
> because they sell the righteous for silver,
>   and the needy for a pair of shoes—
> they that trample the head of the poor into the dust of
>   the earth,
> and turn aside the way of the afflicted."[7]

> Seek good, and not evil,
>   that you may live;
> and so the Lord, the God of hosts, will be with you,
>   as you have said.
> Hate evil, and love good,
>   and establish justice in the gate;
> it may be that the Lord, the God of hosts,
>   will be gracious to the remnant of Joseph.[8]

> "With what shall I come before the Lord,
>   and bow myself before God on high?

[7] Amos 2:6, 7a.
[8] Amos 5:14, 15.

Shall I come before him with burnt offerings,
   with calves a year old?
Will the Lord be pleased with thousands of rams,
   with ten thousands of rivers of oil?
Shall I give my first-born for my transgression,
   the fruit of my body for the sin of my soul?"
He has showed you, O man, what is good;
   and what does the Lord require of you
but to do justice, and love kindness,
   and to walk humbly with your God?[9]

These are not the words of starry-eyed seers who were predicting the future but of men who were busy speaking the word of God to their people. The prophetic movement of ancient Israel stands out as one of the major moral and literary contributions of any religion to the world.

THE EXILE AND THE RETURN

In 922 B.C. the nation of Israel was split into two nations. The northern nation was called Israel, and was the larger and more productive of the two. It was destroyed by the Assyrians in 721 B.C., and ten of the twelve tribes of Israel disappeared from history. The people who made up this nation were either killed or deported and enslaved. Whatever their fate, they were never to be a distinctive people of Israel again; they are known as the ten lost tribes.

The southern nation was called Judah, and was made up of the remaining two tribes. Judah survived the Assyrian years but was eventually destroyed by the neo-Babylonian empire in 586 B.C. With the Babylonian conquest the city of Jerusalem was destroyed, Solomon's temple torn down, and the citizens of Judah either killed or carried into captivity. Whereas the northern nation had simply ceased to exist after its destruction, the nation of Judah clung to its identity, customs, and religion while in captivity. It was led by a man who was both a prophet and a priest, Ezekiel. Ezekiel and others so forged the identity of the Jews in captivity that when the Persians captured Babylon in 538 B.C., many Jews were freed and returned to Jerusalem to reestablish their lives and their temple there.

During the Babylonian captivity certain theological changes were forced upon the Jews. Previously the had thought of YHWH as their local deity, perhaps residing in the temple at Jerusalem. Now the temple

---

[9] Micah 6:6–8.

was destroyed and the people were scattered in a strange land. An unknown poet of that period wrote of their sadness.

> By the waters of Babylon,
>   there we sat down and wept,
>   when we remembered Zion,
> On the willows there
>   we hung our lyres.
> For there our captors required of us songs,
>   and our tormentors, mirth, saying,
>   "Sing us one of the songs of Zion!"
> How shall we sing the Lord's song
>   in a foreign land? [10]

Ezekiel answered that YHWH was mobile and was available to his people in Babylon as easily as he was in Jerusalem.[11] Another prophet, Isaiah,[12] stated that YHWH was no longer just the God of the Israelites but was in fact the one true God for all the people of all the world. Even the Zoroastrian Cyrus, king of Persia, is but an instrument of YHWH.

> Who says of Cyrus, "He is my shepherd,
>   and he shall fulfill all my purpose;"
> saying of Jerusalem, "She shall be built,"
>   and of the temple, "Your foundations shall be laid."[13]

Indeed, the mission of the Jews as YHWH's chosen people is to present his message to all the nations of the world.

> I will give you as a light to the nations,
>   that my salvation may reach to the end of
>   the earth.[14]

Among the most influential of Jews to return from Babylon to Jerusalem was Ezra (ca. 428 B.C.). Ezra was a priest who brought with him a copy of scripture that he read to the citizens of the rebuilt Jerusalem. The nature and exact content of this book are not known, but whatever they were, it had a profound effect upon the people. They reformed their lives according to the laws in this book. For all times Jews became identified, not only as a people of God's laws, but

---

[10] Psalm 137:1–4.
[11] See Ezekiel 1.
[12] Isaiah chapters 40–66 are usually attributed to a sixth century B.C. prophet.
[13] Isaiah 44:28.
[14] Isaiah 49:6b.

as a people centered around a book. Ezra was probably the person who
began the process of canonizing books as the word of God. From this
time onward it was believed that God no longer spoke through the
prophets but through his book. It remained only for the followers of
YHWH to read his book and interpret it for their lives.

In addition to the growth of a scriptural canon, the religion of the
period of the second temple (520 B.C.–70 A.D.) included sacrifices at
the rebuilt temple, with a cult of priests, singers, and attendants. At
first the temple, which was rebuilt in the sixth century B.C., was a
rather simple structure. In the time of Herod the Great (37–4 B.C.)
and later, it was restored and decorated to a magnificent state, far
beyond the glory of Solomon's temple. Just a few years after the second temple was finally finished, it was destroyed by the Romans in
70 A.D.

RELIGIOUS INSTITUTIONS OF
THE DIASPORA

The years following the Assyrian destruction of Israel saw the beginning of the Diaspora. The Diaspora was the scattering of the Jewish
people all over the world. Sometimes it was forced upon them, as it
was in 586 B.C. by the Babylonians. In other cases, Jews moved by
choice to other nations or stayed by choice in nations such as Babylon
and Persia. By the year 250 B.C. there was such a large Jewish community in Alexandria, Egypt, that it was necessary to translate the
Bible from Hebrew to Greek.[15] Jews in Babylon lived well under Persian rule. According to the book of Esther, a young woman from the
Jewish community actually became queen of Persia in the fifth century B.C. In later years, Jews were found in all the cities of the Roman
Empire.

The Synagogue

Judaism away from the land of Israel was forced to accept a new concept of God and new institutions of worship. The notion of YHWH
as the only God of all the peoples of the world, as enunciated by
Second Isaiah, was accepted, and various books were accepted as his
word. Because they could not get to the temple to worship except on
rare occasions, and because blood sacrifices were no longer appropriate for Jews living in such cosmopolitan centers as Rome, Athens,
and Alexandria, the Jews of the Diaspora developed the institution of

---

[15] The Septuagint.

the synagogue. The English word *synagogue* is derived from the Greek word *synagoge*, which means "assembly." The synagogue is literally an assembly. Snyagogue can occur wherever there is a copy of the scripture (Torah) and ten adult (over thirteen years of age) Jewish males. Ten adult males constitute a quorum, or a *minyan*. Whenever this combination exists, there can be prayer and instruction. Synagogue may be held under a tree or in an elaborate building set aside for the purpose. No one knows exactly when the institution of the snyagogue was developed, but whatever the specific date, it arose during the Diaspora, when Jews could no longer worship at the temple in Jerusalem, and it serves Judaism to this day.

Along with the synagogue there arose the figure of the rabbi. The rabbi is not a priest or a minister in the traditional sense. The world *rabbi* literally means "my master." With the establishment of the Torah as the voice of God, there also arose the need for someone to spend time studying the scripture and teaching the community. Those persons who had the time, the interest, and the intelligence to study gradually began to be singled out and sought after by inquiring members of the Jewish community. They eventually became known as rabbis.

As rabbis sought to interpret scripture to Jews living lives very different from those of Abraham, Moses, or David, many problems arose. How does one apply laws intended for nomadic or agricultural peoples of the Iron Age to persons living in imperial Rome in the time of Augustus Caesar? Rabbis struggled with these problems, sought hermeneutical (interpretive) principles, and interpreted God's laws to their people. Outstanding rabbis arose; their fame as wise men and interpreters spread; students came to study with them; great rabbis disagreed with one another and entered into debate with each other. Gradually an accepted corpus of rabbinic opinion developed.

In addition to the synagogue and the rabbis, the Diaspora Jewish communities maintained other distinctive features that set them apart from the gentiles who surrounded them, and Jews maintained their separateness. Jews separated themselves from gentiles by refusing to work on the Sabbath. In the worlds of the Greeks and the Romans, where only religious holidays were days of rest from labor, the Jews were regarded as lazy loafers because of their refusal to work one day out of seven. In addition, Jews refused to eat certain foods that gentiles ate. Kosher food laws in the early Diaspora were not as broad or as complex as they later became, but Jews of the Diaspora doubtless had to refuse many foods that their neighbors ate. The story of Daniel, in which a Jewish captive in Babylon refuses to eat the king's food, must have been representative of the plight of many. Jews also practiced circumcision. This ritual was looked upon with disgust, at

Lifting the Torah after the reading. (*Courtesy of Monkmeyer Press Photo Service.*)

least by the Greeks, who believed in the beauty of the unmarred human body. Undoubtedly circumcision was the object of humor and disgust among other gentile nations also.

In 66 A.D. the cup of bitterness between Jews and Romans in Judea overflowed into violent revolution. As first the Jews were successful, but by 68 A.D. the tide had turned. The Romans, under Titus, gradually subdued the land and finally besieged Jerusalem. By the summer of 70 A.D. the city was defeated. Jewish revolutionaries were slaughtered or enslaved by the thousands. Worst of all, the magnificent temple was looted and burned, never to be rebuilt. This was surely the most severe blow of all to the Jews.

From the ashes of destruction there arose a new Judaism. The phoenix was modest indeed. A rabbi living in Jerusalem during the siege, Yohanan Ben Zakkai, escaped in a coffin borne by his disciples to the tent of Titus. The rabbi asked permission to establish an academy to discuss the future of Judaism on the Mediterranean seacoast at the town of Yabneh. Titus granted permission, and Ben Zakkai gathered about him the rabbis of Israel to discuss and debate the future of Judaism. The debate lasted for years. Among the issues that were decided was the exact list of books that belonged in the sacred Torah. The books of the law (Genesis-Deuteronomy) were widely accepted, as were most of the books of the prophets.[16] The books that were the object of the debate were called "the writings," These were books such as the Psalms, Job, Esther, Ruth, Tobit, Judith, I and II Macabees. After much debate, the canon that we know today was established.

The Mishnah

After the years at Yabneh, the leadership of post 70 A.D. Judaism moved to the region of Galilee. Here the debates over the meaning of the law continued for years. The greatest leader of Jews during the second century A.D. was man named Judah ha-Nasi (Judah the Prince). Judah's great contribution to Judaism was to bring together all the commentary about the law that had been collected since the days of Ezra. The commentary, along with the disputes, was collected into a series of tractates arranged into six divisions. This collection by Judah was called the *Mishnah* (repetition) and became one of the great literary milestones in Jewish history.

Within the pages of the Mishnah the reader finds the attempt of the second-century Jew to live by the law of God. At this time there was no more Jewish nation, and after 135 A.D. there was no hope of rebuilding the temple or reestablishing a priesthood. All that was left was the law. How does one keep the law? By building a structure of additional, complementary laws as an adjunct to the primary law, so that in keeping the second law the first will not be violated. For example, the Ten Commandments say, "Remember the sabbath day and keep it holy." People must not work on the Sabbath, but what does that mean? The only form of work specifically forbidden in the Bible is lighting a fire. Some literalists would have had the observant Jew simply sitting in cold and darkened rooms all the Sabbath. The rabbis who produced the Mishnah tried to interpret what the Torah really meant by keeping the Sabbath. They tried to develop interpretations

---

[16]In the time of Jesus, the Bible was defined as "the law and the prophets."

and secondary laws that would make the Sabbath a day of worship and joy. The Mishnah has one entire section set aside for opinions relating to the Sabbath to make the house more cheerful. Gentiles could be employed to light or extinguish cooking fires on the seventh day.

> If a gentile lighted a lamp an Israelite may make use of the light, but if he lighted it for the sake of the Israelite it is forbidden. If he filled (a trough) with water to give his cattle to drink, an Israelite may give his own cattle to drink after him, but if the gentile did it for the Israelite, it is forbidden. If he made a gangway by which to come down (from a ship) an Israelite may come down after him, but if he did it for the Israelite, it is forbidden. Rabban Gamaliel and the elders were once travelling in a ship, and a gentile made a gangway by which to come down, and Rabban Gamaliel and the elders came down by it.[17]

According to the Mishnah, the Sabbath was to be a happy day. The best food the family could afford was to be served on Sabbath; the best clothes were to be worn on that day; and even emergency situations that might arise on the Sabbath were to be taken care of by the rabbis. Every step was taken to preserve the sanctity of the law, on the one hand, and to make life under the law as comfortable and agreeable as possible on the other.

The Talmud

Following the compilation of the Mishnah, the center of Jewish life and learning gradually moved from Galilee to Babylon, where Jews had lived since 586 B.C. While there was occasional persecution of the Jews by the Zoroastrians of that area, life for the Jews in Babylon was easier and more profitable than it had become in Galilee. In 323 A.D. Constantine became sole emperor of what was left of the Roman Empire. Because of his wife and mother, Constantine was favorably inclined toward Christianity and took steps toward making it the official religion of the empire; this was finally accomplished near the end of the fourth century. The rise of Christianity brought about pressure and hostility against the Jews in Galilee and throughout the rest of the empire.

Christianity had begun as a sect of Judaism, with Jesus and all his immediate disciples as practicing Jews. Christianity drew its scripture, its forms of worship, and its eschatology directly from Judaism. In fact, the early church first met in synagogues throughout the Roman Empire.

---

[17] *The Mishnah*, Herbert Danby, trans. (Oxford: Oxford University Press, 1933) p. 115.

The western or wailing wall is all that remains of the magnificent temple built by Herod. The rest of the temple was destroyed by the Romans in 70 A.D. (*Courtesy of Israeli Government Tourist Office.*)

The New Testament records the first splits between Judaism and Christianity in the middle of the first century, when first Peter and then Paul invite non-Jews into Christianity. In the missionary ministry of Paul not only are non-Jews brought in, but they come without benefit of circumcision or kosher food laws; they did not have to convert to Judaism or keep its laws. Whether it was Judaism drawing away from Christianity or the reverse is not clear, but the schism occurred and was intensified after 70 A.D. Jesus' messiahship was doubtless one of the issues of separation, but it was not the only issue. Jews were willing enough to accept potential messiahs, such as Simon Bar Cochba in the second century and Sabbatai Zevi in the seventeenth century. The greatest issue must have been the Christian acceptance of gentiles who were not required to keep the laws of Judaism. Christian hostility toward Judaism centered on Jewish refusal to accept Jesus as Messiah and the supposed guilt of all Jews for the death of Jesus. Jewish minorities living on Christian-dominated lands began to feel the hostility from the majority. Byzantine Christianity soon made life for Jews in Palestine less pleasant than it had been under pagan Roman domination, and life in Zoroastrian Babylon became more acceptable.

In the Jewish community of Babylon the discussion over the laws of God continued. Additional interpretative, illustrative, and sermonic material was brought together under the title of *Gemara*. Gemara was more than additional commentary on the Mishnah and Torah; it was a body of literature that dealt with every area of Jewish life. Gemara developed in both the Palestiniam and the Babylonian communities. When Gemara was added to the Mishnah the resultant product was called Talmud.

The Palestinian Talmud was completed about 425 A.D. The body of this Talmud is about one-third the size of its Babylonian counterpart. Both Talmuds are written mainly in Aramaic with some Hebrew mixed in, while the Mishnah texts are entirely in Hebrew. The Babylonian Talmud is the larger (it runs to 2.5 million words) and more influential of the two; it was completed about 500 A.D. Both Talmuds are made up of two kinds of material: legal material, discussions, and decisions that are called *Halachah* ("the proper way"), and sections that deal with history, folklore, and sermons that are called *Haggadah* ("tale," "narrative"). About 30 percent of the Babylonian Talmud is Haggadah. The following tale is an example of Haggadic material found in the Talmud.

> Another time the Emperor said to R. Joshua B. Hananiah, "I wish to see your God." He replied, "You cannot see him." "Indeed," said the Emperor, "I will see him." He went and placed the Emperor facing the sun during the summer solstice and said to him, "Look up at it." He replied, "I cannot." Said R. Joshua, "If at the sun which is but one of the ministers that attend the Holy One, blessed be He, you cannot look, how then can you presume to look upon the divine presence!"[18]

As the repository of the oral law, the Talmuds became the most important nonbiblical material in Judaism. Since the time of their completion they have been the object of many commentaries and endless study by all generations of Jews.

With the completion of the Talmuds in Babylon at the beginning of the sixth century A.D., a portion of the life of Judaism came to an end. Those scholars who had complied the Talmud were followed by scholars who funded and ran academies for the study of the Talmud. The presidents of these academies were called *Gaon* (excellency), and the period between 600–1000 A.D. was known as the Gaonic period. These Geonim lived mainly in Babylon and were the leading religious authorities in Judaism during that period. The last of the great Geonim was Saadia ben Joseph (882–942), who became Gaon of the academy at Sura. Saadia was best known as the leading spokesperson of tal-

[18] B. Talmud, Hullin 60a.

The Tower of David, Jerusalem. According to the Bible, David erected the walls of Jerusalem. Tradition has it that this tower may also have been built by David, or possibly by Solomon. (*Courtesy of Israeli Government Tourist Office.*)

mudic Judaism against the Karaites, a group within Judaism that denied the authority of the Talmuds and desired to live exclusively by the legal material within the Hebrew Bible. With the passing of Saadia the great Jewish academies of Babylon faded.

The Cabala

Jewish mysticism is as old as Judaism. Elements of the occult in Judaism have been found in the Bible, in the Talmud, and in the writings of many of its leading figures. The concern for angels, demons, magical incantations, charms, witches, ghouls, interpretation of dreams, the date of the coming of the Messiah, numerology, and the name of God have been lumped together under the heading of *Cabala* (tradition). The codification of these elements in Judaism probably began in Babylon between approximately 500 and 900 A.D. when books containing speculations in these areas began to appear. The outstanding book from this period was the *Sefer Yetzirch* ("the book of creation"), which came from the Babylonian Jewish community. After this period the cabalistic movement shifted to Spain, Italy, Germany, and Poland.

By far the most outstanding compilation of cabalistic material was the *Sefer Hazohar* ("the book of splendor"), which is more simply known as the Zohar. The book is attributed to Tanna Simeon Ben Yohai, a Jewish leader of the second century A.D. Internal evidence has caused modern scholars to assign the Zohar to Moses de Leon, a thirteenth-century Spanish mystic from Cordova. De Leon probably attempted to attribute the book to a figure one thousand years earlier in order to give it more authority. Whoever its author may have been, the Zohar soon became the most widely read book in Judaism, replacing for a time even the Talmud.

The cabalistic literature became popular with Jews during a very difficult time for them. By the late fifteenth century the Jews had been officially expelled from most European nations. The Babylonian Jewish community had also collapsed. World Judaism had entered a period of persecution, exile, poverty, and depression. The Talmud is a book for reasonable people who live under rather normal circumstances. The cabalistic literature is for the oppressed and despised who have little hope. Jews fleeing from Spain and from ghetto to ghetto in Europe needed a Messiah to deliver them more than ever. Therefore they searched the Zohar for magical clues that would lead them to the Messiah and to salvation.

The Zohar is concerned with such themes as the nature of God, the theory of the emanations from God, cosmogony, the creation of humankind and of angels, the existence of evil, and the work of angels in the world. Like some of the Gnostics, the cabalists asked how an essentially good and spiritual God could have created this sensual world. The answer to this question that most satisfied them was that the nature of God is truly incomprehensible to humanity. Therefore God reveals himself to the world through ten emanations. These emanations are named for the various attributes of God, such as "wisdom," "strength," and "beauty." It was by the work of these ten forces that the sensual world was created. Humans are the highest of all creation and are endowed with three souls. These souls are preexistent and immortal. The cabalists also taught that evil is nonexistent. That which is called evil is but the negative side of good. By such teachings the cabalists differed markedly from orthodox Judaism.

In order to achieve its unorthodox teachings the followers of Cabala utilized unique and far-fetched systems of interpretation. For example, in reading the story of Abraham and the angels who visited him at Mamre (Genesis 18:2a), the cabalists found the following phrase: "Behold, three men stood in front of him." Nowhere in the text are the angels named, but the cabalists ascertained that they must have been Michael, Gabriel, and Raphael. They achieved this knowledge by totaling the numbers of the letters in the phrase. Hebrew, like Latin and Greek, utilizes the letters of its alphabet for numerals. Therefore, by adding the numerical values of the letters used in the Hebrew phrase, "Behold, three men stood in front of him," the interpreter totals 701. The numerical value of the names Michael, Gabriel, and Raphael is also 701. Therefore, the cabalists reason, these three must have been the angels who visited Abraham.

One of the outstanding cabalistic groups was founded in upper Galilee in the village of Safed by Jews fleeing from Spain in the sixteenth century. They were led by Isaac Luria (1534–1572). Luria and his friends established a whole system of amulets, words, and numbers that would overcome evil. Luria himself is said to have believed that he was Elijah, the forerunner of the Messiah. Wherever Jews were found during these troubled times, they studied the cabalistic literature and dreamed of the Messiah.

JUDAISM AND THE MODERN WORLD

Because of the misery of the Jews in the ghettos, there arose a strong messianic hope. The object of this hope in the seventeenth century was a charismatic figure named Sabbatai Zevi. Sabbatai Zevi was born in Smyrna in 1626. As a young man he studied the mysticism of the Cabala and eventually gathered about him a band of disciples. Sabbatai Zevi and his followers wandered from place to place in the Middle East. In Egypt he married a girl named Sarah, who claimed that she was destined to be the bride of the Messiah, and Sabbatai Zevi was eventually declared the Messiah by his disciples. These claims raised Jewish hopes all over the world. Jews danced for joy in the streets of many European cities; bets were taken in Lloyd's of London as to the exact day when Sabbatai Zevi would enter Jerusalem. In 1665 the Messiah and his party entered Constantinople with the purpose of dethroning the Sultan of Turkey. The Turkish rulers imprisoned him and gave him the choice of conversion to Islam or death. Sabbatai Zevi converted and thus bitterly crushed the hopes of Jews everywhere.

Where Sabbatai Zevi had failed, another figure arose in Germany, and his life and influence would do much to deliver the Jews from their misery. In 1743 a frail, hunchbacked boy appeared at the only

A Bar Mitzvah Ceremony. Usually at the age of thirteen Jewish young men go through the ritual of Bar Mitzvah (Son of the Commandment). This rite of passage marks entrance into adult status and responsibilities. (*Courtesy of Kapp Photography and Mrs. Peter Knobel.*)

gate through which a Jew could enter Berlin. When asked his purpose in the city, he replied that he had come to learn. This was Moses the son of Mendel of Dessau. He had been born in 1729, and indeed his passion was learning. The long hours spent in studying under poor conditions had ruined his health and stooped his shoulders. After his arrival in Berlin he spent his time learning and soon began to write essays in German that caused him to be widely accepted by the poets and philosophers of eighteenth-century Germany and the court of Frederick the Great. Moses Germanized his name to Mendelssohn. That a Jew could write in German prose and be accepted by the learned of that nation was phenomenal. Mendelssohn became the friend of German critic and dramatist Gotthold Ephraim Lessing, and is believed to be the hero of his play, *Nathan the Wise.* He encouraged the Jews to come out of the ghettos and enter the modern world, to write and speak German rather than Yiddish.

At the same time, another movement that would influence modern Judaism was developing in Poland. About 1750, in Podolia, a simple, uneducated man named Israel ben Eliezer (1699–1760) began to preach to his Jewish brethren that God was not to be found in scholarly research in the Bible or the Talmud but in simple, heartfelt faith.

Israel became known to his followers as Baal Shem Tov ("master of the good name"), and his followers became known as the *Hasidim.* The following is an example of the teaching of the Baal Shem Tov.

Frequently we observe a Zaddik lamenting unto the Lord because of his poverty, yet failing to gain any improvement of his position. This should not be construed to mean that the Lord does not concern himself for the Zaddik. Nay, it is rather a sign of God's great love for him. A parable will illustrate this: A prince of tender age built himself a little house of toy boards. A careless servant inadvertently struck it with his foot, and the fragile structure fell to pieces. The weeping child complained to the king and besought him to punish the servant. The king, however, had secretly intended to surprise his beloved son by building for him a miniature palace of solid and beautiful materials. Therefore, knowing of the rare gift in store for the prince, he did not act upon the lad's complaint.

It is the same with the Zaddik, God's cherished son. The Lord has made ready for him a splendid abode in Paradise. He therefore, gives slight attention to the Zaddik's complaints of temporary discomforts in this insignificant world below.[19]

The Hasidic movement was widely accepted by the Jews of Eastern Europe, although many of them were excommunicated by the orthodox rabbis. One could not find more distant opposites than the two stellar figures of Judaism in the eighteenth century, Moses Mendelssohn and Baal Shem Tov.

The end of the eighteenth century brought new winds of thought to Europe and North America, and these were to have an effect upon Judaism. In North America there was a revolution and a subsequent constitution, which stated that all people are to be treated equally under the law. For the first time in modern history a gentile nation declared that the Jews were to be treated as people with equal rights. In France, the revolution of 1789 was followed by a declaration of the rights of men, including the Jews. Wherever the armies of France went in the following years, ghettos were torn down and Jews were given civil rights. In that same year, Jews were first admitted to the European universities. On the one hand, Mendelssohn encouraged the Jews of Western Europe to come out of the ghettoes and join the Christian societies in the adventure of modernity. On the other hand, the Baal Shem Tov and his followers in the Hasidic movement encouraged the Jews of Eastern Europe to search within their own traditions and find the resources to maintain Judaism as an independent entity in the midst of Christian societies.

[19] Louis I. Newman, trans., *The Hasidic Anthology* (New York: Scribner, 1934), p 3.

Reform Judaism

With Jews following the lead of Mendelssohn and entering European society on all levels, the demand for reforms in Judaism became apparent. If Jews were to be a part of Western civilization, many felt, some of the historical practices of Judaism were out of place. In 1843 a group of German Jewish leaders met and made the following declarations:

1. There is a continuation in the development of Judaism.
2. The Talmud has no authority for the modern Jew.
3. We seek no Messiah, and we know no homeland but the land of our birth.

This declaration became the basis for Reform Judaism. Reform Jews began to use more vernacular and less Hebrew in their worship; their synagogues were called temples; kosher food laws were not stressed; choirs and organs were introduced. Indeed, Reform worship in the nineteenth century was in many respects like Christian worship. Many of the Jewish immigrants to the United States in the early nineteenth century were Reform.

While Jews were enjoying new freedoms and rights in Western Europe in the nineteenth century, the lot of their kinspeople in Eastern Europe had scarcely changed in two hundred years. Czarist Russia allowed fierce pogroms against the Jewish population. Harassment and second-class citizenship were their lot. In Russia, they were squeezed, into certain areas called the Pale of Settlement and forbidden even to travel into other parts of the nation. In 1881, after the assassination of Alexander II, the worst series of pogroms agains the Jews broke out. As a result, a great exodus from Eastern Europe took place. Thousands of Jews fled to any country that would have them; the greatest number took refuge in the United States.

Zionism

In Western Europe the Jewish population may have believed that it had been accepted into the modern world as an equal. Indeed, civil rights had been granted to Jews, and Jews were making great contributions in every profession. But the anti-Jewish feeling of Christian Europe still lay beneath the surface. These feelings were brought into the open by the Dreyfus case. In 1894, Captain Alfred Dreyfus was accused of betraying French military secrets during the Franco-Prussian War. On the basis of flimsy evidence, Dreyfus was convicted and condemned to life imprisonment on Devil's Island. During the trial the hostility of the French toward the Jewish Dreyfus and all Jewish people erupted. Captain Dreyfus was granted amnesty in 1899, and seven years later, his court-martial was declared "erroneous."

The Dreyfus case was to have long-range effects upon modern Judaism because of a young Austrian journalist named Theodore Herzl, who covered the trial for his newspaper. Herzl and others came to realize that regardless of the liberal façade of European countries, Jewish people would never be treated fairly until they had a land of their own. In a movement know as Zionism, Herzl and others pleaded the cause of a Jewish state. Attempts were made to find land anywhere in the world where Jews might develop a state, but in Jewish hearts, all locations took second place to the land they had left hundreds of years before, the land now called Palestine.

In the early 1900s, Jews began buying land and developing settlements in Palestine. Herzl worked himself into an early grave on behalf of Zionism, but the seeds had been sown for what would eventually become the nation of Israel. In 1909, the Jewish city of Tel Aviv was founded, and by 1920 approximately 50,000 Jews had immigrated to Palestine.

With the end of World War I, the defeat of the Turks and the breakup of the Ottoman Empire, Palestine became governed by mandate by the British. In 1917 Chaim Weizmann, a Zionist who had rendered service to the British as a chemist, persuaded the British Foreign Secretary, Lord Balfour, to issue a declaration which said: "His majesty's government views with favour the establishment in Palestine of a national home for the Jewish people . . . ." With the issuance of this document by a sympathetic government that ruled Palestine, it would seem that it should have been clear sailing for Zionists. Their objective, however, was not to be easily achieved.

In many cases, the native populations of Palestine reacted strongly against great numbers of Jewish immigrants and put pressure on the British to restrict the immigration. By 1928 there were 100,000 Jews in Palestine; by 1931, 175,000; by 1933, 220,000. The Arabs reacted with riots and strikes. In 1939, fearing to further offend the Arab nations, the British government issued a white paper in which a quota was set, limiting Jewish immigration to 15,000 per year for the following five years. This quota came at a time when the Jews of Europe were desperately seeking refuge from the Nazi holocaust.

The Nazi Holocaust

In 1933 Adolph Hitler became chancellor of Germany. Very quickly thereafter that nation was changed into an anti-Semitic, Nazi dictatorship. Little by little the rights of the Jews in Germany were taken

Menorah in front of the Knesset, Israel's parliament. The seven-branched cande-labrum is one of the oldest symbols of Judaism. (*Courtesy of Israeli Government Tourist Office.*)

away. The Nuremburg Laws of 1935 reduced Jews to second-class citizens who could not vote, hold office, work in most professions, or marry non-Jews. Jews who could see the handwriting on the wall fled to whatever refuge they could find. Immigration laws in the United States prevented large numbers of them from entering this country. Palestine was virtually closed as a result of the white paper of 1939.

When Hitler began to move into Eastern Europe in 1939, millions of Jews in Poland, Hungary, and Czechoslovakia fell into his hands. In most cases, the non-Jewish citizens of these countries were only too happy to cooperate with the Nazis on the Jewish question. (The yellow badges and ghettos of the Middle Ages were restored for the Jews.) How was the extermination of European Jews to be accomplished? There were millions of Jews trapped in Europe, and their numbers made a solution to the Jewish problem difficult. The first solution was deportation of all Jews in Nazi occupied countries to concentration work camps in the east. Hundreds of thousands were jammed into cattle cars and sent to Eastern Europe, where they were forced to work until they died.

By 1941, a final solution was reached by the Nazis: The Jews were to be biologically annihilated. Many extermination methods were attempted, but the one that was eventually accepted as cheapest and most efficient was death by Zyklon B gas. Methodically, Jews from the concentration camps were driven into gas chambers and asphyxiated. Their bodies were shorn of all valuables, including hair and gold teeth. Skin, bones, and even body fat were put to use by the thorough Nazis. Bodies that were of no more use were then burned in special ovens.

There are various estimates of the number of Jews killed during the Nazi years. The usual number given is six million. In Poland alone, prior to World War II the Jewish population was 3,350,000. In 1945 there remained only 50,000.

One might ask how such a thing could happen in the twentieth century. How could it happen in one of the most civilized nations in the history of the world? Germany had given the world great musicians, philosophers, theologians, scientists, and leaders in nearly every profession, art, and craft. How could such a nation produce such evil? A number of explanations for the Nazi holocaust have been suggested:

1. *German racism.* Adolph Hitler appealed to a very basic emotion in his people when he asserted that the Aryans were the supreme race and that other races, especially the Semites, were inferior.

2. *German troubles following World War I.* Germany had been defeated in World War I and humiliated in the peace treaty that followed. German pride demanded that some reason be found for the defeat. The most common excuse was that Germany had been "stabbed in the back," and the most common traitor was the Jew. Germany also suffered from severe economic conditions following the war, and this too was blamed on the Jews. The fraudulent *Protocols of the Elders of Zion* was believed to be the plan for an international Jewish conspiracy to destroy the economies of Christian nations. At the same time, many Germans also believed that the Jews were behind the international Communist conspiracy. Therefore Jews were accused of being the international bankers and financiers who would wreak havoc in world economy at the same time that they were considered to be the Marxist enemy of capitalist economies!

3. *Nazi madness.* It would seem that in some cases the destruction of the Jews was more important to the Nazis than anything else.

There were occasions when trains that were needed to take German troops and supplies to the front were diverted to take Jews to concentration camps.

4. *Modern efficiency.* The very number of Jews murdered could not have been achieved at any other time in history. Neither the Romans nor the Cossacks could have killed so many persons in such a short period of time. Only modern, efficient technology made it possible.

5. *The silence of the rest of the world.* At a time when Jews most needed a refuge, doors were shut to them all over the world. Christian nations and Christian leaders did very little to rescue the victims, and little protest was raised. No attempt was made by Allied bombers to wreck the machinery of the holocaust. It was as though the rest of the world were willing to allow Hitler to have his way with the unfortunate Jews in his trap.

The holocaust reduced the world population of Jews by as much as one-third. When the enormity of the crime was made public in the Nuremburg trials of the late 1940s and, the Eichmann trial of 1960, it had a profound effect upon Jewish thinking. It was one of the primary causes for the development of the nation of Israel in the years after World War II. The holocaust may have had a lasting effect upon Jewish theology also. At least one Jewish thinker, Richard Rubenstein, has said in his book, *After Auschwitz,* that for Judaism, God died in the holocaust. Before the Nazi years, whenever there was a serious threat to the Jews, no matter how severe it was, God somehow answered the cries of his people. At Auschwitz and in other concentration camps, there seemed to be no answer to their prayers as they were led to the ovens. The full story of the holocaust and its effects upon Judaism has not yet been told.

The State of Israel

The development of the state of Israel came quickly after World War II. By 1947, it was obvious that Britain could no longer control Palestine and its two warring factions. Zionists were determined to build a home for the thousands of displaced Jews, and the Palestinian Arabs were just as determined that it would not be established in Palestine. In 1947 United Nations voted to partition Palestine into a Jewish and an Arab state. The British left Palestine in May of 1948, and immediately Israel proclaimed statehood. Ironically, the United States and Russia vied to see who would be the first to recognize the new nation. Immediately, Israel was attached by five neighboring Arab states. She survived these attacks and others, and has answered, at least in part, the Zionits' dreams of a homeland for the Jews.

Unfortunately, with the development of the state of Israel, thousands of Palestinian Arabs fled their homes in what became the new nation. Since 1948, many of them have eked out miserable existences in various refugee camps. During the war of 1967, other large portions of territory formerly held by the Arab nations fell to the Israelis, including the city of Old Jerusalem and one of the most sacred shrines of all to the Jews, the Wailing Wall, that one portion of the temple area remaining after the war of 70 A.D. The governance of the city of Jerusalem and the west bank of the Jordan, and an equitable solution to the difficulties of the Palestinian refugees, remain serious problems.

Current Varieties in Judaism

Recent statistics estimate that there are 17,000,000 Jews in the world. Three million are in Israel; 2,620,000 are in Russia; and 5,870,000 are in the United States. The largest concentration of Jews anywhere in the world is in New York City, with 1,836,000. As already stated, the term *Jew* covers a multitude of religious practices and beliefs. The Jews of the world are widely divided in terms of their belief and practices.

Those called Orthodox are the largest group within Judaism. The Orthodox attempt to stay as close as possible to the nature of biblical and talmudic Judaism. Kosher food laws are stressed, along with strict observance of the Sabbath. In worship, men and women are separated in the synagogue and both must cover their heads. Hebrew is the language of Orthodox worship.

Reform Judaism is popular mainly in the United States and Europe. It attempts to be as modern as possible in Judaistic beliefs and practices. It worship is usually on Friday evenings, and its synagogues are called temples. Men and women sit together with uncovered heads. The vernacular is used through most of the service, with Hebrew interspersed only occasionally. Organ music and choirs are common. Few members of Reform temples attempt to keep all of the kosher food laws or the talmudic restrictions on the Sabbath.

In between the Orthodox and the Reform is the Conservative movement. It arose in the nineteenth century, led by Sabata Morais, as a reaction against the extremes of the Reform movement. Shocked at the excesses of the Reform leaders at the Pittsburg Conference of American Rabbis in 1885, Sabata Morais and others organized the Jewish Theological Seminary of America in New York City. This seminary has been the voice of Conservative Judaism in America ever since. Conservative Judaism is distinguished from the Orthodox by its greater concern with the scientific study of the Bible and rabbinical material. In its worship the vernacular is used more than Hebrew. Unlike Reform Jews, Conservatives tend to worship on Saturday morning. Men are required to cover their head with the traditional skull cap (*yarmulke*) during worship. There is an attempt by many Conservatives to abide by the biblical and talmudic laws regulating food and Sabbath observance.

Growing out of the Conservative movement is Reconstructionist Judaism. Mordecai M. Kaplan, a professor of homiletics at the Jewish Theological Seminary in the 1930s, is regarded as the founder of Reconstructionism. He understood Judaism to be not only a religion but a culture, with its own history, laws, and arts. Therefore, it is not enough to practice Judaism as a religion only; the entire Jewish culture must be studied and experienced. The numerous Jewish community centers in American cities today are an organizational attempt to deal with Kaplan's ideals. Naturally, the Reconstructionist give complete support to the state of Israel as the home of Jewish culture.

In addition to these groups there are numerous smaller sects of Judaism throughout the world, which because of geographical isolation or differing religious practice, are out of the mainstream. There are the Falashas of Ethiopia, a group of black Ethiopians, numbering between 15,000 and 25,000, who practice a form of Judaism that retains Jewish beliefs and practices from the first century A.D. Other small, variant Jewish groups also exist in India and China.

JEWISH HOLIDAYS

Judaism has always been defined and understood by its adherents in terms of the actions of God on behalf of his people. Therefore, commemorations of these acts of God tend to be extremely important. The holidays on which these great events are remembered are a unifying factor, bringing together Jews of all degrees of belief and practice. Judaism also depends upon community for its very existence. Therefore, although many portions of its annual festivals may be carried out in the Jewish home, most depend heavily upon the community meeting in the synagogue. Because of this reliance upon the group, the events of *Bar Mitzvah*, when the young are officially recognized as adult members of the Jewish community, also are a significant festival.

Sabbath (Shabbat)

The most important and distinctive of all Jewish holidays is the Sabbath. Judaism gave the world the six-day workweek, with the seventh day reserved for worship and rest. The Sabbath begins on Friday at sundown and continues until sundown on Saturday. On Friday night the Sabbath is ushered in with the *Kiddush*, the benediction over wine or bread, and the lighting and blessing of Sabbath candles by the woman of the house. Traditionally, the best food of the week is served at the Friday evening meal. Conservative and Orthodox Jews attend synagogue on Saturday morning and also read the week's section of the Torah. Orthodox observance of the Sabbath forbids lighting or extinguishing fires or lights, riding in automobiles, smoking, carrying money, or performing any type of labor.

Passover (Pesach)

Another important festival in Judaism is the celebration of the Passover. This holiday begins on the fifteenth of the Hebrew month of Nisan[20] (March–April) and lasts for eight days. It commemorates the deliverance of the Israelites from slavery in Egypt. On the first two nights of Passover the Jewish family gathers for a ritual meal called *Seder*. The foods associated with the Exodus (lamb, unleavened bread, bitter herbs, and so on) are eaten as the family engages in rituals that recall the Exodus.

The Feast of Weeks (Shavuot)

Fifty days after *Pesach*, on the sixth and seventh days of Sivan (May–June), the celebration of Weeks, or *Shavuot*, occurs. This holiday is called Pentecost in the New Testament. *Shavuot* was originally a festival celebrating the first grain harvest, but later it was related to the Exodus event—the time when Moses received the Ten Commandments on Mt. Sinai. Jewish homes and synagogues are decorated with plants and flowers during the celebration of this holiday.

New Year (Rosh Hashanah)

The Jewish new year is celebrated on the first and second days of the month of Tishre (September–October). Tradition says that the days of *Rosh Hashanah* were also the first days of creation. The season begins a period of penitence that culminates in the next holiday, the Day of Atonement (*Yom Kippur*). The new year is celebrated by special prayers and by eating sweets, in the hope of a good year to come.

---

[20] For its religious festivals Judaism relies upon an ancient lunar calendar that is synchronized with the solar calendar by adding an extra month each leap year. This calendar is dated from the supposed date of creation, which would make the year beginning in the fall of 1987 A.D. the Jewish year 5748.

The Day of Atonement (Yom Kippur)

The holiest of all Jewish holidays is the Day of Atonement. It is celebrated on the tenth of Tishre and at the end of the period of penitence begun at *Rosh Hashanah.* The day is traditionally celebrated by
an abstinence from work, food, and drink. The day is to be spent in
the synagogue, where prayers are offered for forgiveness of sins and
reconciliation. It is also an occasion for charity.

The Feast of Tabernacles (Sukkot)

Five days after *Yom Kipper,* on the fifteenth of Tishre, the feast of
tabernacles is celebrated. Originally this was a celebration of the autumn harvest. Like many of the other holidays, *Sukkot* became attached to the Exodus experience and is now kept as a remembrance
of the times when the Israelites wandered in the Sinai wilderness and
lived in makeshift tabernacles (*sukkot*). For either reason, the festival
is a joyous one.

The Feast of Dedication (Chanukkah)

On the twenty-fifth of the month of Kislev (November–December),
Jews celebrate one of the few holidays not associated with the Exodus. In 165 B.C., Judas Maccabeus retook the Temple from the Syrian
Greeks and rededicated it. Only one small container of oil was available for lighting the temple. It should have lasted only one day. However, a miracle happened and the oil lasted for eight days. In remembrance of that event, Jews light a candle each day, for eight days. It is
thus a festival of lights as well as a festival of dedication. *Chanukkah*
has been a minor holiday in Judaism until fairly recent times.

The Feast of Lots (Purim)

Another festival not associated with the Exodus is *Purim,* celebrated
on the fourteenth of Adar (February–March) as a remembrance of Jewish victory over gentile foes. The book of Esther says that Esther, who
had become the Queen of Persia, was made aware of a plot to destroy
her people. By boldly approaching the king and revealing this plot to
him, Esther was able to save her people from a massacre and see her
enemies hanged upon the gibbet they had prepared for the Jews. Since
lots were cast to determine the day when the Jews were to be destroyed, the festival is known as *Purim* (lots). On this day the scroll

of Esther is read, gifts are exchanged, and a special meal is eaten. Generally it is a day of great joy and merrymaking.

The Son of the Commandment (Bar Mitzvah)

Though the *Bar Mitzvah* is not an annual festival in the Jewish calendar, it is an important occasion in the life of the community. According to Judaism, when a boy has reached his thirteenth birthday, he is technically a man. He can be a member of the ten adults necessary for a *minyan*. Usually the boy is prepared for the occasion by several years of instruction in his religion and in Hebrew. On the Sabbath after his thirteenth birthday, he reads from the scripture at synagogue, and may deliver a speech. This is a festive occasion for the boy and his parents, and the young man may receive many presents from his friends. The *Bar Mitzvah* may have been introduced as late as the fourteenth century, as a counter to Christian confirmation, although the age of thirteen has always been the age of majority in Judaism. A modern innovation is the *Bat Mitzvah* ("daughter of commandment"), a similar ceremony for girls. The *Bat Mitzvah* is practiced mainly among Reform congregations.

JUDAISM TODAY

In the last part of the twentieth century, one of the primary tasks of Judaism continues to be interpreting the holocaust. Throughout its history Judaism has always sought to understand God through history. The biblical material seeks to understand the Exodus experience. The postexilic books tried to make sense of the Babylonian exile. The Mishnah and Talmud sought to reinterpret Jewish life after the destruction of the temple. Cabalistic literature was the Jewish response to the expulsion from Europe in the fifteenth century. The single greatest tragedy for Judaism in the modern world has been the murder of six million Jews by the Nazis. Does this event mean that God is dead for the Jews, or that he has turned his back upon them, or that they were being punished for some sin? Does it mean that all Christian nations are hostile and murderous toward Jews? These and many other questions continue to be asked by Jewish thinkers today.

As we have noted, one major response to the holocaust was the development of the state of Israel. Although the rest of the world may look upon Israel as just another nation, it is far more to Jews. Israel is seen as a refuge for Jews who need to flee from oppressive governments around the world. Israel is seen as the culmination of all of

Judaism's dreams for a homeland after 2,000 years of wandering. It is seen by many Jews as almost filling the role of God's Messiah. Therefore the peace, safety, and well-being of Israel are central concerns to modern Judaism. Anyone of another religion who does not understand this one fact does not understand modern Judaism. Israel's survival after the battles that occurred in 1948, 1956, 1967, and 1973 are seen in a theological light. The 1978 peace treaty with Egypt is seen as a harbinger of peace with all its neighbors, which is to come in the future.

As has been the case many times in the past, Judaism today struggles with the issue of its place in a predominately Gentile society. There is a long-standing debate about whether a Jew should compromise with the values of society at large, or whether he or she should find his values only in historic Judaism. One compromise that is greatly feared is intermarriage with Gentiles, and the consequent loss of Jewish offspring. This concern has created a revival of interest in such forms of Orthodox Judaism as Hasidism. Many of these movements are of great interest to modern Jewish young people.

STUDY QUESTIONS

1. Is Judaism a religion, a culture, a race, . . . ? Defend your answer.

2. Using material from the Bible, explain how Judaism provided the moral foundation for much of Western culture.

3. Define "prophet," in the biblical sense of the word.

4. How did the Babylonian exile of 586 B.C. change the Jewish understanding of God?

5. Explain the value of the synagogue to a scattered Judaism. Why are some modern synagogues called "temples?"

6. What were the factors in the development of the Talmud? List the various parts that went into it.

7. Why was cabalistic literature important to the Jews of the sixteenth century?

8. List the three major divisions within modern Judaism. Explain how they differ from one another.

9. Explain the importance of the Nazi holocaust to Jewish thinking. Discuss the state of Israel as a response to the holocaust.

SUGGESTED READING

Baron, Salo W. *A Social and Religious History of the Jews.* 3 vols. New York: Columbia University Press, 1952.

Bokser, Ben Zion. *The Jewish Mystical Tradition.* New York: The Pilgrim Press, 1981.

Buber, Martin. *Tales of the Hasidim.* 2 vols. New York: Schocken Books, 1948.

Cohen, A., ed. *Everybody's Talmud.* New York: E. P. Dutton & Co., Inc., 1932.

Hertzberg, Arthur, ed. *Judaism.* New York: George Braziller, 1961.

Lachs, Samuel T. and Saul P. Wachs. *Judaism.* Niles Ill.: Argus Communications, 1979.

Neusner, Jacob. *Between Time and Eternity, the Essentials of Judaism.* Encino, Calif.: Dickenson, 1975.

Trepp, Leo. *Judaism: Development and Life.* Encino, Calif.: Dickenson Publishing Co., 1966.

Selections from Hebrew Scriptures and the Mishnah

Jewish scripture and commentary is so widely available and so abundant that is difficult to select a truly representative collection. However, the following materials tend to be illustrative of at least early Jewish thought. The book of Deuteronomy, from the Old Testament, though it claims to be the words of Moses, is believed by many scholars to be the work of the disciples of the eighth century B.C. prophets. It is also believed to have been the book found in the rubble of the temple in the sixth century B.C. (see II Kings 22). Deuteronomy 5 contains one version of the Ten Commandments, and chapter 6, verses 4 and 5, contain the *shema*. Micah is representative of the prophetic movement in Israel, particularly with his strong emphasis on social justice. The Psalms make up a large part of the poetical material of early Israel. Psalm 1, with its praise for the person who "delights in the law of the Lord," shows the growing concern for scripture in Israel. The Mishnah is representative of rabbinic literature which became so important to later Judaism. It is made up of the comments and opinions of the great rabbis and was compiled in the second century A.D. The selection on the Sabbath illustrates the depth and the controversy involved in these studies.[21]

Deuteronomy

5 And Moses summoned all Israel, and said to them, "Hear, O Israel, the statutes and the ordinances which I speak in your hearing this day, and you shall learn them and be careful to do them. [2] The LORD our God made a covenant with us in Horeb. [3] Not with our fathers did the LORD make this covenant, but with us, who are all of us here alive this day. [4] The LORD spoke with you face to face at the mountain, out of the midst of the fire, [5] while I stood between the LORD and you at the time, to declare to you the word of the LORD; for you were afraid because of the fire, and you did not go up into the mountain. He said:

[6] " 'I am the LORD your God, who brought you out of the land of Egypt, out of the house of bondage.

[7] " 'You shall have no other gods before me.

[21] The source material that follows is taken from the *Holy Bible* Revised Standard Version. (New York: Thomas Nelson & Sons, 1952.) Deuteronomy chapters 5 and 6, Psalm 1, Micah chapter 6.

8 " 'You shall not make for yourself a graven image, or any likeness of anything that is in heaven above, or that is on the earth beneath, or that is in the water under the earth; 9 you shall not bow down to them or serve them; for I the LORD your God am a jealous God, visiting the iniquity of the fathers upon the children to the third and fourth generation of those who hate me, 10 but showing steadfast love to thousands of those who love me and keep my commandments.

11 " 'You shall not take the name of the LORD your God in vain: for the LORD will not hold him guiltless who take his name in vain.

12 " 'Observe the sabbath day, to keep it holy, as the LORD your God commanded you. 13 Six days you shall labor, and do all your work; 14 but the seventh day is a sabbath to the LORD your God; in it you shall not do any work, you, or your son, or your daughter, or your manservant, or your maid-servant, or your ox, or your ass, or any of your cattle, or the sojourner who is within your gates, that your manservant and your maidservant may rest as well as you. 15 You shall remember that you were a servant in the land of Egypt, and the LORD your God brought you out thence with a mighty hand and an outstretched arm; therefore the LORD your God commanded you to keep the sabbath day.

16 " 'Honor your father and your mother, as the LORD your God commanded you; that your days may be prolonged, and that it may go well with you, in the land which the LORD your God gives you.

17 " 'You shall not kill.

18 " 'Neither shall you commit adultery.

19 " 'Neither shall you steal.

20 " 'Neither shall you bear false witness against your neighbor.

21 " 'Neither shall you covet your neighbor's wife; and you shall not desire your neighbor's house, his field, or his manservant, or his maidservant, his ox, or his ass, or anything that is your neighbor's.'

22 " 'These words the LORD spoke to all your assembly at the mountain out of the midst of the fire, the cloud, and the thick darkness, with a loud voice; and he added no more. And he wrote them upon two tables of stones, gave them to me. 23 And when you heard the voice out of the midst of the darkness, while the mountain was burning with fire, you came near to me, all the heads of your tribes, and your elders; 24 and you said, 'Behold, the LORD our God has shown us his glory and greatness, and we have heard his voice out of the midst of the fire; we have this day seen God speak with man and man still live. 25 Now therefore why should we die? For this great fire will consume us; if we hear the voice of the LORD our God any more, we shall die, 26 For who is there of all flesh, that has heard the voice of the living God speaking out of the midst of fire, as we have, and has still lived? 27 Go near, and hear all that the LORD our God will say; and speak to us all that the LORD our God will speak to you; and we will hear and do it.'

[28] " 'And the LORD heard your words, when you spoke to me; and the LORD said to me, 'I have heard the words of this people, which they have spoken to you; they have rightly said all that they have spoken. [29] Oh that they had such a mind as this always, to fear me and to keep all my commandments, that it might go well with them and with their children for ever! [30] Go and say to them, "Return to your tents." [31] But you, stand here by me, and I will tell you all the commandment and the statutes and the ordinances which you shall teach them, that they may do them in the land which I give them to possess.' [32] You shall be careful to do therefore as the LORD your God has commanded you; you shall not turn aside to the right hand or to the left. [33] You shall walk in all the way which the LORD your God has commanded you, that you may live, and that it may go well with you, and that you may live long in the land which you shall possess.

6 "Now this is the commandment, the statutes and the ordinance which the LORD your God commanded me to teach you, and you may do them in the land to which you are going over, to possess it; [2] that you may fear the LORD your God, you and your son and your son's son, by keeping all his statutes and his commandments, which I command you, all the days of your life; and that your days may be prolonged. [3] Hear therefore, O Israel, and be careful to do them; that it may go well with you, and that you may multiply greatly, as the LORD, the God of your fathers, has promised you, in a land flowing with milk and honey.

[4] "Hear, O Israel: The LORD our God is one LORD; [5] and you shall love the LORD your God with all your heart, and with all your soul, and with all your might. [6] And these words which I command you this day shall be upon your heart; [7] and you shall teach them diligently to your children, and shall talk to them when you sit in your house, and when you walk by the way, and when you lie down, and when you rise. [8] 'And you shall bind them as a sign upon your hand, and they shall be as frontlets between your eyes. [9] And you shall write them on the doorposts of your house and on your gates.

[10] "And when the LORD your God brings you into the land which he swore to your fathers, to Abraham, to Isaac, and to Jacob, to give you, with great and goodly cities, which you did not build, [11] and houses full of all good things, which you did not fill, and cisterns hewn out, which you did not hew, and vineyards and olive trees, which you did not plant, and when you eat and are full, [12] then take heed lest you forget the LORD, who brought you out of the land of Egypt, out of the house of bondage. [13] You shall fear the LORD your God; you shall serve him, and swear by his name. [14] You shall not go after other gods, of the gods of the people who are round about you; [15] for the LORD your God in the midst of you is a jealous God; lest the anger of the LORD your God be kindled against you, and he destroy you from off the face of the earth.

¹⁶"You shall not put the LORD your God to the test, as you tested him at Massah. ¹⁷You shall diligently keep the commandments of the LORD your God, and his testimonies, and his statutes, which he has commanded you.

¹⁸And you shall do what is right and good in the sight of the LORD, that it may go well with you, and that you may go in and take possession of the good land which the LORD swore to give to your fathers ¹⁹by thrusting out all your enemies from before you, as the LORD has promised.

²⁰"When your son asks you in time to come, 'What is the meaning of the testimonies and the statutes and the ordinances which the LORD our God has commanded you?' ²¹then you shall say to your son, 'We were Pharaoh's slaves in Egypt; and the LORD brought us out of Egypt with a mighty hand; ²²and the LORD showed signs and wonders, great and grievous, against Egypt and against Pharaoh and all his household, before our eyes; ²³and he brought us out from there, that he might bring us in and give us the land which he swore to give to our fathers. ²⁴And the LORD commanded us to do all these statutes, to fear the LORD our God, for our good always, that he might preserve us alive, as at this day. ²⁵And it will be righteousness for us, if we are careful to do all this commandment before the LORD our God, as he has commanded us.'

The Psalms

Book I

Blessed is the man
who walks not in the counsel of the wicked,
nor stand in the way of sinners,
  nor sits in the seat of scoffers;
but his delight is in the law of the LORD,
  and on his law he meditates day and night.
He is like a tree
  planted by streams of water,
that yields its fruit in its season,
  and its leaf does not wither.
In all that he does, he prospers.

The wicked are not so,
  but are like chaff which the wind drives away.
Therefore the wicked will not stand in the judgment,
  nor sinners in the congregation of the righteous;
for the LORD knows the way of the righteous,
  but the way of the wicked will perish.

180   **Micah**

181 **6** Hear what the LORD says:
Arise, plead your case before the mountains,
and let the hills hear your voice.
² Hear, your mountains, the controversy of the LORD,
and you enduring foundations of the earth;
for the LORD has a controversy with his people,
and he will contend with Israel.

182 ³ "O my people, what have I done to you?
In what have I wearied you? Answer me!
⁴ For I brought you up from the land of Egypt,
and redeemed you from the house of bondage;
and I sent before you Moses,
Aaron, and Miriam.
⁵ O my people, remember what Balak king of Moab devised,
and what Balaam the son of Be'or answered him,
and what happened from Shittim to Gilgal,
that you may know the saving acts of the LORD."

183 ⁶ "With what shall I come before the LORD,
and bow myself before God on high?
Shall I come before him with burnt offerings,
with calves a year old?
⁷ Will the LORD be pleased with thousands of rams,
with ten thousands of rivers of oil?
Shall I give my first-born for my transgression,
the fruit of my body for the sin of my soul?"
⁸ He has showed you, O man, what is good;
and what does the LORD require of you
but to do justice, and to love kindness,
and to walk humbly with your God?

184 ⁹ The voice of the LORD cries to the city—
and it is sound wisdom to fear thy name;
"Hear, O tribe and assembly of the city!
¹⁰ Can I forget the treasures of the wickedness in the house of the
wicked,
and the scant measure that is accursed?
¹¹ Shall I acquit the man with wicked scales
and with a bag of deceitful weights?
¹² Your rich men are full of violence; your inhabitants speak lies,
and their tongue is deceitful in their mouth.

[13] Therefore I have begun to smite you,
   making you desolate because of your sins.
[14] You shall eat, but not be satisfied,
   and there shall be hunger in your inward parts;
you shall put away, but not save,
   and what you save I will give to the sword.
[15] You shall sow, but not reap;
   you shall tread olives, but not anoint yourselves with oil;
   you shall tread grapes, but not drink wine.
[16] For you have kept the statutes of Omri,
   and all the works of the house of Ahab;
   and you have walked in their counsels;
that I may make you a desolation, and your inhabitants a hissing;
   so you shall bear the scorn of the peoples."

The Mishnah: Pesahim (The Feast of Passover)

The Mishnah is a collection of rabbinic opinions about how
to keep the laws of God. It is believed that the Mishnah was
collected and codified in the second century A.D. The following selection is taken from the section that deals with
keeping the feast of Passover. Exodus 12:19 forbade the
presence of any form of leaven or yeast in a Jewish household during the seven days of the feast of Passover. But what
is yeast (*hametz*)? Where is it found? And to what lengths
should one go to get rid of it? This section of the Mishnah
attempts to answer these questions.[22]

3   1. These must be removed at Passover: Babylonian porridge, Median
beer, Edomite vinegar, and Egyptian barley-beer; also dyers' pulp, cooks'
starch-flour, and writers' paste. R. Eliezer says: Also women's cosmetics.
This is the general rule: whatsoever is made from any kind of grain must
be removed at Passover. These are included in the prohibition, yet punishment by Extirpation is not thereby incurred.
   2. If dough remained in the cracks of a kneading-trough and there was
an olive's bulk in any one place, it must be removed. If there was less than
this it is negligible in its scantness. So, too, in a matter of uncleaness: he
that is scrupulous about it must make a partition; if he wishes it to remain
it can be reckoned as (one with) the kneading-trough. Dough that is still
"dumb" is forbidden if other dough like to it has already fermented.
   3. How is the dough-offering set apart on a Festival-day if the dough is

[22] *The Mishnah*. Herbert Danby, trans. (Oxford: Oxford University Press, 1933), pp. 139, 140.

unclean? R. Eliezer says: She should not designate it (Dough-offering) until it is baked. R. Judah b. Bathyra says: She should throw it into cold water. R. Joshua said: Such *hametz* is not included in the prohibitions *Let it not be seen,* and *Let it not be found;* but rather, she should set it apart and leave it until evening, and if it becomes *hametz* it becomes *hametz*.

4. Rabban Gamaliel says: Three women may knead dough at the same time and bake it in the same oven one after the other. But the Sages say: Three women may occupy themselves (at the same time) with the dough, one kneading, one rolling it out, and one baking. R. Akiba says: All women and all kinds of wood and all ovens are not equal. This is the general rule: if the dough swells let her slap it with cold water.

5. Dough beginning to ferment (*si'ur*) must be burnt; but he that eats it is not culpable. Dough wholly fermented (*sidduk*) must be burnt and he that eats it is liable to punishment by Extirpation. What is *si'ur?* (Dough) on which the cracks are all entangled together. So R. Judah. But the Sages say: If a man ate either (of these) he is liable to punishment by Extirpation. But what is *si'ur?* (Dough) whose surface turns palid like a man's face when his hair stands on end.

6. If the 14th falls on a Sabbath all *hametz* must be removed before the Sabbath. So R. Meir. But the Sages say: (Not until) its appointed time. R. Eliezer b. R. Zadok says: Heave-offering (must be removed) before the Sabbath, but common food (not until) its appointed time.

7. If a man was on the way to slaughter his Passover-offering or to circumcise his son or to eat the betrothal meal at his father-in-law's house and he remembered that he had left *hametz* in his house, if he has yet time to go back and remove it and return to fulfil his religious duty, let him go back and remove it: but if not, he may annul it in his heart. (If he was on the way) to render help against ravaging soldiery or a flood or a fire or a falling building, he may annul the *hametz* in his heart; but if it was but to keep the Feast at a place of his own choice he must return at once.

8. So, too, if a man had gone forth from Jerusalem and remembered that he still had with him flesh that was hallowed, if he had already passed Zofim he may burn it there and then; but if not, he must return and burn it before the Birah with wood for the Altar-hearth. By reason of how much (flesh or *hametz*) must they return? R. Meir says: In either case an egg's bulk. R. Judah says: In either case an olive's bulk. But the Sages say: An olive's bulk of hallowed flesh or an egg's bulk of *hametz*.

CHAPTER 12

Christianity

Altar, United Methodist Church. (*Courtesy of Jean-Claude Lejeune; Stockmarket/Los Angeles.*)

Jesus said to him, "I am the way, and the truth, and the
life; no one comes to the Father, but by me."
—John 14:6

In terms of the number of its adherents, Christianity is by far the largest religion in the world. In 1985 the estimated number of Roman Catholics, Eastern Orthodox, and Protestants was 1,063,000,000.[1] This means that approximately one of every four persons on earth is identified in some way with Christianity. Naturally a religion that encompasses so many people contains a great variety of beliefs and practices. In general, Christians share a common belief in the uniqueness of Jesus of Nazareth, that he in some way provided for the redemption of humankind by his death and was himself resurrected from the dead. Christians generally also believe in baptism as initiation into the religion, and in the communion meal. They hold to the idea that the believer has one life in which to determine his or her destiny for life after death. This destiny is usually thought to be either an eternity of bliss in heaven or an eternity of torment in hell. Around these basic themes are many variations within the body of Christianity.

THE WORLD OF THE FIRST CENTURY A.D.

Christianity arose as a sect of Judaism in the first century A.D., when the Roman Empire was at its peak. According to Christian scripture, Jesus was born when Augustus Caesar ruled the world, and Christianity became known in the Roman capital in the last third of the first century. Some knowledge of the condition of both Judaism and the Roman Empire of those days will help us understand the forces that created Christianity.

If there were ever a time in the history of the world when there was "one world"—in the sense that the peoples of Europe, Asia Minor, and North Africa were ruled by one government, with a basic common language and a basic common culture—it was the world of the first century A.D. Under the rule of Augustus Caesar and his successors, the mighty Roman legions had conquered almost everything that could be conquered. Wherever they went they took with them

---

[1] 1985 *Encyclopedia Britannica Book of the Year* (Chicago: Encyclopedia Britannica Inc., 1985), p. 365. Statistics on the number of adherents of any religion are vague, at best. The number of Christians is often determined simply by giving the populations of nations known to be "Christian."

Roman civilization, efficient administrators, and thorough engineers. They built cities and roads. They swept the Mediterranean of the pirates and made sea travel safe. Communication and travel across the vast empire had never been safer and surer. When Christian missionaries such as St. Paul began to spread the gospel of Christianity, the Roman Empire provided the path.

In addition to material benefits the Roman Empire gave the world one language. Of course, each captive nation continued to speak its own native tongue, but wherever one went in the Roman world the leaders of government and business would, in addition, be able to speak koine Greek. Though the language of the common people of Rome was Latin, many of the leaders had been educated by Greek slaves and tutors, and they found Greek to be the more beautiful and expressive language. Furthermore, Alexander the Great had conquered much of the same world that became the Roman Empire, and he had sowed the seeds of Hellenistic culture and its Greek language wherever his armies had gone. Because ancient Greece had been the home of philosophy, the beautiful and accurate language of Greece is considered by many to be one of the best vehicles for expressing philosophical and theological thoughts. A Christian missionary, for example Paul, could go anywhere in the Roman Empire and be sure that he could converse with the populace in koine Greek. He could also write letters or epistles to Christian communities in Greek and know that they would be read and understood.

The world of the first century A.D. was also a world of governmental stability. The Romans governed with great cruelty, but they produced a world of relative peace. Augustus and his successors imposed their *Pax Romana* ("the peace of Rome"), and though it was harsh, it was peace nonetheless. To be sure, there were local revolts against Roman government, such as the Jewish revolt of 66–70 A.D., but there were no major international wars during this period. Christianity developed in a time of stable government and international calm.

The Roman world of the first century had no major religious commitment. The Greeks and the Romans had their pantheons, but belief in them had largely ceased. Sacrifices to the Roman gods were still carried on officially, but there was little popular support for them. The nations within the empire had their own national religions, and many of these were alive and well. In Judaism the rabbis were developing material that would eventually become the Mishnah and Talmud. Indeed, Judaism was finding many converts from other religions. However, the empire itself had no vital religion during this era, and many people were seeking a new religion to take the place of the dead religions. Many sought out astrology as a solution to the problems of life. Others turned to new religious cults that developed from various Eastern religions. Mithraism, which was a development from Persian thought, entered Roman life during the reign of Nero and quickly became a very popular cult among Roman soldiers. The cult of Osiris spread from Egyptian religions into the empire. In Greece, the worship of Dionysus was popular. These and other so-called mystery religions gained large followings from among the citizens of the Roman Empire. Each offered the believer life after death in one form or another. Many had secret rituals to which only the initiated were invited. Many had sacred communion meals and baptisms that aided the participant in the search for eternal life. Most of the mystery religions accepted people into their groups without regard to race or social status. In the homogenized life of the Roman Empire, where a large portion of the population was made up of slaves, this was an important feature indeed.

Another aspect of the first-century world that is becoming increasingly clear today is that, in Judaism at least, and possibly in other religions, there was an anticipation among some that the world was nearing its end or at least a climactic moment. Among the political groups of Palestine there was the hope that a messiah would rise up and lead the people in the overthrow of the Roman monster. This was therefore a time in which many would identify themselves, or at least allow themselves to be identified, as Messiah. Among the people who lived by the Dead Sea and produced those documents popularly called the *Dead Sea Scrolls*, there was an anticipation of a swiftly approaching end of time. These people were so certain that the end was at hand that they had left their normal lives and come to this lonely, godforsaken wilderness to await the coming of the Lord in the wilderness. Into this forlorn and hopeful world came Jesus of Nazareth.

THE LIFE AND TEACHINGS OF JESUS

Jesus of Nazareth was not mentioned in non-Christian literature until the end of the first century A.D. Even then the references to him were vague and not very helpful in constructing the events in his life. Non-Christians sometimes assert that Jesus was not a historical figure, because up until the end of the first century there were only Christian stories about his life. Whether or not this is true cannot be proved, but the limited first-century, non-Christian material on his life is a fact. The only truly objective facts we have about the life of Jesus are that a group of people, who were called Christians, began to be recognized in the Roman Empire around 60–65 A.D., and they aroused hostility and persecution in an empire that was normally tolerant of religious variations. Christianity became the object of many official and unofficial persecutions but continued to grow, until finally, in the fourth century, it became the official religion of what remained of the Roman Empire. While modern students of Christianity may not know exactly what the early church taught, the existence of this group cannot be questioned.

Central to the existence of early Christians was the idea that Jesus of Nazareth had been crucified in Jerusalem during the reign of Pontius Pilate and had been resurrected from the dead. About forty years after his death members of this group began to write biographical statements about Jesus, centering on his death and resurrection. Modern scholarship usually agrees that the earliest Gospel, Mark, was written about 70 A.D. It is the briefest of the four Gospels that have been retained by the church. The Gospel of Mark was followed by those of Matthew and Luke, both written about 85 A.D., and then by that of John, written between 90 and 100 A.D. These Gospels are not biographies in the true sense of the word, but give most of their attention to the last few months in the life of Jesus. Only rarely is Jesus' childhood or early adult years mentioned, and none of the Gospels contains a physical description of Jesus. Even the exact details of Jesus' last few months are in dispute among the four Gospels. If the earliest Gospel was written forty years after the death of Jesus, and if all of the Gospels were written by confessed Christians who had a biased point of view, then admittedly they are not the most reliable sources of objective material. However, with all of their imperfections, the Gospels still provide the best information we have about the life of Jesus.

Two Gospels, Mark and John, begin with the ministry of a mature Jesus. Only Matthew and Luke speak of his birth, and only Luke contains material relating to his childhood. The reader must assume that for the early church, the years before Jesus' actual ministry were not terribly important. In those Gospels that do tell of his birth there are problems in harmonizing details. However, they do agree that Jesus was born in the ancestral home of David, Bethlehem. Matthew places the time of Jesus' birth in the years prior to the death of Herod the Great (4 B.C.)[2] Both Matthew and Luke assert that Jesus' birth was unique in that he was born from Mary, who was a virgin. They tie this event to the words of the eighth century B.C. Hebrew prophet, Isaiah:

---

[2] If Matthew is correct in this, Jesus would have been born between 6 and 4 B.C. This is possible, since those who established the Christian calendar, marking time into B.C. (before Christ) and A.D. (*Anno Domini*, in the year of our Lord), lived several hundred years after the time of Jesus and simply miscalculated the date by a few years.

The remains of a fourth-century synagogue in Capernaum. It is believed that it was built over the site of a first-century synagogue. In such a synagogue in Capernaum Jesus taught and performed miracles. (*Courtesy of Israeli Government Tourist Office.*)

Behold, a young woman [virgin][3] shall conceive and bear a son, and shall call his name Immanuel.[4]

All Gospels agree that Jesus was a native of the village of Nazareth in the province of Galilee. Of his childhood and young maturity we are told only of the event recorded in Luke, in which the twelve-year-old Jesus went to Jerusalem for a festival with his parents and became so involved in discussion with the teachers of the law that he failed to find his way into the party returning to Nazareth. Except for this lone incident, the life of Jesus prior to his thirtieth year is not mentioned. Naturally, this blank has led to all sorts of speculation by Christians and non-Christians.

The Gospel of Luke tells its readers that Jesus was about thirty

[3] The translation of the Hebrew word *almah* has been a source of contention between Christians and Jews for years. In other contexts, the word nearly always means "young woman." Matthew translates it with the Greek word *parthenos*, which always means "virgin."

[4] Isaiah 7:14. This quotation and those that follow are taken from *The Holy Bible: Revised Standard Version* (New York: Thomas Nelson & Sons, 1952).

years of age when he began his ministry, and all the Gospels agree that his first public act was his baptism by John the Baptist in the Jordan River. The figure of John also is not clear in the Gospel accounts. Luke says that he was Jesus' second cousin. Whatever his relationship may have been, John was a powerful charismatic figure in Judea. When he preached his message of repentance, large crowds came down to the Jordan to hear him. A body of disciples followed him. Years later, the apostle Paul encountered Jews in Ephesus who had heard of John but not of Jesus.[5]

Following his baptism Jesus went into the nearby Judean wilderness where he fasted for forty days and pondered the nature of his ministry. According to the Gospels, Jesus was tempted by Satan to accept all sorts of easy paths to glory during this time. After the period of temptations Jesus returned to Galilee, where he began to preach. From the Galilean villages he chose a band of followers who would be his disciples for the next few years. Some of them had originally been disciples of John the Baptist. The Gospels list twelve disciples, but this number must have been flexible. There were times in Jesus' ministry when only three or four of this group were close to him. At other times he seems to have been followed by thousands of disciples.

The exact length of Jesus' public ministry is not known. The events of this ministry that are given in the synoptic Gospels (Matthew, Mark, and Luke) could fit into one year, beginning and ending at Passover. However, the Gospel of John presents Jesus' ministry over several seasons that seem to fit into a three-year period. Traditionally, Christians accept John's outline and talk of a three-year ministry. The location of Jesus' ministry is also a matter of some dispute. The synoptic Gospels present Jesus working mainly in Galilee and appearing in Jerusalem only for special occasions. John's account has Jesus spending more time in the province of Judea, around Jerusalem.

All the Gospels agree that during his public ministry Jesus spent his time teaching and healing. Whether it was to a small group of disciples or to a large crowd in a public place, he was a teacher. In the truest sense of the word he was called *rabbi* by his disciples. Both the form and the content of Jesus' teachings are recognized and respected as outstanding among those of the great religious innovators of the world. Occasionally Jesus conveyed his message in direct, simple statements, such as the Beatitudes of the Sermon on the Mount:

Blessed are the poor in spirit, for theirs is the kingdom of heaven.
Blessed are those who mourn, for they shall be comforted.
Blessed are the meek, for they shall inherit the earth.

[5] Acts 19:1–7.

Blessed are those who hunger and thirst for righteousness, for they shall be satisfied.

Blessed are the merciful, for they shall obtain mercy.

Blessed are the pure in heart, for they shall see God.

Blessed are the peacemakers, for they shall be called sons of God.

Blessed are those who are persecuted for righteousness' sake, for theirs is the kingdom of heaven.

Blessed are you when men revile you and persecute you and utter all kinds of evil against you falsely on my account.

Rejoice and be glad, for your reward is great in heaven, for so men persecuted the prophets who were before you.[6]

Jesus is most often remembered, however, for his use of a teaching device called the parable. The parable is a short, easily recognized story about very human characters and events. Because of the brevity and beauty of these stories, the parables of Jesus are among the best remembered and most quoted teachings of all the religions of the world. The Gospel of Luke is particularly well stocked with Jesus' parables. Here the reader finds the stories of the prodigal son, the lost sheep, and, perhaps the best known of all, the parable of the Good Samaritan.

A man was going down from Jerusalem to Jericho, and he fell among robbers, who stripped him and beat him, and departed, leaving him half dead. Now by chance a priest was going down that road; and when he saw him he passed by on the other side. So likewise a Levite, when he came to the place and saw him, passed by on the other side. But a Samaritan, as he journeyed, came to where he was; and when he saw him, he had compassion, and went to him and bound up his wounds, pouring on oil and wine; then he set him on his own beast and brought him to an inn, and took care of him. And the next day he took out two denarii and gave them to the innkeeper, saying, "Take care of him; and whatever more you spend, I will repay you when I come back."[7]

It is difficult to find one central theme in all of the teachings of Jesus. Different groups within Christianity tend to isolate those statements that seem to support their position and claim that this was indeed the main message of Christ.

Many of Jesus' teachings seem to be pacifistic. For example:

You have heard that it was said, "An eye for an eye and a tooth for a tooth." But I say to you, Do not resist one who is evil. But if any one strikes you on the right cheek, turn to him the other also; and if any one

---

[6] Matthew 5:3–12.
[7] Luke 10:30–35.

would sue you and take your coat, let him have your cloak as well; and if any one forces you to go one mile, go with him two miles.[8]

Yet it would be a mistake to say that his total answer to the problems of his times was pacificism. At one point he urges his disciples to be armed (Luke 22:36), and at another he states that he has not come to bring peace, but a sword (Matthew 10:34).

Other groups within Christianity contend that the central message of Jesus was people's superiority over the Jewish law. Indeed, many of Jesus' actions and teachings seem to suggest an attitude of indifference toward the laws of Judaism. He healed on the Sabbath, and he allowed his disciples to pluck grain on the Sabbath while they walked through the fields. He also stated that

> Not what goes into the mouth defiles a man, but what comes out of the mouth, this defiles a man.[9]

This statement seems to put Jesus in conflict with the kosher food laws. However, at times Jesus has a very reverent attitude toward the laws of Judaism:

> Think not that I have come to abolish the law and the prophets; I have come not to abolish them but to fulfill them. For truly I say to you, till heaven and earth pass away, not an iota, not a dot, will pass from the law until all is accomplished. Whoever then relaxes one of the least of these commandments and teaches men so, shall be called least in the kingdom of heaven; but he who does them and teaches them shall be called great in the kingdom of heaven.[10]

Indeed, many of the teachings of Jesus are similar or parallel to those of the great rabbis of that era, whose words are remembered in the Mishnah.

Still others have chosen to see the central message of Jesus in terms of an overwhelming concern on his part for the coming end of the age. Albert Schweitzer, in his classic *The Quest for the Historical Jesus,* has pointed out the heavy emphasis on eschatology found in the words of Jesus. Those who agree with Schweitzer see Jesus as a leader who believed that the world was very near the end of an old age and the beginning of a new one.

In truth, there are many aspects to the teachings of Jesus as found in the Gospels. Like all great teachers he was concerned with human

---

[8] Matthew 5:38–41.
[9] Matthew 15:11.
[10] Matthew 5:17–19.

values, warning people about the perils of riches and preaching compassion among humans. Yet he was also a man of his times, aware of the hateful oppression of his people by the Romans but similarly aware of the disastrous possibilities of revolution against the Romans. He was a man who had been schooled in the laws of his religion and saw in them the great potential for human good if properly applied, as well as the potential for oppressiveness if improperly applied. Jesus was also a man of his times in that he, like the Essenes of Qumran and others, was acutely aware that the age was drawing to a climax. Therefore, Jesus cannot easily be forced into one dogmatic mold.

All of the Gospels record that Jesus was a worker of miracles. Regardless of the attitude that modern readers may have toward the nature of miracles, and regardless of the embarrassment that the miracles may cause modern Christians as they try to find a rational explanation for them, the Gospels and the sermons of the early Christians are quite clear: Jesus worked miracles. He healed the sick, the blind, and the lame; he fed the hungry; he raised the dead; he cast out demons; he walked upon the waters and stilled the storms. Miracles were a very real part of the world of Jesus, and he performed them regularly, without great fanfare.

After a time of public ministry the opposition against Jesus began to grow. It became necessary for him to go away from the crowds of both friends and enemies and rest periodically. On one such occasion he went to the north to Caesarea Philippi to be alone with his closest disciples. Here he asked his disciples:

> "Who do men say that I am?" And they told him, "John the Baptist; and others say, Elijah; and others one of the prophets." And he asked them, "But who do you say that I am?" Peter answered him, "You are the Christ."[11]

This is the clearest statement of Jesus' identification as a messianic figure by his disciples and by himself. He followed this statement with the warning that he would soon go to Jerusalem and be put to death.

After these events Jesus and his followers began their journey southward to Jerusalem. They arrived at the time of celebration of the Passover. The city was crowded with pilgrims from the Diaspora communities all over the world. It was a season of high theological expectation since it commemorated YHWH's greatest intervention in history on behalf of his people. On the Sunday before his death, Jesus entered the city and was widely accepted and acclaimed by the citizens. On this day and those that followed Jesus spent time in the

[11] Mark 8:27–29.

Crucifixion by Matthias Grunewald (center panel of the exterior of the *Isenheim Altarpiece*); completed in 1515. (*Courtesy of Musée d'Unterlinden—Colmar.*)

temple teaching and engaging in debates with his opponents. Each afternoon he left the city and went a few miles to the village of Bethany, where he stayed at the home of Mary, Martha, and Lazarus.

On Thursday evening Jesus entered Jerusalem and partook of a final meal with his disciples. It is not clear in all of the Gospels whether this was the Passover Seder or simply a common meal. He shared bread and wine with his disciples and indicated that they were symbolic of his broken body and shed blood. Following the meal, Jesus and his party went out of the city to the Garden of Gethsemane, where he prayed for a few hours. Here he was betrayed by Judas, one of his closest disciples, and arrested by the temple guards. He was tried by the Jewish high court, the Sanhedrin, early the next morning. This trial was followed by a series of trials, interviews, and beatings by Pontius Pilate, the Roman Procurator of Judea, and by Herod Antipas.

Finally, at about nine o'clock in the morning he was sent out of the city and crucified with two felons. The Gospels record that a series of cataclysmic events occurred as Jesus was dying. By three o'clock in the afternoon he was dead. He was taken from the cross and buried in a nearby borrowed tomb.

The Gospels state that the opposition to Jesus and the responsibility for his death came mainly from within the body of Jewish leadership, especially from the party of the Pharisees. The Pharisees were a group within Judaism made up mostly of the common people. They were fairly liberal and progressive in their theological outlook. They believed in resurrection of the dead and accepted as canon books in the Bible beyond the first five books of Moses. The New Testament lists several of Jesus' disciples as Pharisees, including Paul, the great missionary of the early church. In truth, there were more similarities between Jesus and the Pharisees than there were differences. Indeed, some have suggested that Jesus himself was a Pharisee.

Other opposition came to Jesus from the Sadducees, an aristocratic group who controlled the temple in Jerusalem. Theologically they were very conservative, accepting only the first five books of the Bible as the word of God. The Gospels present the Sadducean leaders as the ones who tried Jesus in Jerusalem and were ultimately responsible for his death.

Undoubtedly Jesus was opposed by another party within Judaism, the Zealots. The Zealots, who had arisen in Galilee soon after the birth of Jesus, were fanatical anti-Roman patriots who stirred up revolution at every opportunity. Even though one of Jesus' closest disciples is listed as a Zealot, this party could not have been pleased with Jesus because he refused to be the leader of a political revolution against Rome.[12]

Although the Gospels fix the major share of the opposition to Jesus on these groups within Judaism, the ultimate and fatal opposition must surely have come from the Roman government. Because of the Zealots and other dissident groups, Roman rule of Judea was never easy. From the time of Pompey's entry into Jerusalem in 63 B.C., through the reign of Herod the Great in the first century B.C., and into the era of 130–135 A.D., Judea was not quiet for the Romans. The Gospels say that Jesus began the last week of his life by entering the city of Jerusalem during Passover week, riding upon a donkey, and being received by the crowds as though he were a conquering hero. Because Jesus was from Galilee, the home of the Zealots, and because some of his close followers were known to be armed, it was only natural for the Roman authorities to assume that this was a potentially dan-

---

[12]One of the lesser known disciples was called "Simon the Zealot." See Luke 6:15.

gerous man. The Gospel accounts place the responsibility for Jesus' death upon the Jewish leaders and the crowds in Jerusalem who were there for the Passover, and thus lay the foundation for much of the anti-Jewish feeling and persecution that followed in the past two thousand years.[13] But Jesus surely would not have been executed had it not been the wish of the Roman authorities. He was crucified Roman fashion, by a group of Roman soldiers, by the order of the Roman procurator of Judea, Pontius Pilate.

Jesus was crucified on Friday and was in the tomb by Friday evening. The following Sunday morning when women came to tend to his body they found the tomb empty. A reading of the four Gospels about the events that followed is confusing. Mark records that the women found the tomb empty and conversed with a young man there who told them that Jesus has risen and gone into Galilee. The other Gospels present more elaborate statements. In them, Jesus appeared to different groups of disciples in Jerusalem and Galilee at various times over the next forty days. Eventually he gathered his friends together at the Mount of Olives outside of Jerusalem and ascended into heaven. All of the Gospels agree, however, that the tomb was empty and that Jesus had conquered death. Most agree that he was seen after his resurrection by a number of reputable witnesses. The resurrection event became central to the early Christian church.

EARLY CHRISTIANITY

The Jerusalem Church

After Jesus' resurrection and ascension, his followers met in Jerusalem. They probably banded together out of fear that they might share Jesus' fate. However, at the festival of Shavuot[14] fifty days after Passover, the Christians were feeling more courageous because of the coming of the Holy Spirit and went out into the streets of Jerusalem to preach about their faith. Miraculously, they were able to preach in languages that they had not known before, and as a result persuaded many people to join with them.

It is important to note that this original group of Christians in Jerusalem, and those groups that later sprang up throughout the world, were considered by others and by themselves to be another sect of Judaism. The members of this group were Jewish by background; their

---

[13] The Second Vatican Council (1962–1965), after much debate, issued a statement which said that although Jewish authorities were the ones who pressed for the death of Jesus, his execution cannot be charged against all Jews.

[14] Christians refer to this festival by its Greek name, *Pentecost*.

Bible was the Jewish Bible; and they continued to worship at the Temple in Jerusalem. The only thing that distinguished them from other Jews was their belief that Jesus of Nazareth was somehow unique. The exact faith of these early Christians is difficult to define precisely. The systemization of Christian theology was not to come for several centuries, and after long years of debate.

Our knowledge of the Jerusalem church is drawn from the accounts of the New Testament book, Acts of the Apostles. The leadership of the group seems to have resided in two men. The first was Simon Peter, who had been among the inner circle of Jesus' disciples. Though the organization was loose in the early days, Peter was certainly a major spokesperson for the church. Other of Jesus' disciples are mentioned in Acts, but none seems to have had the authority of Peter. A second man who came to have more and more influence in Jerusalem was James, the half-brother of Jesus. Tradition says that James was not a follower of Jesus during his ministry but came to believe in him after the resurrection. James assumed leadership of the Jerusalem church when Peter moved out to other communities. Beyond these two, there seems to have been no official leadership.

The Acts record that seven men were chosen to serve the Christians in the distribution of charity. One of these was Stephen, who not only acted as a servant of the church but also preached in the streets. His preaching so enraged the authorities in Jerusalem that he was officially denounced and stoned to death. Thus Stephen became the first martyr of the Christian faith. His death was but one event in a series of persecutions against the Christians in Jerusalem as hostility against them increased. These persecutions caused many of the Christians to leave Jerusalem and carry their faith elsewhere in Judea and into other centers of the Roman Empire.

The Life of Paul

Because almost one-half of the book of Acts is given over to the missionary activities of Paul, and because he is traditionally considered to be the author of fourteen books in the New Testament, Paul is the best-known early Christian. Undoubtedly there were other missionary figures in the early church who went as far and did as much as Paul, but they escaped the attention of the New Testament. Not only was Paul important as a missionary of the early faith, but he also made a great contribution as a theologian. He was among the first to attempt to state systematically the beliefs of Christianity. Indeed, Paul is sometimes called the "Second Founder of Christianity."

According to the biographical material presented in Acts, and that which may be gathered from his epistles, Paul was reared in the Diaspora Jewish community of Tarsus in Asia Minor. He undoubtedly received an education in both Judaism and in Hellenistic culture. He studied with the great Rabbi Gamaliel and was a member of the Pharisee party. Paul was originally part of the anti-Christian group, and when opposition to the Christian sect in Jerusalem became active persecution, Paul became a leader and observed the stoning of Stephen. On a mission to persecute the Christians in Damascus, he was struck down by a light from heaven and became converted from an enemy of the Christians to a spokesperson for them. After a time of study he began to preach on behalf of Christianity. With various companions he traveled across the Roman Empire, preaching first in the Jewish synagogues and then to gentile audiences. It was Paul, perhaps more than anyone else, who led the movement to allow gentiles to become Christians without first becoming Jews and following the laws of Judaism. This became both the strength and the weakness of Christianity. Its strength lay in the fact that converts could come very easily into the church from almost any background without a lengthy and arduous preparation for Judaism. Its weakness was that it set the wedge between the church and the synagogue, a wedge that has never been removed.

Paul and his companions carried out three missionary journeys, which are discussed in Acts. These journeys took them to many of the great cities of Asia Minor and Greece. Upon completion of his travels, Paul returned to Jerusalem, where he was arrested by the Roman authorities. He was imprisoned in Caesarea for several years and eventually sent to Rome, where he was to be tried by Caesar. Acts concludes with Paul entering Rome somewhere around 60 A.D., and there is no biblical material on the remainder of his life. Tradition says that he was imprisoned in Rome during the period of the Neronic persecution of the church (64 A.D.) and executed. Tradition also states that Peter, who had become bishop of the church at Rome, was executed there at approximately the same time. The *Annals* of Tacitus, a Roman historian who wrote approximately fifty years after the Neronic persecution, claims that Nero set out to persecute the Christians in order to shift the blame from himself for having set a great fire in Rome. This was the first of the official persecutions of the Christians by the Roman government.

The Worship of the Early Church

Clearly, the church modeled its worship after the forms used in the Jewish synagogue. The Jerusalem church, which continued to exist and exert authority until its destruction along with the city in 70 A.D., still used the Temple as a place of worship. It may even have

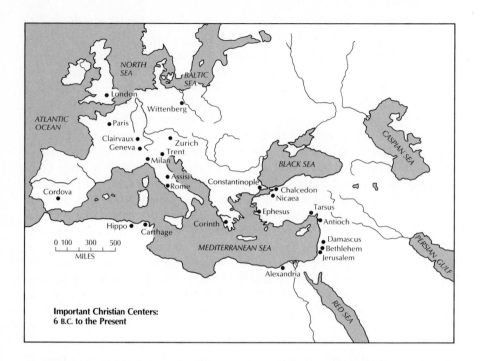

**Important Christian Centers:
6 B.C. to the Present**

continued to practice the animal sacrifice that was a part of Temple worship at that time. Wherever Paul went he first sought out and preached at the local Jewish synagogue. Undoubtedly the prayers, the scripture reading, the hymns, and the simple sermons so much a part of synagogue worship were also a part of early Christian worship.

In addition to these modes of worship Christians added others. Baptism was apparently a part of Christian worship from earliest times. Baptism as an initiation into a new faith was practiced by the Pharisees when they took converts into Judaism. John the Baptist baptized people in the Jordan River as a symbol of repentance. Jesus' disciples baptized converts even during his ministry, and Paul baptized converts wherever he went.

Both the mode and the meaning of Christian baptism have been objects of debate throughout the history of the church. The word *baptize* comes from the Greek word *baptidzo,* which means "to immerse." Presumably John immersed his converts in the Jordan. As Christians grew in number, the inconvenience of finding a body of water large enough to immerse the candidate perhaps argued for a more moderate form of baptism. Pouring or sprinkling water upon the head became accepted as the proper mode of baptism.

It is not clear why Jesus' disciples baptized, nor does the New Testament tell the reader clearly why the early church continued the practice. It appears to have originally been an outward sign of the change in status from the pagan life to the Christian life. In later years it took on deeper meanings. Eventually, baptism was understood to be the washing away of original sin. In the New Testament accounts, the converts who were baptized were adults, but baptism became more and more important to salvation, and eventually infants were baptized in order to wash away the stain of original sin as quickly as possible. Whatever the manner and meaning of baptism may have been, before very long it was administered by a sprinkling of water on the infant children of Christian parents and became a sacrament of the church.

The second addition of the early Christians was the eucharist, or communion meal. This was probably modeled on the Seder meal of Judaism, in which the community recalls divine history as they partake of sacred foods. Specifically, it was adopted by Christians from the model of Jesus' last supper with his disciples on the evening before his death. In the early years of the church it became customary for Christians to gather together and eat a meal recalling the death of Jesus. Perhaps it was simply a meal of bread and wine, or it may have included other foods. Again, both the manner and meaning of the communion meal have been debated within the church. Eventually the eucharist became a sacred meal in which the bread and wine actually became the flesh and blood of Jesus; individuals who received these elements were actually eating and drinking the body of Jesus and thus their souls were somehow sanctified and aided in their journey toward eventual salvation.

Leadership in the Early Church

Apparently the early church was not a highly organized structure. It was small and not quite sure of itself. Both the Acts and the epistles of Paul indicate that many Christians were expecting Jesus to return to earth at almost any time, and therefore the church had no need of a highly organized structure. As the years passed and it became apparent that Jesus was not returning immediately, as the number of Christians grew, and as the various interpretations of Christianity increased, it became necessary for the church to organize more fully.

There had always been outstanding leaders such as Peter, Paul, and James, but apparently they held no titles and drew whatever authority they had from their relationship to Jesus and the force of their personalities. The claim of the Roman Catholic Church is that Peter was intended by Jesus to be the cornerstone of the church. This claim is based upon the following biblical passage:

Simon Peter replied, "You are the Christ, the Son of the living God." And Jesus answered him, "Blessed are you, Simon Bar-Jona! For flesh and blood has not revealed this to you, but my Father who is in heaven. And I tell you, you are Peter [Greek *Petros*], and on this rock [Greek *petra*] I will build my church, and the powers of death shall not prevail against it. I will give you the keys of the kingdom of heaven, and whatever you bind on earth shall be bound in heaven, and whatever you loose on earth shall be loosed in heaven."[15]

Although it is not mentioned in the New Testament, a strong tradition says that Peter went to Rome and became the leader of the church in that city. The bishops who were his successors became the popes of the Roman church.

The New Testament mentions several kinds of leaders in the early church, but their roles are never very clearly delineated. One such leader was the bishop. The Greek word for bishop is *Episcopos*, which literally means "shepherd." Qualifications for this office were laid out by Paul in both the epistles to Timothy and to Titus, and the bishop seems to have managed the church in a certain geographical area. Another officer was the deacon. The first seven servants chosen by the church of Jerusalem are frequently referred to as deacons, although the New Testament never calls them this. The office of deacon was as the word *diakonos* ("servant") implies, one of service. The qualifications for deacon were as stringent as those for the bishop. Elders *(presbeuteroi)* are also mentioned as leaders of the church. Acts makes a clear connection between the elders of Judaism and those of the church. Apparently the latter were older persons who had been given authority to make decisions on religious matters by virtue of their age and wisdom. Paul's letters indicate that the elders also had the function of teaching and preaching. In addition to these offices the New Testament mentions evangelists, prophets, apostles, pastors, and teachers. Never, however, is the reader given a complete list of the functions of these leaders.

The Christian church of the New Testament period (ca. 30–150 A.D.) seems to have been amorphous both in belief and structure. There was no strong organization to impose a creed upon the Christian groups, and therefore they varied greatly in what they believed and practiced. Paul was constantly having to correct what he considered false doctrine among Christians in various parts of the Roman world. He was in disagreement with many of the Jerusalem leaders over the issue of the admittance of gentiles into the church. The churches of the various cities within the Roman Empire seem to have been loosely or-

[15]Matthew 16:16–19.

ganized, meeting in the synagogues when they were welcome and in private homes when no other arrangements could be made. They soon changed their day of worship from the Jewish Sabbath of Saturday to Sunday, the day when Jesus rose from the dead. Their clergy apparently had little official status and usually were not paid for their preaching. Occasionally, offerings were taken for Christian preachers, but for the most part they lived by whatever trade or skills they had.

The Production of the New Testament

The Bible of the early church was the Jewish Bible. Christians read the prophets Isaiah, Micah, and Zechariah and saw in them predictions of the life of Jesus. As the years passed, specifically Christian literature began to be developed. Probably the earliest Christian writings were the letters (epistles) that Saint Paul wrote to the congregations of Christians he had established. These letters began in the 50s and 60s of the first century. Fourteen of the current twenty-seven books of the New Testament are letters attributed to Paul, although modern scholarship doubts that all of the fourteen came from his pen.[16] These letters are an anthology of Pauline thought. They contain advice to the early church on doctrine, leadership, and worship. Additionally, they contain some biographical material about Paul and other early church leaders that is not found elsewhere. In his letters to the Romans and Galatians particularly, Paul sets forth the first systematic understanding of the importance of the life, death, and resurrection of Jesus.

In the years following Jesus' death, Christians undoubtedly wrote their remembrances of the events of his life as well as his sayings. We may speculate that collections of his teachings were compiled for use in the instruction of converts. However, Christians may not have made a careful attempt to write the story of Jesus because they were expecting his imminent return. As the years went by, and as the people who personally knew of Jesus began to die, either from old age or from persecution, fewer and fewer Christians were able to recount the events in Jesus' life with any certainty. In 70 A.D. the Roman armies closed in on Jerusalem to finish off the Jewish revolution that had begun four years earlier. By the end of the summer Jerusalem and its temple were destroyed, along with the Jerusalem church and many witnesses to the life of Jesus. It may have been this event that caused a Christian to collect a brief statement of the events in the last few months of Jesus' life and to publish it as the Gospel of Mark. In the

---

[16] The books that are most commonly questioned are Ephesians, I, II Timothy, and Titus.

next decade, two more elaborate Gospels, Matthew and Luke, used Mark as a base. The Gospel that differs most from the others in terms of content, chronology, and message is the Gospel of John. This supposedly was written between 90 and 100 A.D., although its date is by no means certain. The account of the early church in Jerusalem, Acts of the Apostles, was probably written by the author of Luke as a sequel to that Gospel.[17]

Other epistles by anonymous authors were probably written between 90 and 150 A.D. and make up eight books in the current New Testament. In addition to these books there must have been many other epistles, gospels, and histories written in these early centuries, and circulated and read by Christians; but they were not popular or authoritative enough to have been maintained. The twenty-seven books that make up the New Testament were probably well established as canon in Christendom by the end of the second century.

Early Heresies

As we have noted, because early Christianity was not a highly organized body with an established creed, and because it encompassed a wide variety of members, many different beliefs were held by the early Christians. In subsequent years the church did establish creedal statements and supported an orthodox theology. Later Christians, looking back on the early believers who did not conform to the content of these creeds, referred to such predecessors as heretics.

The most famous heresy within the early church centered around the widespread and diverse group called Gnostics.[18] The term *Gnostic* has come to encompass so many beliefs and practices among early Christians that it is difficult to define accurately. However, most authorities seem to agree that the Gnostics had in common a belief in a divine spark within all humans. This spark is immortal and came from an unknown god. Gnostics also believed that the universe as we know it is controlled by evil forces. Therefore it was necessary for a redeemer figure to come to earth from the unknown god and provide knowledge whereby the divine spark in humanity might be able to rejoin its maker. Some Gnostics seem to have believed that spirit was good and flesh was evil. Therefore the supreme God, who was pure spirit, could not have created this fleshly world; it must have been created by some secondary deity. The major thrust of Gnosticism

---

[17] This paragraph states the most widely accepted pattern for the reason for the development of the Gospels, their sequence of writing, and their dates. However, it is not universally accepted by all Christian scholars.

[18] The name is derived from the Greek word *gnosko*, which means "to know." Those called Gnostics claimed to know certain secrets that mere mortals could not know.

against orthodox Christianity was that it denied that the Godly Christ could have been fully identified with the human Jesus. Many of the Gnostics said that Jesus only appeared to be human but was actually pure spirit, and therefore his life, teachings, death, and resurrection were of little consequence.[19] Gnosticism was also a syncretistic movement, taking its doctrines from late Judaism, Christianity, Greek, Persian, and Egyptian religions, Greek philosophy, and the mystery religions. Though the Gnostics were branded as heretics and their teachings condemned by the early church councils, their belief that flesh was evil and spirit was divine had its long-range effects upon Christianity. The church has historically placed more emphasis on the divinity of Jesus than upon his humanity, and Christians have been encouraged to deny the flesh in order to glorify the spirit.

A representative collection of early Christian gnostic literature was discovered at Nag Hammadi in Egypt in 1945. After many years of study, editing, and translation, the corpus of these gnostic books are available for study in English. (See *The Nag Hammadi Library*. James M. Robinson, General Editor. New York: Harper & Row, 1977.) For the first time students of Gnosticism can rely upon first-hand gnostic materials in the pursuit of an understanding of this fascinating heresy.

Another version of Gnosticism that developed in the second century A.D. was Marcionism. It was named after Marcion, the son of the Bishop of Pontus, who came to Rome in 140 A.D. seeking an office in the church. Although his theology attracted many followers, he was excommunicated from the church in 144. Basically, he taught that the God of the Old Testament was not the true picture of the God of love that Christians found in Christ. Therefore Christians should not waste time reading the Old Testament. Even the Gospels were suspect because they were written by Jewish Christians. Marcion died in 160, but his teachings continued to be popular in some circles. To this day, one still hears Christians saying that the God of the Old Testament is a God of wrath and judgment, while the God of the New Testament is a God of love.

Another heresy that sprang up in early Christianity was Montanism. In the middle of the second century, Montanus taught that the Holy Spirit, the third member of the Trinity (Father, Son, and Holy Spirit), was not to be stifled by dogma but was to be free to move among Christians, causing them to speak in tongues and prophesy. He also taught that the end of the world was coming soon, along with the return of Christ. Although Montanus had a zealous band of disciples, his movement had almost died out by the fourth century. Still,

---

[19] This particular aspect of Gnosticism is called Docetism.

there have been occasional charismatic movements similar to Montanism throughout the history of the Christian church.

To counter these and other heretical groups it became necessary for orthodox Christians to develop a statement of faith. The statement had to be simple enough to be memorized and used regularly; at the same time it had to be thorough enough to combat effectively the heresies. The result was the so-called Apostles' Creed. The critical mind cannot believe that this creed was developed by Peter, James, and John, although it does have the ring of early authority. The following statement of this creed comes from about 340 A.D.

> I believe in God almighty.
> And in Christ Jesus, his only son, our Lord
> Who was born of the Holy Spirit and the Virgin Mary
> Who was crucified under Pontius Pilate and was buried
> And the third day rose from the dead
> Who ascended into heaven
> And sitteth on the right hand of the Father
> Whence he cometh to judge the living and the dead.
> And in the Holy Ghost
> The holy church
> The remission of sins
> The resurrection of the flesh
> The life everlasting.[20]

Growth of the Church of Rome

In the early years of Christianity Jerusalem exercised leadership over the church. After 70 A.D. other cities, such as Alexandria and Antioch, took over this leadership. These cities produced many of the outstanding thinkers, who are known as the church fathers, and whose writings influenced Christianity for all time. Each of the great cities of the Roman Empire had a bishop; the larger and more influential the city, the greater the authority of its bishop. The bishops of Alexandria, Antioch, Caesarea, and Rome all were considered to be leaders in the early church. Eventually the bishop of the Church of Rome came to be recognized as the most important bishop of all and finally was designated pope. There were several reasons for this ascendancy.

First, Peter, whom Jesus had singled out as the rock upon which he would build his church, had become the first bishop of the Roman church and had passed on his authority to the bishops who succeeded him. Thus the Roman church had a very strong tradition.

[20] Martin E. Marty, *A Short History of Christianity* (Cleveland and New York: World Publishing Company, 1958), p. 75.

Second, Constantine, the first Roman emperor to support Christianity, moved his political capital from Rome to Constantinople in 330. This left the city of Rome without a strong political leader. A series of strong bishops of the Roman church filled this void and were looked upon by Western rulers as extremely important people.

Third, the churches of the East were split apart by various doctrinal controversies, and no one bishop could speak for all Eastern Christians. The West, however, was relatively free from these controversies, and the bishop of Rome was the spokesperson for a widely accepted orthodoxy.

Fourth, in the seventh century the Muslims conquered most of the great cities of the Christian Byzantine Empire, and the dominant religion of cities such as Alexandria and Antioch became Islam. This left Rome as the single leading Christian city in what was left of the Roman Empire.

Thus, through a series of fortuitous events and able leadership, the Church of Rome came to be the dominant church in Christendom, and its bishops became the Christian popes.

The Emergence of Christianity As the Religion of the Roman Empire

During the period between 64 and 330 A.D., Christianity went through several periods of persecution and acceptance by the Roman Empire. Officially, the empire was tolerant of all religions. However, the Christians occasionally found themselves in trouble because of their refusal to accept the official Roman gods and to worship them on state occasions. Jews also were in difficulty over this issue. In addition, the Christian sect was accused by the Romans of a variety of evils. Since the Christians were often from the slave classes and often met in secret they were accused of evil secret rituals that included eating flesh and drinking blood. They were also accused of sexual immorality. As their numbers grew, as they refused to give first allegiance to the emperor, and as they occasionally refused to be members of the Roman army, the opposition to them grew. Frequently persecution was the result. Nero's persecution of the Christians was local and brief. The Emperor Domitian (81–96 A.D.) insisted that citizens of the empire worship his person, and he instituted the first widespread persecution of Christians who refused to worship him. This persecution may have formed the background from which the Revelation of John was written.

In the second century there were again quiet periods followed by severe persecutions. The legal status of Christians in the empire was never secure, and at any time local officials could begin to pressure them. Widespread persecution broke out under the Emperors Hadrian (117–138) and Marcus Aurelius (161–180). In this era the old Roman Empire was falling apart from internal and external forces, and the emperors frequently looked upon the Christians as a threat to the unity and the strength of the old Roman ways. Therefore they persecuted Christians in hopes of renewing Rome to what it had been in the days before Christianity.

The on-again, off-again persecution of Christians reached its peak in 303, under the Emperor Diocletian, in an empire-wide movement that lasted for more than ten years. This period was followed by the reign of Constantine. Constantine was not Christian but was strongly influenced by his wife and mother, who were. Although he did not make Christianity the religion of the Roman Empire, he treated it with the same toleration extended to other religions and brought a halt to persecution. In 325 Constantine called the Church Council of Nicea, to stop the warring within Christian factions over the nature of Christ. Twelve years later, when he was dying, Constantine finally accepted baptism and officially became a Christian.

Several of the emperors who followed Constantine tried to reverse the tide and return to the old Roman religions. But with the reign of Theodosius (379–395), Christianity officially became the religion of the Roman Empire, and all other religions were suppressed.

Augustine

Perhaps no other Christian after Paul so deeply influenced the life and the direction of Christianity as did Augustine (354–430). Like many of the other leaders of the early church, he was born in North Africa. His mother was a devout Christian, but his father was pagan. Although he received Christian instruction as a child, he did not accept the faith until later in life. As a young man he took a concubine and had a child by her. For a time he was interested in Manichaeism, a religion that was a syncretism of Christian and Zoroastrian ideas. After a few years with Manichaeism, Augustine followed the teachings of Neoplatonism, but he was not completely satisfied with this either. In Milan he came under the influence of the Christian bishop, Ambrose. In a very dramatic conversion experience Augustine became a Christian. He returned to North Africa, where he became a writer and eventually the bishop of Hippo. Two of his writings have become classics in Christian literature: his autobiographical *Confessions* and his *City of God,* an interpretation of history written in response to those who blamed the Christians for the fall of the city of Rome to the Goths.

Roman Catholic priest consecrating the host or sacred bread during a mass. The bread is believed by many Christians to represent the body of Christ.

Augustine is also widely known for his formulations of the doctrine of original sin, the fall of man, and predestination. Taking his support from Paul's letter to the Romans, he believed that the original man and woman had willfully chosen to sin against God and thus had passed to all future generations a sinful nature. For this reason all humankind was incurably sinful and fallen. To Augustine, God in his infinite mercy had sent his son to die for the sins of a handful of sinners who had been predesinted for salvation. All the rest of humankind was doomed to eternal damnation. Augustine was challenged in these views by the monk Pelagius, who believed that humankind was free to act as it would. Therefore, to Pelagius and his followers, salvation was something initiated and mainly carried through by human will. Only a little help from God was needed. Although the Pelagians were denounced by orthodox Christianity, the teachings of Augustine never really became orthodox, either. It was not until the time of John Calvin, in the Protestant Reformation of the sixteenth century, that Augustine's doctrines received wider attention.

The Monastic Movement

Introduced by the early medieval church, the monastic movement became a major part of Christianity. Of all the major religions of the Western world, Christianity is the only one to encourage monastic orders. Neither Judaism nor Islam has encouraged its members to move apart from the evils of normal life and live alone, although there have been minor movements in both religions.

The monastic movement in Christianity did not really begin to develop until the third century. To be sure, there were statements in the New Testament from both Jesus and Paul that supported some forms of celibacy, fasting, and sharing of possessions with the needy. Nevertheless, the first two and a half centuries of Christianity saw no widespread application of these teachings in the form of monasticism. The tradition of celibacy for the bishops, priests, and deacons was established in the Western churches by the end of the fourth century. The Eastern churches commanded celibacy for the bishops, but priests and deacons were allowed to marry before they were ordained.

The movement toward asceticism and monastic community life apparently began in Egypt in the middle of the third century. Christians in Egypt may have been influenced by the asceticism of Hinduism or native Egyptian religions, or they may have been influenced by the basic distrust of the flesh taught by the Manichaeans, the Gnostics, and the Neoplatonists. Egypt itself, with its deserts and wild places, offered the ideal setting for men and women who wanted to leave the problems of normal life behind them and seek solitude in the wilderness. Some began to sell their possessions and go out into the desert regions to live simples lives dedicated to God. A number of them were widely known for their feats of asceticism. Simeon Stylites (d. 459), for example, is said to have lived atop a pillar in the desert for thirty-six years. Others fasted for long periods, went without sleep, ate only the simplest of food, gave up bathing, and wore irritating garments. Still others gathered together and formed monastic communities.

The first Christian monastery is attributed to Pachomius, who was born in Egypt in the last decade of the third century. For a variety of reasons the monastic movement soon became popular throughout Christendom.

Basically, the monasteries were secluded places where men and women were dedicated to a simple life of hard manual labor, prayer, fasting, and sometimes study. What little learning and scholarship that existed in the medieval period was kept alive in the monasteries. Historically, some of the best minds of the church were produced by these communities. St. Jerome (b. 342), who translated the Hebrew and Greek biblical material into the Latin Vulgate, the standard Bible for the Roman Catholic Church for over 1,500 years, was a product of the monastic movement. Some have suggested that the vitality and strength of the monasteries at any given time was an accurate gauge of the vitality of the entire church.

MEDIEVAL CHRISTIANITY

That period between the fall of the Roman Empire and the rise of the modern European nations is usually called the "medieval" period. During this period the Christian Church was a major force in the total culture of both Eastern and Western Europe.

The Division Between Eastern and Western Christianity

From the time of the establishment of the city of Constantinople and the new capital of the Roman Empire (330) there developed a gradually widening division between the Christians of the East and those of Western Europe. This basic division was political and geographical as well as theological. When Constantine set up his capital in the East he took an active role in the development and direction of the church, and called the Council of Nicea to settle theological differences. His successors followed his example and usually took an active part in directing religion. In the West, Rome had been left without effective political leadership. Into this vacuum stepped the able bishops of the Roman church, who even took some of the titles of the ancient Caesars. When the barbarians massed at the walls of Rome, it was the popes who negotiated with them for the city.

The theological differences between East and West were basic ones. Most of the great thinkers and leaders of the early church were from North Africa and Asia Minor. Most of the early councils that established Christian doctrine were held in the East. Eastern Christians tended to be more interested in theological formulations and became bitterly divided over certain issues. Western Christians tended to be more practical and were concerned with survival in a hostile and decaying world. Eastern theologians tended to emphasize the divine nature of Christ, while those of the West emphasized his humanity.

The largest issue dividing Eastern and Western Christians was the papacy. The great cities of the East each had outstanding bishops who became known as patriarchs. Although Constantinople was the capital, its patriarch could never gain authority over the patriarchs of the other major cities. In the West there was only Rome, and the bishop of that city clearly led the Western church. Gradually the bishop of Rome claimed to be the leader of all Christendom, but the Eastern patriarchs refused to accept his authority.

Numerous minor differences also developed between these churches that came to be known as Eastern Orthodox and Roman Catholic. The Eastern church used icons, two-dimensional pictures of Jesus, Mary, and the disciples, in their worship, while the Western church allowed statues. The East baptized infants by immersion, while the West allowed sprinkling. The East gave the people both bread and wine in the communion meal, while the West gave them only bread. The East allowed its clergy the possibility of marriage before ordination, while the West came to insist upon celibacy. The East used Greek as its language of worship, while the West used Latin until the mid-twentieth century.

The rift between the two branches of Christendom continued to grow during its first thousand years. Western Christians were busy repelling various barbarian invasions and building what has become Western Europe, while the East saw almost all of its empire fall into the hands of Muslim invaders in the seventh and eighth centuries. Antagonism reached a climax in 1054, when Pope Leo IX sent delegates to Constantinople to excommunicate the Patriarch Cerularius. Even this breach might have been healed, but Christian Crusaders from European nations stopped at Constantinople in 1204, on their way to the Holy Land, and sacked the city. Even today the modern ecumenical movement within Christendom is still seeking a reunion between these two branches of the church.

The Medieval Papacy

Because of its great missionary activities and basic attractiveness, by the medieval period Christianity virtually became the only religion of Western Europe. The thrust of the Muslim movement into Europe was stopped by Charles Martel at the Battle of Tours in 732, and although there were Muslims in Spain for another seven centuries, Europe was maintained as a Christian realm. The implications of this for the papacy were immense. For Europeans there was only one Holy Catholic Church and outside it there was no salvation. This church had one head, Christ, who ruled through his vicar, Peter, and his successors on the throne of the church in Rome. The line of succession from Peter to the various popes was said to be an unbroken line of authority. This power and its potential were the occasion for both excellence and abuse by the medieval popes.

In the chaos that followed the decline of the Roman Empire, the papacy was often the only secure leadership in Europe, and the popes

Located within the Vatican City in Rome is St. Peter's Basilica. This structure is built over the traditional site of the burial of Peter, the disciple of Jesus. (*Courtesy of Italian Government Travel Office.*)

of the Christian church exercised much of the same power as did temporal rulers. Indeed, they were the makers of many temporal rulers, as it was the custom of those who would be emperors of the "Holy Roman Empire" to be crowned by the popes. Naturally this power led to abuses. The papacy gathered lands, wealth, and art treasures and went to war in a manner similar to that of any other feudal fiefdom. Frequently, ecclesiastical offices were given to relatives (nepotism) or sold to the highest bidder (simony) because they carried so much potential power and wealth.

The strength of the papacy over European politics was never more clearly illustrated than in the conflict between Pope Gregory VII (1073–1085) and Emperor Henry VI (d. 1106). The issue between them was who was to appoint German bishops, the pope or the emperor. The emperor wished to appoint his own bishops, for obvious reasons, but when he did so, the pope excommunicated him. In order to gain a reversal of this decision, the emperor crossed the Alps in the dead of winter, January 1077, and stood for three days as a barefoot penitent before the palace of the pope. Finally Gregory absolved him. Such was the power of the church over the secular rulers of that time.

In terms of its moral leadership the papacy reached its weakest point between 1309 and 1377, a period called the "Babylonian Captivity of the Church." During this period the headquarters of the papacy moved from Rome to Avignon, near the French border. The popes and most of the cardinals of this era were all French, and at times the papacy was virtually captive to the king of France. This weakened its power and prestige with nations that were not friendly to France. This was also a period of papal wealth, luxury, moral laxity, and abuse. The result was the Great Schism.

In 1378 the Avignon cardinals elected a new pope, Urban VI, who then refused to return to Avignon with them and, instead, restored the papacy to Rome. The cardinals declared Urban's election to be void and elected another pope, who would rule from Avignon. There upon, Urban selected another college of cardinals. The European nations were divided in their support of the two men who claimed to be the successor to Saint Peter. The Council of Pisa was called in 1409 to settle the issue but instead selected a third pope, who also claimed to be Christ's vicar on earth. The Great Schism was finally healed by the Council of Constance, which met from 1414 to 1418, and the papacy was returned to one pope, with his capital in Rome.

Thomas Aquinas

No discussion of medieval Christianity, or Christianity in general, would be complete without some mention of one of the greatest—if not *the* greatest—thinkers the church ever produced, Thomas Aquinas (d. 1274).

The tenth through the fourteenth centuries in Western Europe were a time of intense intellectual activity. During this period many of the great universities were founded, and their main intellectual pursuit was theology. The writings of Plato, Aristotle, and others were preserved from destruction by the Arab philosophers, and by the late medieval period there was enough peaceful contact between Muslim and Christian scholars to allow Christians access to these writings so that they could translate them into Latin. These translations gave impetus to the intellectual movement.

The issue that most concerned Christian thinkers was the relationship between faith and reason. Were Christian beliefs, which had been communicated through scripture and the church, consistent with what people perceived to be the truth by means of their ability to reason?

The most outstanding Christian scholar to address this issue was Thomas Aquinas, a Dominican monk whose entire life was given over to scholarship. He was a student of Albertus Magnus at the University of Paris. Although Aquinas was a prolific writer of hymns, commentaries, and theological studies, he is best remembered for two works. The first was *Summa Contra Gentiles,* a series of arguments defending the Christian faith against infidels. The second and best known of his works was *Summa Theologiae,* a massive systematization of the Christian faith that became the standard theological formulation for the Roman Catholic Church. Aquinas, more than any other, attempted to Christianize Aristotle. He utilized Aristotle's arguments for the existence of God, based upon reason, to prove a part of the Christian scheme. However, Aquinas believed that reason could only take the Christian so far; beyond this point, there had to be divine revelation to complete the message. Therefore both reason and revelation were necessary for Christian belief.

THE PROTESTANT REFORMATION

In the sixteenth century the Western church was torn asunder by a violent revolution from which it has never fully recovered. This revolution has been called the Reformation, but it went far beyond reforming Christianity; it upset it, destroyed its unified hold on Europe, challenged its authority, and disrupted it for centuries. The causes for this revolution are many, varied, and intricate. However, the major ones may be listed broadly as the rise of European nationalism, the new learning of the Renaissance, and the decline of the papacy.

Early Reform Movements

The date of the beginning of the Protestant Reformation is usually established at 1517, when Martin Luther posted his ninety-five theses on the door of the church in Wittenberg, but there were reformers and reform movements more than a century before Luther. One of the earliest reformers was John Wyclif of England (1320?–1384). Wyclif was an Oxford scholar who eventually held most of the ideas that were later representative of the Protestant movement. His greatest contribution was the translation of the official Bible of the church, which was called the Vulgate, from Latin into English. To facilitate the reading of this Bible by the common people, Wyclif organized a band of wandering preachers known as Lollards, who went about the country preaching and teaching. Wyclif died in 1384 but was condemned by the Council of Constance in 1415. His remains were unearthed and burned in 1428 as an expression of this condemnation. Even though the Lollard movement was intermittently persecuted by the kings of England, it survived long after Wyclif.

Early reformation in Bohemia was led by John Hus (1373–1415). Rector of the University of Prague, Hus was influenced by the writings of Wyclif. Hus denounced the evils of the current papacy and drew a large following from the citizens of Prague.

In order to raise money for various reasons, the medieval papacy had approved the sale of so-called indulgences. For a price, a Christian could buy an indulgence that, drawing upon the treasury of good that the saints had developed, would pay for a sin committed by the living or by the dead who were in purgatory. Hus was particularly bold in denouncing this practice (which naturally led to all manner of corruption), and became a target for the wrath of the reformers. Hus was condemned by the Council of Constance in 1415 and burned at the stake.

Early reformation was represented in Italy by the fervent preaching of a Dominican monk, Girolamo Savonarola (1452–1498), urging personal moral reform. Savonarola, who was a preacher to the city of Florence in the 1490s, was convinced that Florence was facing troubled times because of God's judgment on the moral laxity of the city. His preaching was so convincing that the Florentines changed their lives and publicly burned their pornography and objects of amusement. The stern Savonarola soon came into conflict with loose-living Pope Alexander VI, who excommunicated him. Eventually, Savonarola and two of his disciples were hanged and their bodies burned.

Martin Luther

The most outstanding figure of the Reformation was Martin Luther of Saxony (1483–1546). Luther was born into the rapidly developing middle class of German society. Although he was reared in a very religious home he had no intention of pursuing a religious vocation. After completing his master of arts degree he began to study law and planned a career as a lawyer. However, in July 1505, Luther was struck down by a bolt of lightning, and in terror he vowed to become a monk. Against his father's wishes he entered an Augustinian monastery and began his search for the salvation of his soul. Two years later he was ordained a priest and celebrated his first mass. Still, he sought salvation through fasting, vigils, confession, and self-mortification.

Luther's skills as a scholar were noted by his superiors, and he was sent as a teacher of theology to the University of Wittenberg. There he taught, preached, and took his doctorate of theology. While at Wittenberg he lectured on Paul's letters to the Romans and the Galatians. In both these books the phrase "the just shall live by faith" caught his eye and became a source of illumination to him.

Like many others, Luther began to call for moral reform within the church. He was particularly incensed by the sale of indulgences by a local man named Tetzel, who promised people that as soon as their money fell into the coffer, a soul rose from purgatory. On the basis of his opposition to this sale of indulgences Luther chose ninety-five theses as grounds for debate and nailed them upon the door of the castle church of Wittenberg on October 31, 1517. These theses were widely read all across Germany and created an immediate sensation. In the publications and debates that followed, Luther was led into more and more controversy with the papacy. He came to declare that every Christian was a priest who could interpret scripture, and that the popes and the church hierarchy were not superior to the believer. He also challenged the doctrine of transubstantiation, which taught that at the mass the bread and wine literally became the body and blood of Jesus. Luther's writings upon these and many other controversial issues were widely distributed through a new medium, the printing press.

Because of the controversy that Luther had caused, the emperor of the Holy Roman Empire, Charles V, called an imperial diet at the city of Worms in April 1521, to try Luther. When questioned, Luther admitted that the writings under scrutiny were his, but he refused to recant or retract any of their contents. He is reported to have said, "Here I stand. I cannot do otherwise." As a result of his actions before the diet, he was placed under an imperial edict that banned the printing and sale of his books, and forbade anyone to provide hospitality or shelter for him or his friends. It had been expected that Luther would suffer the same fate as Hus one hundred years before, but the emperor was too busy with other matters to properly pursue him. Instead, Luther was kidnapped by his own friends and taken to the Wartburg Castle, where he lived in disguise for almost a year. During this time he wrote nearly a dozen books and translated the New Testament into German. Later he translated the Old Testament, and his translations of scripture became classics in the German language.

In 1522 Luther returned to Wittenberg, where he took charge of the rapidly developing Reformation. He repudiated the acts of radical reformers who wanted to destroy everything in the Christian church that was not specifically mentioned in scripture. His own style was to remove only those things that he felt were contrary to scripture. In the following years Luther was busy in many ways. He was, of course, organizing a reformed church in Germany. He was writing hymns, such as the Protestant classic, "A Mighty Fortress Is Our God." He was encouraging former priests and nuns to marry, and he himself married a nun, Katherine von Bora, and became a father.

In the last years of his life Luther grew more conservative. His writings were sometimes bitterly anti-Jewish, because Jews were no more anxious to accept Lutheran Christianity than they had been to accept Catholic Christianity. He also turned against the peasants who were currently in rebellion, and encouraged the nobility to slaughter them. Against all odds, Martin Luther died peacefully in February 1546.

The Reformation sprang up in other nations during Luther's lifetime and immediately thereafter. In Germany, the decision to be reformed or to remain Catholic lay with the prince of any particular region. If the ruler were reformed, the region became reformed; if the ruler chose to remain Catholic, the region remained Catholic. Thus the religious orientation of Germany became a kind of patchwork. The Scandinavian nations, Sweden, Denmark, and Norway, became Lutheran during the following decades.

Ulrich Zwingli

In Switzerland the reform movement was led by Ulrich Zwingli (1484–1531). Zwingli was a contemporary of Luther and was much influenced by his writings. At first the Reformed Church in Switzerland was very close to the Lutheran movement. However, Zwingli and Luther differed substantially over one central issue. Although Luther denied that the bread and wine of communion actually became the body and blood of Christ, he did believe that Christ was spiritually present in the elements. He believed that the words of Jesus at the Last Supper, "This is my body,"were to be taken literally. Zwingli chose to emphasize the other words of Jesus at the Last Supper, "Do this in remembrance of me." Therefore, to the Swiss reformer, the communion meal was a memorial, a remembrance of Jesus' death. This issue prevented a union between the Swiss and the Lutherans.

John Calvin

Probably the greatest and most influential mind of the Reformation was John Calvin (1509–1564). Calvin was born in France and received a classical education at the University of Paris. By 1534 he had come under the influence of the Protestant movement and made his break with the Roman church. By the time he was twenty-six he had turned his fine mind to theological matters and written the massive book that became the classic of Protestant theology, *The Institutes of the Christian Religion*. This book, originally written in Latin and later translated into French, was revised four times in Calvin's lifetime. In it he set forth his understanding of the nature of the true Christian faith before it was corrupted by Rome. He repeated many of the teachings of Saint Augustine, stressing such ideas as the sovereignty of God, original sin, the total depravity of man, predestination, and election.

Eventually Calvin served as a minister in the Reformed Church of Geneva and then in Strassburg. He was invited back to Geneva a second time and remained there from 1541 until his death in 1564. Although he was never more than a minister in Geneva, Calvin's influence over the life of the entire city was enormous. Despite opposition from both theological and political foes, he was virtually the ruler of Geneva. He himself was given to hard work and simple living, and he impressed this upon the city. He discouraged frivolity of any kind. He encouraged commerce and industry along with the lending of money at reasonable rates of interest.[21] He encouraged education and founded the University of Geneva. Under Calvin's leadership Geneva became the home of oppressed Protestants from all over Europe.

The importance of John Calvin to the Reformed church cannot be stressed enough. His writings set the intellectual base for much of the later Protestant theology. His concern for the rightness of labor and thrift as expressions of religion is felt four hundred years later among those who have been reared in Calvinistic religion.

Other Reformation Leaders and Movements

Although the Reformation first centered on the writings and teachings of people like Luther and Calvin, and although it attracted large numbers of dissatisfied Christians throughout Europe, it soon became a fragmented movement. Within one hundred years of the death of Luther there were hundreds of denominations (and later, subdenominations) of the Reformed church. In the centuries that followed, the fragmentation continued. There were at least two major reasons for these divisions. First, Protestantism derived much of its force and early growth from nationalistic trends in sixteenth-century Western Europe. Whereas in medieval Europe one emperor, who was crowned by the pope, ruled the entire European society, postmedieval Europe began to demand monarchs over each nation, without outside interference from the emperor or Rome. Therefore, when the opportunity came for leaders of European nations to express their freedom from Rome through a new version of Christianity, many were willing to

---

[21] Indeed, some scholars, such as Max Weber, have suggested that John Calvin was the father of modern capitalism.

take it. The best example of this was the establishment of the Church of England. Although England had been the home of Wyclif and had theological differences with Rome, the major reason for the Reformation in that country was political. The strong king of England, Henry VIII, wanted a wife who would bear him a son. Since his wife Catherine could not bear him one, Henry asked the pope for an annulment so that he might remarry. When the pope refused, Henry married Anne Boleyn, established the Church of England, and appointed Thomas Cranmer archbishop of Canterbury in 1533. Although the ostensible cause of the breach between Rome and England was Henry's marital life, the drive toward political independence was perhaps the stronger force behind the establishment of the Church of England.

A second cause for the many divisions within Protestantism was the controversy about the "priesthood of the believer," which had been such a strong part of Luther's teachings. Many of the reformers thought that many priests, who heard confessions, administered the sacraments, and interpreted the Bible for the untrained parishioner— indeed, the institution of the priesthood itself—was corrupt. Therefore these reformers taught that in the spirit of the New Testament each believer was a priest who was qualified to perform many of these tasks alone. The reformers were strongly in favor of the translation of the Bible into vernacular languages so it could be read by every Christian. Obviously, if all Christians could read the Bible and were free to interpret it for themselves, differences of interpretation were bound to occur, and these ultimately caused divisions within Protestantism.

One of the most radical dissident groups was the Anabaptists. Whereas Luther and Calvin had rejected only those elements in the Catholic church that they felt were expressly forbidden in the Bible, the Anabaptists attempted to discard all those elements not expressly found in the New Testament. Luther and Calvin advocated infant baptism because it was not condemned by the New Testament, but the Anabaptists rejected it because they could not find such a practice in the New Testament. They therefore baptized adults who had formerly been baptized as infants—thus the nickname "Anabaptists" (i.e., "those who baptize a second time"). Because this movement was devisive in nature, there were many Anabaptist subgroups with a great variety of beliefs. Because they were different and their numbers were small, the Anabaptists were persecuted by both Catholics and other Protestants, to the point that they were almost eliminated from the European continent. They survived in Britain and America as Mennonites and Amish.

Other Reformation groups existed in nearly every European nation. Many of these were suppressed by their governments and either fled their native lands or were crushed completely. One such group was the French Huguenots. The French were deeply impressed by the teachings of John Calvin, and his Reformation made many converts among the French middle class and even the aristocracy. Hostilities between the Catholic majority and the Protestant minority erupted into a series of wars between 1562 and 1594. Following these wars, the Huguenots were guaranteed freedom of worship in certain specified locations by the Edict of Nantes. One hundred years later, in 1685, the edict was formally revoked, and hundreds of thousands of the Huguenots fled to other parts of Europe and America. Only a tiny minority of Protestants remained in France after the seventeenth century.

Italy, the home of both the papacy and Savonarola, never produced a Protestant Reformation of any magnitude, nor did Czechoslovakia, the home of Hus, nor did Spain. The Scottish Reformation was led by a Calvinist, John Knox, and became the basis for the modern Presbyterian Church.

MODERN CHRISTIANITY

Christianity, like all the other major religions of the world, has been forced to deal with the problems and challenges of the modern world. However, in entering the modern age, Christianity was first required to overcome the trauma of the Reformation.

The Catholic Counter-Reformation

Protestants were not the only ones who saw the problems within the sixteenth-century Catholic church. Others were aware of the same grievances that motivated Luther and Calvin, but they wished to purify the church without establishing another form of Christianity. They wanted a reformation without the attendant revolution. These individuals remained within the Roman Catholic Church and sought a Counter-Reformation as a response to the Protestant Reformation.

When it became apparent that large numbers of Christians were leaving the church and following the Reformers, the Catholic church responded immediately, in 1545, by convening the Council of Trent. Some who came to the council wanted to achieve reforms that would bring reconciliation with the Protestants. Others wished to delineate the Catholic position so clearly that there would be no grounds for reconciliation. Generally, the decisions of Trent favored those who preferred the second path. To counter the Protestant emphasis upon scripture as the sole word of God, the council declared that Catholic tradition was coequal with scripture as a source of truth for Chris-

The First Congregational Church of Evanston, Illinois is built in the traditional New England colonial style. The simple grace and beauty of this architecture is widely used in American Christian churches.

tians. Therefore when Protestants pointed to a practice in the Catholic church that was contrary to scripture, the Catholics replied that the church had written scripture and therefore its traditions were at least equal if not superior.

As a response to Protestants such as Wyclif and Luther, who insisted on translating scripture into the vernacular, the Council of Trent stated that the Latin Vulgate was to be the true sacred canon of the church. This was also a counter to Reformers who had chosen to exclude certain Old Testament books not found in the Jewish scripture. The council further declared that only the Roman Catholic Church had the right to interpret scripture. This too flew in the face of the Protestant doctrine of the "priesthood of the believer."

Whereas most Reformed churches had rejected all of the sacraments except baptism and communion, the Council of Trent reaffirmed the traditional seven sacraments:

1. *Baptism.* Baptism of infants was necessary to wash away the taint of original sin. Any infant who died without the benefit of baptism was technically destined for hell. However, later it became popular to say that the unbaptized infant was to spend eternity in a land called *limbo.*

2. *Confirmation.* At some point before maturity, usually about age thirteen, children must be reconfirmed in the vows that were made for them when they were baptized as infants.

3. *Penance.* Christians must confess their sins regularly in private to priests and receive absolution. Absolution, or forgiveness, may be conditioned upon acts of penance ordered by the priest, depending on the seriousness of the sin confessed.

4. *Eucharist.* This sacrament is known throughout Christendom as the Lord's Supper, communion, or mass. In many Christian communities the bread and wine are given to the laity, but the Roman Catholic Church gives only the bread and reserves the wine for the priesthood. The Council of Trent not only reaffirmed this sacrament but also gave renewed support to the doctrine of transubstantiation. According to this doctrine, during the mass the bread and wine literally become the body and blood of Jesus. The Council held that since the whole Christ was present in both the bread and the wine, it was not necessary to give the wine to the laity.

5. *Extreme unction.* As a Christian nears death he or she is to be visited by a priest and anointed with healing oil. The priest then hears the last confession. In receiving these last rites, the Christian is properly prepared to die.

6. *Marriage.* By the fifteenth century, the marriage of Christians had come to be regarded as a sacrament.

7. *Ordination.* For those Christians who chose the clergy as a career rather than marriage, taking the holy orders was considered a sacrament.

The Council of Trent also strongly supported relics, the veneration of saints, and sacred images, all contrary to most Protestant teaching. As a positive response to the challenge of Luther and others, the sale of indulgences was controlled and other abuses of the medieval church were corrected.

Another result of the Catholic Counter-Reformation was the development of the Society of Jesus (Jesuits). The founder of the society was Ignatius Loyola (1491–1556), a Spanish nobleman whose first career was the military. Loyola was wounded in a battle in 1521, and during his convalescence he read about the life of Christ and the various saints. He was so moved by this literature that upon his recovery he entered a monastery, took the vows of poverty, chastity, and obedience, hung up his armor in the chapel of the Virgin Mary, and dedicated himself to becoming a soldier of Christ. In the following years Loyola developed the *Spiritual Exercises,* which were designed to serve as an agency for examining the conscience and as a guide for meditation. These exercises were usually given under the direction of a spiritual leader, and required about four weeks.

Realizing his need for education, Loyola went back to school and eventually studied theology at the University of Paris. He gathered about him other scholars to whom he introduced the *Spiritual Exercises.* Among these early converts was Francis Xavier (1506–1552), who was to become a Christian missionary to India and Japan. Loyola and his friends went to Rome, and in 1540 the pope gave them official permission to found a new order, the Society of Jesus. This order was characterized by its military organization, its absolute obedience to the pope and the general of the order, its scholarship, and its missionary activities. Scholarship was stressed because Loyola and his early followers were university students. Before Loyola died in 1556 he saw his order grow from just a few friends to over a thousand members. Although it was an object of fear and suspicion by both Protestants and other Catholics, the Jesuit order continued to grow and attracted some of the ablest young men in Catholic Europe.

Catholic Dogmas Since the Counter-Reformation

The heart of the modern Catholic church was established by the end of the sixteenth century. Prior to the second Vatican Council called in 1959, there were no sweeping changes in Catholic theology. A series of dogmas were established by the church during this period, but many of them had been widely held for centuries. Their establishment as dogmas merely put the official seal of approval upon them. The following dogmas have been accepted as major doctrines since the Council of Trent.

1. *The Immaculate Conception of Mary.* It had long been held among Catholics that Mary, the mother of Jesus, not only had conceived as a virgin but that she had been born without the taint of original sin. In 1854 Pope Pius IX formally declared the Immaculate Conception to be a dogma that should be believed by all faithful Catholics.

2. *The dogma of papal infallibility.* After the Council of Trent closed in 1563 the Roman Catholic Church called no general council until

the Vatican Council of 1869. This council dealt with the sensitive issue of papal infallibility. After much debate and controversy the council declared as dogma that the pope was infallible when he spoke *ex cathedra*, that is, as the pastor of all Christians on the issues of dogma and morals. Naturally this dogma widened the gap between Catholics and Eastern Orthodox and Protestant groups.

3. *The dogma of the bodily assumption of Mary.* In 1950, Pope Pius XII declared as dogma the bodily assumption of Mary. This meant that Mary did not suffer decay in a tomb but was taken directly into heaven after her death.

Vatican II

Upon the death of Pius XII in 1958, John XXIII became the pope. John was determined to revitalize the church and bring it into line with the twentieth century. Therefore he called the second Vatican Council, which was to be the most revolutionary council since Trent. Invited to this council were representatives of Eastern Orthodox and Protestant Christian groups acting as observers to the proceedings. Meeting between 1962–1965, this council effected some of the most sweeping changes ever made in the Roman Catholic Church. Non-Catholics were recognized as true Christians, the vernacular was allowed in many parts of the mass, the Index of Prohibited Books was abolished, more congregational participation in worship was encouraged, and the church officially declared that Jews were no longer to be held responsible for the death of Jesus. In general, the second Vatican Council attempted to bring the church up to date, and took several steps toward reconciliation with Orthodox and Protestant groups.

Modern Movements

Modern Protestant Movements. Because of the reasons already discussed, Protestantism has been, until the recent ecumenical movement, a denominational movement. Two Protestants might believe essentially the same doctrines but differ on baptism or on church government and belong to different denominations.

There are so many Protestant denominations that not even the most exhaustive text on the history of Christianity could hope to effectively deal with them all. Basically, however, there are four branches of Protestantism. There are the Lutherans, who are generally found in the Germanic and Scandinavian nations and the immigrants from those nations. There are those Reformed and Presbyterian denominations that sprang from the teachings of John Calvin. A third branch is the group that sprang from the radical Reformers, the Anabaptists.

This group includes the Baptists, the Mennonites, and the Amish. Although the lines of descent are not clear, Anabaptist influence also is apparent in several other Protestant groups, such as the Quakers and the Disciples of Christ. The fourth branch includes the Church of England and the Methodists.

We have already considered all of these groups except the Methodists. Methodists began in the eighteenth century as a response to the emotional coolness of the Church of England and the plight of urban dwellers in the early industrial revolution. The founder of Methodism was John Wesley (1703–1791). Wesley, the fifteenth child in the family of an Anglican clergyman, attended Oxford and was ordained as an Anglican priest in 1728. While at Oxford he and his brother Charles organized a small group for the purpose of religious support. The group was first called the Holy Club but because of its disciplined ways was nicknamed the Methodists.

In 1735 John and Charles were sent to Georgia as missionaries, and on the voyage to America they encountered another Protestant group called Moravians, who spoke to them of religious conversion. The Wesley brothers experienced this conversion in 1738 in London. They began to preach about their experience, first in the churches and to religious societies and later in the fields and town squares. They were joined by an eloquent and fiery preacher, George Whitefield. Their emotional sermons mainly appealed to the lower and middle classes, and soon there was a large Methodist following. John organized the Methodists into societies that were formed into circuits and attended by preachers who traveled from society to society. Charles became the hymn writer and contributed hundreds of songs that are still treasured by many Protestants.

Although John Wesley had no desire to separate himself from the Church of England and form a new denomination, by the time he died, the break between the two groups was obvious. At the end of the eighteenth century there were over 70,000 Methodists in England, but the denomination's greatest growth came among the colonists in America. The Methodist meeting and its circuit rider were a familiar part of the American frontier, and Methodism became one of the largest Protestant denominations in the United States, second only to the various Baptist groups.

The squalor, poverty, despair, and alcoholism of the industrial society produced other Protestant movements. In the nineteenth century, in England, William Booth founded the Salvation Army in an attempt not only to save the souls of the ragged edges of humanity in the slums of industrialized cities but also to provide food, clothing, and warmth for their bodies. In 1844, a similar concern for the total person produced the Young Men's Christian Association in London.

The Second Vatican Council meets in Rome's majestic St. Peter's Basilica, where 2,400 high church dignitaries gathered. (*Courtesy of Pix, Inc.*)

A concern for the ignorance of slum children caused Robert Raikes to organize the first Sunday school in Gloucester, England, in 1780. Raikes' first objective was to teach the children to read the Bible. Since then the Sunday school has become almost universally accepted by Protestant denominations as an agency of religious instruction.

The Missionary Movement.   Christians have been missionaries from the earliest days. The great theologian of the early church, Paul, was a far-traveling, zealous missionary. There is a strong tradition that Thomas, the doubting disciple of Jesus, went to India to spread the Christian gospel. We have already spoken of Catholic missionaries such as Francis Xavier, who preached Christianity in Japan. Catholic missionaries accompanied the Spanish explorers in the sixteenth century. The Wesleys served as Anglican missionaries in America. Still, Protestant groups, especially those that had been influenced by John Calvin, were slow to enter the mission fields. They were probably impeded by Calvin's doctrine of predestination, which taught that the sovereign God would save only those persons whom he chose to save, and it was therefore folly to send missionaries to the heathen. If God wished to save them, they would be saved without the help of missionaries; if God did not wish to save them, it was a waste of time and money. By the nineteenth century, however, this attitude had changed except among the sternest Calvinists, and most Protestant groups came to support some form of mission work. Occasionally this missionary activity was directed at the Roman Catholic population in areas such as Latin America, but generally it was carried on in non-Christian areas in Africa and Asia. The rising nationalism among many nations in these areas inn the late twentieth century has brought an end to much missionary activity.

The Ecumenical Movement. The most outstanding movement among Christians in the twentieth century has been the ecumencial movement. As we have noted, Christianity has long been divided into two main branches, Eastern and Western, and, since the sixteenth century, the Western church has been divided into Protestant and Catholic. However, in the twentieth century, Christians have begun the long, hard journey to reunion. The Roman Catholic contribution to this journey was the second Vatican Council.

The most visible attempt at reunion was the organization of the World Council of Churches in Amsterdam, in 1948. This organization has been supported by many Protestant denominations and some representatives of Eastern Orthodoxy. Although the World Council is organized to promote church unity, little actual unification has been produced. In fact there are few concrete examples of reunion within Christendom. One has been the uniting of a small number of Protestant denominations that had no great theological differences. Other, more dramatic, unions stemmed from the pressing needs of the mission fields in nations like India, where factions within Christianity had weakened its case for conversions. Still, the reunification of Christianity is a long way off. Eastern Orthodoxy, whose largest branch, the Russian Orthodox Church, is beset by a hostile government, maintains an aloofness toward the Western church. The post-Vatican II Roman Catholic Church is more open to non-Catholic Christians than ever before, but the Protestant–Catholic dialogue, while progressing, still has many hurdles to clear. Protestants, as always, are vastly divided, and although some are quite anxious for church union and willing to pay almost any price for it, the majority apparently still prefer to go it alone.

CHRISTIANITY TODAY

Christianity faces many unique problems today. Of all the religions of the world, Christianity has the largest number of adherents. It is also spread over a wider geographical area than any other religion. However, its very size and diversity give Christianity unique problems. Since there are so many branches of Christianity, it is also difficult to say that "the Church" is doing this or that.

In the last years of the twentieth century, the Christian community presents many different faces. In Europe, with its patterns of state churches, Christianity idles. It is financially supported by governments and enjoys prestige. European universities and churches continue to produce the leading scholars in Christianity. However, popular support is low. In some European countries church attendance is estimated at 2 percent of the population. In the United States, where there are seemingly endless varieties of Christianity competing for popular support, church attendance is remarkably high. While the Roman Catholic Church in America remains healthy, the most remarkable growth of Christianity in the United States in recent years has been in the ranks of evangelical Protestant groups. Many of the more traditional or "mainline" Protestant denominations are struggling to maintain their memberships.

Whereas Christianity may be idling in Europe and remaining stable in the United States, it is one of the world's most rapidly growing religions in other parts of the world. In sub-Sahara Africa, Christianity is quickly catching up to Islam as the religion of choice. In Korea, which is traditionally Buddhist and Confucian, Christianity is also growing rapidly. Most of this growth does not seem to be attributed to the missions of Western Christians, but is a grassroots movement. The last decades of the twentieth century may be remembered in the future as one of the great eras of the growth of Christianity.

By far the hottest issue in modern Christianity is Liberation Theology. This theology, which grew out of the needs of the poor of Latin America, tends to see religion in political or revolutionary terms. It purports to read the Bible through the eyes of the poor and the oppressed. It believes that the proper role for Christianity is a political identification with the struggles of the poor. The opponents of Liberation Theology see it as very close to Marxist doctrine. Liberation Theology has been mainly expressed by Roman Catholic clergy in Latin America, but it also has Protestant supporters.

STUDY QUESTIONS

1. Discuss Christianity as a product of first-century Judaism and the Graeco-Roman world.

2. In what sense did Jesus fulfill the role of Jewish messiah? In what sense did he not fulfill this role?

3. According to the New Testament, what were the two basic rituals of early Christianity?

4. In the production of the New Testament, which section was likely to have been written first? When were the Gospels written?

5. Discuss the importance of Constantine to the survival of Christianity. Why is Asoka called "the Constantine of Buddhism"?

6. What are the major differences between Eastern Orthodox and Western Christianity?

7. List several of the causes for the Reformation.

8. List the seven sacraments of the Roman Catholic Church as defined by the Council of Trent.

9. Discuss Vatican II. Relate its actions to the ecumenical movement.

SUGGESTED READING

Adam, Karl. *The Spirit of Catholicism.* New York: Macmillan Publishing Company, 1962.

Filson, Floyd V. *Opening the New Testament.* Philadelphia: Westminster Press, 1952.

Hordern, William. *A Layman's Guide to Protestant Theology.* New York: Macmillan Publishing Company, 1957.

Klausner, Joseph. *Jesus of Nazareth.* New York: Macmillan Publishing Company, 1934.

Marty, Martin E. *A Short History of Christianity.* Cleveland: World Publishing Company, 1959.

Reynolds, Stephen. *The Christian Religious Tradition.* Encino, Calif.: Dickenson Publishing Company, 1977.

Selections from the New Testament

The following selections from the New Testament illustrate some of the key issues and themes of early Christianity. Matthew 5, 6, and 7 contain Jesus' Sermon on the Mount. In this sermon one finds many of the distinctive Christian materials, such as the Beatitudes (Matthew 5:3–12) and the Lord's Prayer (Matthew 6:9–13). Romans 3 is selected as one of the bases for the Christian understanding of human sinfulness. I Corinthians 13 is perhaps the most beautiful passage from the New Testament as it describes human and divine love. I Corinthians 15 is one of the best statements of early Christian understanding of the resurrection. Finally, Revelation 20–22 is the clearest statement of Christian eschatology.[22]

Sermon on the Mount

5 Seeing the crowds, he went up on the mountain, and when he sat down his disciples came to him. [2] And he opened his mouth and taught them, saying:

[3] "Blessed are the poor in spirit, for theirs is the kingdom of heaven.

[4] "Blessed are those who mourn, for they shall be comforted.

[5] "Blessed are the meek, for they shall inherit the earth.

[6] "Blessed are those who hunger and thirst for righeousness, for they shall be satisfied.

[7] "Blessed are the merciful, for they shall obtain mercy.

[8] "Blessed are the pure in heart, for they shall see God.

[9] "Blessed are the peacemakers, for they shall be called sons of God.

[10] "Blessed are those who are persecuted for righteousness' sake, for theirs is the kingdom of heaven.

[11] "Blessed are you when men revile you and persecute you and utter all kinds of evil against you falsely on my account. [12] Rejoice and be glad, for your reward is great in heaven, for so men persecuted the prophets who were before you.

[13] "You are the salt of the earth; but if salt has lost its taste, how shall its saltness be restored? It is no longer good for anything except to be thrown out and trodden under foot by men.

[14] "You are the light of the world. A city set on a hill cannot be hid.

―――――――――――――

[22] The source material that follows is taken from the *Holy Bible,* Revised Standard Version (New York: Thomas Nelson & Sons, 1952) Matthew chapters 5, 6, 7; Romans chapter 3; I Corinthians chapters 13 and 15; Revelation chapters 20, 21, 22.

[15]Nor do men light a lamp and put it under a bushel, but on a stand, and it gives light to all in the house. [16]Let your light so shine before men, that they may see your good works and give glory to your Father who is in heaven.

[17]"Think not that I have come to abolish the law and the prophets; I have come not to abolish them but to fulfil them. [18]For truly, I say to you, till heaven and earth pass away, not an iota, not a dot, will pass from the law until all is accomplished. [19]Whoever then relaxes one of the least of these commandments and teaches men so, shall be called least in the kingdom of heaven; but he who does them and teaches them shall be called great in the kingdom of heaven. [20]For I tell you, unless your righteousness exceeds that of the scribes and Pharisees, you will never enter the kingdom of heaven.

[21]"You have heard that it was said to the men of old, 'You shall not kill; and whoever kills shall be liable to judgment.' [22]But I say to you that every one who is angry with his brother shall be liable to judgment; whoever insults his brother shall be liable to the council, and whoever says, 'You fool!' shall be liable to the hell of fire. [23]So if you are offering your gift at the altar, and there remember that your brother has something against you, [24]leave your gift there before the altar and go; first be reconciled to your brother, and then come and offer your gift. [25]Make friends quickly with your accuser, while you are going with him to court, lest your accuser hand you over to the judge, and the judge to the guard, and you be put in prison; [26]truly I say to you, you will never get out till you have paid the last penny.

[27]"You have heard that it was said, 'You shall not commit adultery.' [28]But I say to you that every one who looks at a woman lustfully has already committed adultery with her in his heart. [29]If your right eye causes you to sin, pluck it out and throw it away; it is better that you lost one of your members than that your whole body be thrown into hell. [30]And if your right hand causes you to sin, cut it off and throw it away; it is better that you lost one of your members than that your whole body go into hell.

[31]"It was also said, 'Whoever divorces his wife, let him give her a certificate of divorce.' [32]But I say to you that every one who divorces his wife, except on the ground of unchastity, makes her an adulteress; and whoever marries a divorced woman commits adultery.

[33]"Again you heard that it was said to the men of old, 'You shall not swear falsely, but shall perform to the Lord what you have sworn.' [34]But I say to you, Do not swear at all, either by heaven, for it is the throne of God, [35]or by the earth, for it is his footstool, or by Jerusalem, for it is the city of the great King. [36]And do not swear by your head, for you cannot make one hair white or black. [37]Let what you say be simply 'Yes' or 'No'; anything more than this comes from evil.

[38]"You have heard that it was said, 'An eye for an eye and a tooth for a tooth.' [39]But I say to you, Do not resist one who is evil. But if any one

strikes you on the right cheek, turn to him the other also; [40] and if any one would sue you and take your coat, let him have your cloak a swell; [41] and if any one forces you to go one mile, go with him two miles. [42] Give to him who begs from you, and do not refuse him who would borrow from you.

[43] "You have heard that it was said, 'You shall love your neighbor and hate your enemy.' [44] But I say to you, Love your enemies and pray for those who persecute you, [45] so that you may be sons of your Father who is in heaven; for he makes his sun rise on the evil and on the good, and sends rain on the just and on the unjust. [46] For if you love those who love you, what reward have you? Do not even the tax collectors do the same? [47] And if you salute only your brethern, what more are you doing than others? Do not even the Gentiles do the same? [48] You, therefore, must be perfect, as your heavenly Father is perfect.

6 Beware of practicing your piety before men in order to be seen by them; for then you will have no reward from your Father who is in heaven.

[2] "Thus, when you give alms, sound no trumpet before you, as the hypocrites do in the synagogues and in the streets, that they may be praised by men. Truly, I say to you, they have their reward. [3] But when you give alms, do not let your left hand know what your right hand is doing, [4] so that your alms may be in secret; and your Father who sees in secret will reward you.

[5] "And when you pray, you must not be like the hypocrites; for they love to stand and pray in the synagogues and at the street corners, that they may be seen by men. Truly, I say to you, they have their reward. [6] But when you pray, go into your room and shut the door and pray to your Father who is in secret; and your Father who sees in secret will reward you.

[7] "And in praying do not heap up empty phrases as the Gentiles do; for they think that they will be heard for their many words. [8] Do not be like them, for your Father knows what you need before you ask him. [9] Pray then like this:

Our Father who art in heaven,
Hallowed be thy name.
[10] Thy kingdom come,
Thy will be done,
On earth as it is in heaven.
[11] Give us this day our daily bread;
[12] And forgive us our debts,
As we also have forgiven our debtors;
[13] And lead us not into temptation,
But deliver us from evil.

¹⁴For if you forgive men their trespasses, your heavenly Father also will forgive you; ¹⁵but if you do not forgive men their trespasses, neither will your Father forgive your trespasses.

¹⁶And when you fast, do not look dismal, like the hypocrites, for they disfigure their faces that their fasting may be seen by men. Truly, I say to you, they have their reward. ¹⁷But when you fast, anoint your head and wash your face, ¹⁸that your fasting may not be seen by men but by your Father who is in secret; and your Father who sees in secret will reward you.

¹⁹"Do not lay up for yourselves treasures on earth, where moth and rust consume and where thieves break in and steal, ²⁰but lay up for yourselves treasures in heaven, where neither moth nor rust consumes and where thieves do not break in and steal. ²¹For where your treasure is, there will your heart be also.

²²"The eye is the lamp of the body. So, if your eye is sound, your whole body will be full of light; ²³but if your eye is not sound, your whole body will be full of darkness. If then the light in you is darkness, how great is the darkness! ²⁴"No one can serve two masters; for either he will hate the one and love the other, or he will be devoted to the one and despise the other. You cannot serve God and mammon.

²⁵"Therefore I tell you, do not be anxious about your life, what you shall eat or what you shall drink, nor about your body, what you shall put on. Is not life more than food, and body more than clothing? ²⁶Look at the birds of the air: they neither sow nor reap nor gather into barns, and yet your heavenly Father feeds them. Are you not of more value than they? ²⁷And which of you by being anxious can add one cubit to his span of life? ²⁸And why are you anxious about clothing? Consider the lilies of the field, how they grow; they neither toil nor spin; ²⁹yet I tell you, even Solomon in all his glory was not arrayed like one of these. ³⁰But if God so clothes the grass of the field, which today is alive and tomorrow is thrown into the oven, will he not much more clothe you, O men of little faith? ³¹Therefore do not be anxious, saying, 'What shall we eat?' or 'What shall we drink?' or 'What shall we wear?' ³²For the Gentiles seek all these things; and your heavenly Father knows that you need them all. ³³But seek first his kingdom and his righteousness, and all these things shall be yours as well.

³⁴"Therefore do not be anxious about tomorrow, for tomorrow will be anxious for itself. Let the day's own trouble be sufficient for the day.

7 "Judge not, that you be not judged. ²For with the judgment you pronounce you will be judged, and the measure you give will be the measure you get. ³Why do you see the speck that is in your brother's eye, but do not notice the log that is in your own eye? ⁴Or how can you say to your brother, 'Let me take the speck out of your eye,' when there is the log in your own eye? ⁵You hypocrite, first take the log out of your own eye, and then you will see clearly to take the speck out of your brother's eye.

⁶"Do not give dogs what is holy; and do not throw your pearls before swine, lest they trample them under foot and turn to attack you.

[7] "Ask, and it will be given you; seek, and you will find; knock, and it will be opened to you. [8] For every one who asks receives, and he who seeks finds, and to him who knocks it will be opened. [9] Or what man of you, if his son asks him for bread, will give him a stone? [10] Or if he asks for a fish, will give him a serpent? [11] If you then, who are evil, know how to give good gifts to your children, how much more will your Father who is in heaven give good things to those who ask him! [12] So whatever you wish that men would do to you, do so to them; for this is the law and the prophets.

[13] "Enter by the narrow gate; for the gate is wide and the way is easy, that leads to destruction, and those who enter by it are many. [14] For the gate is narrow and the way is hard, that leads to life, and those who find it are few.

[15] "Beware of false prophets, who come to you in sheep's clothing but inwardly are ravenous wolves. [16] You will know them by their fruits. Are grapes gathered from thorns, or figs from thistles? [17] So, every sound tree bears good fruit, but the bad tree bears evil fruit. [18] A sound tree cannot bear evil fruit, nor can a bad tree bear good fruit. [19] Every tree that does not bear good fruit is cut down and thrown into the fire. [20] Thus you will know them by their fruits.

[21] "Not every one who says to me, 'Lord, Lord,' shall enter the kingdom of heaven, but he who does the will of my Father who is in heaven. [22] On that day many will say to me, 'Lord, Lord, did we not prophesy in your name, and cast out demons in your name, and do many mighty works in your name?' [23] And then will I declare to them, 'I never knew you; depart from me, you evildoers.'

[24] "Every one then who hears these words of mine and does them will be like a wise man who built his house upon the rock; [25] and the rain fell, and the floods came, and the winds blew and beat upon that house, but it did not fall, because it had been founded on the rock. [26] And every one who hears these words of mine and does not do them will be like a foolish man who built his house upon the sand; [27] and the rain fell, and the floods came, and the winds blew and beat against that house, and it fell; and great was the fall of it."

[28] And when Jesus finished these sayings, the crowds were astonished at his teaching, [29] for he taught them as one who had authority, and not as their scribes.

Romans

3 Then what advantage has the Jew? Or what is the value of circumcision? [2] Much in every way. To begin with, the Jews are entrusted with the oracles of God. [3] What if some were unfaithful? Does their faithlessness nullify the faithfulness of God? [4] By no means! Let God be true though every man be false, as it is written,

"That thou mayest be justified in thy words,
and prevail when thou art judged."
⁵But if our wickedness serves to show the justice of God, what shall we
say? That God is unjust to inflict wrath on us? (I speak in a human way.)
⁶By no means! For then how could God judge the world? ⁷But if through
my falsehood God's truthfulness abounds to his glory, why am I still being
condemned as a sinner? ⁸And why not do evil that good may come?—as
some people slanderously charge us with saying. Their condemnation is
just.

⁹What then? Are we Jews any better off? No, not at all; for I have already charged that all men, both Jews and Greeks, are under the power of
sin, ¹⁰as it is written:

"None is righteous, no, not one;
¹¹no one understands, no one seeks for God.
¹²All have turned aside, together they have gone wrong;
     no one does good, not even one."
¹³"Their throat is an open grave,
     they use their tongues to deceive."
"The venom of asps is under their lips."
¹⁴Their mouth is full of curses and bitterness."
¹⁵"Their feet are swift to shed blood,
¹⁶in their paths are ruin and misery,
¹⁷and the way of peace they do not know."
¹⁸"There is no fear of God before their eyes."

¹⁹Now we know that whatever the law says it speaks to those who are
under the law, so that every mouth may be stopped, and the whole world
may be held accountable to God. ²⁰For no human being will be justified
in his sight by works of the law, since through the law comes knowledge
of sin.

²¹But now the righteousness of God has been manifested apart from
law, although the law and the prophets bear witness to it, ²²the righteousness of God through faith in Jesus Christ for all who believe. For there is
no distinction: ²³since all have sinned and fall short of the glory of God,
²⁴they are justified by his grace as a gift, through the redemption which is
in Christ Jesus, ²⁵whom God put forward as an expiation by his blood, to
be received by faith. This was to show God's righteousness, because in his
divine forbearance had had passed over former sins; ²⁶it was to prove at
the present time that he himself is righteous and that he justifies him who
has faith in Jesus.

²⁷Then what becomes of our boasting? It is excluded. On what principle? On the principle of works? No, but on the principle of faith. ²⁸For we
hold that a man is justified by faith apart from works of law. ²⁹Or is God
the God of Jews only? Is he not the God of Gentiles also? Yes, of Gentiles

also, ³⁰ since God is one; and he will justify the circumcised on the ground of their faith and the uncircumcised through their faith. ³¹ Do we then overthrow the law by this faith? By no means! On the contrary, we uphold the law.

I Corinthians

13 If I speak in the tongues of men and of angels, but have not love, I am a noisy gong or a clanging cymbal. ² And if I have prophetic powers, and understand all mysteries and all knowledge, and if I have all faith, so as to remove mountains, but have not love, I am nothing. ³ If I give away all I have, and if I deliver my body to be burned, but have not love, I gain nothing.

⁴ Love is patient and kind; love is not jealous or boastful; ⁵ it is not arrogant or rude. Love does not insist on its own way; it is not irritable or resentful; ⁶ it does not rejoice at wrong, but rejoices in the right. ⁷ Love bears all things, believes all things, hopes all things, endures all things.

⁸ Love never ends; as for prophecies, they will pass away; as for tongues, they will cease; as for knowledge, it will pass away. ⁹ For our knowledge is imperfect and our prophecy is imperfect; ¹⁰ but when the perfect comes, the imperfect will pass away. ¹¹ When I was a child, I spoke like a child, I thought like a child, I reasoned like a child; when I became a man, I gave up childish ways. ¹² For now we see in a mirror dimly, but then face to face. Now I know in part; then I shall understand fully, even as I have been fully understood. ¹³ So faith, hope, love abide, these three; but the greatest of these is love.

15 Now I would remind you, brethren, in what terms I preached to you the gospel, which you received, in which you stand, ² by which you are saved, if you hold it fast—unless you believed in vain.

³ For I delivered to you as of first importance what I also received, that Christ died for our sins in accordance with the scriptures, ⁴ that he was buried, that he was raised on the third day in accordance with the scriptures, ⁵ and that he appeared to Cephas, then to the twelve. ⁶ Then he appeared to more than five hundred brethren at one time, most of whom are still alive, though some have fallen asleep. ⁷ Then he appeared to James, then to all the apostles. ⁸ Last of all, as to one untimely born, he appeared also to me. ⁹ For I am the least of the apostles, unfit to be call an apostle, because I persecuted the church of God. ¹⁰ But by the grace of God I am what I am, and his grace toward me was not in vain. On the contrary, I worked harder than any of them, though it was not I, but the grace of God which is with me. ¹¹ Whether then it was I or they, so we preach and so you believed.

¹² Now if Christ is preached as raised from the dead, how can some of

you say that there is no resurrection of the dead? [13] But if there is no resurrection of the dead, then Christ has not been raised; [14] if Christ has not been raised, then our preaching is in vain and your faith is in vain. [15] We are even found to be misrepresenting God, because we testified of God that he raised Christ, whom he did not raise if it is true that the dead are not raised. [16] For if the dead are not raised, then Christ has not been raised. [17] If Christ has not been raised, your faith is futile and you are still in your sins. [18] Then those also who have fallen asleep in Christ have perished. [19] If for this life only we have hoped in Christ, we are of all men most to be pitied.

[20] But in fact Christ has been raised from the dead, the first fruits of those who have fallen asleep. [21] For as by a man came death, by a man has come also the resurrection of the dead. [22] For as in Adam all die, so also in Christ shall all be made alive. [23] But each in his own order: Christ the first fruits, then at his coming those who belong to Christ. [24] Then comes the end, when he delivers the kingdom to God the Father after destroying every rule and every authority and power. [25] For he must reign until he has put all his enemies under his feet. [26] The last enemy to be destroyed is death. [27] "For God has put all things in subjection under his feet." But when it says, "All things are put in subjection under him," it is plain that he is excepted who put all things under him. [28] When all things are subjected to him, then the Son himself will also be subjected to him who put all things under him, that God may be everything to every one.

[29] Otherwise, what do people mean by being baptized on behalf of the dead? If the dead are not raised at all, why are people baptized on their behalf? [30] Why am I in peril every hour? [31] I protest, brethren, by my pride in you which I have in Christ Jesus our Lord, I die every day! [32] What do I gain if, humanly speaking, I fought with beasts at Ephesus? If the dead are not raised, "Let us eat and drink, for tomorrow we die." [33] Do not be deceived: "Bad company ruins good morals." [34] Come to your right mind, and sin no more. For some have no knowledge of God. I say this to your shame.

[35] But some one will ask, "How are the dead raised? With what kind of body do they come?" [36] You foolish man! What you sow does not come to life unless it dies. [37] And what you sow is not the body which is to be, but a bare kernel, perhaps of wheat or of some other grain. [38] But God gives it a body as he has chosen, and to each kind of seed it's own body. [39] For not all flesh is alike, but there is one kind for men, another for animals, another for birds, and another for fish. [40] There are celestial bodies and there are terrestrial bodies; but the glory of the celestial is one, and the glory of the terrestrial is another. [41] There is one glory of the sun, and another glory of the moon, and another glory of the stars; for star differs from star in glory.

[42] So is it with the resurrection of the dead. What is sown is perishable,

what is raised is imperishable. [43] It is sown in dishonor, it is raised in glory. It is sown in weakness, it is raised in power. [44] It is sown a physical body, it is raised a spiritual body. If there is a physical body, there is also a spiritual body. [45] Thus it is written, "The first man Adam became a living being"; the last Adam became a life-giving spirit. [46] But it is not the spiritual which is first but the physical, and then the spiritual. [47] The first man was from the earth, a man of dust; the second man is from heaven. [48] As was the man of dust, so are those who are of the dust; and as is the man of heaven, so are those who are of heaven. [49] Just as we have borne the image of the man of dust, we shall also bear the image of the man of heaven. [50] I tell you this, brethern: flesh and blood cannot inherit the kingdom of God, nor does the perishable inherit the imperishable.

[51] Lo! I tell you a mystery. We shall not all sleep, but we shall all be changed, [52] in a moment, in the twinkling of an eye, at the last trumpet. For the trumpet will sound, and the dead will be raised imperishable, and we shall be changed. [53] For this perishable nature must put on the imperishable, and this mortal nature must put on immortality. [54] When the perishable puts on the imperishable, and the mortal puts on immortality, then shall come to pass the saying that is written:

"Death is swallowed up in victory."
[55] "O death, where is thy victory?
O death, where is thy sting?"

[56] The sting of death is sin, and the power of sin is the law. [57] But thanks be to God, who gives us the victory through our Lord Jesus Christ.

[58] Therefore, my beloved brethren, be steadfast, immovable, always abounding in the work of the Lord, knowing that in the Lord your labor is not in vain.

Revelation

20 Then I saw an angel coming down from heaven, holding in his hand the key of the bottomless pit and a great chain. [2] And he seized the dragon, that ancient serpent, who is the Devil and Satan, and bound him for a thousand years, [3] and threw him into the pit, and shut it and sealed it over him, that he should deceive the nations no more, till the thousand years were ended. After that he must be loosed for a little while.

[4] Then I saw thrones, and seated on them were those to whom judgment was committed. Also I saw the souls of those who had been beheaded for their testimony to Jesus and for the word of God, and who had not worshiped the beast or its image and had not received its mark on their foreheads or their hands. They came to life, and reigned with Christ a thousand years. [5] The rest of the dead did not come to life until the thousand years

were ended. This is the first resurrection. [6] Blessed and holy is he who shares in the first resurrection! Over such the second death has no power, but they shall be priests of God and of Christ, and they shall reign with him a thousand years.

[7] And when the thousand years are ended, Satan will be loosed from his prison [8] and will come out to deceive the nations which are at the four corners of the earth, that is, Gog and Magog, to gather them for battle; their number is like the sand of the sea. [9] And they marched up over the broad earth and surrounded the camp of the saints and the beloved city; but fire came down from heaven and consumed them, [10] and the devil who had deceived them was thrown into the lake of fire and brimstone where the beast and the false prophet were, and they will be tormented day and night for ever and ever.

[11] Then I saw a great white throne and him who sat upon it; from his presence earth and sky fled away, and no place was found for them. [12] And I saw the dead, great and small, standing before the throne, and books were opened. Also another book was opened, which is the book of life. And the dead were judged by what was written in the books, by what they had done. [13] And the sea gave up the dead in it, Death and Hades gave up the dead in them, and all were judged by what they had done. [14] Then Death and Hades were thrown into the lake of fire. This is the second death, the lake of fire; [15] and if any one's name was not found written in the book of life, he was thrown into the lake of fire.

The Martyrdom of St. Polycarp

> For the first three hundred years of its existence Christianity underwent an on-again, off-again period of persecution by the Roman government. At times, and in certain places in the Empire, Christianity was tolerated. At other times the persecution was severe. Christians were a special target because they refused to offer simple sacrifices to the emperors. Therefore they were accused of being atheists and of being unpatriotic. Many stories of martyrdom come from this era. None is more touching or telling than that of Polycarp. In the mid-second century, Polycarp was the aged bishop of the Church of Smyrna, in Asia Minor. The following is an account of his martyrdom.[23]

V. But the most wonderful Polycarp, when he first heard it, was not disturbed, but wished to remain in the city; but the majority persuaded

[23] *The Writings of the Apostolic Fathers*, Roberts, Donaldson, and Crombie, trans. Vol. I (Edinburgh: T. & T. Clark, 1867), pp. 86–92.

him to go away quietly, and he went out quietly to a farm, not far distant from the city, and stayed with a few friends, doing nothing but pray night and day for all, and for the Churches throughout the world, as was his custom. And while he was praying he fell into a trance, three days before he was arrested, and saw the pillow under his head burning with fire, and he turned and said to those who were with him: "I must be burnt alive."

VI. And when the searching for him persisted he went to another farm; and those who were searching for him came up at once, and when they did not find him, they arrested young slaves, and one of them confessed under torture. For it was indeed impossible for him to remain hid, since those who betrayed him were of his own house, and the police captain who had been allotted the very name, being called Herod, hastened to bring him to the arena that he might fulfil his appointed lot by becoming a partaker of Christ, while they who betrayed him should undergo the same punishment as Judas.

VII. Taking the slave, then police and cavalry went out on Friday about supper-time, with their usual arms, as if they were advancing against a robber. And late in the evening they came up together against him and found him lying in an upper room. And he might have departed to another place, but would not, saying, "the will of God be done." So when he heard that they had arrived he went down and talked with them, while those who were present wondered at his age and courage, and whether there was so much haste for the arrest of an old man of such a kind. Therefore he ordered food and drink to be set before them at that hour, whatever they should wish, and he asked them to give him an hour to pray without hindrance. To this they assented, and he stood and prayed—thus filled with the grace of God—so that for two hours he could not be silent, and those who listened were astounded, and many repented that they had come against such a venerable old man.

VIII. Now when he had at last finished his prayer, after remembering all who had ever even come his way, both small and great, high and low, and the whole Catholic Church throughout the world, the hour came for departure, and they set him on an ass, and led him into the city, on a "great Sabbath day." And the police captain Herod and his father Niketas met him and removed him into their carriage, and sat by his side trying to persuade him and saying: "But what harm is it to say, 'Lord Caesar,' and to offer sacrifice and so forth, and to be saved?" But he at first did not answer them, but when they continued he said: "I am not going to do what you counsel me." And they gave up the attempt to persuade him, and began to speak fiercely to him, and turned him out in such a hurry that in getting down from the carriage he scraped his shin; and without turning round, as though he had suffered nothing, he walked on promptly and quickly, and was taken to the arena, while the uproar in the arena was so great that no one could even be heard.

IX. Now when Polycarp entered into the arena there came a voice from heaven: "Be strong, Polycarp, and play the man!" And no one saw the speaker, but our friends who were there heard the voice. And next he was brought forward, and there was a great uproar of those who heard that Polycarp had been arrested. Therefore when he was brought forward the Pro-Consul asked him if he were Polycarp, and when he admitted it he tried to persuade him to deny, saying: "Respect your age," and so forth, as they are accustomed to say: "Swear by the genius of Caesar, repent, say: 'Away with the Atheists,' "; but Polycarp, with a stern countenance looked on all the crowd of lawless heathen in the arena, and waving his hand at them, he groaned and looked up to heaven and said: "Away with the Atheists." But when the Pro-Consul pressed him and said: "Take the oath and I let you go, revile Christ," Polycarp said: "For eighty and six years have I been his servant, and he has done me no wrong, and how can I blaspheme my King who has saved me?"

X. But when he persisted again, and said: "Swear by the genius of Caesar," he answered him: "If you vainly suppose that I will swear by the genius of Caesar, as you say, and pretend that you are ignorant who I am, listen plainly: I am a Christian. And if you wish to learn the doctrine of Christianity fix a day and listen." The Pro-Consul said: "Persuade the people." And Polycarp said: "You I should have held worthy of discussion, for we have been taught to render honour, as is meet, if it hurt us not, to princes and authorities appointed by God. But as for those, I do not count them worthy that a defence should be made to them."

XI. And the Pro-Consul said: "I have wild beasts, I will deliver you to them, unless you repent." And he said: "Call for them, for repentance from better to worse is not allowed us; but it is good to change from evil to righteousness." And he said again to him: "I will cause you to be consumed by fire, if you despise the beasts, unless you repent." But Polycarp said: "You threaten with the fire that burns for a time and is quickly quenched, for you do not know the fire which awaits the wicked in the judgment to come and in everlasting punishment. But why are you waiting? Come, do what you will."

XII. And with these and many other words he was filled with courage and joy, and his face was full of grace so that it not only did not fall with trouble at the things said to him, but that the Pro-Consul, on the other hand, was astounded and sent his herald into the midst of the arena to announce three times: "Polycarp has confessed that he is a Christian." When this had been said by the herald, all the multitude of heathen and Jews living in Smyrna cried out with uncontrollable wrath and a loud shout: "This is the teacher of Asia, the father of the Christians, the destroyer of our Gods, who teaches many neither to offer sacrifice nor to worship." And when they said this, they cried out and asked Philip the Asiarch to let loose a lion on Polycarp. But he said he could not legally do this, since he had closed the Sports. Then they found it good to cry out with one mind that he should burn Polycarp alive, for the vision which had appeared to him on his pillow must be fulfilled, when he saw it burning, while he was praying, and he turned and said prophetically to those of the faithful who were with him, "I must be burnt alive."

XIII. These things then happened with so great speed, quicker than it takes to tell, and the crowd came together immediately, and prepared wood and faggots from the work-shops and baths and the Jews were extremely zealous, as is their custom, in assisting at this. Now when the fire was ready he put off all his clothes, and loosened his girdle and tried also to take off his shoes, though he did not do this before, because each of the faithful was always zealous, which of them might the more quickly touch his flesh. For he had been treated with all respect because of his noble life, even before his martyrdom. Immediately therefore, he was fastened to the instruments which had been prepared for the fire, but when they were going to nail him as well he said: "Leave me thus, for He who gives me power to endure the fire, will grant me to remain in the flames unmoved even without the security you will give by the nails."

XIV. So they did not nail him, but bound him, and he put his hands behind him and was bound, as a noble ram out of a great flock, for an oblation, a whole offering made ready and acceptable to God; and he looked up to heaven and said: "O Lord God Almighty, Father of thy beloved and blessed Child, Jesus Christ, through Whom we have received full knowledge of thee, the God of Angels and powers, and of all creation, and of the whole family of the righteous, who live before thee! I bless thee, that Thou has granted me this day and hour, that I may share, among the number of the martyrs, in the cup of thy Christ, for the Resurrection to everlasting life, both of soul and body in the immortality of the Holy Spirit. And may I, today, be received among them before Thee, as a rich and acceptable sacrifice, as Thou, the God who lies not and is truth, hast prepared beforehand, and shown forth, and fulfilled. For this reason I also praise Thee for all things, I bless Thee, I glorify Thee through the everlasting and heavenly high Priest, Jesus Christ, thy beloved Child, through whom be glory to Thee with him and the Holy Spirit, both now and for the ages that are to come, Amen."

XV. Now when he had uttered his Amen and finished his prayer, the men in charge of the fire lit it, and a great flame blazed up and we, to whom it was given to see, saw a marvel. And we have been preserved to report to others what befell. For the fire made the likeness of a room, like the sail of a vessel filled with wind, and surrounded the body of the martyr as with a wall, and he was within it not as burning flesh, but as bread that is being baked, or as gold and silver being refined in a furnace. And we perceived such a fragrant smell as the scent of incense or other costly spices.

XVI. At length the lawless men, seeing that his body could not be consumed by the fire, commanded an executioner to go up and stab him with a dagger, and when he did this, there came out a dove, and much blood, so that the fire was quenched and all the crowd marvelled that here was such a difference between the unbelievers and the elect. And of the elect was he indeed one, the wonderful martyr Polycarp, who in our days was an apostolic and prophetic teacher, bishop of the Catholic Church in Smyrna. For every word which he uttered from his mouth both was fulfilled and will be fulfilled.

CHAPTER 13

Islam

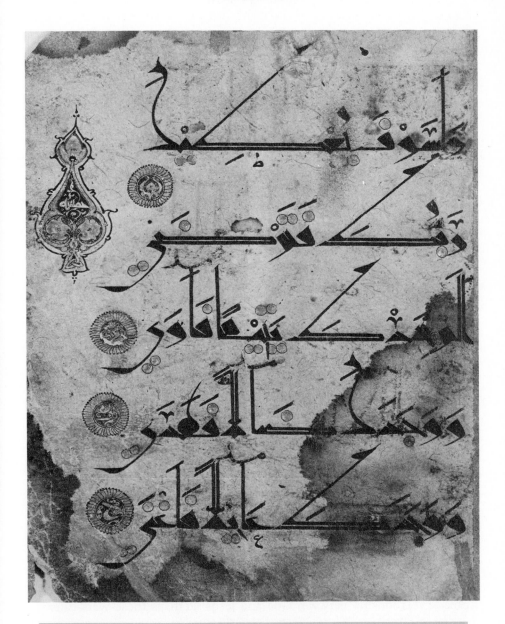

A page from the Quran written in Kufic script, one of the two Arabic styles.
(*Courtesy of Museum of Fine Arts, Boston.*)

387

There is no God but Allah; Muhammad is the messenger of Allah.

—The Shahadah

The youngest of the world's major religions is Islam. It is also one of the largest, with more than one-half billion adherents. It is also the dominant religion of many of the so-called third world nations in the Middle East, Africa, and Asia. These factors, coupled with a colorful founder and a rapid expansion period, make Islam one of the most interesting and important of all religions.

The basic belief of this religion is that there is only one God, who is called Allah, the same God worshiped by other religions under other names. He is the sole and sovereign ruler of the universe. Though Allah has made himself known through other prophets at other times, his best and final revelation was to the prophet Muhammad in the seventh century A.D. According to his teachings, the believer has only one life to live. How believers live this life will determine how they spend their eternal existence. During this one life believers must submit to the will of Allah. Thus, the adherents of this religion are called *Muslims* ("submitters").[1]

PRE-ISLAMIC ARAB RELIGION

Islam began with the Arabian desert peoples in the seventh century A.D. It did not spring out of a religious vacuum. The people of this area had developed religious forms of their own and had been exposed to various other religions for centuries. Although the influence was not strong, Byzantine Christianity had been a factor in the lives of these people. Judea, the home of Christianity, was not too distant from Arabia. Cities such as Damascus, Caesarea, Antioch, and Alexandria were neighbors to Mecca and Yathrib (Medina). Christian princes ruled from these cities, and many of the early Church fathers wrote and taught in them. Christian influence on the early Arab people was weakened by two factors. First, in the Byzantine world Christian theology was internally divided into many factions regarding the nature of Christ. Battles, both theological and physical, were fought over the precise relationship between God and Jesus. Perhaps these wars caused

[1] Technically, it is a misnomer to refer to this religion as "Mohammedanism" and its adherents as "Mohammedans" since they are not followers of the man Muhammad, but are submitters to the will of Allah.

a yearning for a prophet who would say, "There is no God but Allah." Second, the Byzantine rulers on many occasions had treated the Arab Christians with hostility and cruelty. Undoubtedly this caused many to welcome the conquests of a new Arab religion, in the seventh century.

The people of Arabia were also familiar with Judaism. Several of the desert tribes were Jewish. Although their origins are not clear, many historians believe that these tribes were the descendents of Jews who had been forced out of Judea when the Romans put down rebellion in the land in 70 A.D. and again in 135. When Muhammad, the prophet of Islam, entered Medina in 622 A.D. many of the citizens of that city were Jewish.

Another religion that may have had some influence upon the formulation of Islam was Zoroastrianism. While the effects upon Islam were not as strong as on Judaism and Christianity, it is possible that Muhammad and some of his disciples may have been in contact with the Persian Zoroastrians.

Perhaps the major religious force from which Islam grew—and which it reacted against—was the native religions of the Arab people. Actually we know very little about the basic religion of these people because the only material we have about them is the Muslim scripture, the Quran, which naturally is hostile. Apparently, the pre-Islamic people worshiped a variety of gods. They recognized one supreme high god, who was separated and unapproachable by people, whom they called Allah (literally, "the God"). The deities that received most worship and attention were the local and tribal gods. Images of these gods were carved and cherished, and blood sacrifices were made to them. In addition to a great pantheon of the gods of heaven and earth, there were lesser divine creatures. There were angels and fairies who were kind and helpful spirits, and there were demonic creatures called *jinn* who usually sought to do harm to humans. There were also the universally evil spirits, such as the ghouls who devoured the bodies of the dead.

Perhaps the most obvious characteristic of basic pre-Islamic religion is its animism. Gods and spirits were found in stones, trees, wells, and animals, and these spirits had to be placated and implored for aid. The city of Mecca became a holy place because of animistic associations. Mecca is located on the central western coast of Arabia, and lay on the major north-south caravan route. Its claim to fame was rooted in a meteoric stone that had fallen there centuries before. The stone became an object of veneration to the animistic population, and by the time of Muhammad, pilgrims had built an enclosure around it called the Kaaba. The Kaaba gradually filled with images, relics, and paintings. One report claims that it even contained a painting of Jesus and Mary. Islamic legend says that the black stone fell from heaven during the time of Adam and Eve and that Abraham and his son Ishmael built the Kaaba. A period of several months each year was set aside as a time of truce so that pilgrims could travel safely to Mecca to worship at this shrine. Naturally the black stone was an object of both pride and profit to the Meccans, and there was a constant struggle between the various clans of Mecca over who would control the Kaaba.

THE LIFE OF MUHAMMAD

Because Islam is one of the youngest of the world's religions, the details of the life of its founder are more available than those of other founders. No one seriously questions the fact that Muhammad was a historical figure who lived in the seventh century A.D. From information on the life of the Prophet, we assume that he was born about 570 A.D. into the clan of Hashim of the tribe of Quraysh, the group that controlled the Kaaba in Mecca. His father, Abd-Allah, died before Muhammad was born and his mother died before he was six years of age.[2] Thereafter Muhammad was reared by his uncle, abu-Talib, chief of the Quraysh tribe. Life for an orphan in those times must have been difficult. There was no chance for any kind of formal education, and Islam makes much of the fact that Muhammad was illiterate. Thus the revelation of the Quran to him was the more miraculous. The only occupation open to him was that of a caravan worker, and many of his formative years probably were spent in traveling across the Middle East as a camel driver. Of course, this in itself must have been quite an education. During these travels the young Muhammad had an opportunity to come into contact with representatives of the religions and the cultures of the world. Covering the Arabian peninsula, traveling to Byzantine cities such as Damascus, he doubtless met Christians, Jews, and perhaps even Zoroastrians. Each of these religions had several things in common and must have had an influence upon Muhammad. They all believed in one God, though Byzantine Christians were in a constant state of dispute over the persons within the Trinity, and the Zoroastrians had developed a dualism of a god of light and a god of darkness. All of these religions had a scripture that was believed to be the word of God. All of them had an

[2]It has often been observed that many of the founders of religions spent at least a portion of their formative years in homes without a father figure. This was the case in the lives of Moses, Muhammad, Confucius, Mencius, and others. Freud, in *Moses and Monotheism*, makes a great deal of this fact.

eschatology that taught that the world would one day end and that the righteous would be rewarded while the evil would be tormented in hell. Muhammad seems to have been especially affected by eschatology and began to be concerned about the future of his people, who worshiped a multitude of gods and idols.

These years as a camel driver also afforded Muhammad the opportunity to meet the woman who would become his wife, the owner of the caravan, Khadija. Khadija was a wealthy widow, who was about forty years old when she married the twenty-five-year-old Muhammad. Although it was permissible to have more than one wife, Muhammad was married only to Khadiju as long as she lived. During their marriage of twenty-five years she bore him two sons and four daughters. The sons died in infancy and only one daughter, Fatima, survived her father. Khadija provided the wealth and love that the orphaned Muhammad had never had as a child. She became his strongest supporter and one of his first converts, and her wealth gave him the freedom to consider theological questions.

In the years following his marriage to Khadija, Muhammad began to go into the hills surrounding Mecca and ponder the fate of his people. He was especially concerned about their idolatry and the fate they would have on judgment day when the world ended. During these periods of meditation he received a visit from an angel, whom he later identified as Gabriel, mentioned in both the Jewish and Christian bibles. Tradition says that during the month of Ramadan, in a cave on Mt. Hira, Gabriel brought the following command from God:

> Read in the name of thy Lord who created, who created man of blood coagulated. Read! Thy Lord is the most beneficent, who taught by the pen, taught that which they knew not unto men.[3]

At frequent intervals during the rest of his life, Muhammad received revelations from God in this fashion. Islamic tradition says that the Prophet received many of these revelations through what must be called ecstatic seizures. Inspiration came like the painful sounding of a bell; his forehead became covered with sweat. At times visions came to him in his sleep. These traditions have caused unfriendly critics to suggest that Muhammad may have been an epileptic. Superficial interpreters of religious experience often seek to explain religious ecstasy in terms of epilepsy, but this can seldom be proved. Muhammad memorized the contents of these divine messages and eventually they were committed to writing, to become the scriptures of Islam, called the Quran.

---

[3] Quran 96:1–5. This quotation and those that follow are taken from *The Quran*, translated by J. M. Rodwell, Everyman's Library, J. M. Dent & Sons, London, 1909.

After a series of revelations, Muhammad became convinced that there was only one God, whom his people had called Allah and whom other religions called by other names. He also became convinced that he was the last and the greatest in a series of prophets of this God, which included Abraham, Moses, and Jesus, among others. These former prophets had only an incomplete revelation of Allah, but Muhammad had the complete and final revelation. Thus, Islam at its very inception did not deny the validity of other religions but rather looked upon itself as the completion of what others had begun. It is also worthy of note that Muhammad never considered himself any more than a prophet. He was not divine; he died like any other person. His mission was much like that of the classical Hebrew prophet: to present the word of God to his people.

As the Prophet of Allah, Muhammad began to preach his new understanding of religion to the citizens of Mecca. He received little encouragement from his neighbors; indeed, there was much discouragement and open hostility. He was preaching that there was only one God, who was not to be worshiped with idols, and this of course worked against the livelihood of many Meccans who depended upon pilgrims coming to Mecca to worship idols at the Kaaba. Muhammad's first convert was his wife, Khadija. There is debate in the traditions as to who was his first male convert. It was either Ali, a cousin, or Zayd, a slave boy who had been freed by Muhammad. The third convert was a friend, abu-Bakr. In the following years a handful of other converts joined the Muslim movement. Mainly they came from the younger and poorer classes in Mecca. As opposition from the older, richer, and established clan leaders of the city grew stronger, Muhammad received protection from his uncle abu-Talib and other members of his clan, even those who were not Muslims. However, as the opposition and persecution became more severe, Muhammad finally had to urge some of his followers to leave the country. In the year 615 about fifteen Muslim families fled Mecca and took refuge in the Christian kingdom of Abyssinia. The Prophet and the remainder of the Muslims stayed behind in Mecca to continue to preach and face persecution. This persecution took the form of a boycott against Muhammad and his entire clan by the rest of the Meccans, but it proved ineffective.

In 619 Muhammad suffered the loss of his two greatest benefactors, his uncle abu-Talib and his beloved Khadija. After the death of his wife, the Prophet married the first of a number of wives whom he was to have during the remainder of his life. The death of abu-Talib left him without the protection of his clan, and life became very difficult for the Muslims. Muhammad tried to move out of Mecca to a nearby town but was rejected there and had to return.

One of the most significant events in the history of Islam occurred in the year 620, when a group of six men journeyed from the city of Yathrib (later renamed Medina in honor of the Prophet), located 250 miles to the north, to Mecca to confer with Muhammad. They were impressed with the power of his personality. Medina was a city torn by clan warfare and internal strife. It needed one who would come as an impartial judge and settle the disputes within the city, and the delegation believed that Muhammad might be the person. The following year twelve delegates came from Medina to meet the Prophet. Curiously enough, ten of the twelve were from Jewish tribes who believed that Muhammad might possibly be the Messiah. An invitation was extended to him to come and be the judge over the city. It was 622 before Muhammad could leave Mecca because a group of assassins had pledged to kill him, and he had to avoid them with great care. His followers slipped out a few at a time, and finally the Prophet made his escape in September. On September 24, 622, Muhammad arrived to be the judge of the city of Medina. The journey from Mecca to Medina is called *Hijrah* ("migration"), and it is the time from which Muslims have since dated their calendars. Dates are listed as A.H. *(Anno Hegirae).*

In Medina, the Muslims were established as a clan among other clans, and although Muhammad had been brought to the city as an arbitrator, his religion was by no means widely accepted. Many of the tribes in Medina were Jewish, and perhaps to gain their favor Muhammad commanded the Muslims to pray toward Jerusalem. With the passing of time, the divisions between Muslims and Jews increased, and the Prophet commanded his disciples to pray toward Mecca instead.

In 623 Muhammad married Aishah, the nine-year-old daughter of his friend abu-Bakr. This was also the year of the first conflict between the Medinans, under the leadership of Muhammad, and the Meccans. The natural rivalry between these two cities was of course intensified by Hijrah. At first the conflicts were merely scattered raids against the Meccan caravans, but later they developed into full military campaigns.

The process of raiding caravans was not a dishonorable matter among Arabs of this era, and it gave the Muslims a way not only to take vengeance against the Meccans but also to acquire money and goods. The most successful of these early encounters was the battle of Badr in 624, when the Muslims defeated the Meccans, killed up to seventy, and took many prisoners and much booty. Tradition says that this was accomplished because the Prophet was at the battle praying for his troops. A victory like this was a great stimulus for the Muslims. It reinforced their loyalty to the Prophet and his cause, and it at-

Old man reading the Quran. (*Courtesy of Liaison. Photograph by Gamma-Liaison.*)

tracted many others to Islam. The following year brought another battle with the Meccans. In this battle the Muslims lost more men than the Meccans, and Muhammad himself was wounded. Because the forces of Mecca had not altogether wiped out the Muslims, however, it was considered a victory for the Prophet.

Conflict between the Muslims and the Jewish tribes in the area also intensified during this period. The Jews apparently had rejected any notion that Muhammad was the Messiah and often ridiculed him publicly. At times they supported the Meccans against the Prophet. As a result, the Jewish tribes were either expelled from Muslim territory or offered the choice of conversion or death. According to Muslim tradition, the final break occurred when Zainab, a matron from the Jewish community, invited the Prophet and his friends to dinner and fed them poisoned lamb. Although Muhammad ate only a little of the meat, he suffered from the effects for the rest of his life.

In 627 a force of 10,000 Meccans attacked Medina, but no decisive battles were fought and the Meccans withdrew. The following year Muhammad attempted to go to Mecca for pilgrimage with his followers, but the Meccans barred the way. A peace treaty was arranged, and the Muslims were allowed to make the pilgrimage the following year. By 629 Islam had grown so strong that when the Muslims entered Mecca on their pilgrimage, no one dared to stop them. In 630 Muhammad, with a force of 10,000 men, entered Mecca as its complete conqueror. He went to the Kaaba and, although he respected the black stone and its enclosure, he destroyed the idols and images. With this symbolic act the Prophet became virtually the sole leader of the Arabian people.

During the next few years Islam grew stronger still. Muhammad sent out messages to surrounding nations inviting them to join the nation of Islam. His followers returned from Abyssinia to rejoin him. He married new wives, many of whom were the widows of Muslims who had died in battle. Other marriages strengthened political ties. Only one of his late marriages was open to criticism. This was his marriage to his cousin Zaynab, who was also the wife of Zayd, his adopted son. Because of her love for the Prophet, Zaynab is supposed to have made life unbearable for her husband until he divorced her. After a suitable period she and the Prophet were married. Muhammad was not criticized so much for taking another man's wife as for marrying his own cousin, which was considered incestuous by the Arab culture of the time.

In 632 Muhammad led the Muslims in another pilgrimage to Mecca. By this time he was sixty-two years of age and in poor health, having never fully recovered from the effects of the poison he had eaten a few years before. Upon his return to Medina he gave a farewell message to the Muslims and then died in the arms of his wife, Aishah. He had made no arrangements regarding his successor, and for a time there was confusion among the Muslims as to leadership. It was finally agreed that abu-Bakr should be the caliph, or successor. At Muhammad's funeral the following words, attributed to abu-Bakr, summed up the Muslim understanding of the Prophet:

O ye people, if anyone worships Muhammad, Muhammad is dead, but if anyone worships God, He is alive and dies not.[4]

[4]W. Montgomery Watt, *Muhammad: Prophet and Statesman* (London: Oxford University Press, 1961), p. 228.

THE QURAN

The scripture of Islam is called the Quran (sometimes spelled "Koran" in English). The word *quran* literally means "reading" or "recitation." Thus the title indicates the basic belief that all Muslims hold about this book, that it is a copy of a recitation of an eternal scripture, written in heaven and revealed, chapter by chapter, to Muhammad. The title may also reflect the words of the first *surah* or chapter, "Read, in the name of the Lord who created . . ."

Perhaps no scripture has ever been so influential upon its people as the Quran. Surely no scripture is read so much or committed to memory so often. Although Christians and Jews take their bibles seriously, they have subjected them to textual and literary criticism for centuries. Therefore all but the most orthodox believe that the current texts of the Bible mean something less than the absolute word of God. Such is not the case in Islam; the Quran *is* the word of God: It is eternal, absolute, and irrevocable. It was literally revealed to Muhammad, who acted only as a stenographer for Allah, and it has been transmitted virtually unchanged since the days of the Prophet. Therefore it is recited and memorized by all Muslims. The first things Muslims hear when they are born are selections from the Quran. It is the source of their education and becomes a textbook for the study of Arabic. It is not unusual for a Muslim schoolchild to memorize the Quran in its entirety. Verses from it are inscribed upon the walls of the Muslim's home for decoration; its words may be the last a person hears before death.

The Quran is said to contain the exact words of Allah to the Prophet from the time of the first revelation to the end of Muhammad's life. Because Muhammad was illiterate, the messages were memorized by him and passed on to Zayd, his secretary, who wrote them upon leaves, stones, bones, or parchments. After Muhammad's death these materials were collected. Tradition says that an early caliph, Uthman, worked with Zayd and others to develop an authorized version of the Quran which replaced several variations of the text.

The revelations that make up the Quran are organized into chapters called *surahs*. With the exception of a brief introductory statement, the text is arranged according to the length of the *surah* in descending order. Therefore the non-Muslim reader is sometimes confused because there is no topical or chronological arrangement of the material. The revelations are a great deal like the materials one finds in the prophetic books of the Jewish Bible, an anthology of prophetic material without regard to arrangement. The longest *surah* contains 287 verses, the shortest only three.

The Nature of God

Because the Quran is the word of God, its messages become the authority for all Muslims on God, how God expects people to live, and the eternal destiny of humankind. Allah is revealed to be the one sovereign God over all the universe. The religion of Islam demands the strictest of monotheism, and its creed is this: "There is no God but Allah and Muhammad is his messenger." In contrast to the polytheists of Mecca and the Byzantine Christians who were in dispute over what part Jesus played in the Godhead, Muslims state that there is only the one God, complete, eternal, and undivided. Of all the world's other religions only Judaism insists on such absolute monotheism.

> He unto Whom belongeth the sovereignty of the heavens and the earth, He hath chosen no son nor hath He any partner in the sovereignty.[5]

> Say: He is God, One,
> God, the Everlasting Refuge,
> Who has not begotten, and has not been begotten,
> and equal to Him is not any one.;[6]

Allah is the omnipresent, omniscient, and omnipotent creator of the universe, and this role is heavily emphasized in the Quran.

> Lo! your Lord is Allah Who created the heavens and the earth in six Days, then mounted He the Throne. He covered the night with the day, which is in haste to follow it, and hath made the sun and the moon and the stars subservient by His command. His verily is all creation and commandment. Blessed be Allah, the Lord of the Worlds![7]

According to Muslim tradition, Allah had ninety-nine names, such as the Holy One, the Keeper of Faith, the Guardian, and the Creator. Devout Muslims repeat these names in a manner similar to a Catholic Christian saying the rosary.

While Allah possesses the characteristics of power, sovereignty, and majesty, he is also characterized by his justice and mercy. He will repay the evil with justice and the righteous with mercy.

> To God belongs every one dwelling in the heavens and the earth, that he may requite all those who have done evil and requite all those who have done good with the fairest recompense, even them who avoid the great sins and abominations (save for the trifling faults). Truly your Lord is am-

[5] Quran 25:2.
[6] Quran 112.
[7] Quran 7:54.

ple in forgiveness: very well He knew you, when He formed you of the earth and while you were yet hidden in your Mother's womb. Boast not therefore of your own worth: very well He knows who is truly godly.[8]

Though Allah is alone as the God figure in Islam he is surrounded and aided by certain other heavenly figures. There are his angels who act as his messengers, as did Gabriel when he revealed the Quran to Muhammad, and as his warriors who fight at the side of believers against the infidels. There is another creation halfway between humans and angels who are called the *jinn*. The jinn are created of fire. Some are beneficial creatures who act as guardian angels for humankind while others are demons. The leader of the jinn is a fallen angel called Iblis.[9] Iblis acts very much like the Satan figure in the biblical book of Job. He is not so much a secondary god of evil as Angra Mainyu in Zoroastrianism, but he acts as tempter and prosecuting attorney against humankind. According to Muslim legend Iblis was responsible for the fall of Adam.

Predestination

In the Quran it is revealed that humans are the creation of Allah and must be obedient to him. Righteous persons who would win the favor of God must submit to his will. Because of the Muslim emphasis upon God's power and sovereignty, the words *fatalism* and *predestination* have been used to describe this religion. Carried to its ultimate extreme in Islam, Calvinism, and early Greek philosophy, the belief in an all-powerful force that rules the universe and knows all things leads one to believe that people have no choice in life. Whether one does good or evil, enjoys success or failure, is all in the hands of the God who rules the world and has planned each event in advance. When carried to this extreme people do not possess freedom of choice and therefore are not responsible for their acts. God is all and people are but his puppets. Indeed there is a strong strain of fatalism in Islam. The most frequent statement among devout Muslims is *im shallah* (if God wills it). Nevertheless it is not accurate to call Islam purely a fatalistic religion. All sects within it do not agree on this issue, although they do hold in common the idea that people are somehow responsible for the evil that they commit and will be judged for this. Allah in his wisdom and mercy allows human beings to make choices in the areas in which they will be judged. From this point of view, people do have freedom.

[8] Quran 53:32, 33.
[9] It is believed that this word is the Arabic version of the Greek word for devil, *diabolos.*

Eschatology

The judgment of humanity at the conclusion of time by Allah is one of the basic beliefs of Islam. The eschatology of Jews, Christians, and Zoroastrians had a profound effect upon Muhammad, and the Quran reflects these influences. The Quran says that when a person dies the body returns to the earth and the soul goes into a state of sleep until resurrection day. On this day the angel of Allah will sound his trumpet, the earth will be split, and the bodies will rejoin their souls.[10] The resurrected are then judged by Allah. Those who have been faithful and virtuous will be rewarded, and those who have been evil will be punished. All people are judged on the basis of the record of deeds in a book kept for the purpose.

> And the Book is placed, and thou seest the guilty fearful of that which is therein, and they say: What kind of a book is this that leaveth not a small thing nor a great thing but hath counted it! And they find all that they did, confronting them, and thy Lord wrongeth no one.[11]

Both the hell and paradise of Islam are very real places, which are graphically described.

> When the day that must come shall have come suddenly,
> None shall treat that sudden coming as a lie:
> Day that shall abase! Day that shall exalt!
> When the earth shall be shaken with a shock,
> And the mountains shall be crumbled with a crumbling,
> And shall become scattered dust,
> And into three bands shall ye be divided:
> Then the people of the right hand—Oh! how happy shall be the people of
>   the right hand!
> And the people of the left hand—Oh! how wretched shall be the people of
>   the left hand!
> And they who were foremost on earth—the foremost still.
> These are they who shall be brought nigh to God,
> In gardens of delight;
> A crowd of the former
> And few of the latter generations;
> On inwrought couches
> Reclining on them face to face:
> Aye-blooming youths go round about to them
> With goblets and ewers and a cup of flowing wine;
> Their brows ache not from it, nor fails the sense:

[10] Quran 82.
[11] Quran 18:50.

And with such fruits as shall please them best,
And with flesh of such birds, as they shall long for:
And theirs shall be the Houris, with large dark eyes, like pearls hidden in
    their shells,
In recompense of their labours past.
No vain discourse shall they hear therein, nor charge of sin,
But only the cry, "Peace! Peace!"
And the people of the right hand—Oh! how happy shall be the people of
    the right hand!
Amid thornless sidrahs
And tall trees clad with fruit,
And in extended shade,
And by flowing waters,
And with abundant fruits,
Unfailing, unforbidden,
And on lofty couches.
Of a rare creation have we created the Houris,
And we have made them ever virgins,
Dear to their spouses, of equal age with them,
For the people of the right hand,
A crowd of the former,
And a crowd of the latter generations.
But the people of the left hand—Oh! how wretched shall be the people of
    the left hand!
Amid pestilential winds and in scalding water,
And in the shadow of a black smoke,
Not cool, and horrid to behold.
For they truly, ere this, were blessed with worldly goods,
But persisted in heinous sin,
And were wont to say,
"What! after we have died, and become dust and bones shall we be raised?
And our fathers, the men of yore?"
Say: Aye, the former and the latter:
Gathered shall they all be for the time of a known day.
Then ye, O ye the erring, the gainsaying,
Shall surely eat of the tree Ez-zakkoum,
And fill your bellies with it,
And thereupon shall ye drink boiling water,
And ye shall drink as the thirsty camel drinketh.
This shall be their repast in the day of reckoning! [12]

The student of world religions is immediately aware of the similarities among the Muslim eschatological scheme and those of Zoroastrianism, Judaism, and Christianity. The only differences in the
Islamic heaven and hell are those that would be particularly appealing
or distasteful to a desert dweller. Heaven is located in a beautiful

[12] Quran 56:1–56.

One of the holiest mosques in Islam is the Dome of the Rock. This mosque was built in Jerusalem over the site of Solomon's temple in the seventh century A.D. (*Courtesy of Israeli Government Tourist Office.*)

garden with flowing water and shade. The righetous are fed wine—normally forbidden to Muslims—that does not disturb the senses and does not leave the drinker with a hangover. Hell is a horrid place filled with scalding winds, black smoke, and brackish water.

RELIGIOUS INSTITUTIONS

From the Quran and from the early years of Islamic life there developed certain religious institutions that are almost universally recognized by Muslims.

The Mosque

Islam is not a temple-oriented religion. Although certain places are venerated by Muslims it would not have suited the nomadic life of the Arab people to require that they worship in a temple of any sort.

The nature of their lives demanded that they be free to worship Allah everyday, wherever they might be. Generally, Muslim worship is carried on in a variety of places. Muhammad decreed that Friday should be a special day of Muslim worship, as Saturday was Sabbath for the Jews and Sunday for the Christians. Unlike the Jewish and Christian Sabbath, however, Friday is not a day of rest; rather, it is the only day of the week when the Muslim is required to pray with his fellow Muslims at a mosque. There believers are led in prayer by an *imam*. The *imam* is not a priest in any sense of the word but rather a member of the community who has been chosen to lead the prayers because of his reputation as a pious man. The remainder of the religious duties of a Muslim can be performed away from the mosque and its leadership.

The Five Pillars

Those things that one must do to be a good Muslim are usually referred to as "the five pillars of Islam." These five pillars or obligations are repetition of the creed, daily prayer, almsgiving, the fast during the month of Ramadan, and the pilgrimage to Mecca.

1. Repetition of the Creed (shahadah). The most common religious act of the Muslim is his frequent repetition of the creed of Islam: *La ilaha illa Allah; Muhammad rasul Allah.* ("There is no God but Allah; Muhammad is the messenger of Allah.") This statement is known as *Shahadah* (bearing witness). These are the first words that a Muslim child hears, and they are likely to be the last words uttered by the dying Muslim. The devout will utter this statement as often as possible everyday, and the mere utterance of it makes the reciter a Muslim.

2. Daily Prayer (salah). In addition to the recitation of the creed, the Muslim is expected to pray daily. The Prophet commanded three prayers daily during his lifetime, but in later years this number was revised upward to five daily prayers. The five accepted times for prayer are dawn, midday, midafternoon, sunset, and nightfall. In Muslim communities strong-voiced men called *muezzins* climb to the tops of graceful towers known as minarets five times a day and cry out that it is time for prayer.[13] Wherever Muslims are they pause for a prescribed prayer. Before they pray, however, they must wash themselves and be cleansed of any impurities. Mosques are frequently built

---

[13] Regrettably, the muezzin is being replaced in many modern Muslim communities by tape recordings and loudspeakers.

Muslims are required to pray five times per day. Sometimes the prayers are private and sometimes large groups of Muslims pray together. In this picture thousands of Muslims pray in Teheran, Iran. (*Courtesy of the United Nations.*)

with facilities for washing the hands, feet, and face before prayer. If no water is available Muslims may cleanse themselves with sand. Properly cleansed, the worshipers prostrate themselves, facing toward Mecca, and offer their prayers. Prayer in the mosque is usually limited to men, as women are instructed to pray at home.

3. Almsgiving (zakah). Proper Muslims are expected to share their possessions with the poor of the community.

> Establish worship and pay the poor-due and obey the messenger, that haply ye may find mercy.[14]
> Lo! those who give alms, both men and women and lend unto Allah a goodly loan, it will be doubled for them, and theirs will be a rich reward.[15]

Originally, almsgiving was intended to be simply an act of charity toward the poor, widows, and orphans of the community, but in later Islamic life it became obligatory and was assessed as a tax amounting to between 2 and 3 percent of one's wealth. Because of its emphasis

[14]Quran 24:56.
[15]Quran 57:18.

upon almsgiving, Islam has never looked upon begging as dishonorable.

4. Fasting (sawm).   Many religions require fasting in one form or another during the year, but usually it is for a very brief period of time. Jews, for example, are to fast on the Day of Antonement. Other religions restrict certain foods at special times; for example, Roman Catholic Christians are expected to avoid meat during the season of Lent. Islam, however, requires the longest and most stringent fast of all. Each year during the entire month of Ramadan, Muslims are expected to abstain from all food, drink, smoking, and sexual relations during the daylight hours. The fast is kept in remembrance of the month when the Prophet first received his revelation, which became the Quran. Because of the Muslim lunar calendar the month of Ramadan varies from year to year. On some years it may fall in the summer months when abstinence from water during the long daylight hours is very difficult. By Muslim tradition all food and drink must cease when there is enough light in the morning to distinguish a black thread from a white thread. Nourishment may be taken again in the evening when light has passed so that the threads may not be distinguished. The only Muslims who are excused from this fast are those who are sick, those who are traveling, mothers nursing infants, and small children. When the month of Ramadan is concluded Muslims celebrate with a feast that lasts three days.

5. Pilgrimage (hajj).   A pilgrimage to Mecca was part of pre-Islamic Arab worship for many years before the time of Muhammad. During a special season each year pilgrims came to Mecca, worshipped at the Kaaba, and paid respect to the sacred black stone. Although the Prophet purged the Kaaba of its idols, he incorporated it and its black stone into his religion. It has become a requirement for every Muslim who can afford the trip to make the pilgrimage to Mecca and venerate the sacred shrines of Islam.

The pilgrimage takes place during a special month in the Muslim calendar called the dhul-Hijah. During this month pilgrims from all over the world arrive at Mecca. The poor sometimes use their life's savings to make this trip. Others who are elderly and sick begin the long journey with no real hope of completing it or of returning, but no devout Muslim could ask for a more blessed way to die than on the *hajj* to Mecca. Outside Mecca the pilgrims must leave whatever mode of transportation they used for the journey, and walk the rest of the way. They must be clad in simple pilgrims's garment with no head covering and only the briefest of sandals, so that rich and poor cannot be distinguished by their apparel. During most of the *hajj* the pilgrims must abstain from food and drink during the daylight hours, they must abstain from sexual intercourse, and they must not cut their hair and nails.

During the days of the pilgrimage visitors to Mecca visit the well of Zemzen established by Hagar and Ishmael. They make seven trips around the Kaaba and kiss the sacred black stone. They offer a sacrifice of a sheep or goat on the tenth day of the *hajj*. After these duties they may visit Medina and perhaps Jerusalem. When the pilgrims return home, they may have the title *hajj* attached to their names so that all the world will know that they have fulfilled this religious obligation.

Calendar

Islam has its own distinctive calendar, which is made up of twelve lunar months of between twenty-nine and thirty days for a total of 354 days each year. To make up some of the difference between the lunar year and the solar year, one day is added to the last month of the year eleven times each thirty years. Even with this correction, however, 103 Muslim years are the equivalent of 100 solar years. Muslims date their calendars from the Hijrah, so the date of the Prophet's death is not known as 632 A.D. but as 10 A.H.

Islam and Women

The position of women in pre-Islamic Arabia was very low. Female infanticide was apparently common as a means of keeping down the female population. A woman was considered as chattel owned by her father, husband, or elder brother. If she displeased her husband, he could divorce her without any recourse on her part. Women like Khadija, the first wife of the Prophet, who could control their own wealth and destinies must have been extremely rare. While Muhammad did not raise the status of women to that of men, he did raise it significantly.

The practice of murdering female babies was forbidden by Islam. While Muhammad allowed polygamy[16] to continue and was married to many women himself, he limited the number of wives a Muslim could have to four, provided a man could afford them. In a society whose males were frequently killed in tribal warfare and in which marriage was the only acceptable state for a women, the polygamy rules probably worked to the benefit of women. Many of the wives of

[16]Technically "polygyny."

the Prophet were the widows of Muslims who had been killed in battle.

If a Muslim wished to divorce his wife it was an easy process compared to modern Western methods. When the husband said, "I divorce you, I divorce you, I divorce you," the divorce was in effect. However, the Muslim woman was not left totally destitute. She had as her possession the dowry that the husband paid the wife when the marriage was initially arranged. If there was a divorce, the property of the dowry remained the wife's.

In spite of the elevation of the position of women in Islam, they are still regarded as inferior to men. Generally women are not encouraged to pray at the mosque. Their status is mentioned in the Quran:

> Men are in charge of women, because Allah hath made the one of them to excel the other, and because they spend of their property [for the support of women]. So good women are obedient, guarding in secret that which Allah hath guarded. As for those from whom ye fear rebellion, admonish them and banish them to beds apart, and scourge them. Then if they obey you, seek not a way against them. Lo! Allah is ever High Exalted, Great.[17]

Muslim Taboos

The Quran and Muslim tradition have established a series of taboos that in many ways are similar to those established in the Jewish Bible. Pork is forbidden to the Muslim as the most unclean of all meats. In Muhammad's day, there must have been little temptation for the desert-dwelling nomads to eat pork, because their major meat supply was sheep and goats. Unlike Jews and Christians, Muslims are also forbidden to drink wine. Again this may have been an expression of the contempt that desert nomads felt for the settled farmer. Because Muslims are forbidden wine, they gave the world coffee as a drink. Gambling is also forbidden to Muslims.

The Holy War (Jihad)

One of the more controversial requirements placed upon Muslims by their religion is that of the holy war. In the strictest sense, a Muslim might feel a religious obligation to go to war and wipe out the infidel in the name of Allah. This requirement was invoked several times in the early days of Islam as its forces spread out across the Middle East, and in later years when the movement was directed eastward. The Muslim warrior was offered two enticements to do battle with the

---

[17]Quran 4:34.

infidel. One of course was the booty that he might win for himself, and the other was the promise that if he died in battle he would go straight to a reward in paradise. In modern times *jihad* has never been a clear issue. Although the rewards are still there, modern Arab states have been less than anxious to enter wars as unified Muslims against non-Muslims. Even the modern wars against Israel have not enjoyed the complete support of all Muslim nations against a common enemy.

THE SPREAD OF ISLAM

Islam appeared and developed at exactly the right time in history for expansion. It came at a time when the Arab people were ready for a unifying force; when the Byzantine Empire was on the verge of collapse from internal corruption and misrule; and when the Persian Empire was also vulnerable. Within a century of the death of the Prophet the religion of Islam had become the unifying force for the Arab people; it had conquered Palestine, Persia, and Egypt and had swept across North Africa into Spain. In the centuries that followed, Islam conquered all the Middle East and moved on into India, China, and eventually the islands of the Pacific. There were several reasons for this rapid and massive expansion.

1. Islam is a militant religion that rewards those who go into battle on its behalf.
2. Islam is a universal religion. Though it arose from the Arab world it recognizes no national barriers and knows no distinction between races. All are the children of Allah and all are accepted as Muslims.
3. Islam is a simple religion. Unlike religions that require learning or meditation or great sacrifice, Islam is a simple and clear religion. A person who repeats the creed is a Muslim; a person who keeps the five pillars of Islam is a good Muslim.
4. The world that surrounded the early Muslims was a confused and corrupt one. Byzantine Christian rulers had mistreated and abused Arab Christians, and therefore the Muslim conquerors were frequently received not as an invading army but as deliverers.

Before the death of Muhammad, Islam had begun to conquer and unite the Arabian peninsula. With every conquest and every addition to Islam others were encouraged to join and share in the benefits. After the death of the Prophet the movement gathered momentum and moved outside Arabia. Damascus was taken in 634; Persia fell by 636; Jerusalem became Muslim in 638; Caesarea was conquered, after stubborn resistance, in 640; and Egypt was also taken in 640. In the following decades Islam consolidated its victories. Most of North Africa became Muslim by the end of the seventh century. In 711 the Muslims entered Spain, where they were dominant for the next seven centuries. In 732 they were turned back from further conquest in Europe by Charles Martel, at the Battle of Tours. On the eastern side of the Mediterranean the expansion also began to slow down. Constantinople, the capital of the Byzantine Empire, was able to resist the attacks of the Muslims until 1453. The island of Sicily fell to the Muslims in the ninth century, and for a period was a base for raids against Italy. With the consolidation of the Islamic Empire of Spain, North Africa, and the Middle East, the Muslims moved eastward. In the eleventh century the caliphs of Baghdad extended their conquests into India and China. Today large portions of India and Pakistan are Muslim, and there are an estimated thirty million Muslims in China. In the fourteenth century, Indonesia was virtually converted to Islam, and in the fifteenth and sixteenth centuries Islam made converts in the Pacific Islands. The Muslim world remained within these boundaries until the end of the nineteenth century, when missionary activity began to make renewed and rapid strides in Africa.

THE CALIPHATE

Islam is not a highly structured religion in the sense that Roman Catholic Christianity is. One of the reasons for this is the fact that Islam is a religion that can be practiced privately. Most of the duties of a good Muslim can be practiced at home, without the presence of a priest. Another reason for its lack of structure is that Muhammad never clearly left a successor or a plan for the succession of his leadership. Only one of his children, Fatima, lived longer than the Prophet, and he never clearly designated her as the leader who was to follow him. The only hint of succession that the Prophet made was to appoint his friend abu-Bakr to lead the community in prayers. Following the death of Muhammad there was great confusion among the Muslims, but after a time it was agreed that abu-Bakr should be the caliph (from *khalifa*, "deputy" or "representative") who would rule the Muslims in temporal matters. It was presumed that spiritual rule would be left to the Quran.

The caliphate is the one central unifying office in the history of Islam. At first, the caliphs were friends of the Prophet and acted as pious leaders of the faithful. They were chosen by election or com-

From the time of Muhammad to the present day, the lifestyle of the Middle Eastern nomad has changed little. (*Courtesy of FAO.*)

mon consent. In later years, the caliphate became hereditary, and the office was more like that of a king. The first four caliphs are often referred to as the "orthodox caliphs" because they were selected from the circle of friends of the Prophet and ruled from Arabia. These four were abu-Bakr, Umar, Uthman, and Ali, the husband of the Prophet's daughter, Fatima. Life was not easy for these caliphs: abu-Bakr had to suppress rebellion and also try to unify the nation that the Prophet had built; Umar and Uthman were murdered; and Ali had the caliphate wrested from his hands in 661 by those who formed the first dynasty of Islam, the Umayyads.

Between 661 and 750 Islam was ruled by the Umayyad caliphs, who made their headquarters in Damascus, Syria. The Umayyads were more interested in ruling as kings, in conquering territory, and in sharing booty than they were in being leaders of a religious community. They were succeeded by the Abbasid dynasty, which ruled from Baghdad in Persia between 750 and 1258. The Abbasids outdid the Umayyads and ruled with great pomp and splendor, in the style depicted in the *Arabian Nights*. It was during the years of the Abbasid caliphate that Islam reached the peak of its civilization. It was in Baghdad that Jews and Muslims worked together in studying and preserving the texts of the Greek philosophers and scientists. After the tenth century, however, the golden age of Muslim civilization began to decline, and the caliphate began to lose its power. The Abbasids were replaced by the Mamelukan Turks, who ruled the Muslim Empire from Egypt. The Mamelukes were replaced in the sixteenth century by the Ottoman Turks, who made the title *caliph* synonymous with that of *sultan* of Turkey. When the Ottoman Empire was broken up after World War I, the caliphate ceased to exist. However, by that time it was only a title, and carried with it none of the glory and power it had once held in the days of the Abbasid caliphs.

VARIATIONS WITHIN ISLAM

Like most large religions, Islam is not a monolithic body. Although most Muslims would agree on the basic principles of Islam, there are many variations in beliefs and practice.

The Sunnis

Eighty-five percent of all Muslims are classified as Sunnis (traditionalists) and are regarded as the orthodox of Islam. These representatives of normative Islam attempt to follow the path of their religion exactly as it was established by the Prophet and the first four orthodox caliphs. However, this is not always easy to do because Muhammad was a man who lived in Arabia in the seventh century, and there are difficulties in applying his teachings to persons living in other regions and in other centuries. It became necessary for Muslims to collect those sayings of Muhammad and his immediate disciples that are not found in the Quran, and to interpret them as guides for problems not anticipated in the Quran. For example, the Quran orders very severe punishment for thieves.

> As for the thief, both male and female, cut off their hands. It is the reward of their own deeds, and exemplary punishment from Allah. Allah is Mighty, Wise.[18]

Although this punishment may have been fair and effective for a few Muslims living in Medina in the seventh century, it could scarcely have worked in Damascus in the ninth century, after Islam had grown into a world power. Therefore a tradition developed whereby thieves were punished by flogging. These traditions and interpretations relating to the laws of the Quran became known as *hadith*.

As Islam grew and took on the character of the many nations into which it spread, there arose schools of interpretation that varied in the amount of weight they gave to the Quran, the hadiths, and human reason in interpreting the life of Islam. There are four of these

[18] Quran 5:38.

schools of thought, and every Sunni Muslim is a member of one of these schools. Generally, the four schools represent different geographical regions. The first is the Hanifite group, which follow the teachings of abu-Hanifah (d. 767 A.D.). The Hanifites are found today in western Asia, India, and lower Egypt. The second are the Malikites, who follow the teachings of Malik ibn-Anas (d. 795 A.D.) and are found in North and West Africa and upper Egypt. The third is the Shafi'ite group, who follow the patterns established by al-Shafi'i (d. 820 A.D.) and are found in lower Egypt, Syria, India, and Indonesia. The last group are the Hanbalites, who follow Ahmad ibn-Hanbal (d. 855 A.D.) and are today found in Saudi Arabia. Generally, the Hanbalites are the most conservative of the four groups.

The Shi'ites

The Shi'ite element within Islam represents a basic rupture in the body of this religion. It began as a political dispute over the leadership of Islam, but it later took on theological overtones. Because Muhammad had left no clear message as to who was to succeed him, he was followed by three men who had been his close associates. However, some Muslims believed that Muhammad should have been succeeded by Ali, who was his cousin and son-in-law. Ali was finally named the Caliph in 656 A.D. but gradually lost control of the Muslim world. At his death in 661, the Umayyad dynasty took the Caliphate. Ali's youngest son, Husain, challenged the Umayyad Caliphs in 680 but was defeated at the battle of Karbala. After the battle, Husain was executed.

Throughout the history of Islam certain elements have always believed that the descendants of Ali should be the leaders of the faith. In earlier times these people were called "Alids," but they gradually became known as "Shia Ali" (the party of Ali), and, finally, as "Shi'ites." The Shi'ites differ from Sunni Muslims in the following ways:

1. The Shi'ites believe that revelation did not end with Muhammad and the Quran, but that in later generations there were further revelations through figures called "imams." To Sunnis, an *imam* is one who leads community prayers, but the word carries far more important connotations for Shi'ites.
2. Shi'ites believe that after the disasterous events of 680 the next imam was another son of Ali, Zain. Some believe that Zain was followed by a series of six other imams. These Shi'ites are called "Seveners" because they believe there was a total of seven imams in history. Others believe that Zain was followed by eleven other imams, and they are called "Twelvers." Both the Seveners

and the Twelvers believe that some of these imams did not die but went into hiding and are now waiting to return to earth.

3. Shi'ites have also traditionally believed in the existence of a *mahdi* ("guided one"), a messiah figure who will one day appear on earth and lead the world into an era of justice.

4. Because of the importance of the martyrdom of Husain, Shi'ites tend to prize martyrdom. Each year, on the tenth of the month of Muharran, the passion of Husain is reenacted. The site of his execution, and other locations that are important in his life, are places of special pilgrimages to Shia Muslims. Husain almost takes on the character of a redeeming figure, whose death aids the Shi'ite to achieve paradise.

5. The traditional reading and interpretation of the Quran is mistrusted by the Shi'ites. It is reasoned that, since the current version of the Quran does not mention the name of Ali, it must have been tampered with by his enemies. The Quran must have hidden meanings which can only be known through allegorical interpretations.

All of these factors make Shia Islam suspicious of the world at large. Like chiliastic sects in Christianity, Shi'ites tend to look at the present order of the world with great distrust. Instead, they look to the future, when promised messiahs or messianic movements will arise and bring justice to the oppressed. The Shi'ite movements favor the true believer, who has clung to his faith and has not sold out to the established order of the world.

In 1502, Shia Islam became the established religion of Persia and has maintained its hold on Iran; Shi'ites are also found as minority groups in Iraq, India, Yemen, in some areas in East Africa, and in scattered pockets throughout the Muslim world. It is estimated that approximately 14 percent of all the Muslims of the world are Shi'ites.

The Mystical Element

Islam, like Judaism, has always been a religion that emphasized obedience to the will of God in the here and now. Therefore it has never encouraged the ascetic life, which is so characteristic of the Indian religions. In addition to its emphasis upon this world, Islam has been essentially an unemotional religion. Good Muslims need not enter a mystical experience with God; but must only obey the teachings of the Quran. Nevertheless, in every religion there is a hunger for the mystical experience. Furthermore, Islam arose in a land dominated by Byzantine Christianity, which highly prized the ascetic life; and in later years it developed in India, where there is also a strong concern for communion with God through asceticism.

In Islam the concern for mystical union with God was expressed through a group called the Sufis. The word *sufi* means "woolen" and refers to the coarse wool garments worn by the members of this order as a symbol of their poverty and rejection of worldly niceties. The Sufis claim that they have always been a part of Islam and trace their origins back to the days of the Prophet and the first four orthodox caliphs. In Islam's earlier days, Muslims were supposed to have been more pious and more concerned with true spiritual matters than they were later. With the expansion of Islam into a world empire it became more materialistic than it had been during the first fifty years of its history. With the development of the Abbasid dynasty and its grandeur, in Baghdad, there came a cry among some for a simpler, more austere life. Therefore the ninth century probably was the era when the Sufi movement began.

One of the most outstanding Sufis of the early period was Mansur al-Hallaj. His quest for mystical oneness with God brought him to the point where he finally proclaimed, "I am the truth." For this offense and others, his fellow Muslims crucified him in 922 A.D. He went to his death asking forgiveness for his persecutors. The martyrdom of one of their number, and similar persecutions in the following years, forced the Sufi movement to go underground and to teach its more unorthodox beliefs in secret. However, as the orthodox Muslim teachers emphasized more and more the formal and legalistic aspects of Islam, the Sufis emphasized the emotional and mystical aspects, and thus came to appeal to the common people. Islam finally accepted the major teachings of the Sufis in the twelfth century, because of the life and teachings of Abu-Hamid al-Ghazali. Al-Ghazali, a professor of theology at the Nizamiyah school in Baghdad, found no personal satisfaction in orthodox Muslim doctrine. He abandoned his position and his family and, like the Christian Saint Francis, set out to find God in poverty and mystical experiences. He found his satisfaction among the Sufis. His books, *The Revivification of the Religious Sciences*, *The Folly of the Philosophers*, and the *Niche of the Lights*, had a great impact upon Islam and served to make orthodox doctrine more mystical.

Also in the twelfth century, the Sufis began to organize themselves into monastical orders. These orders were usually centered on a Sufi saint. When a convert came to join the order, he was known as a *fakir* or a *dervish*.[19] Traditionally, novices stayed in the order and studied with the master until they became masters themselves. Sufi monastic practices vary, but generally they emphasize discipline, poverty, ab-

[19] The word *faqir* (fakir) literally means "a poor man," and the word *darwish* (dervish) connotes "one who comes to the door," i.e., a beggar. Thus both words indicate the monk's universal practices of poverty and begging.

stinence, and in some cases celibacy. Sometimes there were the extremes of asceticism and emotionalism, which Westerners have come to associate with the titles *fakir* and *dervish*. There are recorded reports of Sufis swallowing live coals, walking on coals, swallowing snakes, and so on, and of course there are the various Turkish dervishes who seek oneness with God by whirling in one spot for hours. These are only the extremes of the Sufi movement, however, and are not representative of the totality in any sense. The real contribution of the Sufis to Islamic thought is their insistence on the possibility of union with God through a mystical experience.

ISLAM IN THE MODERN WORLD

In the years following the glories of the Caliphate of Baghdad, Islam settled down to a relatively routine existence. There were the battles with the Christian Crusaders over the holy sites in Palestine in the twelfth and thirteenth centuries, which produced one of the most outstanding Muslim leaders of all time, Saladin; there was the eastward spread of Islam into India, China, and the Pacific Islands; and there was the development of the Ottoman Empire in the sixteenth century. But on the whole, Islam never achieved the golden era of wealth, power, and intellectual life that it had enjoyed during the reign of the Abbasid caliphs.

When the European nations were moving out of the medieval twilight into the industrial age, many Islamic nations continued to live in preindustrialized societies. Several reasons are suggested for this era of quiet in the Islamic world. One of the most obvious is the conservative nature of the religion itself. Most religions are essentially conservative, but Islam is especially so. The Prophet came as the last word from God to humankind, and the Quran is God's last great message. All that is necessary is to know the Quran and how to apply it to one's life. Therefore, after the great era of the Baghdad caliphs, there was little internal stimulus to encourage Muslims to seek new knowledge or to change their lives.

Another reason for the lack of change among Muslims may have been their sense of self-satisfaction relative to European nations. The Muslims had decidedly defeated the Christian crusaders who had invaded their lands. Later, they had taken the supposedly invincible city of Constantinople from its Christian defenders. The Islamic world therefore had a sense of military and cultural superiority toward the Christian nations. Some have suggested that it was not until the conquest of Egypt by Napoleon in the early nineteenth century that Islamic nations became aware that Europeans might be superior in any way.

A third reason for the slowness with which the Muslim nations moved into the modern era was the development of extremely conservative groups within Islam which took active leadership in a struggle against any change. The most outstanding force against change was the Wahhabi movement, founded in 1744 by Muhammad ibn-Abdalal-Wahhab. The Wahhabis were traditionalists who opposed all forms of change. Naturally they opposed any acceptance of European ways, but they also opposed internal innovations, such as those proposed by the Sufis. The Wahhabi movement came to be attached to the house of the Su'ud family, and when the Su'ud family came to control Arabia, this puritanical religious movement came with them. In the nineteenth century the Wahhabis suppressed the Sufis and others whom they considered to be compromising with change. Today the Wahhabi movement is not strong in the Islamic world, but its existence in the last century does speak to the latent desire among many Muslims to resist change.

The isolation of the Muslim world from the modern world came to an end in the early part of the twentieth century. By that time, transportation and communication had advanced to the point that the Muslim world came within easy reach of the European world. World War I brought the Ottoman Empire into the struggle on the side of the Axis powers. With the defeat of the Axis forces the Ottoman Empire was broken up, and European powers took control of some parts of the Middle East. During the post-World War I years the various Muslim states that had constituted parts of the Ottoman Empire developed into independent nations. They eventually broke their ties with the European governments and achieved independent status. In addition, many of the Middle Eastern Arab nations were found to have the world's largest supply of crude oil, thus raising the level of their wealth and political power almost overnight. These factors have caused a resurgence of interest in Islam, both internally and externally. Whether the world chooses to or not, the Muslim states of the Middle East can never again be overlooked; they are extremely important.

The internal resurgence of interest in Islam has manifested itself in several ways. First is the reform movements from within. Some Muslims have suggested, and practiced, textual criticism of the Quran in a manner similar to that practiced by Christians and Jews on their bibles. No one has yet suggested the higher criticism of the Quran. Other reformers have changed marriage and divorce laws in Muslim communities, to help make them more compatible with those of the Western nations. Other reform movements in Islam have been syncretistic, picking up features from other world religions and changing the nature of Islam altogether.

The most obvious result of the resurgence of Islam in the twentieth century is its very active missionary movement in Africa. The

Modern-day pilgrimage to Mecca. (*Courtesy of Liaison. Photograph by Gamma-Liaison.*)

move south of the Sahara by Muslim missionaries began in the late nineteenth century when the slave trade had ended and conversion of blacks was possible. Yet Islam has existed in portions of Africa since the seventh century. North Africa was among the first lands to be conquered and converted to Islam. Portions of the interior, particularly the cities, have also known Muslim influence for a long time. Muslim merchants and traders worked in many parts of the continent. However, the colonial forces of the European nations in the eighteenth and nineteenth centuries made Muslim missionary activity in the interior possible. The colonial powers opened Africa to both Christian and Muslim missions, with maps, modern transportation, and communication. The abuses of the Africans by the colonial nations also opened doors for Islam; when the African nations gained their independence, hostility toward the white Europeans and their religion could be expressed by conversion to Islam. Although Islam is a religion that knows no bias of color or ethnic origin, it can be thought of as the religion of the peoples of the third world who have been victimized by the Christian colonial powers.

ISLAM TODAY

In recent decades Islam has become an increasingly important force in world politics. Many of the newly emerging nations of the third world are Muslim. Some of these nations are very important to the world's economy because they control vital natural resources such as oil, natural gas, and minerals. In order to understand there nations, one must understand Islam.

Mention has already been made of Muslim missionary activity in Africa. Islam is growing in other parts of the world as well. The Muslim population of Western Europe has been increasing because of the immigration of workers from Muslim nations. Immigration has also been a factor in the growth of Muslims in the United States. It is estimated by some that in the mid-1980s the number of traditional Muslims in the United States exceeds the number of Jews. In the Soviet Union, the number of Asian Muslims continues to grow faster than the European population. If current trends continue, at some point in the future Russia may be regarded as a Muslim nation.

The most dramatic change that is occurring in world Islam today is the emergence of Islamic fundamentalism. One sees this movement particularly in Iran, but it can be found, to some extent, throughout Islam. In the 1960s and 70s Iran, like many other Muslim nations, became rich with oil profits. In many cases, it turned to Western society as a model. The rise of Western universities and Western customs, such as the increased role of women in public life, was perceived as a threat by some Muslims. In 1979 the Shi'ite Muslims of Iran deposed their Shah and accepted as their leader the Ayatollah Khomeini. The new government called itself an Islamic Republic, and was based upon a return to the laws and traditions of the Quran. It was an attempt to stop the flow of Western influence in an Islamic nation. It remains to be seen if Iran or any Muslim nation can exist in the modern world with a culture that is based upon ancient nomadic customs.

STUDY QUESTIONS

1. Contrast the role of Muhammad as founder of Islam with that of Jesus and Christianity. How are they similar?

2. Trace the roots of Islam in Jewish, Christian, and traditional Arab religions.

3. What were the factors that made Islam so widely accepted by so many diverse people in the first two centuries of its life?

4. List the five pillars or duties of a good Muslim.

5. Locate the various places in the modern world where one would find an Islamic majority.

6. Distinguish between Sunni and Shi'ite Muslims. Where are Shi'ites a majority?

SUGGESTED READING

Arberry, A. J. *The Holy Koran.* New York: Macmillan Publishing Company, 1953.

Cragg, Kenneth. *The House of Islam.* Encino, Calif.: Dickenson Publishing Co., 1975.

Denny, F. M. *An Introduction to Islam.* New York: Macmillan Publishing Company, 1985.

Guillaume, Alfred. *Islam.* Baltimore: Penguin Books, 1954.

Rahman, Fazlur. *Islam,* 2nd. ed. Chicago: The University of Chicago Press, 1979.

Watt, W. Montgomery. *Muhammad, Prophet and Statesman.* London: Oxford University Press, 1964.

Watt, W. Montgomery. *What Is Islam,* 2nd ed. London: Longman, 1979.

The Muslim Vision of Allah

In the following selections from the Quran the qualities of Allah as absolute creator and ruler, the only God, are presented.[20]

God
there is no god but He, the
Living, the Everlasting.
Slumber seizes Him not, neither sleep;
   to Him belongs
all that is in the heavens and the earth
Who is there that shall intercede with Him
   save by His leave?
He knows what lies before them
   and what is after them,
and they comprehend not anything of His knowledge
   save such as He wills.
His Throne comprises the heavens and earth;
the preserving of them oppresses Him not;
He is the All-high, the All-glorious.
No compulsion is there in religion.
Rectitude has become clear from error.
So whosoever disbelieves in idols
and believes in God, has laid hold of
the most firm handle, unbreaking; God is
   All-hearing, All-knowing.
God is the protector of the believers;
He brings them forth from the shadows
   into the light.
And the unbelievers—their protectors are
idols, that bring them forth from the light
   into the shadows;
those are the inhabitants of the Fire,
   therein dwelling forever. (II, 256–259)

That then is God your Lord;
there is no god but He,
the Creator of everything.

[20] A. J. Arberry, trans., *The Koran Interpreted* (London: Allen & Unwin, 1955). Vol. I, pp. 65, 66, 161; Vol. II, pp. 81, 82, 110, 111, 142, 258, 264, 270.

So serve Him,
for He is Guardian over everything.
The eyes attain Him not, but He attains the eyes;
He is the All-subtle, the All-aware. (VI, 102, 103)

He who created the heavens and earth, and sent down for you
    out of heaven water;
and We caused to grow therewith gardens full of loveliness
    whose trees you could never grow.
    Is there a god with God?
Nay, but they are a people who assign to Him equals!
    He who made the earth a fixed place
    and set amidst it rivers
    and appointed it firm mountains
    and placed a partition between the two seas.
    Is there a god with God?
Nay, but the most of them have no knowledge.
He who answers the constrained, when he calls unto Him,
    and removes the evil
    and appoints you to be successors in the earth.
    Is there a god with God?
Little indeed do you remember.
He who guides you in the shadows of the land and the sea
    and looses the winds,
    bearing good tidings before His mercy.
    Is there a god with God?
High exalted be God, above that which they associate!
Who originates creation, then brings it back again,
    and provides you out of heaven and earth,
    Is there a god with God? (XXVII, 61–65)

God is He that looses the winds, that stirs up clouds,
and He spreads them in heaven how He will, and shatters them;
    then thou seest the rain issuing out of the midst of them,
    and when he smites with it whomsoever of His servants
    He will, lo, they rejoice,
although before it was sent down on them before that
    they had been in despair.
    So behold the marks of God's mercy,
    how He quickens the earth after it
    was dead; surely He is the quickener
    of the dead, and He is powerful
    over everything.
But if We loose a wind, and they see it growing yellow,

they remain after that unbelievers.
Thou shalt not make the dead to hear,
neither shalt thou make the deaf to hear the call
when they turn about, retreating.
Thou shalt not guide the blind out of their error
neither shalt thou make any to hear
except for such as believe in Our signs, and so surrender.
God is He that created you of weakness, then He appointed
after weakness strength, then after strength he appointed
weakness and grey hairs; He creates what He will, and
    He is the All-knowing, the All-powerful. (XXX, 47–54)

God knows the Unseen in the heavens and the earth;
    He knows the thoughts within the breasts.
It is He who appointed you viceroys in the earth.
So whosoever disbelieves, his unbelief shall be
charged against him; their unbelief increases
the disbelievers only in hate in God's sight;
their unbelief increases the disbelievers only in loss.
Say: "Have you considered your associates on whom
you call, apart from God? Show what they have
created in the earth; or have they a partnership
in the heavens?" Or have We given them a Book,
so that they are upon a clear sign from it?
Nay, but the evildoers promise one another
    naught but delusion.
God holds the heavens and the earth, lest they remove;
did they remove, none would hold them after Him.
Surely He is All-clement, All-forgiving. (XXXV, 36–39)

In the Name of God, the Merciful, the Compassionate
All that is in the heavens and the earth magnifies God;
    He is the All-mighty, the All-wise.
To Him belongs the Kingdom of the heavens and the earth;
He gives life, and He makes to die, and He is powerful
    Over everything.
He is the First and the Last, the Outward and the Inward;
    He has knowledge of everything.
It is He that created the heavens and the earth in six days
    then seated Himself upon the Throne.
He knows what penetrates into the earth
    and what comes forth from it,
what comes down from heaven, and what goes up into it.

He is with you wherever you are; and God sees
the things you do.
To Him belongs the Kingdom of the heavens and the earth;
and unto Him all matters are returned,
He makes the night to enter into the day
and makes the day to enter into the night
He knows the thoughts within the breasts. (LVII, 1–5)

Hast thou not seen that God knows whatsoever is in the heavens, and whatsoever is in the earth? Three men conspire not secretly together, but He is the fourth of them, neither five men, but He is the sixth of them, neither fewer than that, neither more, but He is with them, wherever they may be; then He shall tell them what they have done, on the Day of Resurrection. Surely God has knowledge of everything. (LVIII 7, 8)

He is God;
There is no God but He.
He is the knower of the unseen and the Visible;
He is the All-merciful, the All-compassionate.
He is God;
There is no God but He.
He is the King, the All-holy, the All-peaceable.
the All-faithful, the All-preserver,
the All-mighty, the All-compeller,
the All-sublime.
Glory be to God, above that they associate!
He is God;
the Creator, the Maker, the Shaper.
To Him belong the Names Most Beautiful.
All that is in the heavens and the earth magnifies Him;
He is the All-mighty, the All-wise. (LIX, 23–25)

Muhammad Proclaims the Prescriptions of Islam

In the following selections from the Quran many of the duties of a faithful Muslim are detailed.[21]

O believers, eat of the good things
wherewith We have provided you, and give thanks
to God, if it be Him that you serve.
These things only has he forbidden you;

[21] Ibid. Vol. I, pp. 50–54.

carrion, blood, the flesh of swine,
what has been hallowed to other than God.
Yet whoso is constrained, not desiring,
nor transgressing, no sin shall be on him;
God is All-forgiving, All-compassionate.

Those who conceal what of the Book God has sent down
on them, and sell it for a little price—they shall eat
naught but the Fire in their bellies; God shall not
speak to them on the Day of Resurrection
neither purify them; there awaits them
    a painful chastisement.
Those are they that have bought error at
the price of guidance, and chastisement at
the price of pardon; how patiently they
    shall endure the Fire!
That, because God has sent down the Book
with the Truth, and those that are
at variance regarding the Book
    are in wide schism.

It is not piety, that you turn your faces
    to the East and to the West.
    True piety is this:
to believe in God, and the Last Day,
the angels, the Book, and the Prophets,
to give of one's substance, however cherished,
    to kinsmen, and orphans,
the needy, the traveller, beggars,
    and to ransom the slave,
to perform the prayer, to pay the alms,
And they who fulfill their covenant
when they have engaged in a covenant,
    and endure with fortitude
    misfortune, hardship and peril,
these are they who are true in their faith,
    these are the truly godfearing.

O believers, prescribed for you is
retaliation, touching the slain;
freeman for freeman, slave for slave,
female for female. But if aught is pardoned
a man by his brother, let the pursuing
be honorable, and let the payment be

with kindliness. That is a lightening
granted you by your Lord, and a mercy;
and for him who commits aggression
after that—for his there awaits
    a painful chastisement.
In retaliation there is life for you,
men possessed of minds; haply you
    will be godfearing.

O believers, prescribed for you is
the Fast, even as it was prescribed for
those that were before you—haply you
    will be godfearing—
for days numbered; and if any of you
be sick, or if he be on a journey,
then a number of other days; and for those
who are able to fast, a redemption
by feeding a poor man. Yet better
it is for him who volunteers good,
and that you should fast is better for you,
    if you but know;
the month of Ramadan, wherein the Koran
was sent down to be a guidance
to the people, and as clear signs
of the Guidance and the Salvation.
So let those of you, who are present
at the month, fast it; and if any of you
be sick, or if he be on a journey,
then a number of other days; God desires
ease for you, and desires not hardship
for you; and that you fulfill the number, and
magnify God that he has guided you, and haply
    you will be thankful.

Permitted to you, upon the night of
the Fast, is to go in to your wives;
they are a vestment for you, and you are
a vestment for them. God knows that you have been
betraying yourselves, and has turned to you
and pardoned you. So now lie with them,
and seek what God has prescribed for you.
And eat and drink, until the white thread
shows clearly to you from the black thread
at the dawn; then complete the Fast

unto the night, and do not lie with them
while you cleave to the mosques. Those are
God's bounds; keep well within them. So God
makes clear His signs to men; haply they
    will be godfearing.

And fight in the way of God with those
who fight with you, but aggress not; God loves
    not the aggressors.
And slay them wherever you come upon them,
and expel them from where they expelled you;
persecution is more grievous than slaying.
But fight them not by the Holy Mosque
until they should fight you there;
then, if they fight you, slay them—
such is the recompense of unbelievers—
but if they give over, surely God is
All-forgiving, All compassionate.
Fight them, till there is no persecution
and the religion is God's; then if they
give over, there shall be no enmity
    save for evildoers.
The holy month for the holy month;
holy things demand retaliation.
Whoso commits aggression against you,
do you commit aggression against him
like as he has committed against you;
and fear you God, and know that God is
    with the godfearing.

And expend in the way of God;
and cast not yourselves by your own hands
into destruction, but be good-doers; God
    loves the good-doers.
Fulfil the Pilgrimage and the Visitation
unto God; but if you are prevented,
then such offering as may be feasible.
And shave not your heads, till the offering
reaches its place of sacrifice. If any
of you is sick, or injured in his head,
then redemption by fast, or freewill offering,
or ritual sacrifice. When you are secure,
then whosoever enjoys the Visitation
until the Pilgrimage, let his offering

be such as may be feasible; of if he
finds none, then a fast of three days
in the Pilgrimage, and of seven when
you return, that is ten completely;
that is for him whose family are not
present at the Holy Mosque. And fear
God, and know that God is terrible
   in retribution. (II, 166–175, 180–182, 186–193)

Baha'i

One of the entrances to the North American Baha'i Center in Wilmette, Illinois. *(Courtesy of the Baha'i Office of Public Affairs.)*

All the prophets of God proclaim the same faith.
       —Bahaullah

Baha'i began as a sect of Islam but has moved so far away from that religion as to be considered a separate religion altogether. Several themes are central to Baha'i. Baha'i assumes that all the religions of the world spring from one source, that there is a basic unity of all religious truth, and that all the prophets have had a partial message from the one God. Baha'i further maintains that religion must work in harmony with science and education to provide a peaceful world order; Baha'is also believe in the equality of opportunity among the races and between the sexes. By emphasizing these themes, Baha'i has attracted followers in many of the nations of the world.

ORIGIN AND DEVELOPMENT OF BAHA'I

The Shi'ite sect of Islam, particularly in Persia, has always taught that there were twelve legitimate descendants of Ali, the son-in-law and legitimate successor to Muhammad. These twelve *imams* were often referred to as "gates" whereby the believers gained access to the true faith. The twelfth of these successors disappeared in the ninth century A.D., and the Shi'ites have always believed that one day he would reappear as a messiah.

In 1844, a Shi'ite Muslim, named Mirza Ali Muhammad, declared that he was the promised twelfth *imam* and called himself Bab-ub-Din ("the gate of faith"). He advocated sweeping religious and social reforms, such as raising the status of women, and thus the Bab gathered around him a group of disciples, who called themselves Babis. The movement was short-lived as both the religious and political forces of Persia moved to crush it. The Bab was publicly executed in 1850, and many of his disciples were imprisoned or executed. Before he died, however, the Bab predicted that he had prepared the way for one yet to come who would found a universal religion. The body of the Bab was rescued by some of his followers and preserved for several years. Ultimately it was transported to the city of Haifa, in Palestine, where it was finally buried.

One of the Bab's imprisoned disciples was a man named Mirza Husayn Ali, the son of one of the most distinguished families in Persia. Because of his family Mirza was not executed with the Bab but was imprisoned in Tehran. In 1852, another of the Bab's followers attempted to assassinate the Shah of Iran, and this brought further persecution upon the group. Mirza Ali was exiled to Baghdad, and there he spent the next ten years of his life. During his imprisonment and exile it was revealed to Mirza that he was the one whom the Bab had foretold. In 1863, Mirza and the remaining Babis were exiled from Baghdad to Constantinople, and on the eve of their departure he revealed to the Babis that he was the one promised by the Bab. This revelation was made in Ridvan, near Baghdad, and today is commemorated annually by Baha'is, with a feast. Mirza assumed the name Bahaullah ("the glory of God"), and those Babis who accepted him and followed his teachings became known as Baha'is.

In the following years Bahaullah and the Baha'is were forced from one capital city in the Middle East to another. From Constantinople they went to Adrianople. Finally, they were banished to the Turkish prison city of Acca, in Palestine. At first Bahaullah and about eighty of his followers were incarcerated for two years in an army barracks, where they suffered from hunger and disease. After this period the group was transferred to other quarters, which were somewhat more comfortable. Eventually, more freedom was given to Bahaullah, but he spent the remainder of his life as a prisoner of the Turkish government in Acca. Although he was imprisoned during his years in Acca, Bahaullah was able to send out missionaries and receive guests and thus spread his teachings of unity and world peace. During this period he wrote many letters and books. One series of letters was sent to the pope and to the world heads of state, announcing his mission and calling for their help in furthering world peace. He wrote books such as the *Kitab-i-Aqdas* ("The Most Holy Book"), the *Kitab-i-Iqan* ("The Book of Certitudes"), and *The Hidden Words*. He died in Acca in 1892, at the age of 75.

Leadership of the movement passed to the son of Bahaullah, Abbas Effendi, who became known as Abdul Baha (the servant of Baha). Abdul Baha carried on his father's program of writing, and in 1908 he was freed by the Turks. For the remaining years of his life he traveled widely in Europe and North America preaching the doctrines of Baha'i and establishing Baha'i assemblies in many nations. In 1920, the British conferred the knighthood of the British Empire upon Abdul Baha because of his work for world peace. Upon Abdul Baha's death in 1921, leadership of the movement was passed to his grandson, Shoghi Effendi, who continued the work of establishing local and national assemblies in many nations, until his death in 1957. At this point Baha'i came to be governed, not by one of the descendants of Bahaullah, but by a body elected from Bahai'is all over the world.

THE TEACHINGS OF BAHA'I

Although Baha'i originated within the Shi'ite sect of Islam it soon came to differ radically from it. Baha'i does not revere the Quran to the same degree that Islam does. Much of the Quran is modified, explained allegorically, or treated symbolically. Belief in angels and evil spirits has been discarded by Baha'i, while heaven and hell are treated symbolically. The Quran takes its place, along with the Christian and Jewish bibles and the sacred writings of other religions, as a source for Baha'i worship. This attitude toward the Quran has made Baha'i most unpopular among Muslims, and it has even been outlawed in Iran, the land of its birth. Persecution against Baha'is in Iran became especially harsh after the so-called Islamic revolution of 1979.

The basic belief of Baha'i is that all religions come from the same source. In nearly every era God has revealed his truth through prophets. Moses, Zoroaster, Jesus, Muhammad, Krishna, Buddah, and Bahaullah were the prophets of God, and all presented a portion of the truth of God in their times, but Bahaullah, as the last and the greatest of these prophets, revealed the final truth from God. Bahaullah's greatest message was the oneness of the human race. All of humankind, all races, both sexes, and all religious truths are the work of the one God. In the words of Bahaullah:

> There can be no doubt whatever that the peoples of the world, of whatever race or religion, derive their inspiration from one heavenly Source and are the subjects of one God.[1]

On the basis of these religious truths found in the writings of Bahaullah, Abdul Baha went out from Acca to preach the following Baha'i doctrines of the world.

1. The oneness of the entire human race is the pivotal principle and fundamental doctrine of the faith. This principle is essential to Baha'i. It is the basis for most of its teachings and practices.

2. There must be an independent search after truth, unfettered by superstition or tradition. Anyone who wishes to be a Baha'i must be willing to search out the truth of God without relying on the prophets and the traditions of the past. "The freedom of man from superstition and imitation, so that he may discern the Manifestations of God with the eye of Oneness, and consider all affairs with keen sight. . . ."[2] is one of the basic teachings of Baha'i.

---

[1] Bahaullah, *Gleanings from the Writings of Bahaullah* (Wilmette, Ill.: Baha'i Publishing Trust, 1952), p. 217.
[2] J. E. Esslemont, *Bahaullah and the New Era* (Wilmette, Il: Baha'i Books, 1976), p. 85.

3. There is a basic unity of all religions. Growing out of the belief that there is a oneness in the human race is the teaching that all religions essentially teach the same message. This is not to say that differences do not exist among the religions of the world, but Baha'i doctrine states that the basic message of every religion is the same and that all minor differences should be forgotten. In a conversation with a visitor, Bahaullah said:

That all nations should become one in faith and all men as brothers; that the bonds of affections and unity between the sons of men should be strengthened; that diversity of religion should cease, and differences of race be annulled . . . these strifes and this bloodshed and discord must cease, and all men be as one kindred and one family. . . .[3]

4. All forms of prejudice, whether religious, racial, class, or national, are condemned. In one of his speeches in Paris Abdul Baha said:

Religion should unite all hearts and cause wars and disputes to vanish from the face of the earth; it should give birth to spirituality, and bring light and life to every soul. If religion becomes a cause of dislike, hatred and division, it would be better to be without it. . . . Any religion which is not a cause of love and unity is no religion.[4]

5. Harmony must exist between religion and science. Baha'i arose in the nineteenth century when great battles were fought between the established religions and the newly emerging sciences. These two forces must be harmonized.

Ali, the son-in-law of Muhammad, said: "That which is in conformity with science is also in conformity with religion." Whatever the intelligence of man cannot understand, religion ought not to accept. Religion and science walk hand in hand, and any religion contrary to science is not the truth.[5]

6. There is equality of men and women. Baha'i may be the only religion of the world that has asserted from the beginning that women are equal to men.

Humanity is like a bird with its two wings—the one is male, the other female. Unless both wings are strong and impelled by some common force, the bird cannot fly heavenwards. According to the spirit of this age, women

[3] Ibid., p. 126.
[4] Ibid., p. 165.
[5] Ibid., p. 202.

must advance and fulfill their mission in all departments of life, becoming equal to men.[6]

7. Compulsory education must prevail. Although neither Bahaullah nor Abdul Baha had the opportunity of formal education, both preached that universal education was a necessary condition for world peace and stability.

8. In addition to universal education, Baha'i teaches that there should be a universal language. Bahaullah said:

> We commanded the Trustees of the House of Justice, either to choose one of the existing tongues, or to originate a new one, and in like manner to adopt a common script, teaching these to the children in all the schools of the world, that the world may become even as one land and one home.[7]

Abdul Baha was an advocate of the adoption of Esperanto as the universal language.

9. Extremes of wealth and poverty should be abolished. Coming from a family of high rank and then spending much of his life in prisons, Bahaullah was acutely aware of the extremes of wealth and poverty in the world. Believing that both extremes were unhealthy and abnormal, he urged their abolition. He did not offer an elaborate plan that would bring about this change. Rather, he suggested to the rich of the world that they should open their hearts and contribute to the poor. He also advocated that the governments of the world should pass laws to prevent the two extremes.

10. A world tribunal for the adjudication of disputes between nations should be instituted. Forty years before the establishment of the League of Nations, Bahaullah was urging such an organization from his prison cell in Acca. However, when the League of Nations was formed after World War I, Abdul Baha considered it too weak to be effective.

11. Work performed in the spirit of service should be exalted to the rank of worship. According to Baha'i, a good society is one in which everyone works at some task. There are to be no loafers or idlers.

> It is enjoined on every one of you to engage in some occupation—some art, trade, or the like. We have made this—your occupation—identical with the worship of God, the true One.[8]

Thus Bahaullah, like Calvin and the ancient Jewish Pharisees, believed in the religious efficacy of labor.

---

[6] Ibid., p. 154.
[7] Ibid., p. 170.
[8] Bahaullah, *Glad Tidings*.

12. Justice should be glorified as the ruling principle in human society and religion, for the protection of all peoples and nations.

13. Finally, as a capstone to all of the teachings of Baha'i, the establishment of a permanent and universal peace should be the supreme goal of humankind.[9]

Unlike Islam and other Western religions, Baha'i believes that heaven and hell are not places but conditions of the soul. The soul, which is the reality of humankind, is eternal and in continuous progress. When the soul is near to God and God's purposes, that is heaven; when the soul is distant from God, that is hell. Thus the descriptions of heaven and hell that are found in other religions are regarded as symbolic rather than actual. When Baha'is speak of the unity of humankind, they mean not only the unity of humanity in this life but unity of the living and the dead as well. Thus it is possible that the living and the dead may commune with each other. Abdul Baha believed that this was the reason for the peculiar powers of the prophets and saints to see into the other world and commune with it.

According to the Baha'i belief in the total unity of God, there can be no such thing as positive evil. If God is one and all, there can be no Satan figure in the universe. Just as darkness is only the absence of light, so that which appears to be evil is only the absence of good. According to Abdul Baha:

> In creation there is no evil; all is good. Certain qualities and natures innate in some men and apparently blameworthy are not so in reality.[10]

BAHA'I PRACTICES

The daily life of Baha'is is governed by many regulations. The Baha'i is required to pray daily. In fact, the entire life of a Baha'i is supposed to be a prayer. One's work, one's thoughts, and one's deeds are all to be done in the spirit of a prayer. This is one of the most important aspects of Baha'i life. Bahaullah stressed this in the *Kitab-i-Aqdas*.

> Chant (or recite) the Words of God every morning and evening. The one who neglects this has not been faithful to the Covenant of God and His agreement, and he who turns away from it today is of those who have turned away from God.[11]

[9] These thirteen principles are taken from information supplied by the Public Information Department, National Baha'i Headquarters, 112 Linden Avenue, Wilmette, Illinois.

[10] Abdul Baha, *Some Answered Questions* (Wilmette, Ill: Baha'i Publishing Trust, 1964), p. 250.

[11] Bahaullah, *Kitab-i-Aqdas*.

The North American Baha'i Center. Each of the Baha'i centers is built with nine sides. Since nine is the largest unit number, this symbolizes the unity that Baha'i wishes to bring to humanity. (*Courtesy of the Baha'i Office of Public Affairs.*)

Although there are many formal prayers a Baha'i may recite in daily devotions, Bahaullah established three obligatory prayers. Baha'is are free to choose any one of these three as a part of their meditations.

Baha'is are also encouraged to fast for one of the nineteen months in their calendar. During the month of *Ala* (loftiness), which begins near the first of March, Baha'is are expected to fast for nineteen days. A full fast, with a complete abstinence from food, is not required; Baha'is must not eat during the daylight hours only. Since the fast occurs during the early spring each year, no food or drink is taken between about 6 A.M. and 6 P.M. According to Abdul Baha:

> Fasting is a symbol. Fasting signifies abstinence from lust. Physical fasting is a symbol of that abstinence, and is a reminder; that is, just as a person abstains from physical appetites, he is to abstain from self-appetites and self-desires. But mere abstention from food has no effect on the spirit. It is only a symbol, a reminder. Otherwise it is of no importance.[12]

At other periods during the Baha'i year, followers engage in certain feasts which celebrate various events in the history of Baha'i. These

[12] Abdul Baha, cited by J. E. Esslemont, *Bahaullah and the New Era*, p. 189.

include the feast of the new year, celebrated on March 21, and the feast of Ridvan, celebrated between April 21 and May 2, which commemorates Bahaullah's declaration that he was the promised one.

For Baha'is, monogamy is the rule in marriage. Baha'is may marry only after they have the consent of both sets of parents. Bahaullah taught:

> Verily in the Book of Bayan (the Bab's Revelation) the matter is restricted to the consent of both (bride and bridegroom). As We desired to bring about love and friendship and the unity of the people, therefore We made it conditional upon the consent of the parents also, that enmity and ill-feeling might be avoided.[13]

Divorce is permitted for Baha'is, but only in extreme cases of incompatibility. At such a point the couple must wait for one full year and seek to re-establish their relationship. If this does not happen, then a divorce may be granted. If a Baha'i couple have children, they are obligated to provide their children with the best possible education. Alcohol and narcotics are forbidden to Baha'is.

Baha'i differs from many other religions in its manner of worship. The basic unit of worship is the Local Spiritual Assembly. This group may meet in the homes of members or in other buildings, but there are no special houses of worship as in other religions. Neither is there a special clergy to conduct the worship. Worship for Baha'is tends to be very simple, with a minimum of form and no ritual. A respected member of the community reads from the writings of Bahaullah and from the scriptures of other world religions. The remainder of the service consists of private prayers and readings. Baha'i community worship is so simple in form that it rejects two elements that Christians and others often find essential, the sermon and the offering. While Baha'is are expected to contribute to the support of their religion, they refuse to take offerings from non-Baha'is.

Baha'is are organized on three levels. The most basic is that of the Local Spiritual Assembly already mentioned. In every community where there are nine or more adult Baha'is, a nine-member administrative body is elected each April 21 to govern the affairs of those Baha'is. As of 1968, there were 6,828 of these assemblies in the world. The second level of administration is the National Spiritual Assembly. This too is a nine-member body made up of people elected annually by delegates to the national conventions. In 1968 there were eighty-three National Assemblies. The top level of the Baha'i organization is the Universal House of Justice. This is a nine-member body

---

[13] Bahaullah, *Kitab-i-Aqdas.*

elected by the members of the National Spiritual Assemblies throughout the world. These representatives serve a five-year term.

Although the Baha'is do not have local houses of worship they have constructed several magnificent temples around the world, and plan eventually to construct one on every continent. Those already in existence are located in Frankfurt, Germany; Sydney, Australia; Kampala, Uganda; and Wilmette, Illinois, U.S.A. Each of these temples reflects a somewhat different style of architecture, but all must be nine-sided and covered with a dome. The number nine is symbolic for Baha'i because it is the largest unit number and thus represents the worldwide unity that Baha'i seeks to develop. In addition to these temples, the world center of Baha'i is located on Mt. Carmel in Haifa, Israel, near Acca, where Bahaullah spent his last days. In the midst of splendid gardens stand the gold-domed shrine of the Bab and the archive building.

Like other religions, Baha'i has established its own calendar and its own holy days. The calendar is a solar one made up of nineteen months, each containing nineteen days. To achieve 365 days, four days are added after the last month of the year (five days are added in leap years). The new year begins on March 21, at the birth of spring. As is the case with the Jewish calendar, the day begins at sunset.

Although exact statistics are not available, it is estimated that there may be as many as five million Baha'is in the world today. Although still relatively small in terms of members, this religion appears to be growing.

STUDY QUESTIONS

1. Relate the beginnings of Baha'i to the messianic hopes of Shia Islam.

2. Why do some consider Baha'i to be the religion most in tune with the modern world?

3. How do Baha'is regard the scriptures of other religions?

SUGGESTED READING

Bahaullah. *The Kitab-I-Iqan* [The Book of Certitudes]. Translated by Shoghi Effendi. Wilmette, Ill.: Baha'i Publishing Trust, 1931.

———. *Gleanings from the Writings of Bahaullah.* Translated by Shoghi Effendi. Wilmette, Ill.: Baha'i Publishing Trust, 1952.

Effendi, Shoghi. *God Passes By*. Wilmette, Ill.: Baha'i Publishing Trust, 1970.

Esslemont, J. E. *Bahaullah and the New Era*. Wilmette, Ill.: Baha'i Books, 1976.

Lee, Anthony A., ed. *Circle of Unity: Baha'i Approaches to Current Social Issues*. Los Angeles: Kalimat Press, 1984.

Selection From the Writings of Bahaullah

> Although the Baha'i religion believes that all the scriptures
> of the world contain God's revelation and are sacred, it still
> holds a special place of reverence for the writings of its
> founder, Bahaullah.

It is incumbent upon every man, in this Day, to hold fast unto whatsoever
will promote the interests, and exalt the station, of all nations and just
governments. Through each and every one of the verses which the Pen of
the most high hath revealed, the doors of love and unity have been un-
locked and flung open to the face of men. We have erewhile declared—
and Our Word is the truth—: "Consort with the followers of all religions
in a spirit of friendliness and fellowship." Whatsoever hath led the children
of men to shun one another, and hath caused dissensions and divisions
amongst them, hath, through the revelation of these words, been nullified
and abolished. From the haven of God's Will, and for the purpose of ennobling the world of being and of elevating the minds and souls of men,
hath been sent down that which is the most effective instrument for the
education of the whole human race. The highest essence and most perfect
expression of whatsoever the peoples of old have either said or written
hath, through this most potent Revelation, been sent down from the heaven
of the Will of the All-Possessing, the Ever-Abiding God. Of old it hath been
revealed: "Love of one's country is an element of the Faith of God." The
Tongue of Grandeur hath, however, in the day of His manifestation proclaimed: "It is not his to boast who loveth his country, but it is his who
loveth the world." Through the power released by these exalted words He
hath lent a fresh impulse, and set a new direction, to the birds of men's
hearts, and hath obliterated every trace of restriction and limitation from
God's holy Book.[14]

Lay not aside the fear of God, O kings of the earth, and beware that ye
transgress not the bounds which the Almighty hath fixed. Observe the in-
junctions laid upon you in His book, and take good heed not to overstep
their limits. Be vigilant, that ye may not do injustice to anyone, be it to the
extent of a grain of mustard seed. Tread ye the path of justice, for this,
verily is the straight path.

Compose your differences, and reduce your armaments, that the burden
of your expenditures may be lightened, and that your minds and hearts
may be tranquillized. Heal the dissensions that divide you, and ye will not

[14] Bahaullah, *Gleanings from the Writings of Bahaullah,* trans., Shoghi Effendi (Wilmette, Ill.:
Baha'i Publishing Trust, 1952), pp. 94—96.

longer be in need of any armaments except what the protection of your cities and territories demandeth. Fear ye God, and take heed not to outstrip the bounds of moderation, and be numbered among the extravagant.

We have learned that you are increasing your outlay every year, and are laying the burden thereof on your subjects. This verily, is more than they can bear, and is a grievous injustice. Decide justly between men, and be ye the emblems of justice amongst them. This, if ye judge fairly, is the thing that behoveth you, and beseemeth your station.

Beware not to deal unjustly with any one that appealeth to you, and entereth beneath your shadow. Walk ye in the fear of God, and be ye of them that lead a godly life. Rest not on your own power, your armies, and treasures. Put your whole trust and confidence in God, Who created you, and seek ye His help in all your affairs. Succor cometh from Him alone. He succoreth whom He will with the hosts of the heavens and of the earth.

Know ye that the poor are the trust of God in your midst. Watch that ye betray not His trust, that ye deal not unjustly with them and that ye walk not in the ways of the treacherous. Ye will most certainly be called upon to answer for His trust on the day when the Balance of Justice shall be set, the day when unto every one shall be rendered his due, when the doings of all men, be they rich or poor, shall be weighed.[15]

Be generous in prosperity, and thankful in adversity. Be worthy of the trust of thy neighbor and look upon him with a bright and friendly face. Be a treasure to the poor, an admonisher to the rich, an answerer of the cry of the needy, a preserver of the sanctity of thy pledge. Be fair in thy judgment, and guarded in thy speech. Be unjust to no man, and show all meekness to all men. Be as a lamp unto them that walk in darkness, a joy to the sorrowful, a sea for the thirsty, a haven for the distressed, an upholder and defender of the victim of oppression. Let integrity and uprightness distinguish all thine acts. Be a home for the stranger, a balm to the suffering, a tower of strength for the fugitive. Be eyes to the blind, and a guiding light unto the feet of the erring. Be an ornament to the countenance of truth, a crown to the brow of fidelity, a pillar of the temple of righteousness, a breath of life to the body of mankind, an ensign of the hosts of justice, a luminary above the horizon of virtue, a dew to the soil of the human heart, an ark on the ocean of knowledge, a sun in the heaven of bounty, a gem on the diadem of wisdom, a shining light in the firmament of thy generation, a fruit upon the tree of humility.[16]

[15] Ibid, pp. 250, 251.
[16] Ibid, p. 285.

Glossary

Agama The scripture of Jainism, believed by some to be the actual sermons given by Mahavira to his disciples.

Agni Aryan god of fire.

Agnostic Literally, "one who does not know." This term is usually taken by those persons who say that they do not know for certain the nature or reality of God. This is in contrast to the atheist who is certain that there is no God.

Ahura Mazda The one true god recognized by Zoroastrians.

Ajwaka African religious functionary whose primary purpose it is to heal by driving out the evil spirits believed to cause the sickness.

Allah Literally "the God." Muslim name for the deity.

Amaterasu Sun goddess in Japanese mythology.

Amesha-Spenta Literally "Holy Immortals." Six modes through which Ahura Mazda revealed himself to humanity in Zoroastrianism.

Amitabha A Dhyani Buddha who presides over the paradise called "the pure land of the west."

Anabaptist Literally "rebaptizer." A radical group of Protestant reformers that insisted that baptism was for adult believers only.

Anatman The state of nonsoulness which, according to the Buddha, was the natural state of humanity.

Ancestor Veneration The veneration of deceased members of the family. It frequently involves the upkeep and care of graves, memorizing the names of past generations, and prayers and sacrifices in honor of the dead.

Angra Mainyu (Shaitin, Satan) The evil spirit recognized by Zoroastrians.

Animism The belief that all nature is alive and filled with unseen spirits that may be worshipped or placated. The animist would see a soul or a self existing in trees, stones, rivers, and the heavenly bodies.

Apocalypse Literally, "that which is revealed." This word is used to describe certain forms of literature that were popular in Christianity, Judaism, and Zoroastrianism in the second century B.C. to the second century A.D. Apocalyptic books often were written in secret or coded language and spoke about a dramatic end of the world.

Aranyakas "Forest treatises," instructions for hermits found in the Vedic literature.

Arhat The state of sainthood in Buddhism.

Arjuna One of the major characters in the Bhagavad-Gita.

Aryan This is a Sanskrit word that basically means "the noble ones" and is applied to those migrants who moved into the Indus valley in the second millenium B.C. from the regions of Persia.

Ashkenazim Jews who lived in Europe, especially Eastern Europe.

Atharva Veda The fourth book in the Vedic collection. It contains rituals and prayers used in the worship of the Aryan gods.

Atheist One who believes there are no gods.

Avatar An incarnation of a deity. In Hinduism, the god Vishnu is believed to have taken human or other forms on several occasions.

Avidya A term found in the Upanishads, which means "ignorance."

Baalim Fertility gods worshipped by the ancient Canaanite people.

Babi The religious group that was the immediate forerunner of the Baha'is.

Babylonian Captivity of the Church That period between 1309–1377 when the papacy was at Avignon, France.

Baptism The Christian initiatory ritual.

Bardo Thodol Tibretan name for the Book of the Dead.

Bar Mitzvah, Bat Mitzvah Jewish rituals in which the young men and women are officially recognized as adult members of the community.

Beatitudes The first ten verses of Jesus' Sermon on the Mount.

Bhagavad-Gita "The Song of the Blessed Lord." The epic poem of Indian culture and religion.

Bhakti Devotion to the gods of Hinduism.

Bhakti Marga "The way of devotion." Salvation in postclassical Hinduism through devotion to a specific god.

Black Stone   A meteorite stone located in the city of Mecca, which was an object of veneration in pre-Islamic Arabia.

Bodhidharma   A legendary monk who brought intuitive Buddhism from India to China in the sixth century A.D.

Bon   Pre-Buddhist native religion of Tibet.

Bot   A hall found in Wats, dedicated to the purpose of teaching, preaching, and meditation.

Brahma   One of the three most important gods in Indian worship. He is generally regarded as the creator of the world.

Brahman   The impersonal god who is seen as total reality in the Upanishads.

Brahmana   Ritual instruction found in Vedic literature.

Brahmin   The priestly caste of Indian society.

Bushido   The code of the Samurai.

Butsu-dan   A Japanese Buddhist household altar.

Cabala   General term for mystical elements in Judaism.

Caliph   From *khalifa*, literally "deputy, representative." The successors of Muhammad in leading Islam. At first the Caliphate was limited to the friends of Muhammad, but as Islam grew it took on the role of a dynastic political leadership.

Caste   From the Portuguese word, *casta*, race. The multiple classes into which traditional Indian society has been divided.

Chanukkah   The Jewish festival that celebrates the rededicating of the temple by Judas Maccabeus in 165 B.C.

Chinvat Bridge   The bridge that connects the point of judgment with the region of reward or punishment in Zoroastrianism.

Consubstantiation   The presence of the body and blood of Jesus along with the bread and the wine of communion.

Copt   A version of Christianity found in North Africa, particularly in Egypt, and which traces its history back to the earliest Christian communities.

Council of Trent   That Council convened in 1545 by the Roman Catholic Church, which acted to reform the Church and to oppose the actions of the Protestants.

Cro-Magnon   That predecessor of the current human race, who lived upon the earth from approximately 25,000 to 7,000 B.C.

Daeva   Pre-Zoroastrian Aryan deity.

Dakhma   A round structure, open to the sky, in which Zoroastrians expose their dead for disposal by the birds.

Dalai Lama   The leader of the so-called Yellow Hat group of Tibetan Buddhists and, up until 1950, the spiritual and political ruler of Tibet.

Deacon   Literally "servant, attendant, minister." A functionary within the Christian Church.

Dervish   Literally "one who comes to the door." A member of a Muslim monastic order.

Dharma   The duties incumbent upon a person in traditional Hindu life, based upon his caste and station in life.

Dhyani Buddha   A Buddhist deity who dwells in heaven and can aid humans in their struggles through life.

Diaspora   The scattering of the Israelite people away from their homeland, which began with the Assyrian destruction of Israel in 722 B.C.

Digambara   Literally "the sky clad." The more conservative sect of Jainism, which holds nudity as an ideal for its monks.

Divination   Prediction of the future through various magical means. Examples: Tarot cards, *I Ching*, reading tea leaves.

Docetism   The belief held by some Gnostics that Jesus only appeared to be human while he was actually pure spirit.

Ecumenical Movement   That action within the modern Christian Church that attempts to minimize the differences between various groups and achieve some form of Christian unity.

Elohim   Literally "gods." One of the names by which the God of the biblical patriarchs was known.

Eschatology   Doctrines concerning the end of the world.

Essenes   A monastic Jewish community whose primary headquarters may have been Wadi Qumran near the Dead Sea. They existed mainly during the first century B.C. and the first century A.D. and were extremely interested in eschatology.

Eucharist   Literally "Thanksgiving." The Christian memorial meal of bread and wine that celebrates the sacrifice of Jesus.

Extreme Unction   The last rite of the Roman Catholic Church which is given to one who is dying.

Fakir   Literally "poor man." A member of a Muslim monastic order.

Falasha   A form of Judaism that is found in Ethiopia.

Fetish   Any object used to control nature in a magical fashion. *Example:* lucky coin, rabbit's foot, religious charm.

Gaon   The president of early medieval Jewish academies.

Gatha   Zoroastrian hymn that takes on the quality of scripture.

Gemara   The commentary upon the Mishnah compiled from the rabbinic academies of Palestine and Babylon. In addition to the commentary upon the Mishnah, there is a great body of material that has no connection to the Mishnah. There are two Gemaras: Palestinian and Babylonian.

Ghetto   That section of certain European cities where Jews were forced to live.

Gnostic   A family of early Christian heresies that claimed to know the secrets of the universe and thus were superior to orthodox Christians.

Gospel   Literally "Good News." The four books appearing at the beginning of the New Testament, which tell the story of Jesus' ministry.

Granth   The scriptures of Sikhism.

Gurdwara   Sikh temple.

Guru   In Hinduism the word has the connotation of "teacher." In Sikhism it refers to the leaders of the religion.

Haggadagh   Literally "narrative." History, folklore, and sermons found in the Talmud.

Hajj   The pilrimage each Muslim is supposed to make once in his lifetime to the shrines in and around Mecca.

Halachah   Legal material, discussions, and rabbinic decisions that are found in the Talmud.

Hasidim   Movement founded in the seventeenth century in Poland by Israel ben Eliezer. He taught that God was not to be found in scholarly research or in the Talmud but in simple faith.

High God   Among certain basic religions it is believed that one supreme god created the world and then withdrew from active participation. Although this god is often recognized and given token worship, the bulk of active worship is given to the lesser deities, who participate more fully in the activities of the world.

Hijrah   Literally "migration." The migration of Muhammad and his disciples from Mecca to Medina in 622 A.D.

Horse Sacrifice   An elaborate, year-long sacrifice carried out in ancient India, which involved the sacrifice of thousands of animals.

Iblis   The fallen angel who is the Satan figure in Islam.

I Ching   The ancient Chinese book of Divination.

Imam   To Sunni Muslims, the Imam is one who leads the community in prayers. To Shi'ite Muslims, the Imams were a group of the legitimate descendants of Ali.

Immaculate Conception of Mary That dogma of the Roman Catholic Church that teaches that Mary was born without the taint of original sin.

Indra Aryan god of thunder, rain, and the ruler of heaven.

The Institutes of the Christian Religion John Calvin's statement of Christian theology that became a classic for Protestant theology.

Izanagi and Izanami Mythological male and female who participated in the creation of the Japanese islands.

Jen A Confucian principle which has been translated by words such as "love," "goodness," and "humaneness."

Jihad The concept of holy war in Islam.

Jinn Demonic creatures who were recognized in pre-Islamic Arabia.

Jiva and Ajiva Soul and matter in the Jain philosophy.

Jnana Marga The way of knowledge. Salvation is achieved in studying the philosophical implications of Indian sacred writings.

Kaaba The enclosure surrounding the black stone in Mecca that became an object of veneration by pilgrims in pre-Islamic Arabia.

Kali Consort of Shiva. Also known as Durga.

Kami Japanese word for spirits. Some scholars see this word as equivalent to *mana* but no exact English translation has been achieved.

Kami-dana Literally "god shelf." The center of domestic Shinto in a Japanese home. A shelf where sacred objects are kept and where daily prayers are said.

Karaites A medieval Jewish group that denied the authority of the Talmud and tried to live exclusively by the rules of the Hebrew Bible.

Karma In Indian thought, that which binds us to the endless cycles of life, death, and rebirth is karma.

Koan Literally "case study." A riddle, tale, or short statement that is used by the Zen masters to bring the students to sudden insight.

Kojiki Literally "Chronicles of Ancient Events." The source book of Japanese mythology.

Kosher Literally "fit, proper." That which is ritually clean or acceptable in Judaism. The term is usually applied to food or food preparation.

Krishna An incarnation of the Hindu god, Vishnu, who appears as a main character in the Bhagavad-Gita.

Kshatriya The warrior caste of Indian society.

Kusti The sacred belt worn by Zoroastrians.

Kwei Evil spirits recognized in early Chinese religions.

Lama Literally "the superior one." Tibetan Buddhist clergy.

Li A Confucian term that has been translated as "propriety," "rites," "ceremonies," and "courtesy." It probably means, "the course of life as it is intended to go."

Lollards A group of wandering preachers, instituted by John Wyclif in the fourteenth century A.D.

Magic An attempt to influence the action of nature through special practices, dances, rituals, incantation. The magician believes if he performs his rituals properly he will cause nature to react favorably toward him.

Mahayana Literally "the larger vehicle." The larger and more liberal branch of Buddhism.

Mantra A ritual sound, word, or phrase that is used to evoke a certain religious effect.

Mana A term taken from the language of the Melanesian Islands. It is used to describe a mysterious, invisible, and impersonal force that causes nature to act as it does.

Manu The mythological survivor of the Indian flood story.

Manu, Code of Classical Hindu literature that describes life in India between 300 B.C. and 300 A.D.

Marcionism An early Christian heresy named for Marcion of Rome. Marcionism rejected the God of the Old Testament and all theological and literary attachments to the Old Testament.

Marrano Spanish Jews who openly converted to Christianity but who secretly continued to practice Judaism.

Maya Illusion. In the Upanishads, all that is not Brahman is maya.

Medicine Man A religious functionary among American Indians whose primary task it was to heal by religious means.

Megalith Large stone monuments apparently raised in connection with religious practices. Examples: Stonehedge, the statues on Easter Islands, the megalith fields in Brittany.

Mishnah A collection of oral laws gathered by Judah ha Nasi (born c. 135 A.D.) that contained the bulk of extra-biblical Jewish law up to the second century A.D.

Mithra (Mithras) A pre-Zoroastrian Aryan deity. He appears in the Hindu Vedic literature as Mitra, in Zoroastrianism as the judge of the dead, and as the leading figure in a Roman mystery religion.

Moghul Empire The Muslim rule of portions of India between the sixteenth and the eighteenth centuries A.D.

Moksha Release from the cycle of death and rebirth, in Indian religions.

Mosque Muslim house of prayer.

Muezzin One who calls the Muslim community to prayer five times per day.

Muslim Literally "submitter." One who submits to the will of God.

Neandertal That predecessor of *Homo sapiens* who lived upon the earth from approximately 125,000 to 30,000 B.C.

Neolithic The late stone age; that era in human history between approximately 7,000 and 3,000 B.C., when most tools, weapons, etc. were constructed from stone.

Nichiren Literally "sun lotus." A sociopolitical sect of Mahayana Buddhism found primarily in Japan.

Ninety-five Theses The ninety-five points of controversy that Luther submitted as grounds for debate in 1517.

Nirvana Literally "blowing out." The cessation of human individuality and desires and absorption into Brahman, in Indian religion.

Nyaya A Hindu philosophical system that uses logical analysis as a means of arriving at truth about the world.

Om mani padmi hum A phrase used in Tibetan Buddhism, which means "Om, the jewel of the lotus, hum."

Orisha Lesser deities who participated in the creation of the world, according to African mythology.

Parable The short, meaningful story that was one of Jesus' chief teaching devices.

Parsee The name by which Zoroastrians are known in India.

Passover (Pesach) Jewish holiday celebrated in the spring of each year, remembering the deliverance of the Israelites from Egyptian slavery.

Penance That sacrament of the Roman Catholic Church in which the Christian confesses sin and receives absolution.

Pentecost A Christian festival, which comes fifty days after the Passover and celebrates the coming of the Holy Spirit upon the Church.

Peyote A cactus plant that bears small button growths. These buttons contain mescaline, a hallucinogenic that is sometimes used in the religious rites of the Native American Church.

Prophet Spokesman for the god YHWH to the people of Israel.

Pure Land Buddhism A version of Mahayana Buddhism popular in Japan. It teaches that its devotees can achieve a paradise, called "the pure land of the west," after their deaths.

Purim A Jewish holiday that celebrates the deliverance of the Jews from destruction at the hands of the Persians.

Purva Mimansa A Hindu philosophical system that taught the avoidance of rebirth by adhering to the laws found in the Vedic literature.

Quran Literally "reading, recitation." The Muslim scripture.

Rabbi Literally "my master." A teacher associated with the Jewish synagogue.

Rajah Originally, this word was applied to Aryan chieftains but later came to be used to describe Indian rulers in general.

Ramadan The month during which true Muslims do not eat or drink between sunrise and sunset. The fast celebrates the month in which the Prophet received the Quran.

Rig-Veda The basic book of the Vedic literature. It consists of over 1,000 hymns and other mythological elements dedicated to the gods of the Aryan pantheon.

Rite of Passage Those rituals that make the passage from one distinct point in a person's life to another. Examples: baptism, circumcision, puberty rites, marriage, death rituals.

Rosh Hashanah The Jewish New Year.

Ryobu An attempted amalgamation between Shinto and Buddhism.

Sabbath (Shabbat) The seventh day, set aside as a day of rest and worship in Judaism.

Sahajdhari A conservative sect in Sikhism.

Sama Veda The third book in the Vedic collection. A collection of verses from hymns dedicated to the gods of the Aryan pantheon.

Samkhya A dualistic system of philosophy in postclassical Hinduism.

Samsara In the Upanishads, samsara refers to the endless cycle of birth, life, death, and rebirth that all humans experience.

Samurai Medieval Japanese knights.

Sangha Buddhist monastic order.

Sannyasin A wandering beggar, in traditional Indian life. This is the fourth stage in the life of a Hindu male.

Satori The state of enlightenment that one can achieve in Zen Buddhism.

Saoshyant Prophet or reformer whom pre-Zoroastrian Aryans believed came to restore the purity of religion.

Sefer Hazohar Literally "The Book of Splendor." The most outstanding example of cabalistic literature in Judaism.

Sephardim Jews who fled from Spain and Portugal and took refuge in the Ottoman Empire.

Seppuku (hari-kiri) Ritual suicide by disembowelment, dictated for certain dishonors and crimes among the Samurai.

Shahadah The creedal statement of Islam, "There is no God but Allah and Muhammad is his messenger."

Shaivite Devotee of the god Shiva.

Shaman The term is taken from the religious life of Siberian people. The Shaman is one who is literally possessed by the gods and who can therefore predict the future.

Shang Ti The supreme god recognized by the Chou dynasty of ancient China.

Shavuot "Feast of Weeks" Jewish holiday in remembrance of the giving of the Ten Commandments.

Shema Deuteronomy 6:4, "Hear (shema) O Israel: The Lord our God is one Lord; and you shall love the Lord your God with all your heart, and with all your soul, and with all your might."

Shen Beneficial spirits recognized in early Christian religion.

Shi'ite Literally "the party of . . ." This group, which accounts for approximately 14 percent of all Muslims, began as "the Party of Ali." They were those who believed that the legitimate successor to Muhammad was his cousin and son-in-law, Ali.

Shinto (Shen Tao) Literally "the way of the gods." The Japanese equivalent is Kami-no-michi. The native religion of Japan.

Shirk Muslim word for polytheism.

Shiva The most popular god in postclassical Hinduism. Shiva is regarded as the god of death and destruction but also of rebirth and reproduction.

Shu The Confucian law of reciprocity.

Shudra The slave or servant caste of Indian society.

Sikh Literally "disciple." An Indian religion made of elements of Hinduism and Islam.

Singhs In Sikhism, the Singhs constitute a corps of warriors.

Soma A sacred plant whose juice was used as a libation to the gods of India. The exact identification of the soma plant is lost to the modern world.

Sufi Literally, "woolen." A monastic group within Islam that seeks a mystical knowledge of God.

Sukkot The Jewish autumn festival of thanksgiving.

Summa Theologiae The massive systematic theology written by St. Thomas Aquinas, which became the standard for Catholic theology.

Sunni The majority of Muslims are Sunnis (traditionalists), who accept orthodox Muslim theology and the traditional line of Caliphs.

Surah Chapter divisions within the Quran.

Suttee The practice followed in India for many years, in which a widow allowed herself to be burned upon her husband's funeral pyre or to be buried alive in his grave.

Svetambara Literally "the white clad." The more liberal sect of Jainism.

Sympathetic or Imitative magic Magic that seeks to operate on the basic notion that "look alikes act alike." The voodoo doll and the various rain dances are examples of sympathetic magic.

Synagogue Literally "assembly." The meeting of Jews of the Diaspora for study and prayer.

Synoptic Gospels Matthew, Mark, and Luke. The three Gospels that share the same basic outline and chronology.

Taboo (tabu) An action that must be avoided lest it release harmful effects upon a person or his group. Examples: walking under a ladder, breaking a mirror, marrying in violation of cultural rules.

Takht The throne of Sikhism at Amritsar, which is a pilgrimage site.

Talmud The encyclopedic collection of Mishnah and Gemara, which is the literary source of postbiblical Judaism. There are two Talmudim: Palestinian and Babylonian.

Tanha Desire, thirst, or craving. This concept was identified by Buddha as that which causes karma.

Tantras Manuals that teach magical words and spells. Primarily found in Tibetan Buddhism but also present in other Buddhist sects and in Hinduism. In these religions, *tantric* religion takes on the element of enlightenment by carrying passion to excessive lengths.

Tao Literally "The Way," or "The Way of Nature."

Tao Tê Ching Literally "The Classic of the Way and its Power or

Virtue." The book that became the basis for the philosophy of Taoism.

Tenri-kyo Literally "Teaching of Heavenly Reason." A sect of Shinto that gives emphasis to faith healing.

Theravada or Hinayana Literally "the tradition of the elders." The smaller and more conservative version of Buddhism.

Thugee A cult of devotees of Kali, who specialized in murdering victims as sacrifices to her.

Tien-t'ai, Tendai Rationalist sects of Mahayana Buddhism.

Torah A general term found in the Hebrew bible referring to divine law and instruction. It is usually translated "law" but can also refer to the first five books of the Bible or to revelation in general.

Totem Taken from the Ojibwa word *ototoman*. It involves the recognition of a relationship between a certain animal and a group of people. The animal becomes sacred to the group and may not be killed by its members except under certain ritual conditions.

Transubstantiation The change that occurs at the blessing of the elements of the Eucharist in the Roman Catholic Church, in which the bread and wine become the body and blood of Jesus.

Udasis An order of holy men in Sikhism.

Upanishads Philosophical materials found in the Vedic literature.

Vaisheshika A Hindu philosophical system that teaches that the universe is made up of nine distinct and uncreated elements.

Vaishya The merchant caste of Indian society.

Vatican II That council called by the Roman Catholic Church in 1962, which took broad steps to modernize the Church and mend relationships with Jews, Eastern Orthodox, and Protestants.

Veda Basically, a collection of hymns to the Aryan gods. The term is also used to apply to the entire collection of Indian sacred literature, including the Vedas, the Brahmanas, the Aranykas, and the Upanishads.

Vedanta Literally "the end of the Vedas." This Hindu philosophical system takes its major materials from the Upanishads and assumes that there is only one true reality in the world, Brahman.

Vishnu One of the three most popular gods of postclassical Hinduism. Vishnu is known as the god of love.

Vohu Mana An angelic figure who revealed the nature of Ahura Mazda to Zoroaster.

Vulgate Latin translation of the Bible by St. Jerome.

Wahhabi   An ultraconservative movement in Islam; it was founded in the eighteenth century and opposed all forms of change within religion and culture.

Wat   A complex of buildings used in Theravada Buddhism, for worship and teaching.

Wu-Wei   The Taoist principle of nonaggression and pacifism.

Yajur Veda   The second book in the collection of Vedic literature. It is a collection of materials to be recited during sacrifice to the Aryan gods.

Yang   The positive force in nature recognized in early Chinese religion.

Yarmulke   Skull cap worn by Jewish males at times of worship.

Yazata   Literally "Adorable Ones." The hosts of angels surrounding the throne of Ahura Mazda in Zoroastrianism.

YHWH   The name of the God who revealed himself to Moses and who became the God of the Israelite people.

Yiddish   The language of Ashkenaz Jews. Essentially, it is Middle High German written in the Hebrew alphabet.

Yin   The negative force in nature recognized in early Chinese religions.

Yoga   A philosophical system in postclassical Hinduism that teaches a dualistic world view.

Yom Kippur   The Jewish Day of Atonement.

Zen, Ch'an Buddhism   A form of Mahayana Buddhism that teaches that the real truth about life comes from intuitive flashes of insight.

Zionism   Movement founded in the late nineteenth century by Theodore Herzl, which sought to find a national home for the Jews scattered throughout the world.

Index